Designing More-than-Human Smart Cities

Beyond Sustainability, Towards Cohabitation

Edited by

SARA HEITLINGER
MARCUS FOTH
RACHEL CLARKE

OXFORD
UNIVERSITY PRESS

Great Clarendon Street, Oxford, OX2 6DP,
United Kingdom

Oxford University Press is a department of the University of Oxford.
It furthers the University's objective of excellence in research, scholarship,
and education by publishing worldwide. Oxford is a registered trade mark
of Oxford University Press in the UK and in certain other countries

Published in the United States of America by Oxford University Press
198 Madison Avenue, New York, NY 10016, United States of America

British Library Cataloguing in Publication Data
Data available

Library of Congress Control Number: 2024936389

ISBN 9780192884169
ISBN 9780198904892 (pbk.)

DOI: 10.1093/9780191980060.001.0001

Printed and bound by
CPI Group (UK) Ltd, Croydon, CR0 4YY

Contents

SECTION 3 JUSTICE

SECTION 4 FUTURES

Notes on contributors

Editors

Sara Heitlinger is a UKRI Future Leaders Fellow and Senior Lecturer in Computer Science, in the Centre for Human-Computer Interaction Design at City, University of London. She leads the More-than-Human Sustainable and Inclusive Smart Cities (MoSaIC) project. Her research at the intersections of urban sustainability, computation, and participatory design draws on methods from the arts and humanities to find ways for co-designing more just and inclusive smart cities.

Marcus Foth is a Professor of Urban Informatics in the School of Design and a Chief Investigator in the QUT Digital Media Research Centre (DMRC), Faculty of Creative Industries, Education, and Social Justice, Queensland University of Technology, Brisbane, Australia. For more than two decades, Marcus has led ubiquitous computing and interaction design research into interactive digital media, screen, mobile, and smart-city applications. Marcus founded the Urban Informatics Research Lab in 2006 and the QUT Design Lab in 2016. He is a founding member of the QUT More-Than-Human Futures research group. Marcus is a Fellow of the Australian Computer Society and the Queensland Academy of Arts and Sciences, a Distinguished Member of the international Association for Computing Machinery (ACM), and currently serves on Australia's national College of Experts.

Rachel Clarke is a design researcher and practitioner combining visual communication with qualitative research, performance and storytelling on the climate emergency, sustainability, and social inequality. She has exhibited work internationally and co-authored research papers across design research, human–computer interaction (HCI), and social sciences. She is course leader of the BA (Hons) Design for Climate Justice, an innovative new course that develops student skills in diverse design practices for climate action and changemaking at London College of Communication, University of the Arts London. She is a member of DEFRA's Futures Advisory Group informing UK agricultural and environmental policy and practice.

Authors

Yoko Akama is a design researcher in the School of Design, RMIT University, near Naarm (Melbourne) on lands now called Australia. Her practice is shaped by various Japanese philosophies, where designing to her means a way to enhance qualities of inter-relating, by respecting difference and accommodating diversity. She brings this practice to research and teaching, where she collaborates with various communities, both in Australia and elsewhere, to self-determine shared futures. She is a recipient of several national and international design awards and has been recognised by *The Australian* as the country's leading researcher in Visual Arts in 2020 and 2022. She co-leads the Designing Entangled Social Innovation in Asia–Pacific network (https://desiap.org/).

Rachel Armstrong is Professor of Regenerative Architecture, at the Department of Architecture, Faculty of Architecture, Campus Sint-Lucas, Brussels/Ghent, KU Leuven, Belgium. Her work concerns the transition from an industrial to an ecological era of development with fundamental changes to the impacts on our health, ecosystems, and how we live. Drawing together the fields of architectural design, natural, and medical sciences, the 'living architecture' synthesis that occurs shares some of the properties of organisms. This simultaneously ecological, technological, and humanistic practice considers the implications for designing and engineering in a world thrown off balance by proposing new standards for sustainable living.

Andy Boucher is an Associate Professor and co-director of the Interaction Research Studio, based at Northumbria University's London campus. He is a designer and maker, who over the past twenty years has developed a practice-based approach to the production of interactive research devices and design-led methodologies for user studies. A co-founder of the Studio, he has helped it grow into an internationally recognised team of multi-disciplinary designers and technologists. His work centres on the design of research products that offer an alternative present for how technology is produced, distributed, and used, ranging from highly finished prototypes for long-term field studies to self-build designs that anybody can make at home.

Dean Brown is a 3D designer and researcher in the Interaction Research Studio. He has worked on ProbeTools, My Naturewatch, and Yo–Yo Machines and is adept at creating engaging designs from humble materials. In addition, he has used his network to create links between the Studio and the wider design community. Dean studied Product Design at DJCAD, Dundee (2003–7) followed by a residency period at Fabrica Research Centre, Italy (2010–14). In parallel to his research Dean is the founder of Brown Office—a multidisciplinary studio creating objects, installations, and interiors. Among other things he has designed vases, cameras, kitchens, and sunglasses for puffins.

Ruth Catlow is an artist, researcher, and curator of emancipatory network cultures, practices, and poetics. She is Co-Director of Furtherfield for art, technology, and eco-social change, and Co-PI at Serpentine Galleries Blockchain Lab. She specialises in critical group-driven discovery and playful co-creation that embraces more-than-human interests for fairer and more connected cultural ecologies and economies. Projects include Larps for planetary-scale interspecies justice and the CultureStake app for collective cultural decision making using quadratic voting on the blockchain. She is co-editor of *Radical Friends: Decentralised Autonomous Organisations and the Arts* with Penny Rafferty.

Carl DiSalvo is a designer, writer, educator, and artist based in Atlanta, Georgia, where he is a Professor in the School of Interactive Computing at the Georgia Institute of Technology. His work explores the relationship between design, technology, and politics. DiSalvo's design and art have been exhibited and supported by the ZKM, Grey Area Foundation for the Arts, Science Gallery Dublin, and the Walker Arts Center. DiSalvo is the author of two books, *Adversarial*

Design (2012) and *Design as Democratic Inquiry* (2022), and an editor of the journal *Design Issues.*

Laura Forlano, a Fulbright award-winning scholar, is a disabled writer, social scientist, and design researcher. She is Professor in the departments of Art + Design and Communication Studies in the College of Arts, Media, and Design and Senior Fellow at The Burnes Center for Social Change at Northeastern University. She is the author of *Cyborg* (with Danya Glabau, MIT Press 2024) and an editor of three books: *Bauhaus Futures* (MIT Press 2019), *digitalSTS* (Princeton University Press 2019), and *From Social Butterfly to Engaged Citizen* (MIT Press 2011). She received her PhD in communications from Columbia University.

Bill Gaver is Professor of Design and co-leader of the Interaction Research Studio at the University of Northumbria, London. With the Studio, he has developed novel approaches for pursuing design as research over the course of numerous practice-based projects, many of which have been published and exhibited internationally. He came to Design as a lapsed psychologist and cognitive scientist with a background in HCI and Politics and long-standing engagements with Sociology and Science, Technology, and Society (STS). This has allowed him to make distinctive contributions to a portfolio of work that includes research products, methodologies, and conceptual insights for and about practice-based design research, with an emphasis on ambiguity, ludic design, and emergence.

Mary Graham is an Adjunct Associate Professor in the School of Political Science & International Studies at the University of Queensland. She grew up in South-East Queensland, and is a Kombumerri person through her father's heritage and a Wakka Wakka Elder through her mother's heritage. For more than thirty years, Mary has been a dedicated community development leader, philosopher, and educator. For her leadership in the fields of Aboriginal history, politics, and comparative philosophy, the University of Queensland awarded Mary with an Honorary Doctorate in 2023.

Mennatullah Hendawy is an Assistant Professor at Ain Shams University in Cairo. She is an interdisciplinary urban planner working at the intersection of cities, media, ethics, and technology to promote equity and sustainability. She earned her PhD summa cum laude in 2021 from the Faculty of Planning Building Environment at TU Berlin, Germany.

Jean Hillier is an Emeritus Professor at RMIT University, Melbourne, Australia. Her research interests include post-structural planning theory and methodology for strategic practice in conditions of uncertainty, more-than-human planning theory and practice, and cultural heritage practices in spatial planning, particularly in China.

Orit Hirsch-Matsioulas is an anthropologist specialising in human–animal relations. She is a research associate at the Tech4Animals Lab in the Information Systems Department of Haifa University and a young researcher at the Centre for Research and Study of Aging (University of Haifa). She is also a co-founder of the Israeli Human–Animal Studies Academic Community and the Human–Animal Studies Forum (Tel Aviv University). Through empirical and interdisciplinary projects on animal–human relations, her scholarship focuses on multispecies ethnography, Animal–Computer Interaction, multispecies wellbeing, and politics of belonging. Her articles were published in various academic journals, such as the journal *Society & Animals.*

Alexander Holland is a designer and researcher at the Deep Design Lab and the University of Melbourne. He studies characteristics of past and future environments. Alexander's work focuses on the political and practical implications of disappearing habitat structures, including trees. His research combines methods from conservation ecology, computer science, and digital design to include non-human as well as human stakeholders. Alexander has won several awards and disseminated his findings in leading scientific, artistic, and architectural venues.

Donna Houston is an urban and cultural geographer. Her research focuses on environmental justice in climate-changing worlds; geographies of extinction; and urban planning, politics, and places in more-than-human cities. She is particularly interested in how cultural methodologies such as storytelling, visual methods, and cultural memory can be used to address current social and environmental challenges.

Lara Houston is a social scientist who investigates sustainability through grassroots, citizen-led practices. She studies how citizens create alternative ways of producing knowledge—particularly when they are excluded or marginalised from large-scale institutions. This has included collaborations with electronics repairers, citizen scientists, and urban farmers. She specialises in using creative, inventive, and participatory methods, and her work often takes the form of inter- and trans-disciplinary collaborations. She is also a co-author of the CreaTures Framework.

Owain Jones is a cultural geographer and became the first Professor of Environmental Humanities in the UK in 2014 at Bath Spa University and was deputy director of the Research Centre for the Environmental Humanities, 2016–19. He has published over eighty scholarly articles on various aspects of nature–society relations, many focusing particularly on tidal cultures and tree cultures. He has co-authored/edited five books: *Art and Creativity in an Era of Ecocide* (2023); *Visual Culture in the Northern British Archipelago: Imagining Islands* (2018); *Participatory Research in More-Than-Human Worlds* (2017); *Geography and Memory: Identity, Place and Becoming* (2012); and *Tree Cultures: Places of Trees* (2002). He led a £1.5-million Arts and Humanities Research Council Connected Communities project with eight UK universities, community partners and artists in four UK case study areas (2014–17). This project sought to creatively explore and transform connections within and between communities, and communities and nature, in relation to water issues. He has supervised four Environmental Humanities PhDs with art practice and conducted various creative/academic collaborations with artists.

Lasse Kantola is a drama and youth educator, teacher and director of the arts-based learning theatre Theatrum Olga. This is part of vocational education and training (VET) Diakonia College of Finland/ Suomen Diakoniaopisto (SDO). He has pioneered a unique multi-professional way of organizing phenomena-based learning spaces and arts-based learning processes. Theatrum Olga also offers possibilities for work experience and voluntary work in props, clothing, graphic design, fine arts, and music in this unique, innovative, and sustainable setting.

Shaimaa Lazem is an Associate Research Professor at the City of Scientific Research and Technological Applications (SRTA-City), Egypt. She is interested in participatory design, co-design, decolonising HCI, and HCI education. She worked on designing educational and heritage documentation technologies for rural populations in Egypt. She is a Leaders-in-Innovation Fellow with the Royal Academy of Engineering in London since 2018, and the co-founder of the Arab-HCI community. She works on localising responsible human-centred AI in the African tech ecosystem with support from Google 2020 Award for Inclusion Research and Google AI 2021 Award in partnership with Professor Anicia Peters from Namibia.

Ann Light is an interaction theorist and professor of design specialising in participatory practice, human–technology relations, and collaborative future-making. Her twenty-five-year research career has focused on the politics, ethics, and agency of design, especially co-design in communities, exploring social activism at neighbourhood level. Regarding the social and ecological as inextricably linked and believing creative remaking of relations is needed, she has been studying cultural aspects of climate collapse and the stress that current systems put on the planet. She is co-creator of the CreaTures Framework, part of the European Union project *Creative Practices for Transformative Futures* (CreaTures: https://creaturesframework.org/).

Michelle Maloney holds a Bachelor of Arts (Political Science and History) and Laws (Honours) from the Australian National University and a PhD in Law from Griffith University. She has more than thirty years' experience designing and managing climate change, sustainability, and community building projects in Australia, the United Kingdom, Indonesia, and the United States. This includes working in solidarity with Indigenous colleagues in Central Queensland, South-East Queensland, and other regions, on a range of community building, natural resource management, and cultural heritage projects.

Clara Mancini is Professor of Animal–Computer Interaction at The Open University's School of Computing and Communications and founding head of the Animal–Computer Interaction (ACI) Laboratory, whose mission is researching and designing interactive systems for and with animals. Her work aims to advance animal welfare and justice through animal-centred technologies that can monitor animals with minimal interference, and afford them environmental control, experiential enrichment, and enhanced societal status. Founding member of the ACI International Steering Committee and co-founder of the ACI International Conference, Clara has published and lectured extensively on the theory, methodology, and ethics of animal-centred research and design.

Naho Matsuda, with a background in visual communication and interaction design, primarily takes responsibility for graphic design, photography, publication, and web design for the Interaction Research Studio, as well as studio publicity. She has a personal practice as an artist working in print, publications, writing, installation, and performance.

Jessica McLean does research on how humans, more-than-humans, environments, and technologies interact to produce geographies of change. Her research focuses on digital technologies, water politics, climate action, and activism. As an Associate Professor in the School of Social Sciences (Macquarie University), she teaches smart urbanism, Anthropocene politics, and environmental justice. Her book *Changing Digital Geographies: Technologies, Environments and People* (2020) contributed to the emerging subdiscipline of digital geographies. Jess is an Associate Editor of *Transactions of the Institute of British Geographers*; she enjoys writing for and speaking with multiple audiences, both within and beyond academia, and builds collaborations across disciplines and in applied settings.

Daniel Metcalfe is a designer, researcher, and visiting senior lecturer in the Technion's Faculty of Architecture and Town Planning. His work includes large-scale environmental design and planning projects that integrate more-than-human perspectives into the design and planning of both natural and urban landscapes. His research looks at developing design methods for addressing the needs of non-human species and ways to compensate for lost and degraded habitats in human-dominated areas, in addition to addressing the growing alienation of people from nature. His teaching includes courses on multispecies design, digital design and manufacturing, social innovation, and design research.

Jonathan Metzger is a Professor in Urban and Regional Studies at the KTH Royal Institute of Technology in Stockholm. Most of his research deals with decision making concerning complex environmental issues—often (but not exclusively) with a focus on urban and regional policy and politics. In his work he relates to, and finds inspiration in, research debates within the subject areas of planning studies, human geography, science and technology studies, and organisation studies.

Natalie Osborne is a critical urban geographer and Senior Lecturer in the School of Engineering and Built Environment, Griffith University, and a white settler living on unceded Jagera and Turrbal Country. She is interested in feminist, queer, anti-colonial, and crip practices of thinking and organising around urban and climate justice, and how we can resist alt-right, eco-fascist, and neo-colonial responses to social and environmental crises while working towards collective liberation. She is a co-producer of Radio Reversal, a critical theory and politics programme broadcast on 4ZZZ 102.1FM, and an organiser with the Brisbane Free University.

Allan Owens has a doctoral degree in applied drama within intercultural contexts. His practice and research focus on learning through critical-creative pedagogy for understanding of self, organisation, and society. His specialisations are in drama and education and in particular the use of Pretext Drama as a method to create spaces for understanding. Currently Professor Emeritus at the centre for Research into Education, Creativity and the Arts through Practice (RECAP), and Phillip Barker Centre for Creative Learning, University of Chester, Allan is also a UK National Teaching Fellow.

Liliana Ovalle is a Senior Research Fellow with over ten years of experience at the Interaction Research Studio. Liliana has worked on a wide range of research projects focusing on the design and production of research devices and design-led methodologies for public engagement. Liliana studied Industrial Design at Universidad Nacional Autonoma de Mexico followed by an MA at the Royal College of Art in London. She is now pursuing a PhD in which she explores the role of design in creating ludic engagements through craft practices in cross-cultural settings in Mexico. Parallel to her research Liliana runs her design practice where she works on experimental one-off projects and collaborations with industry.

Anne Pässilä, PhD, MA, drama educator is Senior Researcher in the School of Engineering and Science at Lappeenranta-Lahti University of Technology (LUT), Finland and Visiting Research Fellow at the University of Chester, UK. She is a pioneer in designing and applying arts-based research approaches (ABR) and arts-based methodology (ABM) in technological and industrial management contexts. As a scholar she has published extensively on these areas. As a practitioner, she is in demand for her expert facilitation skills in co-creation processes both within and beyond the academy.

Alison Powell is Associate Professor in Media and Communications at the London School of Economics. She directed the JUST AI Network: Joining Up Society and Technology for AI, supported by the AHRC and Ada Lovelace Institute. JUST AI creates alternative ethical spaces, practices, and orientations towards the issue of data and AI ethics; its work is documented at https://just-ai.net. Alison's research focuses on the ways technology-driven governance influences citizenship, especially in 'smart cities'. She is also interested in just transitions, deep sustainability, and radical futures. Alison is the author of *Undoing Optimization: Civic Action and Smart Cities* (Yale University Press).

Stanislav Roudavski is a founder of the Deep Design Lab and an academic at the University of Melbourne. His work explores more-than-human design, engaging with ecology, technology, design, and architecture. Stanislav's publications and creative work address non-human agents in design imagination, creative computing, and digital fabrication. He won multiple awards for teaching, research, and design. Prior to his current position, Stanislav has worked at the University of Cambridge, MIT, and architectural practices in Europe.

Andy Sheen is a creative technologist with a strong background in hardware design as well as software. Joining the Interaction Research Studio from Tech Will Save Us, he is very experienced in working with the technologies needed for stand-alone computational products, and moreover for designing electronics that are accessible for novices to make. He has a background in audio design and also works with electronic installations in his personal practice.

Manuela Taboada is a designer, researcher, and senior lecturer working across environmental sciences and design. Her background in complex emergency, design activism, and decolonial design defines the way she critically engages transdisciplinary multi-cultural teams to design change and systems transitions.

Alex Taylor is a Reader in Design Informatics at the University of Edinburgh. With a fascination for the entanglements between social life and machines, his research ranges from empirical studies of technology in everyday life to speculative design interventions. He draws on feminist technoscience to ask questions about the roles human–machine composites play in forms of knowing and being, and how they open up possibilities for fundamental transformations in society.

Jane Turner is a game and interaction design educator and researcher. Her research embraces game design, story making, and the more-than-human through frames informed by narrative, meaning making, and place. She focuses on narrative methodologies and the material and cultural aspects of game designing, particularly the ways that design and designing are mimetic 'story-ing' practices.

Mike Vanis is a creative technologist who joined the Interaction Research Studio from Tech Will Save Us. He has strong software skills particularly in working with the microprocessor platforms and networking we use in our designs and is also well-versed in hardware design. He pursues his personal practice with his partner Cindy Strobach as Unit Lab, making playful products inspired by science and the natural world.

Ron Wakkary is a Professor in the School of Interactive Arts and Technology, Simon Fraser University in Canada where he founded the Everyday Design Studio (eds.siat.sfu.ca). In addition, he is a Professor and Chair of Design for More-Than-Human-Centred Worlds in Industrial Design, Eindhoven University of Technology in the Netherlands. Wakkary is the author of the book *Things We Could Design for More Than Human-Centered Worlds* (MIT Press, 2021). His research investigates the changing nature of design in response to new understandings of human–technology relations, multispecies worlds, and posthumanism. He aims to reflectively create new design exemplars, theory, and emergent practices to contribute generously and expansively to understanding ways of designing that are more accountable, co-habitable, and equitable.

Annika Wolff has a BSc in Cognitive Science and a doctoral degree in knowledge modelling and HCI. Her specialisations are in co-design and human–data interaction, at the intersection between complex data, machine, and human learning. Her research focuses on how people make sense of, interact with, and design from complex data and how data can be used to build empathy for sustainability.

Prologue

Carl DiSalvo

There are two sweetgum trees in my yard, and my yard is small. Every year they produce thousands of gumballs that fall to the ground and spill into the street. The gumballs are nasty. They are spiky and sticky, make walking treacherous, and rip the soil underfoot. After the first year living with them, I wanted to cut the trees down. I asked my neighbour for suggestions for an arborist, and he told me I couldn't cut them down due to 'the tree ordinance'. I had no idea what he was talking about, and he didn't have any more to say about the matter. I went home to look this ordinance up, falling into a rabbit hole of policy and regulations and ending up in a fascinating database.

The City of Atlanta's Tree Protection Ordinance regulates which trees can be cut down and under what circumstances. It also stipulates consequences, in the form of fees, for violating the ordinance. The ordinance exists to protect the tree canopy of Atlanta, which is exceptionally robust. Indeed, some people refer to Atlanta as a 'city in a forest'. It's widely accepted that having trees in the city is good for aesthetic and environmental reasons. Many of those environmental reasons are amplified in a city like Atlanta, which is hot and car-centric: trees provide a respite of all sorts. The specific part of the ordinance my neighbour was referring to when he told me I couldn't cut down the sweetgum trees is section 158–101:

> No person shall directly or indirectly remove or destroy [or injure] any tree located on public property that is subject to the provisions of this article, or any tree having a diameter at breast height (DBH) of six inches or more which is located on private property subject to the provisions of this article, without obtaining a permit as provided in this section.

Like all legislation, the ordinance contains myriad definitions, procedures, and exceptions. To cut down a tree that is six inches or more in DBH, you (the owner of the property) need to arrange for an inspection by an arborist. The arborist evaluates the tree on several factors, including its health and whether the growth and location of the tree is a public safety concern, and then determines if the tree can be cut down. Over the years, there have been suggestions for various adjustments to the ordinance, such as giving some species of trees heritage status (and thus more protection) or allowing trees to be cut down when making space for affordable housing. Overall, the Tree Protection Ordinance is a fascinating thing relevant to the topic of this edited collection because it's a policy developed to contribute to the design of the city. Furthermore, it's a policy that takes the environment seriously. It seeks to give standing to a particular aspect of the environment, over the will of people to simply

Carl DiSalvo, *Prologue* In: *Designing More-than-Human Smart Cities*. Edited by: Sara Heitlinger, Marcus Foth, and Rachel Clarke, Oxford University Press. © Oxford University Press (2024). DOI: 10.1093/9780191980060.003.0001 do whatever they want to the environment. We might consider it a step toward a more-than-human urbanism.

But there is more than just an ordinance; there's also a database. Like many cities, especially those striving to be smart, the City of Atlanta municipal government maintains an online portal to access data about the city. Much of the available data relates to planning and permits, and the tree protection ordinance falls under the purview of the Department of City Planning. Within that portal, in one of the drop-down menus, is the item 'Arborist Illegal Activity'. Selecting this and then performing a search returns all the verified incidents relating to cutting or fatally damaging trees without a permit. The data in this table is not big, but it's also not inconsequential. A search over the past year (2022) returns 416 violations of the ordinance. And that's more than 416 trees because many records account for multiple trees. For instance, on 8 February 2022 a citation was given for removing sixty-seven trees from a single plot of land! For each record, we can view the date, the address, a description, a label for the category of the infraction, and the status, such as if a fine was levelled or the issue is pending investigation, or in a few cases, if in fact there was a permit, and the case was closed. The data is messy but informative. For instance, there are differences between illegal removal and illegal destruction, which refers to activities that cause a tree to die, such as damaging the root system by installing drainage. There is also a category of 'Complaint', which suggests that in some cases, neighbours or other residents call in to report these (alleged) illegal activities.

We can assume some of these happen by mistake. After all, it's an unusual law, and people may not know you cannot cut down a tree on your property. And sometimes, accidents happen when you are digging a trench for a drain. Others, however, are not a mistake. They are a wager and investment. A wager that they won't be caught. And an investment that, even if they are caught, it was worthwhile. Case that could be worthwhile include if you are a developer building housing, or an individual looking to extend your house. If the land upon which those trees stand can be monetised for more than the fees for illegally cutting down a tree (or sixty-seven trees), then that fee is an investment in future financial returns. And looking across the entries in the database, it seems that's often the case. A single lot might have five, ten, or more trees cut down. That lot is not being pruned; it's being cleared. And the reason to clear a lot is for development.

From the perspective of more-than-human smart cities, this database and what it expresses is thought provoking. These trees are counted, and their demise is recorded because someone—many people, in fact—cares. Bringing this policy into being required the effort of residents, non-profit organisations, politicians, and others working in concert. Data about the value of trees to the city would have needed to be collected and presented compellingly to persuade the city council to pass and uphold such an ordinance. Maintaining this policy takes work. It's one more responsibility of the Office of City Planning in their ongoing and ever-more challenging work of urban design in a rapidly growing city.

Maintaining this data also takes work. Municipal employees are assigned to investigate events, and data about those events is collected and entered into the database. If we consider the Tree Protection Ordinance as a step-in policy toward a more-than-human urbanism, then the database is how that policy is operationalised, and becomes a smart city project. It reflects a standard discourse among smart-city advocates regarding the value of collecting and maintaining data. Ostensibly, that data might be used to inform decision making. In this case, that data might be used to inform the ongoing design of Atlanta. We might also query the database further to gain insights. We could, for example, look for patterns. Are there neighbourhoods where more trees are being illegally cut down? Are there repeat offenders? Could this data be correlated with other data to create a proxy to register broader phenomena, such as gentrification? Focusing on the perspective of a more-than-human smart city, we might also consider how this database, and the work of collecting and maintaining the data, attunes us to the world of trees and how we live with them. Yes, trees are just a single kind of plant, but accounting for trees counts for something.

At the same time, the database and the regulatory apparatus it's meant to support give us insight into the shortcomings of such approaches. In her fantastic essay 'Tree Thinking', Shannon Mattern traces some of the ways trees have affected, and continue to affect, our lives, connecting varied histories of trees and thinking to current technology trends and discourses (2021). Discussing several computational tools designed to study and model tree canopies and their environmental effects, she states that 'It's easier to plant a tree—and to allow a generative design dashboard to tell you precisely where to plant it—than it is to change our individual and collective consumption habits or to muster the political will to eliminate fossil fuels.' While the systems Mattern is describing relate to climate change specifically, and the Tree Protection Ordinance is more general, there's a connection to make and a lesson to learn. Yes, we can count these illegally removed trees, and we can enter those numbers and locations into a database. And we can use that data to hold people accountable for such actions. But such data, systems, and procedures may fail to address the fundamental concerns and conditions they mark and measure. We can fine people for illegally clearing trees, but in a culture where economics is the arbitrator of value, such ordinances and data may have little efficacy. Although we might consider it to be wrong in some moral sense to cut down those trees, some might argue that, economically, it is quite all right, in that the cost of the fines is far less than the profit gained from developing that land.

And it's not that the ordinance is poorly crafted or the process for collecting data is flawed. We can imagine the question that spurred the Tree Protection Ordinance. It could have been a question such as 'How might we protect the tree canopy of Atlanta so that it continues to flourish?' In response to such a question, a series of policies and systems were designed that leveraged existing mechanisms of governance. The question is a good question. The policies and systems may be good, too, in that they do the work they were intended to do. In other words, these may be good designs. But—by themselves—they may also be insufficient to sustain an approach to the city that prioritises the welfare of the environment because, in much of contemporary society and governance, the market trumps the environment.

We need policies like the Tree Protection Ordinance. Such ordinances will produce data, and collecting and sharing that data seems useful. What's also needed is something in addition to such ordinances and data. And that 'something in addition' is found in the pages of this edited volume. What's needed are different and diverse framings of what it means to live together. Part of that is framings that de-centre the human and begin to move us towards more-than-human encounters and worlds. It will take a bit of work for designers, planners, policymakers, and philosophers to get there. So many of our methods and discourses, particularly in design, have become an exceptionally perverse version of human-centredness that manipulates people's behaviour and desire toward the accumulation of capital. These methods and discourses need to be replaced. The essays and projects in the following pages begin to do some of that work.

Reference

Mattern, S. (2021). Tree Thinking. Places Journal. https://doi.org/10.22269/210921.

Editorial Introduction

Sara Heitlinger, Marcus Foth, and Rachel Clarke

Cities are changing across the planet. Climate change, rapid urbanisation, pandemics, as well as innovations in technologies such as blockchain, artificial intelligence (AI), and the Internet of Things (IoT) are all impacting urban space. In turn, cities are changing the planet, too. One response to such changes has been to make cities ecologically sustainable and 'smart'. The 'eco smart city' for instance uses networked sensing, cloud, and mobile computing to optimise, control, and regulate urban processes and resources. From real-time bus information, autonomous electric vehicles, smart parking, and smart street lighting, such initiatives are often presented as a social and environmental good.

Critics, however, increasingly argue that technologically driven and efficiency-led approaches are too simplistic to deal with the complexities of the urgent and widespread transformations needed. Sustainability in the smart city predominantly focuses on resource optimisation and efficiencies and is thus performed in limited ways that leave little room for participation and citizen agency despite government efforts to integrate innovative technologies in more equitable ways. More importantly, there is a growing awareness that a human-centred notion of cities, in which urban space is designed for, and inhabited by, humans only, is no longer tenable. Within the age of the Anthropocene[1]—a term used to refer to a new geological era in which human activity is transforming Earth systems, accelerating climate change, and causing mass extinctions—scholars and practitioners are working generatively by acknowledging the entanglements between human and non-human others (including plants, animals, and insects, as well as soil, water, and sensors and their data) in urban life.

In *Designing More-than-Human Smart Cities*, renowned researchers and practitioners from urban planning, architecture, environmental humanities, geography, design, and computing systematically and critically consider smart cities beyond a human-centred approach. They respond to the complex interrelations between human and non-human others in urban space. Through theory, policy, and practice (past and present), and thinking speculatively about how smart cities may evolve in the future, the book makes a timely contribution to lively, contemporary scientific and political debates on what counts as genuinely sustainable smart cities. This is of particular relevance now, given how the climate emergency, growing pollution, and species decline, as well as the COVID-19 pandemic and wars, are shifting urban land use and mobility, and bringing issues of environmental and social injustices much more visibly into the public domain.

Sara Heitlinger, Marcus Foth, and Rachel Clarke, *Editorial Introduction.* In: *Designing More-than-Human Smart Cities.*
Edited by: Sara Heitlinger, Marcus Foth, and Rachel Clarke, Oxford University Press.
DOI: 10.1093/9780191980060.003.0002

The aim of this book is to move discourse and practice for the design of sustainable smart cities forward by demonstrating how concepts and theories from the more-than-human paradigm are being brought into a range of emergent design practices, while offering a direction for future work. The book brings together different disciplinary perspectives to explore what it means to co-design with humans and non-humans, embrace our interrelatedness and interdependencies, and co-create more liveable, just, sustainable, and resilient urban environments that contribute to planetary health and wellbeing. The chapters in this book illustrate key concepts using case studies, methods, policies, and frameworks. Our book sits at a timely and unique intersection between smart city and sustainability engineering and conceptual and methodological explorations of more-than-human design.

Our Personal Motivations and Positioning

With a book such as this, which inevitably asks that we acknowledge and limit human-centric approaches, we feel it is important to also represent our interests and concerns in the current research and practice landscape and recognise how taking a more-than-human view requires acceptance of a double bind. The act of writing and editing a book of this kind is, in and of itself, a very human-centric thing to do: we are creating a thing with words and sections designed specifically for other humans to read and design with. We are therefore coming to this work from a particular set of histories, herstories, and perspectives that are grounded in our collective experiences, senses, and knowledges as people, which has its limits. At the same time, we are encouraging our authors and readers to question and decentre human dominance and exceptionalism to empathise, engage, and be compassionate with more-than-human perspectives and not only advocate for other ways of knowing, but other ways of being with.

The more-than-human turn in design signifies a fundamental shift in perspective, acknowledging the intricate web of interactions between not only humans and their surroundings, but also the myriad non-human entities that coexist within our urban landscapes (Clarke et al. 2019; Forlano 2016; Giaccardi & Redström 2020). We connect with and extend long-standing discourse in the environmental humanities on more-than-human ontologies (Abram 1997; Franklin 2017; Galloway 2017; Panelli 2010). As a result of this scholarly history and development across different disciplines, the authors of the chapters in this book employ the term 'more-than-human' in diverse and innovative ways, reflecting a rich tapestry of ideas. Some contributors delve into the realms of ecology and biology, emphasising the symbiotic relationships between urban ecosystems and their human inhabitants. Others explore the infusion of smart-city technology, examining how artificial intelligence (AI), the Internet of Things (IoT), and autonomous systems can foster a deeper integration of human and non-human elements in the city. Additionally, several chapters probe the cultural, epistemological, and ethical dimensions of more-than-human urbanism, offering critical reflections on how this concept can redefine our understanding of community, belonging, and cohabitation. As we embark on this journey through the pages of this book, readers will encounter a pluriversal discourse that challenges conventional wisdom, inviting us to reimagine our cities as vibrant, harmonious ecosystems where humans, nature, and technology coalesce to create a sustainable and inclusive urban future.

Sara

My interest in the topics of the book developed through long-term participatory design research with urban community food-growers at Spitalfields City Farm, a community farm in inner East London, in the UK. This farm was the site of my PhD work, and subsequent research in a project called Connected Seeds and Sensors that explored how networked sensors, data visualisation, and an interactive seed library could help support more sustainable food production and consumption in the smart city. It was at the farm that I first learned from urban food-growers the importance of plants, insects, birds, and microbes, as well as the role of less-defined entities such as soil, the air, and a changing climate in the urban food web, and this changed how I think about smart cities. I have continued to work with food-growing communities, as well as more recently with different urban nature-based communities such as river activists, and together we have been co-designing digital prototypes for more-than-human smart cities. The aim is not to make urban processes more efficient, but to tell the stories of bio-cultural diversity, share knowledge, distribute benefits of the smart city more evenly, and celebrate practices of care in the web of life, particularly in the context of densely populated, culturally diverse cities (see Nichols & Heitlinger 2022 for a write-up of some of these experiments).

It was at the farm in 2017 that I met Marcus on one of his visits to London, and I remember after showing him the Connected Seeds Library, we hatched the germ of the idea to edit a book on the topic of More-than-Human Smart Cities. Rachel joined us, and the three of us subsequently co-organised two international and interdisciplinary workshops that were important in the development of our book proposal. The first workshop, called *Avoiding Ecocidal Smart Cities: Participatory Design for More-than-Human Futures* took place at the Participatory Design Conference in 2018. It was co-organised together with Ann Light, Carl DiSalvo, and Laura Forlano, and involved seventeen accepted position papers (Heitlinger et al. 2018; Clarke et al, 2019). The second workshop, *Digital Cities #11—Communities and Technologies for More-than-Human Futures*, at the Communities and Technology conference in 2019, was co-organised with Martin Tomitsch and had sixteen position papers accepted (Foth et al. 2019). Together these workshops helped us refine the focus for the book and understand the relevance of the topic for different disciplines and contexts. Many of the participants have contributed chapters here.

Marcus

My scholarly journey from championing human-centred design in urban informatics to co-founding the More-than-Human Futures research group at QUT has been an evolving exploration of the ever-changing relationship between people, place, and technology. Back in 2006, when I established the Urban Informatics Research Lab at QUT, the prevailing industry and governmental approaches to urban computing were distinctly technocratic. I was thus motivated to steer urban computing research and development towards *human-centred* design principles. However, as our group went through the heydays of the smart city, a profound shift in perspective began to take root. This was accompanied by Paul Dourish's (2010) reflections on the limits of 'use' and 'usability' notions in sustainable HCI, Laura Forlano's (2016) article about decentring the human in the design of cities, Mike Monteiro's (2017, 2019) poignant call for ethics in design, and our own early engagement with notions of sustainability in design (Foth et al. 2009; Paulos et al. 2008). All of this contributed to an epiphanic moment of self-reflection that made me recognise design's deep-rooted complicity in the complex, interconnected challenges humanity has wrought upon the planet. This introspection resonated with my colleagues at QUT, leading to the inception of the More-than-Human Futures research group in 2020.[2] Our collective vision is to strive for socio-ecological justice by co-creating inclusive pathways rooted in Indigenous wisdom, focusing on environmental humanities, ecological justice, and decolonial theory. This self-reflection on my design research practice also fuelled my motivation to co-edit this book alongside Sara and Rachel, exploring the multifaceted dimensions of more-than-human smart cities and their potential to reshape urban futures. With this book, we want to provoke critical discussions and inspire innovative solutions in our pursuit of a more harmonious and sustainable cohabitation between humans and the diverse species and systems of our cities.

Rachel

As a design researcher I have a background in digital live and performance art practice. Prior to joining academia, I worked with environmental organisations and youth groups on mining and quarry restoration projects exploring digital representation of landscape and biodiversity in the United Kingdom and internationally. Now I have a particular interest in how more-than-human sensibilities can be brought into particular design practices in urban environments and the challenges and tensions this creates between organisations. I have had many postgraduate and undergraduate students struggle with the theories and concepts discussed in the works of brilliant authors such as Puig de la Bellacasa in finding practical routes into design that can take an ethical and speculative stand on more-than-human life. For me the exciting part of working on this edited collection has been reading how designers interpret and work with these ideas and apply them, build on them or struggle with them. First of all, this is understanding where the generative potential of such work is, but also where the limits of our practice and mindsets might be and what change can happen as a consequence of doing design from these perspectives.

Book Sections

The book is divided into four sections: Cultures, Practices, Justice, and Futures, with a Prologue from Carl DiSalvo and an Epilogue from Laura Forlano, experts we invited to provide overarching critical reflections and personal commentaries for the main chapters to sit with. Taken together, these sections trace the different perspectives and approaches pertinent to the topic of designing more-than-human smart cities, including methods and practices, bringing together different actors and disciplines, and finally reflecting on possible smart cities of the future that are more sustainable and just. In order to compile state of the art knowledge and appeal to a diverse audience, *Designing More-than-Human Smart Cities* draws on academics and practitioners' knowledge, and features studies from established and emerging scholars, as well as aiming to include an internationally diverse array of voices and cases. Each of the four sections—Cultures, Practices, Justice, and Futures—is populated by original chapters that address different aspects of each theme and that together showcase the diversity of thoughts and praxis within each theme.

Cultures

In our first section on cultures, authors provide readers with an overview of frames, theories, and concepts from different cultural epistemologies, highlighting work from indigenous ways of knowing, postcolonial perspectives, and design anthropology. This section provides readers with examples of practices and perspectives that have privileged kinship and alliances over extraction and exploitation of natural resources. Authors introduce pluriversal knowledges across data, organic matter, and indigeneity, while providing a theoretical and conceptual grounding for the book by drawing on feminist ethics of care. Authors in this section expand on recent thinking from social sciences and humanities to consider the political and practical imperative for attending to the marginalised, for making the invisible visible, and understanding the ways in which to move beyond a human-centred perspective of dominance and privilege to consider feral assemblages and more-than-human alliances. This section helps trace the move from technocratic and efficiency-based approaches to smart cities, towards care and interdependent relationships within urban space.

Donna Houston, Jessica McLean, and Natalie Osborne's chapter considers many of the infrastructural frictions and the necessity of care in the face of ruins in the multispecies smart city. They consider different theoretical critiques of smart cities, and through feminist thinking about care, shadows, and ruins in multispecies worlds, they introduce a series of 'glitch vignettes' to surface the edges of the smart city to mobilise different forms of interdependence.

Through questions around smart, stupid, and wise cities, Owain Jones's chapter asks how a focus on water can help us move beyond narrow and problematic notions of urban smartness. Drawing on a project called *Hydrocitizenship*, his explorations use water as a lens to rethink technocentric and modernist ideas of smartness in cities and move towards a more ecologically inflected notion of the wise city.

Yoko Akama flips notions of growth and control associated with the smart city on their heads, instead reflecting on the importance of spirits, death, and destruction in relation to Japanese culture and the uncontrollable power of seismic geological forces.

Manuela Tabouda and Jane Turner delve into the realm of decolonial thought to illuminate the intricate relationships between humans and the more-than-human in urban design. Drawing from narratives of Meanjin/Brisbane, Australia, their chapter uncovers the often-unseen 'abyssal lines' in cities that delineate humans from non-human others.

Practices

In our second section, authors consider the different practices that bring some of these theories to life and engage others in the processes of design. The focus here is on strategies and methods aimed at moving beyond a human-centred perspective of design in the urban realm. Here we see how practitioners, including artists, researchers, designers, and policy makers, approached the design of digital infrastructures, monitoring and sensing, data collection, and visualisation aimed at improving more-than-human cities, socially, economically, environmentally, and democratically.

Alexander Holland and Stanislav Roudavski pioneer an innovative approach to addressing the environmental crisis through more-than-human design. By reimagining trees as designers, birds as clients, and humans as assistants, the chapter empowers non-human lifeforms and advocates for their active inclusion in the design process. Through the use of AI, field observations, and computation, the authors provide both a conceptual framework and practical tools to foster cohabitation and sustainability.

In their chapter, Bill Gaver, Andy Boucher, Dean Brown, Naho Matsuda, Liliana Ovalle, Andy Sheen, and Mike Vanis recount their journey as newcomers to the field of smart cities, seeking to incorporate more-than-human perspectives, particularly non-human living beings, into their design practice. Through participatory and design-led engagements with stakeholders, they developed a workbook of design proposals and fictions, challenging conventional notions of smart-city design by opening up new possibilities for cohabitation and reshaping our urban landscapes.

Jonathan Metzger and Jean Hillier explore the unintended consequences of suburban development on mosquito populations in Australia. By emphasising the co-becoming of humans and mosquitoes and drawing from the philosophies of thinkers like Bruno Latour and François Jullien, the chapter advocates for an 'upstream' investigation approach that challenges traditional 'downstream' mosquito-management practices. This thought-provoking perspective suggests that smarter urban planning should prioritise understanding development environments over relying solely on technology and offers a fresh outlook on the coexistence of humans and non-human entities in the smart city context.

Annika Wolff, Anne Pässilä, Allan Owens, and Lasse Kantola tackle the challenge of harnessing environmental data for urban planning and its impact on nature. They introduce the concept of 'data drama' as an innovative approach that goes beyond traditional data storytelling and actively involves the audience in embodying and understanding data. This chapter bridges the worlds of drama, education, critical pedagogy, and data science and emphasises the role of emotions and imagination in fostering empathy for the hidden concerns that data can unveil, ultimately facilitating a deeper exploration of the more-than-human dimensions of urban development.

Justice

In the third section, authors discuss different issues associated with achieving justice in smart cities when we consider moving beyond a human-centred perspective. Special attention is given to the tensions around which species we are prepared to live with, and those we are not prepared to tolerate, as well as a consideration of the sacrifices humans may need to make in order to make space for other species. This section also presents a critical analysis of what democracy might mean when non-human stakeholders are brought to the table of urban governance processes.

The chapter by Clara Mancini, Daniel Metcalfe, and Orit Hirsch-Matsioulas advocates for extending the principles of equity and inclusivity to the realm of animal inhabitants within smart cities. Grounded in multispecies justice theory, the authors posit that truly just smart cities should facilitate animals' pursuit of biologically relevant goals and species-specific capabilities. By providing cases of human–animal cohabitation, the authors highlight the importance of supporting animals' interaction in cities.

Mennatullah Hendawy, Shaimaa Lazem, and Rachel Clarke explore complex notions of decentring human exceptionalism in the context of urban development and conflict, where communities are spatially marginalised in East Jerusalem. They argue for more-than-human speculations that recognise multiple perspectives, including human inequality when considering designs for cohabitation towards a just smart city.

Alex Taylor and Alison Powell explore the consequences of reimagining our interactions with multispecies neighbours in smart cities. They argue that these encounters can generate new forms of solidarity between humans and non-humans but also bring forth tensions that highlight the political dimensions of 'partial perspectives' and asymmetries in recognising others. This chapter encourages reflection on the connections that can be forged through encounters with animal others.

Futures

In our final section, authors present speculations, demonstrators, and futuring approaches to more-than-human smart cities to consider higher levels of impact making. What does it mean to scale up the potential for impact, and at the same time respect the specifics of local communities and practices? How can we reconcile the urgency of the climate crisis and the need to act now with the need to consider long-term even geological—timescales? What might sustainable smart cities of the future look like and what are the drivers of change?

The chapter by Mary Graham, Michelle Maloney, and Marcus Foth offers a longer-term perspective on the future of more-than-human cities. Drawing inspiration from the enduring governance systems of Australian Aboriginal societies, they introduce the concepts of the Relationist Ethos and Custodial Ethic to advocate for regenerative habitats and social justice within cities. The chapter encourages urban governance professionals to embrace thinking across generations and envision cities that act as 'good ancestors' for both future generations of humans and non-human others.

At the forefront of engineering and design innovation, Rachel Armstrong explores the practice of working with microbes to build programmable bricks that produce electricity from human waste and AI through biofilms that support a culture of life to inform a new vision of the bio-digital city. Through a series of high-profile international demonstrator projects, Armstrong questions what the future of urban democracy in the smart city might look like when we cohabit with autonomous bio-digital structures inextricably linked to our bodily fluids.

Ann Light, Lara Houston, and Ruth Catlow describe the experiences of developing the *Treaty of Finsbury Park* in London and the significance of intimacy in the process of transforming the urban imagination. They argue intimacy acts as a counter to urban smart-city development that often focuses myopically on efficiency and data abstraction.

In the final chapter, Ron Wakkary provides a unique glimpse into the future of cities by focusing on the lifecycles and endings of designed elements within urban environments. Drawing from the concept of biography in the context of designing-with, Wakkary explores the intertwined narratives of human and non-human agencies and sheds light on the fragility, breakdown, and evolving ontologies of waste that play pivotal roles in shaping and reshaping cities. This chapter ultimately invites readers to perceive cities as intricate interweavings of biographies and multispecies gatherings and offers a thought-provoking perspective on the evolving dynamics of urban spaces and their more-than-human constituents.

What Next?

In editing this book, between its inception in 2019 and throughout the COVID-19 pandemic, we have been constantly reminded of the ever-present challenges when multispecies relations are focused on human dominance over others. We see repeatedly across the globe that this dominance has resulted in extinction, loss, viruses, and disease. While many of the chapters respond to visible Earth systems and species, when faced with viruses such as COVID-19, monkeypox, and bird flu, the significance of microbes and bacteria is clear (Mitchell 2011; Searle & Turnbull 2020). When a species is under threat for long periods of time, the results can be unpredictable, as species adapt and mutate. From our own gut biome, where stresses can cause certain bacteria to thrive, to the changing land use across the planet due to intensification of animal food production and rapid urbanisation causing habitat loss, these drivers inevitably support the conditions for disease and threaten the wellbeing of much life on Earth. This is yet another reason we should opt for cohabitation and not control.

Amidst these challenges, the urgency of our collective and planetary mission becomes clearer than ever. The lessons gleaned from the intricate web of multispecies interactions, including the microbial realms, underscore the necessity of embracing a paradigm shift towards more-than-human smart cities. While the past may be riddled with tales of extinction and pandemics arising from human-centric approaches, our journey forward must be paved with radical and urgent systemic transformations. As we strive towards thriving cohabitation, rather than control, let us develop together new practices and perspectives that recognise the entanglements and interdependencies between humans and other species. At the same time let us remain critically optimistic about the possibilities for harnessing computation to help us advance planetary wellbeing, including in urban space. Let us aim for a future where resilience, adaptability, and a profound respect for the more-than-human world offer a beacon of hope.

Acknowledgements

We express our profound thanks to all the author teams who have played an integral role in making this book possible. Their dedication and meticulous efforts in not only crafting their chapters but also in diligently revising and refining them through the peer review process have been amazing. Collaborating with the editors, fellow chapter authors, and external reviewers, the author teams have exemplified scholarly rigour and dedication. It is through their collective expertise and commitment that this edited volume has become the rich collection it is, shedding light on the fascinating scholarship and practice of designing more-than-human smart cities. Our authors' contributions have been invaluable, and for that, we offer our sincere thanks.

We extend our heartfelt gratitude to our dedicated external peer reviewers who played an instrumental role in shaping the content and quality of each chapter. Their invaluable feedback and constructive comments on earlier drafts have been pivotal in ensuring the quality and rigour of this book. We deeply appreciate their expertise, time, and commitment to academic service. Thank you: Patrick Bresnihan, Simon Bowen, Nic Bidwell, Glenda Caldwell, Nicole Cook, Marketa Dolejsova, Cally Gatehouse, Dave Kirk, Catherine Oliver, Yin Paradies, Doina Petrescu, Larissa Pschetz, Hira Sheikh, Kristine Samson, Martin Tomitsch, and Michelle Westerlaken.

Our thanks and appreciation also go to the dedicated and tireless Oxford University Press staff who have been our guiding stars throughout the journey of producing this book. Their support, guidance, and expertise have been instrumental in shepherding us through the OUP internal review and approval processes. Their patience in answering our myriad questions—from image permissions to epigraph copyright issues—and their commitment to keeping us on track have been invaluable. We are truly grateful for their professionalism, attention to detail, and their commitment to ensuring the timely production of this publication. Their contributions have made the complex task of bringing this book to fruition a smoother and more rewarding process. Thank you for your exceptional support and dedication: Giulia Lipparini, Dan Taber, and Bethany Williams.

Sara thanks her colleagues and members of the Centre for Human–Computer Interaction Design at City, University of London, who have provided feedback and support over the years. She also thanks all the co-organisers and participants who attended the workshops at the PDC 2018 and C&T 2019 conferences who helped develop the ideas for this book.

Marcus extends his thanks and gratitude to members of the QUT More-Than-Human Futures research group who participated in debates, discussions, events, and offered thoughts, ideas, and provocations. Marcus is also grateful for the support and patience from his partner Troy who has cooked dinner on many occasions and endured him working late at night while neglecting his domestic duties. Thank you, hun!

Rachel thanks students, peers, and colleagues at Open Lab at Newcastle University and London College of Communication, University of the Arts London, who have helped provide inspiration and insight into what it means to grapple with more-than-human design in these troubled times. Rachel also thanks her co-editors, collaborators, and other creatures who have brought energy and kindness with them along the way.

Notes

1. We acknowledge that Capitalocene may be a more fitting term considering that not all human activity is equal across the planet, and it is largely the dominant neoliberal economic-political system from the Global North fuelling consumerism that is at the core of the issues we are facing (Monbiot 2016; Moore 2017).
2. https://research.qut.edu.au/morethanhuman/

References

Abram, D. (1997). *The spell of the sensuous: Perception and language in a more-than-human world.* Vintage Books.

Clarke, R., Heitlinger, S., Light, A., Forlano, L., Foth, M., & DiSalvo, C. (2019). More-than-human participation: Design for sustainable smart city futures. *Interactions, 26*(3), 60–63. https://doi.org/10.1145/3319075

Dourish, P. (2010). HCI and environmental sustainability: The politics of design and the design of politics. Proceedings of the 8th ACM Conference on Designing Interactive Systems - DIS '10, *1*. https://doi.org/10.1145/1858171.1858173

Forlano, L. (2016). Decentering the human in the design of collaborative cities. *Design Issues, 32*(3), 42–54. https://doi.org/10.1162/DESI_a_00398

Foth, M., Heitlinger, S., Tomitsch, M., & Clarke, R. (2019). Digital cities #11: Communities and technologies for more-than-human futures [Conference presentation]. *Proceedings of the Communities & Technologies Conference 2019*, Vienna, Austria. https://eprints.qut.edu.au/129010/

Foth, M., Paulos, E., Satchell, C., & Dourish, P. (2009). Pervasive computing and environmental sustainability: Two conference workshops. *IEEE Pervasive Computing/IEEE Computer Society [and] IEEE Communications Society, 8*(1), 78–81. https://doi.org/10.1109/MPRV.2009.13

Franklin, A. (2017). The more-than-human city. *The Sociological Review, 65*(2), 202–217. https://doi.org/10.1111/1467-954X.12396

Galloway, A. (2017). More-than-human lab: Creative ethnography after human exceptionalism. In L. Hjorth, H. Horst, A. Galloway, & G. Bell (Eds.), *The Routledge companion to digital ethnography* (pp. 496–503). Routledge. https://www.taylorfrancis.com/chapters/edit/

10.4324/9781315673974-61/human-lab-creative-ethnography-human-exceptionalism-anne-galloway?context=ubx&refId=89e6a87a-7dd1-4a8d-817f-38228635b198

Giaccardi, E., & Redström, J. (2020). Technology and more-than-human design. *Design Issues, 36*(4), 33–44. https://doi.org/10.1162/desi_a_00612

Heitlinger, S., Foth, M., Clarke, R., DiSalvo, C., Light, A., & Forlano, L. (2018). Avoiding ecocidal smart cities: Participatory design for more-than-human futures. *Proceedings of the 15th Participatory Design Conference: Short Papers, Situated Actions, Workshops and Tutorial, Volume 2*, Article 51. https://doi.org/10.1145/3210604.3210619

Mitchell, P. (2011). Geographies/aerographies of contagion. *Environment and planning D: Society and Space, 29*(3), 533–550. https://doi.org/10.1068/d9009

Monbiot, G. (2016). *How did we get into this mess? Politics, equality, nature.* Verso Books. http://www.monbiot.com/2007/08/28/how-did-we-get-into-this-mess/

Monteiro, M. (2017, March 20). Ethics can't be a side hustle. *Dear Design Student.* https://deardesignstudent.com/ethics-cant-be-a-side-hustle-b9e78c090aee

Monteiro, M. (2019). Ruined by Design: How Designers Destroyed the World, and What We Can Do to Fix It. Independently Published. https://www.ruinedby.design

Moore, J. W. (2017). The Capitalocene, Part I: On the nature and origins of our ecological crisis. *The Journal of Peasant Studies, 44*(3), 594–630. https://doi.org/10.1080/03066150.2016.1235036

Nichols, P., & Heitlinger, S. (2022). Farm lab: Ten years of participatory design research with Spitalfields City Farm. *Interactions, 29*(1), 16–19. https://doi.org/10.1145/3505275

Panelli, R. (2010). More-than-human social geographies: Posthuman and other possibilities. *Progress in Human Geography, 34*(1), 79–87. https://doi.org/10.1177/0309132509105007

Paulos, E., Foth, M., Satchell, C., Kim, Y., Dourish, P., & Choi, J. H.-J. (2008, September 21–24). *Ubiquitous Sustainability: Citizen Science and Activism* [Conference presentation]. In Tenth International Conference on Ubiquitous Computing (UbiComp), Seoul, South Korea. https://eprints.qut.edu.au/14130/

Searle, A., & Turnbull, J. (2020). Resurgent natures? More-than-human perspectives on COVID-19. *Dialogues in Human Geography, 10*(2), 291–295. https://doi.org/10.1177/2043820620933859

SECTION 1
CULTURES

1
Infrastructural Frictions
Care, Shadows, and Ruins in Multispecies Smart Cities

Donna Houston, Jessica McLean, and Natalie Osborne

> There is a politics to shadow that is not simply resolved by illuminating what has been previously forgotten, remembering what has been damaged or lost. Being in the light does not mean anything will necessarily change for the better. At the same time, while much suffers in the shadows, some things thrive, as they are hidden from the gaze and protected from encounters.
>
> Shadow Places Network, *A Manifesto for Shadow Places*[1]

Infrastructures, Smart and Shadowy

Is 'smart' a good measure to think with, for, or about multispecies cities? We ask this question because we are interested in the many manifestations of digital, social, biological, and infrastructural lives that comprise more-than-human cities. But we are uncertain and hesitant about how to proceed. We think it important to trouble how *smartness* becomes attached to specific ways of 'knowing/doing/seeing' cities (Williams 2017). At the same time, we do not wish to position the multispecies liveliness or the inhuman intensities that inhabit, nest, weather, erode, inundate, chew-away at, disrupt, and co-create the city as an antidote to smart urbanism. We begin this chapter by situating smart cities practices and theories in the context of shadow geographies, particularly the shadow geographies of urban infrastructures in multispecies cities.

Smart cities have a short but complex material-semiotic history. This history coheres and diverges around different but interrelated framings of digital/data/algorithm/innovation enabled urbanisms focused on aspirations, power relations, and liminalities. Via various aspirations and programmes that seek to envision, affirm, and enact the 'smart city', narratives and practices of *smartness* can be tracked through an array of urban growth logics, platforms, data-driven solutions, and strategic visions for urban innovation (Sadowski 2018; Barns 2019; Datta & Odendall 2019). The ways in which *smartness* cleaves to urban forms, objects, and places are not especially new as far as mainstream planning/design imaginaries in neoliberal and globally competitive cities go. They are commonly found in smart urban policies and strategies from local municipal plans to comprehensive metropolitan visions (e.g. 'Smart London'), which aim to integrate smart platforms

Donna Houston, Jessica McLean, and Natalie Osborne, *Infrastructural Frictions*. In: *Designing More-than-Human Smart Cities*. Edited by: Sara Heitlinger, Marcus Foth, and Rachel Clarke, Oxford University Press. © Oxford University Press (2024). DOI: 10.1093/9780191980060.003.0003 and technologies across many different areas of urban and public life (Dowling et al. 2021). *Smartness* is thus a combination of promissory ideations and techno-fixes that will bring about the next, better city via digital aids, improved data legibility/connectedness, and new digital and technology-enabled infrastructures (Clark 2020; Dowling et al. 2021; Kitchin 2022).

The visibility and legibility of the smart city is thus already storied and fixed in specific ways. *Smartness* operates to illuminate the futurity of places by proposing to smooth out their messy inefficiencies, and in this way, it adheres to linear logics of urban growth and development. Yet, the very presence of the smart city is dependent on what exists within and between: that which endures within and is produced by its shadows (McLean 2020a, 2020b). We find it useful to think with and about smart cities alongside *shadow places* (Plumwood 2008; Potter et al. 2020) and *shadow infrastructures* (Power et al. 2022), which highlight the diverse and unstable interactions of injustices and possibilities, care and ruins in multispecies smart cities.

The *smartness* of the smart city relies on and co-configures shadow places—places that facilitate its existence and yet must be sacrificed, neglected, or obfuscated to maintain the promises and ideals the smart city offers. Shadows also draw attention to the hidden and ignored relations that exist within and between dominant frames of the smart city (Power et al. 2022, p.1166). Following the work of Potter et al. (2020) and Power et al. (2022), herein we seek to think infrastructurally about shadow places, to help foreground the connections and patterns between forms and the organisational structures that produce them. We understand *infrastructures* to mean the systems—comprised of social, technical, political, economic, organic, material, and immaterial, formal, and informal elements—that organise and distribute the resources and byproducts of systems of production, reproduction, and indeed of co-constituted, interdependent life (Grealy et al. 2019; Alam & Houston 2020; Power et al. 2022).

Stokes and De Coss-Corzo (2023) note that infrastructures have been the subject of considerable scholarly attention which have diversified questions of 'what it is and what it is not'. Similar to our definition above, Stokes and De Coss-Corzo 'understand infrastructures as being distinct socio-material assemblages which mediate the lively and repeated processes that underpin and sustain collective life, governance and power, and/or capital accumulation' (2023, pp.428–429). These definitions of infrastructure track beyond the concreteness and appearances of 'things' to emphasise relationalities, labours, politics, affects, and entanglements (see also Star 1999; Amin 2014; Lawhon et al. 2018; McFarlane 2018). In turn, this invites a consideration of what gets relegated to the static, mundane, invisible—*shadowed*—backgrounds concerned with 'sustaining life' (Alam & Houston 2020; Power et al. 2022; Stokes & De Coss-Corzo 2023). Scholars of digital worlds work on similar sets of concerns around how representations of the digital and digital infrastructures (data, clouds, networks) are abstracted from their materialities—again relegating their uneven geographies of production, reproduction, and byproducts as invisible (McLean 2020a, 2020b; Furlong 2021). As Furlong (2021, p.191) writes: 'the infrastructures of our increasingly digital worlds call for a more nuanced engagement with (in)visibility, one that goes beyond visibility as a switch that occurs 'upon breakdown'.

Jess McLean (author two) uses the term *more-than-real* to refer to digital spaces as it enables a serious engagement with the generative and destructive capacities of the digital, capacities that can be too easily overlooked if we describe them as 'virtual' or not IRL (in real life) (McLean 2020b). The interplay of and between more-than-real and more-than-human in multispecies smart cities can be similarly overlooked. We are therefore curious about *glitches*, which Berlant (2016) defines as 'an interruption within a transition, a troubled transmission . . . the revelation of an infrastructural failure' (p.393), how glitches in the smart city are always already multispecies, more-than-human experiences, and what these glitches demand of a feminist ethic of care (Leszczynski 2020). Though not writing about smart cities or digital life, Power et al. (2022) introduce 'shadow care infrastructures' to convey cross-cutting themes where:

> the shadows metaphor purposefully directs attention toward those relations and spaces that sit within and between dominant frames. Productively brought together with feminist ethics of care and new infrastructural studies, this framework conceptualises and can ground efforts to trace a more comprehensive set of relations through which life is sustained, across different domains . . . (2022, p.1166).

Echoing Power et al. (2022), we find the intersecting ideas of shadows, care, infrastructures, and ruins useful for unravelling *smartness* in cities. Indeed, the slick veneers of the smart city are too often fed by the ruins of elsewhere and Others, and these sites, structures, and experiences must be attended to. The promise of *smartness* rarely acknowledges its shadows: the capacities to exclude, extract, colonise, harm, or simply not work as planned (Luque-Ayala & Marvin 2015; Datta 2018; Sadowski 2021). The smart city, it is noted by critical urban and technology scholars, is no panacea for urban injustices (Clark 2020) and can further exacerbate them through increased surveillance and data extraction (Sadowski 2021), socio-technological divides (Datta 2018; Datta & Odendaal 2019), and through displacement and gentrification associated with its various spatial manifestations (Ash et al. 2018; Datta 2018). In the universalising rush towards *smartness*, that is, the city of networks, platforms, algorithmic logics, surveillance, clouds, and big data, it is important to consider what remains in the shadows and what is revealed in the glitches (Berlant 2016; Mah 2017; Leszczynski 2020; McLean 2020b).

It is, at least in part, from these shadows that the frictions, troubles, and resistance that can transform and remake the smart city along more just lines will emerge. *Smartness*, as the digital transformation of urban economies, cultures, labours, intimacies, and places breaks down when it interacts with the unruly bodies, entities, histories, and places of the actually existing city (Dowling et al 2021). Feminist politics of care among and alongside the ruins of smart cities may emerge from that unruliness, seizing and collectivising the powers to engage in creative disruption and destruction, to create ruins; following in the Luddite tradition, to break the machines of the smart city as '*practices of political (re)composition*' (Mueller 2021, p.16, italics in original).

These critiques give rise to understandings and critiques of the smart city's velocities, contradictions, inequities, multiple antagonisms, and invisibilities. Ayona Datta and Nancy Odendaal (2019, p.338), for example, use Achille Mbembe's concept of 'the banality of power' to highlight the normalised (and therefore de-politicised) routine of 'measuring, monitoring and calculating' in the smart city. The routine entanglement of bodies, homes, spaces, infrastructures, and mobilities with the smart city reshapes and reconfigures relations of power in hidden and overt ways. Datta and Odendaal write: 'the banality present in the routineness of events or in the predictability of routine opens up the symbolic and spectacular nature of power in the smart city' (2019, p.338). It is in this regard that the collection, correlation, and mining of 'intimate' (Datta 2020) and 'big' (Mah 2017) data have become significant sites of contestation over digital and place-based rights to the city and its governance (Vadiati 2022). While potentially opening up new affordances for citizen-expert coalitions to mobilise data for social and environmental justice, struggles over the extraction of labour and data continue to reveal persistent racial, class, and gendered blind spots in 'voice, speed and expertise' (Mah 2017). In other words, digital tools tend to reproduce the systems that make them. Akin to being in a hall of mirrors, the aspirations of the smart city are transfixed by its own image (see Rose 2004). There are significant limits on what problems the smart city might be able to story or solve absent of other subjects, and of more transformative, changes.

The spectacular imaginaries of smart cities, socially-connected techno-capitalism, and the banality of power bound up in their everyday arrangements, are contingent on their shadowy geographies—the antagonistic struggle over imaginaries and rights, urban places and infrastructures, publicness and privacy, and data sovereignties (Barns 2019; Galic and Schuilenburg 2020; Burns and Andrucki 2021; Sadowski 2021). Expanding on these contestations, we argue that digital lives and materialities in cities might be understood via infrastructural frictions. Here, different entities, labours, atmospheres, and multiple aspirations and agendas coalesce in the generative interactions of care and ruins. These interactions are not (only) traced through the spectacular and banal presence of *smartness*, but rather (also) though the contours of entangled and in-between spaces of the smart city: its glitchy, shadowy infrastructures of care and ruin. In this emergent framing of smart cities, the appearance of *smartness* falls away and shadows draw attention not only to what is suppressed and unseen but to what other possibilities and practices of care might thrive in the in-betweens. In attending to the shadow places and infrastructures of smart cities, the object of the smart city is not only decentred but decidedly unravelled (Leszczynski 2020; Kitchin 2022). The liminal, ungovernable, unrepresentable habitations, frictions and interrelations of smart cities can then be explored to plot alternative and ethical possibilities.

In what follows, we draw on interdisciplinary feminist thought from the environmental, digital and urban humanities to offer a counterfactual storying of infrastructural frictions in multispecies smart cities. Our aim is to explore how the smart city might be unravelled by thinking about the frictions and interdependent realities that entangle and transgress the dominant smart frame (Heitlinger et al 2018; Kitchin 2022). We ask what emancipatory affordances of smart city assemblages can be brought into democratic and emplaced relations of care, repair, and restoration? And where repair is liable to, however inadvertently, be co-opted into the reproduction of harmful structures (Berlant 2016), when might we turn to the emerging tradition of neo-Luddism (see Mueller 2021) and engage in creative destruction—to not only work and care among the ruins, but to help create them?

The narrative unfolds in the form of three vignettes where we each reflect on that which catches on the static and glitchy edges of smart city configurations. We conclude by asking for a greater consideration of how multispecies smart cities may be thought and lived differently when traced through the frictive and lively entanglements of care and ruins.

Infrastructural Frictions: Three Vignettes

Before sharing the vignettes, we first situate our thinking about the 'in-between' multispecies and more-than-human relationalities of smart cities. Thinking about the relationalities of smart cities pushes back against the intensifying rush toward universality that is bound up with the ideation and the manifestation of *smartness*. New urban technological and economic configurations that aim to smooth out or replace the messy inefficiencies of the unsustainable city seem a worthy goal. But as we have argued in the previous section, fixing the 'object' of the smart city produces only a certain (and always partial) field of vision of urban progress, development, and improvement. To decentre and unravel the object of the smart city, different vocabularies and coordinates for considering entangled and endangered lifeworlds are required.

Through our vignettes we explore some of the 'infrastructural frictions' of multispecies smart cities. 'Friction', which is inspired by Anna Tsing's book of the same name, describes 'the awkward, unequal, unstable and creative qualities of interconnection across difference' (2005, p.4). For Tsing, frictions are sites of practical engagement which interfere with the 'self-fulfilling prophecies' of global capitalism (2005, p.257). Tsing proposes an ethnography of encounter to disrupt the 'dichotomy between global force and local response' to show 'the importance of contingent and botched encounters in shaping both business-as-usual and its radical refusals' (p.258). Friction is a useful method for thinking for/about/with multispecies smart cities because of its focus on 'contingent and botched encounters'. Friction forces a slowing down of the smart city's velocities to emphasise interrelations and interconnections. Such a focus shows how the hopes and ruins of smart cities do not always sit in opposition but rather exist and rub along together in complicated ways. As Tsing contends, friction helps us to write against the 'structures of self-fulfilment'. She adds that it is important to attend to states of emergence and of emergencies where 'hope and despair huddle together, sometimes dependent on the same technologies (2005, p.269).

We are also inspired by Agnieszka Leszczynski's (2020) work on the 'glitchy vignettes' of platform urbanism as an exemplary example of an embodied and frictive approach. Leszczynski shares a similar concern about how the universalising narratives of platform cities produce a dichotomy of utopian/dystopian futures. Leszczynski uses the 'glitch' to propose a minor theory of platform urbanism. Glitches and glitchiness offer glimpses into the in-between of smart cities, Leszcynski uses vignettes to illustrate that which eludes cohesion 'to identify unique spatio-temporalities where the comings-together of cities and platforms are observably glitchy, evading distillation to pattern, process or expected outcome' (2020, p.197). While we are not focused on platforms, we argue that smart city constellations also require minor theories that are attuned to frictions, glitches, and refusals, disruptions to the 'patterning of social form' (Berlant 2016 p.393). Multispecies smart cities do not cohere to sustainable efficiencies, nor will they herald a better 'more ecological' version of the smart city. This assumption is precisely what we aim to disrupt.

Vignette 1: The smart pole

During one evening of a research trip to Meanjin/Brisbane in 2019, I took a walk along the footpath adjacent to Maiwar River and, amidst the graceful eucalyptus and concrete overpass, came upon this smart pole (Figure 1.1). Meanjin/Brisbane is often framed as a leader in smart cities interventions and this was my first glimpse of such infrastructure; the City of Brisbane local government has adopted policies to digitise infrastructure with an intention to leverage these for more sustainable urban places.

I wondered what the green-glowing digital numbers meant. Passers-by might reasonably infer that the figures are indicative of how many people cycle and walk along this riverside path. But how significant was it that on that one particular day there were 2597 cyclists and 1175 pedestrians? And what about non-walkers and non-cyclists—where do they fit? Infrastructural tensions relating to mobilities and access accompany these shiny figures on the smart pole.

Yet I was also happy to see this version of smart infrastructure. Hundreds and thousands of people evidently walk and ride along this waterway throughout the year and these are recorded for city planning. Perhaps these people are experiencing being with water bodies in a different way than when encased in a vehicle; walking and riding with non-humans potentially opens up possibilities for a broader sense of the urban.

When moving with water, noticing multispecies presences is possible. Watching the rakali (native water rat) clambering about the rocky edges could be amusing as people amble along the river. Smelling the sweet and rank odours wafting from the water surface could prompt reflections on what is happening up- and downstream in this catchment. More-than-human lifeworlds, including biological beings and hydrological water bodies as Whatmore (2002) offers, are easier to encounter on these pathways than on overhead roads in tonnes of metal.

And I wanted to add to the smart pole figures. These were (supposedly) moments that I could see that I was contributing to a more sustainable Meanjin/Brisbane! So, I continued to walk many kilometres along the riverbank during that research trip, mostly because I really enjoy walking, and incidentally adding to the figures lighting up that pole each day—while also worrying about what this digital data was doing.

As one data point in the smart machine, I thought and felt like my small walking efforts counted, but I was not clear as to how or why they mattered. Cutting the issue another way, then, what do these smart pole numbers actually do? How do they

Figure 1.1 The smart pole.

change anything? Who is made to feel responsible for contributing to change here, and should they carry that burden? Who is left out of the counting, and why? Where is the multispecies city in this smart technology?

The smart pole, on the one hand, would visibly render the cumulative efforts of individuals and communities as collective efforts. People might garner a sense of pride that they are one of the 417,945 people walking and 999,246 people riding their bikes along that path in the nine and a half months before I saw that smart pole. They might get a sense of empowerment that they are part of a thing that is bigger than themselves and that collectively they can make a difference. That they are active transport—using their feet and wheels—to get somewhere rather than relying on cars that currently dominate so much of Australian city movement. Walkers and cyclists could potentially feel enlivened that they are making more room for more-than-humans by reducing the number of cars on the road. Or they may have just ignored the figures all together.

But individuals are responsibilised here, too, asked to change their own behaviours as a means of building better cities. Social problems are reforged in the creation of this smart pole so that individuals are constructed as in charge of, and having to manage, the huge task of making Meanjin/Brisbane more sustainable. This particular form of smart pole application can be read as responsibilisation in action. Responsibilisation is a key plank in neoliberal strategies to devolve accountability and effective action away from government and corporations, and towards citizens (Stonehouse et al. 2015). As a practice, responsibilisation is problematic as it assumes that individuals have unfettered control over their choices (in this case with respect to mobility) and that they will make the 'right' decision if they have the 'right' information. It also signals to communities and other institutions that the organisation doing the responsibilisation has taken effective action, in this case by doing something about making cities more sustainable, while having only performed this work in tokenistic gestures.

Assumptions about the ever-ready urban dweller are embedded in this digital counting and visualising that forms a dominant smart urban frame. The able-bodied, easily active individual is a part of the count while those with different mobility are rendered somewhat invisible. It is not clear how a pram, for example, is counted on this smart pole, and people using mobility aids such as wheelchairs, motorised scooters, or walking frames seem to be similarly overlooked. Bodies are collapsed into two possible categories of being: as individuals that are cycling or walking.

Resource Man is invoked here, too—an idea put forward by Strengers (2013) to challenge the reductive framing of technological solutionism. 'Rational and rationalising', Strengers (2013) wrote, Resource Man is supposedly constantly able to make the best decisions, ensuring that society as a whole is one step closer to a smart utopic future where digital technologies support flourishing and sustainable cities. Each walking or cycling figure on that smart pole exists as a sort of mini-Resource Man, empowered and enabled to save us all through their active transport decisions.

The geographic scope of these smart meters and other smart cities interventions in Meanjin/Brisbane is quite limited and a sort of smart enclave is produced by these bounded offerings (Rebentisch et al. 2020). While the rambling ways of tourists and more directionally focussed commuters are caught in these numbers on a pole, anything outside the confines of the inner city is not brought into the smart city fold. Who then is the smart pole for? The rich, powerful, and able, it could be inferred.

Ambivalence sits with me as I think back on this moment with a smart pole. I admire and am troubled by its somewhat misplaced efforts to smooth out and displace the messy inefficiencies of the unsustainable city while also wondering how it could become a better intervention, a more useful machine. And I wish for more inclusive offerings in future digital world-making, that facilitate flourishing multispecies cities and all mobilities, rather than reductive smartified environments.

Vignette 2: A squeeze of lime

Riding along the banks of Maiwar, on Jagera and Turrbal Country here in Meanjin (Brisbane), I am stopped by the sight of some of the e-waste, smart waste, dumped in the slick brown waters. Revealed by the receding tide (Figure 1.2), wedged up against the rocks are several Lime e-scooters (Figure 1.3)—the micro-mobility device operated and paid for via smart phone app trialled in Meanjin from 2018 to 2021. In places where the mangroves have not been entirely concreted over, fingery pneumatophores rise from the mud to claim the scooter as part of the at once vestigial and nascent swamp.

I wonder if the mangroves mind—if they'll be troubled by the presence of the cold metal, the corroding lithium batteries, the rubbery wheels and grips, the electrical wires and tiny chips. Or perhaps these are as nothing to the opportunistic forests, growing as they are along a river that carries the waste of a city and the run-off of motorways and freight trains and pastoral and agricultural and extractive hinterlands. Perhaps the intrusion is even welcomed by some: perhaps they provide a sheltering structure for small fish, or crabs evading the ibises keen to test their skills in this proxy of their ancestral hunting grounds, instead of the bins that give them their affectionate

Figure 1.2

Figure 1.3

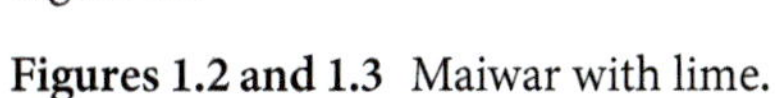

Figures 1.2 and 1.3 Maiwar with lime.

and derogatory nickname of 'bin chicken'. The commercial Lime scooters have an estimated operational life of twelve months (White 2019); I wonder how long their mangrove life is.

I consider the person—probably a person?—who threw the scooter into the lapping waters. Perhaps it was an accident, and they were careening out of control. Perhaps the scooter stopped working and they threw it off in disgust. Perhaps they were a pedestrian or cyclist frustrated by a thoughtless or dangerous parking spot, and they wanted to convey their discontent to the company, or the City Council that permitted them. Or perhaps they were drunk, or in a silly goofy mood, and it was funny.

Electric micro-mobility devices like e-bikes and e-scooters are a promising solution to the 'last mile' problem in transport planning. In a hilly city like Meanjin, where the banks of the southside rise sharply from the river, the climate almost always warm and sticky, only varying in degree, and laid out in winding, sprawling patterns. Public transport has inadequate coverage, and the distances between train stations, bus stops, home, and other destinations are often too far to be easily or comfortably walked in the steep, rolling heat.

Instead of managing the roll-out of e-scooters through the existing public transport agencies, Brisbane City Council outsourced it, first to Lime, and then to Neuron and Beam. In private hands there is much we don't know about the success and impact of these devices. We don't know how many scooters are lost or tossed. We don't know the number of crashes, accidents, injuries, or how much damage. The scooters take up space on already constrained shared paths and active transport networks, and somehow seem particularly prone to being parked just around a sharp bend.

And some, of course, wind up in drains, in trees, in ditches, in creeks, and in the river.

One night, when Lime scooters were still on the streets, I was out fairly late with my partner; we'd been to a show and were walking back to our bikes along quiet streets, near the parklands on the south side of Maiwar. A young man pulled up beside us in a white rental van. He began unloading e-scooters, placing them in a neat row along the edge of the parkland. He was a 'juicer'; a person who collects the scooters that haven't been planted in swamps, takes them home, charges them up, and disperses them back around the city at strategic locations. It was an odd moment; the scooters had been hyper-visible to me for some time, often to the point of being in my way, and yet this was the first time I'd seen one of the people doing the labour that made the system run.

Tech scholar and neo-Luddite Jathan Sadowski talks of Potemkin Artificial Intelligence (AI) and Potemkin tech—technology which 'constructs a façade that not only hides what's going on but deceives potential customers and the general public alike... Potemkin AI provides a convenient way to rationalize exploitation while calling it progress'. This was a reminder that the 'smart city' is in fact a Potemkin village. Every incidence of frictionless technological encounter is in fact a displacement of friction, not its removal. The friction—the work, the danger, the trouble—is displaced, to shadow places, and onto more vulnerable, more precarious, more exploited and exploitable people, often people of colour. The geographies of the smart city are an uneven terrain, steeper and more treacherous than the rolling hills of Meanjin.

I wonder how far that man is driving, in that rented van, and how much it costs in fees and fuel. I wonder how much charging the scooters drives up his electricity bill. I wonder about the timing of the work—late nights and early mornings—affects the rest of his day, his other commitments, his relationships. I wonder how much fossil fuel is burned driving these scooters around and charging them up. I wonder if he has a hard time finding them sometimes. I wonder if he gets sick of fetching them from weird places. I wonder if he has a quota—a number of scooters he is supposed to charge, or is it all of them within a certain catchment? I wonder how many powerboards and extension cables he uses. I wonder if he has housemates, and if they're annoyed by it or if they help. Or both.

I don't ask any of these things. He's busy and my idle curiosity is not his problem.

I wonder how long a scooter takes to rust. I wonder how long it takes for a scooter to rust to nothing. I wonder if the scooter will still be there when the waters rise up, when the city erodes away, and the sand and coral embedded in glass fronted high-rise towers return to the ocean.

Vignette 3: Sensing, loss?

I took this picture (Figure 1.4) on Gadigal Country at Bondi Beach in January 2020 during the Australian bushfire crisis.[2] The photo wasn't taken during the worst of the bushfire smoke, which rolled for months in noxious waves over Sydney and much of the east coast of Australia. But the smoke is there in the hazy background of the picture: permeable, lived, and inhaled. I suffer from seasonal allergies and asthma, so in response to the smoke, I purchased a portable HEPA air purifier for our home (a middle-class luxury to be sure). During that long, hot summer, tracking the indoor and outdoor air quality via the machine and apps using the Australian Air Quality Index Data became a daily (if not hourly) routine.

Along with tracking the air quality, I spent quite a bit of anxious time on the NSW Rural Fire Service 'Fires Near Me' app, worried for friends living in the path of the fires. Largely confined to indoors with smoke creeping through the windows and cloying in the back of my throat, I despaired over the immense scale of the loss of life, the unravelling of places, ecosystems, of earthly life. Blanche Verlie in her book *Learning to Live With Climate Change* (2022) writes that anger, heartbreak, grief, and loss are our climate and extinction companions. And humming along in these climate-driven atmospheres and affects are digitally enabled connections that partially and unevenly trace intimate ecologies of crisis. These are fraught and fragile relations as much as capable of harm as they are of care.

The apps and the HEPA filter offered some (very) minor affordances in the face of the uncontrollable and unfathomable. But while they 'connected' me to the smoke and fires, the HEPA filter and the apps also have material lives that are enmeshed in globalised systems of extraction, labour, production, exchange, and waste. They are embedded in relations that co-produce and exacerbate climate change (McLean 2020b).

Figure 1.4 Bondi Beach, January 2020.

I have been thinking about these affordances and distractions of data in multispecies cities. About how those raging infernos powerful enough to generate their own weather were reduced to fire symbols on maps. What does it mean to be able to measure PM2.5 levels in my living room but not be able to stop from breathing it in, from the fine particulate matter travelling into my lungs and bloodstream?

What does it mean that I could only read the data that had already been interpreted and presented to me in colour coded icons: green (very good); angry dark purple (extreme, very, very bad)? What does this tell me about my health and wellbeing, and the health and wellbeing of earth others? What did the angry purple icon convey about how the air quality in my house that was so poor because we were literally inhaling the charred remains of burned animals and ruined ecosystems? What was it then that the HEPA filter was attempting to 'purify'?

An unknown person taped the plush koala to the pole at Bondi Beach as a form of witness to the climate and the biodiversity crisis. The image tells a story about life and death in multispecies smart cities because it tells a story about how abundance, decline, and interdependence occupy liminal spaces between the 'more-than-human' and the 'more-than-real' (McLean 2020a; Prebble et al 2021). Building on more-than-human thinking, the more-than-real concept challenges binary thinking about digital spaces and highlights the entanglement of the digital with the non-digital. In this liminal space then, between the more-than-human and more-than-real, the plush koala stands in silent testimony: a reminder about whom and what becomes visible and legible and whom and what slips away unseen and unnoticed.

The interconnection between the more-than-human and the more-than-real is glitchy: the former highlights the complex entanglements of earthly and urban dwelling, while the latter is a critique that highlights the 'not realing' of digital technologies and spaces as somehow sitting outside of historical and material relations (Prebble et al. 2021). The more-than-real also helps us understand new digital presences, such as digital peregrines (Searle et al. 2022) or other wildlife under digital surveillance (von Essen et al. 2022), that are not representations of 'true' non-digital beings, but partial and productive renderings of human and more-than-human relations.

There is a growing interest in how disparate and temporally uneven environmental loss, harm, and repair are traced through intimate ecologies, digital cultures, and citizen-science in cities. Environmental justice groups use crowd-sourced data to map and measure air and water quality and to tell stories about environmental inequity. Citizen-science projects are increasingly used by urban ecologists and environmental organisations to help track human–plant–animal mobilities and cultures in cities. First Nations' communities, artists, and local councils use digital apps to assert sovereign relationships with Country and to unsettle settler-colonial representations of nature, place and public space.

The proliferation of these convivial ways of collaborating are in different and disparate ways, mapping multispecies smart cities 'from below'. The *Whadjuk Walking Trail* in Whadjuk/Perth (Western Australia), narrated by Noongar elder Dr Len Collard uses QR codes to share Noongar stories and histories in urban parks. The *Hollows as Homes* joint initiative run by the Australian Museum, Royal Botanic Gardens, and Sydney University is a crowd-sourced program that assesses and digitally maps tree hollow availability across urban and agricultural landscapes. Many Australian parrots and cockatoos require tree hollows, which take many decades to form in mature trees, for roosting and nesting. The *Urban Field Naturalist* project (Sydney) and the *Feral Atlas* (California) are digital storytelling collaborations between scientists, artists, designers, environmental humanities researchers, and citizens illuminating the invisible, the everyday, novel, and in the case of the latter, toxic entanglements that span out across space, place, species, and time.

This sort of work in multispecies smart cities encourages us to look beyond them and more deeply into them. Sensing/digital ecologies tell stories about intimacies and injustices, create different possibilities for care. But as they proliferate, can such imaginings and mappings of the more-than-human and the more-than-real maintain their frictive edges?

I love the idea of the conviviality of the multispecies smart cities, the clever ways of noticing and collaborating, the vivid multiplatform storytelling. But I worry about the consequences of the 'not realing' of relations because it all gets caught up in the busy-ness and banality of measuring and monitoring, where data becomes another distraction claiming to solve problems that it is not solving at all. So, I wonder: does all this sensing and mapping also offer different opportunities to 'look away' from social and environmental injustices? As we begin to shape landscapes of public data and more-than-human digital relations in multispecies cities, does sensing loss make us care more or less about shadow places and infrastructures? Have we already forgotten the margins of digital maps and apps?

Care and Ruins in Multispecies Smart Cities

We began this chapter with the question: is smart a good measure to think with and about multispecies cities? Smartness as it currently manifests in a variety of material-semiotic urban configurations becomes set in a hall of mirrors—endlessly reflecting back on its own shallow image and thus illuminated by the continual affirmation of its own narrow view (Rose 2004, p. 20). It is hard to 'see' the smart city (or more precisely, it is hard for the smart city to see itself) because it cannot attend to the complexities of its emergence or the responsibilities of its interdependencies. The unrepresentable, uninhabitable, and unknowable zones of smart cities remain in the shadows, as do the extractive labours and practices that make them materially possible.

We have argued that being attentive to the glitches and frictions highlights the ambivalences and disjunctures that exist in the entanglement of digital, more-than-human, multispecies worlds. Ambivalence arises from trying to think beyond the object of the smart city and beyond objects in smart cities to consider more-than-human/more-than real interdependencies and relations. Disjunctures arise from the reality that glitches and frictions are sometimes, but not always, generative of alternate ethical doings and possibilities. The smart pole diligently tracking ableist mobilities, the lime scooter slowly leaching heavy metals into Maiwar, the affective atmospheres of sensors, digital maps, and apps that convivially track some socio-ecological relations but not others, all point to our hesitancy and uncertainty about thinking/doing multispecies smart cities. And what of the banality of power in multispecies smart cities? What does it mean to configure human and nonhuman difference through urban-technological mediations?

We have argued that emergent forms and alternate possibilities in smart cities come into relation via the heterogeneous work of living in actually existing cities and through minor theoretical interventions (Katz 1996). Peering through glitches into the shadows helps us better understand the infrastructures that created them. Each of the smart city objects and imaginaries that we have reflected on in the vignettes come with their worlds and with their particular relations of care and ruins, ambivalence and disjuncture, in the sense that Maria Puig de la Bellacasa explains:

> Feminist ethics of care argue that to value care is to recognize the inevitable interdependency essential to the existence of reliant and vulnerable beings . . . Interdependency is not a contract, nor a moral ideal—it is a *condition*. Care is therefore concomitant to the continuation of life for many living beings in more than human entanglements – not forced upon them by a moral order, and not necessarily a rewarding obligation (emphasis in original) (de la Bellacasa 2017, p.70).

These fragments and encounters of smart cities offer glimpses of actually existing smart citizens (Shelton and Lodato 2019) and imagined digital worlds that generate, and are also in turn produced by, infrastructural tensions. Thinking with shadow places, and shadow infrastructures, helps us to examine who and what is included and represented, how everyday lives and moments of crises are navigated, what counter-infrastructures of care and repair are used to survive the failures and harms of dominant systems, what rights are respected and upheld in digital transformations, and what glitches in socio-technical systems reveal.

In the shadow places and infrastructures of smart cities lies interdependent, uneven and entangled relations that do not cohere into particular narratives or imaginaries of *smartness*, but rather, illuminate the ethics of care involved with negotiating life lived in common and in difference in shared multispecies /technological worlds (de la Bellacasa 2012, 2017; Harcourt 2021). Frictions, fissures, cracks in the intersections and interfaces of multispecies smart cities—their botched encounters—reveal different registers for more-than-human lives lived in urban and digital spaces. Botched encounters illuminate pathways into the elsewheres: into local and global historical, economic, cultural, and material relations that co-produce weeds and wires, artefacts, waste, datasets, sensors, rare earth minerals, apps, pollinator meadows, or digital forests (Gabrys 2022).

Care that foregrounds multispecies thinking in smart urbanism involves identifying presences and absences—shadowy infrastructures—in various worlds. If we draw, as de la Bellacasa does, on Fisher and Tronto's (1990) broad definition of care, compelling possibilities emerge for repositioning smart cities practices to prioritise multispecies thinking. In their holistic framing, care 'includes everything that we do to maintain, continue, and repair our "world" so that we can live in it as well as possible. That world includes our bodies, ourselves, and our environment, all of which we seek to interweave in a complex, life-sustaining web' (Fisher and Tronto 1990, p.40). Maintaining, continuing, and repairing our worlds involves recognising complexity and more-than-humans as vital agents, whether they are flourishing or impaired. Caring for digital urban ruins, then, involves respecting and repairing damaged places, engaging in care-full destruction and ruining of systems of harm and exploitation, attending to infrastructural frictions and glitches, while also working to avoid (re)producing digital shadows in that process.

Notes

1. Shadow Places Network, A Manifesto for Shadow Places. Online https://www.shadowplaces.net/manifesto (last accessed 29/9/2023). Excerpt reproduced with permission from the Shadow Places Network.
2. The catastrophic Australian bushfires burned from September 2019 to March 2020. Three billion animal lives were lost or displaced, 5.5 million hectares were burned, twenty-six human lives were lost, and over fourteen thousand homes destroyed.

References

Alam, A., & Houston, D. (2020). Rethinking care as alternate infrastructure. *Cities*, *100*, 102662.

Amin, A. (2014). Lively infrastructure. *Theory, Culture, & Society*, *31*(7–8), 137–161.

Ash, J., Kitchin, R., & Leszcynski, A. (2018). Digital turn, digital geographies? *Progress in Human Geography*, *42*(1), 25–43.

Barns, S. (2019). Negotiating the platform pivot: From participatory digital ecosystems to infrastructures of everyday life. *Geography Compass*, *13*, Article e12464.

Berlant, L. (2016). The Commons: Infrastructures for troubling times. *Environment and Planning D: Society and Space*, *34*(3), 393–419

Burns, R., & Andrucki, M. (2021). Smart cities: Who cares? *Environment and Planning A: Society and Space*, *53*(1), 12–30.

Clark, J. (2020). *Uneven innovation: The work of smart cities*. Columbia University Press.

Datta, A. (2018). The digital turn in postcolonial urbanism: Smart citizenship in the making of India's 100 smart cities. *Transactions of the Institute of British Geographers*, *43*, 405–419. https://doi.org/10.1111/tran.12225

Datta, A. (2020). Self(ie)-governance: Technologies of intimate surveillance in India under COVID-19. *Dialogues in Human Geography*, *10*(2), 234–237. https://doi.org/10.1177/2043820620929797

Datta, A., & Odendall, N. (2019). Smart cities and the banality of power. *Environment and Planning D: Society and Space*, *37*(3), 387–392.

de la Bellacasa, M. P. (2012). Nothing in the world comes without its care. *The Sociological Review*, *60*(2), 197–216.

de la Bellacasa, M.P. (2017). *Matters of care: Speculative ethics in more than human worlds*. University of Minnesota Press.

Dowling, R., McGuirk, P., Maalsen, S., & Sadowski, J. (2021). How smart cities are made: A priori, ad hoc and post hoc drivers of smart city implementation in Sydney, Australia. *Urban Studies*, *58*(16), 3299–3315.

Fisher, B., & Tronto, J. (1990). Towards a feminist ethics of care. In E. K. Abel & M. K. Nelson (Eds.), *Circles of care: Work and identity in women's lives* (pp. 35–62). State University of New York Press.

Furlong, K. (2021). Geographies of infrastructure II: Concrete, cloud and layered (in)visibilities. *Progress in Human Geography*, *45*(1), 190–198.

Gabrys, J. (2022). The forest that walks: Digital fieldwork and distributions of site. *Qualitative Inquiry*, *28*(2), 228–235.

Galic, M. and Schuilenburg, M. (2020). Reclaiming the smart city: Toward a new right to the city. In J. C. Augusto (Ed.), *Handbook of smart cities* (pp. 1419–1436). Springer Nature.

Grealy, L., Brooks, A., Lorange, A., Cornell, C., & Lea, T. (2019). Introduction: Tending a social infrastructure. *Infrastructural Inequalities*, *1*. https://infrastructuralinequalities.net/issue-1/introduction/

Harcourt, W. (2021). Rethinking life-in-common in the Australian landscape. *Environment and Planning E: Nature and Space*, *4*(4), 1330–1345. doi:10.1177/2514848621989602

Heitlinger, S., Foth, M., Clarke, R., DiSalvo, C., Light, A., & Forlano, L. (2018, 20 August). Avoiding ecocidal smart cities: Participatory design for more-than-human futures. In *PDC '18: Proceedings of the 15th participatory design conference: Short papers, situated actions, workshops and tutorial* (Vol. 2, pp. 1–3), Article No. 51. https://doi.org/10.1145/3210604.3210619

Katz, C. (1996). Towards minor theory. *Environment and Planning D: Society and Space*, *14*(4), 487–499.

Kitchin, R. (2022). Conceptualising smart cities. *Urban Research & Practice*, *15*(1), 155–159. doi: 10.1080/17535069.2022.2031143

Lawhon, M., Nilsson, D., Silver, J., Ernston, H., & Lwasa, S. (2018). Thinking through heterogeneous infrastructure configurations. *Urban Studies*, *55*(4), 720–732.

Leszczynski, A. (2020). Glitchy vignettes of platform urbanism. *Environment and Planning D: Society and Space*, *38*(2), 189–208.

Luque-Ayala, A., & Marvin, S. (2015). Developing a critical understanding of smart urbanism? *Urban Studies*, *52*(12), 2105–2116. doi:10.1177/0042098015577319

Mah, A. (2017). Environmental justice in the age of big data: Challenging toxic blind spots of voice, speed and expertise. *Environmental Sociology*, *3*(2), 122–133.

McFarlane, C. (2018). Fragment urbanism: Politics at the margins of the city. *Environment and Planning D: Society and Space*, *36*(6), 1007–1025.

McLean, J. (2020a). *Changing digital geographies: Technologies, environments and people*. Palgrave MacMillan.

McLean, J. (2020b) D: Digital. *A–Z of Shadow Places Concepts*. https://uploads-ssl.webflow.com/5ba9c6933815356bf0faa5f8/5f8fc08c82d90d1f24ecea0e_Digital%20-%20Jessica%20McLean%20(Final%20Proof).pdf

Mueller, G. (2021). *Breaking things at work: The Luddites were right about why you hate your job*. Verso Books.

Plumwood, V. (2008). Shadow places and the politics of dwelling. *Australian Humanities Review*, *44*, 139–150.

Potter, E., Miller, F., Lövbrand, E., Houston, D., McLean, J., O'Gorman, E., Evers, C., & Ziervogel, G. (2020). A manifesto for shadow places: Re-imagining and co-producing connections for justice in an era of climate change. *Environment and Planning E: Nature and Space*, *5*(1), 272–292.

Power, E. R., Wiesel, I., Mitchell, E., & Mee, K. J. (2022). Shadow care infrastructures: Sustaining life in post-welfare cities. *Progress in Human Geography*, *46*(5). https://doi.org/10.1177/03091325221109837

Prebble, S., McLean, J., & Houston, D. (2021). Smart urban forests: An overview of more-than-human and more-than-real urban forest management in Australian cities. *Digital Geography and Society*, *2*, 100013. https://doi.org/10.1016/j.diggeo.2021.100013

Rebentisch, H., Thompson, C., Côté-Roy, L., & Moser, S. (2020). Unicorn planning: Lessons from the rise and fall of an American 'smart' mega-development. *Cities*, *101*, Article 102686.

Rose, D. B. (2004). *Reports from the wild country: Ethics for decolonisation*. University New South Wales Press.

Sadowski, J. (2018, August 6). Potemkin AI. *Real Life*. https://reallifemag.com/potemkin-ai/

Sadowksi, J. (2021). Who owns the future city? Phases of technological urbanism and shifts in sovereignty. *Urban Studies*, *58*(8), 1732–1744.

Searle, A., Turnbull, J., & Adams, W. M. (2022) The digital peregrine: A technonatural history of a cosmopolitan raptor. *Transactions of the Institute of British Geographers*, *48*(1), 195–212. https://doi.org/10.1111/tran.12566

Shadow Places Network (2020). Manifesto for Shadow Places. *Shadow Places*. https://www.shadowplaces.net/manifesto.

Shelton, T., & Lodato, T. 2019. Actually existing smart citizens. *City*, *23*(1), 35–52. doi: 10.1080/13604813.2019.1575115

Star, S. L. (1999). The ethnography of infrastructure. *American Behavioral Scientist*, *43*(3), 377–391.

Stokes, K., & De Coss-Corzo, A. (2023). Doing the work: Locating labour in infrastructural geography. *Progress in Human Geography*, *47*(3), 427–446.

Stonehouse, D., Threlkeld, G., & Farmer, J. (2015). 'Housing risk' and the neoliberal discourse of responsibilisation in Victoria. *Critical Social Policy*, *35*(3), 393–413.
Strengers, Y. (2013). *Smart energy technologies in everyday life: Smart utopia?* Springer.
Tsing, A. (2005). *Friction: An ethnography of global connection*. Princeton University Press.
Vadiati, N. (2022). Alternatives to smart cities: A call for consideration of grassroots digitalism. *Digital Geography and Society*, 3, Article 100030. https://doi.org/10.1016/j.diggeo.2022.100030
Verlie, B. (2022). *Learning to live with climate change: From anxiety to transformation*. Routledge.
von Essen, E., Turnbull, J., Searle, A., Jørgensen, F. A., Hofmeester, T. R., & van der Wal, R. (2022). Wildlife in the digital Anthropocene: Examining human–animal relations through surveillance technologies. *Environment and Planning E: Nature and Space*, *6*(1). https://doi.org/10.1177/25148486211061704
Whatmore, S. (2002). *Hybrid geographies: Natures Cultures Spaces*. Sage.
White, M. (2019, November 8). The scooters that ate Brisbane. *Australian Financial Review*. https://www.afr.com/companies/transport/the-scooters-that-ate-brisbane-20190913-p52r21
Williams, M. J. (2017). Care-full justice in the city. *Antipode*, *49*(3), 821–839. doi:10.1111/anti.1227

2
From 'Smart City' to Wise City?
Thinking with Ecology, Water, and Hydrocitizenship

Owain Jones

> [h]ow [can] the eco-city be re-imagined . . . as a site of more-than-human flourishing and a context for the enactment of bio-inclusive forms of ecological citizenship? . . . This entails a cultural shift: one that re-situates humankind ecologically while re-situating otherkind (plants, animals, and fungi, but potentially also rivers, wetlands, and woods, for example) ethically. To do this would be to break through the walls of human self-enclosure through the enactment of what Australian ecophilosopher Val Plumwood termed cultural practices of 'deep sustainability' (Rigby 2018, p.73).

We drive to attend a gig in a pub in the city (the city of Bristol, UK, but could be many other cities). We find a nearby car park. I notice, at my feet, in the road, a street drain. This is clearly a place where workers, or revellers, habitually stand and smoke cigarettes. Around the drain are dozens of discarded cigarette ends (Figure 2.1), marooned until the next flush of heavy rain washes them down into the sewers, the treatment works, and after that, to the nearby river. The flow finally carrying some of their material remains, more certainly their lingering toxic chemicals traces, into the ocean waters.

Street drains, plugholes, and toilets in buildings of various kinds, habitually treated as disposal portals for all manner of waste beyond the obvious, deliberately and otherwise, are perfect exemplars of modern human self-enclosure. The environmental consequences of our bodily and material everyday actions are invisible, denied, and ignored. The ecologies of watery flows through bodies, buildings, streets, water infrastructures, streams, rivers, and oceans are rendered invisible, and are often toxic. City sewers are clogged with huge 'fatbergs', reinforced with entangled wet wipes and other discarded material waste. Excreted and disposed-of pharmaceuticals find their way to the water courses and oceans as toxins. The modern city, as a human-techno-material system is stupid about waste and water, as it is about so many other things.

If cities really are to become 'smart', or, I would prefer, *wise*, they need to break from the disastrous modern human, increasingly technologised and digitised, self-enclosure that modernity has constructed. They somehow need to move towards an ethically enacted ecology as an underlying foundation of all future planetary co-becoming, urban or otherwise. This includes the vital issue in how cities live with water, which, in its various states and flows, is an underpinning force and matrix of

Owain Jones, *From 'Smart City' to Wise City?* In: *Designing More-than-Human Smart Cities.* Edited by: Sara Heitlinger, Marcus Foth, and Rachel Clarke, Oxford University Press. © Oxford University Press (2024). DOI: 10.1093/9780191980060.003.0004

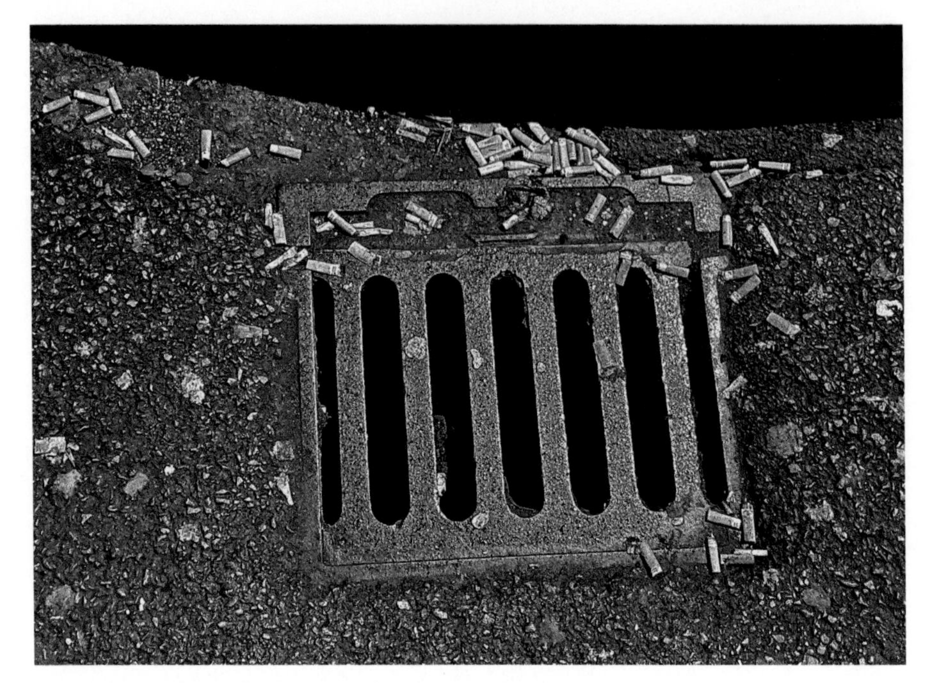

Figure 2.1 Drain and cigarette ends. The stupid city.
Owain Jones 2023.

the ecologies of human and non-human life on earth. Will smart technologies and the 'smart city' they might enable, in current ideological frames of technocentricism, liberalism, and capitalism, help address these kinds of predicaments? Or is some radical re-imagining needed? This is the fundamental challenge and question that has run through environmental thinking about modern society since the era of crisis began to be revealed (e.g. Carson 1962).

This chapter then reflects the wider aims of the book. I seek to push the idea of the smart city towards the more-than-human, and more-than-technology/data visions and practices. I seek to support thinking in which ecology and the nature (plants, animals, minerals, elements (water), natural processes, and so on), that embody and enact ecology, are seen as just as much *key parts* of the future, flourishing, 'eco-wise city' as the techy bits of 'smart' are.

How cities interact with, and effect, global water is a vital question. Living wisely with water is a prerequisite in itself for any flourishing shared life, and water also presents foundational challenges about the city as an ultimate site of human non-human flow, exchange, and ecology. I seek to explore a series of interrelating questions. What can more-than-human perspectives on water tell us about cities? How do more-than-human perspectives on water help us rethink ideas around smartness in cities, and help us move beyond narrow and problematic notions of (urban) smartness?

To do this I firstly reflect briefly on the 'stupid city' idea in wider frames of deeper ecological thinking. I then begin to reflect upon ideas of ecologically inflected senses of what I term the *wise city*. I then turn more specifically to thinking about water in the city and what it might say about wise cities. To do so I draw broadly on a UK-based water and communities focused project called the 'Towards Hydrocitizenship' project, which ran from 2014–2018. That project critically creatively studied water-society relations in four UK case studies: one rural and three urban. The concept and term hydrocitizenship was chosen as a deliberate, and underpinning, component of the wider idea of ecological citizenship.

Stupid Cities

The emergence of the 'smart city' idea stems from the fact that cities are currently pretty stupid. They are so in senses that range from the broadly ecological to a range of evolved, specific dysfunctionalities. Firstly, cities are ruptures in the living, flourishing, life-creating fabric of the biosphere. In his book on forests and civilisation, Harrison (1993) claims that the city starts as a clearing in the forest—a space where nature is excluded, or at least severely constrained and managed. Cities as currently configured are disruptions, or distorters, of the flourishing of ecology. And that is not least through their impact on water. This is not a good start.

Ecology, entwined from cosmic, planetary, and biological evolution, combined as Gaia (Lovelock 2000), is the most creative and smartest system, or process, we are in touch with. It is these processes, in creative combination, that have produced the dazzling variety of life on earth. Cities are stupid spaces if they are ruptures in this ecological flow and mesh of becoming. The fact that some cities are now seen as wildlife-rich islands, offering habitat to a range of flora and fauna, is of course encouraging in one sense. However, it is also testament to the fact that, in the developed world, cities often sit in intensively managed and exploited wider landscapes where biodiversity has been decimated by modern agricultural and other land use practices such as intensive forestry and dense road networks.

Secondly, modern cities also have become engines of the era of global environmental destruction and even ecocide (Pindar and Sutton 2000) that we are sadly in. Rupprecht et al. (2021, p.4) state that not only '[were] cities seen as outside nature', but they also have 'the highest ecological footprints [and are] *the heart of capitalism and power*' (emphasis added). Atkinson et al. (2023) agree that 'cities have become machines designed to build surpluses, finances and futures for the few. [They] are the anchors of the modern, capitalist economy' (2023, p.1). And Reuter (2020) suggests that the smart cities movement is not addressing urban challenges (societal or environmental), but instead 'reinforce[s] digital divides, inequality, and power asymmetries by catering to political elites, prioritising vested interests, and deepening existing socioeconomic divisions' (p.3).

With cities as key nodes of power and agency, modernity has, in some way or other, overlain and largely despoiled the entire world, not least through colonialism, capitalism, climate change, and trace element pollution (hence, the idea of the Anthropocene). Ghandi, who witnessed the early years of the modern urbanisation of India, declared:

> I regard the growth of cities as an evil thing, unfortunate for mankind and the world, unfortunate for England and certainly unfortunate for India. The British have exploited India through its cities. The latter have exploited the villages. The blood of the villages is the cement with which the edifice of the cities is built. I want the blood that is today inflating the arteries of the cities to run once again in the blood vessels of the villages. (23-6-1946) (Jivani 2018, p.2).

Modernism and capitalism have undoubtedly been woven from connectivities such as wired (and then wireless) communication, trade routes, and so on. And they have also in many ways, been dazzlingly (literally) creative; from endless inventions, amazing technologies, to branding, and all the glare of modern consumer culture. The modern city is at once a spectacular product of, and a vehicle for, such forces. But it turns out this kind of creativity was shallowly embedded in the modern human realm alone and has worked at the expense of ecological sustainability. It is a form of creativity to be highly wary of (Mould 2018). Its creativity is, in fact an illusion, a trick of the neon light. In the context of ecocide, any action of design, change, or creativity needs to be explicitly assessed as either contributing to or fighting against the forces of extinction and destruction—the forces driving ecocide. If smart city thinking is just a deepening of the socio–techno–economic weave, will it deepen the crisis, rather than challenge it?

What is ecocide? It is the destruction of the living weave of the biosphere through the related processes of climate change; direct species and habitat extinction through pollution; land use degradation and change; over exploitation; and waste disposal. What drives all this (along with other, related, human-centric ideologies and religions) is the ongoing advancement of the values, practices, economies, technologies, sciences, and politics of the enlightenment and modernity, expressed as globalised industrial consumer capitalism. If the city can be said to be the apotheosis of this grinding modernity, the challenge to become really smart, or wise, is profound.

For smart city thinking to be wise, it needs to think not only about any given city space itself, but also how that space is networked into global systems. So, while many smart city projects are, understandably, geographically specific to their city spaces, a topological view means that they are global spatial entities. To put it another way, any large modern city will have a global footprint in terms of resource procurement and waste disposal and all the networked flows of capital, power, people, and so on. To be locally, topographically smart in those circumstances could be one thing: to be globally, topologically smart, another, probably much harder thing.

Lastly, many, if not most, cities have grown up stupid through the incremental development of systems and patterns. Much urban housing, transport, energy, water supply, and waste disposal are largely dysfunctional. For example, old street patterns and sizes created before the advent of motorised transport and for much smaller populations are dysfunctional. And old public transport hubs that have now inadequate facilities and space are often inappropriately located and hugely difficult or seemingly impossible to relocate or expand. Many city buildings built using old assumptions, techniques, materials, and spatial logics are utterly unfit for what is needed now. Often these endemic urban problems are now being amplified by climate change. For example, in increasingly severe heat waves, cities can become 'heat islands' with even higher temperatures that are a direct threat to human and non-human health and even the very viability of the city itself. Often core service infrastructure, which when new, might have been innovative and transformative of the city, such as the Victorian sewage systems created in London and other cities in the mid- to late nineteenth century, are now not fit for purpose in design, scale, or condition.

Not unreasonably, the smart city idea has arisen in part to address at least some of the worst aspects of the stupid city. However, the idea seems very heavily weighted towards what has been termed the technocentric end of environmental/sustainability thinking (O'Riordan 1976) and thus stands in uncertain relationship to the wider questions of the systemic unsustainability of modernism and capitalism. Colding and Barthel (2017) offer a short commentary on the 'blind spots' they see in the smart cities literature from an urban ecology perspective, first explaining that they 'adhere to a broad definition of Smart City as "a city in which ICT is merged with traditional infrastructure, coordinated and integrated using new digital technologies"' (quoting Batty et al. 2012). One of the 'blind spots' they highlight is the smart city relationship to biosphere stewardship. Seeing 'a real danger that Smart City policies un-intentionally serve to further disconnect citizens from nature experiences' (p.481).

Rupprecht et al. (2021) in their edited collection of essays and stories about multispecies city futures seen through the lens of solarpunk say about the smart cities idea:

> Take a look at ecomodernist dreams of smart cities, efficient and clean in their celebration of green growth and capitalism. Built solely for humans, yet no people to be found. The trees and vertical gardens uniform and functional, deployed as green infrastructure, used and discarded as required. There are no more-than-human-heroes here. Without the radical changes required to transform cities, such urban designs may simply serve as green-washing (p.4).

They argue, as do Rigby (2018) and others, that cities need to be co-productions of multispecies ecology not just from a point of view of justice, but also from the point of view of practical, sustainable functionality. A noble lineage of thinkers on what is required for sustainable futures, such as Lawrence Buell (1995) and Mary Midgley (1996) have argued that transformative change will only come from imaginative, creative transformations of the underpinning cultural 'norms' of everyday life. Others arguing from similar ecocentric positions such as deep ecology, ecofeminism, political ecology, ecological economics/politics, and indigenous cultures/knowledge suggest that, unless key underlying principles and values of modernity change, a turn to ecological sustainability globally is not possible.

The implications and future directions of smart and digital technologies need to be under scrutiny in terms of this wider sense of ecological imagination and transformation. Ecocide should not simply been seen as the eradication of ecological entities such as habitats, species and non-human individuals, but also the richnesses of alterity (as Guattari (2000) has it) and complexity as otherness in social and cultural ecologies. If ecology is about thriving, even flourishing, rich densities of interconnection and interaction, then ecocide is the slow unpicking of these interconnections by eradicating elements and connections between elements. Clearly digital culture and smart cities are about—on the face of it—creating interconnectivities. But the question is, between what and what exactly, and in what form? And what is currently excluded?

Water and the Modern City

Water [. . .] constitutes a central factor of urbanity (Chiarenza et al. 2020, p.1).

The amount of water on earth has been more or less constant since the end of the early planet-forming era. Water can't easily be created or destroyed. It is just in ongoing cycles, flows, and states. In terms of water sustainability, the question is not so much if there is enough water to sustainably serve life on earth, but rather, where it is, in what form, in what condition, and in what relations? Cities, with their huge demands for water supply and their need for waste disposal, are particularly important in this regard. As the United Nations point out, 'the relationship between water and cities is crucial. Cities require a very large input of freshwater and in turn have a huge impact on freshwater systems' (United Nations, no date, p.1).

All urban hydrospheres are unique in their mix of physical (catchment/ground waters), social, and economic geographies, cultures, infrastructures, and histories. All cities need to be seen as extended water catchments; complex and contested hydrosocial cycle spheres as Swyngedouw (2009) famously suggested. First and foremost a city will sit on an actual water catchment in physical terms, as in the terrain it occupies, and the possible deltas, rivers, streams, lakes, wetlands, ponds, and ground waters of that space. But any city might not be contiguous with some 'natural catchment', and instead lie partially on one river catchment, or across more than one catchment, and also share a catchment with other settlements. This is famously so for large rivers that can run from city to city and even from country to country. The implications of impacts on, and responsibilities for, the water in cities are profound. The cities of Bristol and Bath (UK) are both located on the River Avon catchment but the river extends quite far beyond their city limits. This immediately extends, and complicates, relationships and responsibilities within the cities, between the cities, and with surrounding districts.

Secondly, all cities will live with the rainfall patterns of their immediate geographical area, and in the areas of their supply catchment. This might raise questions ranging from severe flood to drought. The cycles and flows of water, linked to catchment dynamics, pose many challenges. For example, sadly, in the UK, urban sewage systems are often overwhelmed by heavy rainfall events leading to untreated sewage being discharged into rivers, thus severely damaging the rivers' ecological and amenity values.

Some cities are trying to be smart, or wise, about their water by monitoring and carefully managing pollution, water extraction, biodiversity, rates of flow (for access, recreation, flood protection, and so on), and are often pushed to do so by extreme pressures (see Whitehead 2016). This smartness is welcome, but is partial, and partially blind, if it stops at the city boundary.

Water is quintessentially a matter of flows, connections, and exchanges. These are also central tenants of smart city thinking. Any form of ecologically sustainable future, urban or otherwise, must have water sustainability as a foundation. But modern city–water relationships are often troubled, or stupid. In the modern city, water is largely invisible beyond its crudely instrumental and immediate presence. Modern water has become lifeless and placeless. As Hayman explains:

> Firstly, the increasing technological manipulation of water and the ambitious water infrastructure provision to western European city households in the nineteenth century led to water's increasing invisibility and abstraction. In his book *What is Water? The History of a Modern Abstraction*, Jamie Linton illustrates this by reflecting on how the 'placelessness of modern water (perhaps best symbolised by the tap) is the transfer of water control to placeless discourses of hydrological engineering, infrastructural management, and economics' (Hayman 2018, p.25).

This echoes Ivan Illich's (1985) famous essay on the historicity of modern unban waters and how the ancient sacred, mythical, and poetic aspects of water were stripped away to just leave some bare technocentric notion of pure H_2O.

Many cities are beset by a whole raft of water-related problems, including flooding, drought, pollution, loss of aquatic biodiversity, loss of water cultures, denials of water as a right and amenity, and upstream–downstream implications and politics. As Savelli et al. (2023) summarise:

> The sustainable management of urban water supply constitutes one of the key challenges of our time. During the first two decades of the twenty-first century alone, more than 80 large metropolitan areas have experienced extreme drought and water shortages. Urban water crises are expected to become more frequent, with over one billion urban residents projected to experience water shortages in the near future. In both the Northern and the Southern hemispheres, metropolitan areas experience extreme droughts and unsustainable levels of water consumption. In the face of fluctuating supplies, meeting the growing urban water demands and finding a sustainable balance among the city, its rural hinterland and environmental flow requirements is becoming increasingly challenging (p.1)

Water is a good 'indicator element' for a city. For a city to look after its water, in all its forms, situations, and relations, from water supply, to amenity, to landscape, biodiversity, and waste management and water quality, all always joined up, it needs to function well in a whole range of joined up ways. Others also think there is a relationship to be had between urban waters and a range of social (and environmental) goods.

> We believe a deeper connection to local water bodies can bring a new cycle of community hope and energy that will lead to healthier urban waters, improved public health, strengthened local businesses, and new jobs, as well as expanded educational, recreational, housing, and social opportunities (Urban Waters Federal Partnership 2016, p.1).

But much of the more pervasive, hidden, flows, seepages, and transpirations of water in urban settings are discounted or disrupted. As Ingold puts it:

> Under the rubric of the 'built environment', human industry has created an infrastructure of hard surfaces, fitted out with objects of all sorts, upon which the play of life is supposed to be enacted. Thus the rigid separation of substances from the medium that Gibson took to be a natural state of affairs has in fact been engineered in an attempt to get the world to conform to our expectations of it, and to provide it with the coherent surface we always thought it had. Yet while designed to ease the transport of occupants across it, the hard surfacing of the earth actually blocks the very intermingling of substances with the medium that is essential to life, growth and habitation. (2011, p.124)

It is now well understood that large areas of hard, impervious surfaces in many cities, such as tarmac roads and paved areas, contribute not only to urban flood risk but also to pollution risk and other problems. This is because rainwater cannot soak into the ground and has to flow somewhere, risking flooding and sewage overflow, and carrying whatever debris and residue is on the surface to the drains. One welcome development in this respect, and maybe a small step to wiser cities, is the development of surface products and systems such as paving stones, which still perform their primary function effectively, but which are permeable, thus allowing surface water to become ground water, reducing flood risk and filtering at least some elements of pollution.

In terms of space, Rodney Giblett (1996) suggests that one of the main tenants of modernity was to drain, confine, and exclude water from wetland and wilderness areas, and to create instead dry hard land, often for urban development. And in terms of water supply, in her detailed case study of New York's water history, Beisaw (2023) points out that modern cities often have violent and oppressive water regimes, which, historically, given the level of water needed, have displaced communities, drowned valleys, and commandeered waters from other catchments—lakes and rivers—that were once serving neighbouring, or even more remote, landscapes and their human and non-human communities. There are many examples of cities around the world seeking to reverse at least some of the worst excesses of modern water oppression, for example, by 'daylighting' culverted waters, and rewilding rivers and streams. This can help biodiversity, city cooling, greening, and human well-being. But there is still a very long way to go to make modern cities truly wise about water in an ecological sense.

Trying to think about sustainable life and water is vitally important in itself, but it can also present a vision of wiser futures of ecological citizenship. Water offers striking opportunities in this regard because of its undeniable importance. In palpable and vicarious ways, it links our own bodies, buildings, and everyday lives to the atmosphere, rivers, streams, and oceans, as well as our lives with others, our streets, taps and toilets, into the water cycle and thus into planetary ecological becoming.

While climate change is disrupting and reducing rainfall patterns that provide fresh water in many parts of the UK and elsewhere, leaks in old water supply systems, buried under busy streets and tangled with other services, continue to waste huge volumes of water. On occasions, older city systems can turn out to be even more dysfunctional than simply out-dated or worn out. For example, the city of Flint, Michigan has faced a prolonged water and health crisis due to old pipe infrastructure leaching lead into the water supply after changes to water management prompted by the financial crisis and city budget cuts.

The neo-liberal belief that the market will answer all, for example, by privatising public water supply in United Kingdom, has failed to deliver the supposed benefits of the 'invisible hand', but it still prevails! Savelli et al. (2023) suggest that in the United States, 'due to stark socioeconomic inequalities, urban elites are able to overconsume water while excluding less-privileged populations from basic access' (2023).

The fundamental and historically novel task of the wise city is to change this relationship from the city as a space of exclusion and destruction of nature to a space of creative co-habitation. Rupprecht et al. (2021, p.4) suggest that, '[i]n re-imagining cities as gentle, as contributing to the ecosystem and landscapes, as more-than-human habitats home to diverse forms of life, we can learn to negotiate, coexist, and flourish together'. And, also as already stated, this does not just apply to the contiguous space of the city itself, but also to the ecological footprints of the city, which, in modern society (but maybe historically, too) are global in reach.

Re-designing city spaces with an emphasis on green and blue processes, elements, and spaces is central to what Rose and McCay (2021) have termed 'the restorative city'. Even though they point to nature and even ideas of biophilia as key to a healthy city, somehow the ecological still feels marginalised in this vision. At one point they state that 'imagining the city of 2050 means learning how to address challenges of mass urbanisation. This calls for careful thought about our political, economic and social fabric' (2021, p.1).

Towards (Urban) Hydrocitizenship?

In its four case studies—three urban and one rural—the 'Towards Hydrocitizenship'[1] project sought to produce a series of co-produced (with artists, policy makers, social activists, and communities) interventions in local eco-social hydro-settings and issues. It also sought to connect to other global perspectives on decolonising 'urban water' in terms of modern/western approaches to urban water in both modern/western settings and in other political, economic, ecological, and cultural locations. Further, it sought to decolonise the notion of community from the narrowly modern human/social and the notion of water from modernist constructions and manipulations. As the project soon found, the challenges to fully map and critically and creatively intervene in the local eco–socio–cultural–tech hydrospheres of a city are daunting.

Taking hydrocitizenship as a subset of ecological citizenship, the overall approach was to work with local partners and local communities in the four case study locations to begin to tease out not only the multiple presences of water in a given area, but also the issues and communities connected to and through them, in as full a spectrum of ways as possible. The case study teams (including social science and arts and humanities scholars; art practitioners with skills in social engagement and environmentally inflected practice; and community enablers) sought to initially 'mind map' their areas for their watery ecologies, cultures, challenges, assets, and conflicts. And then, from within the complexity that began to emerge from that process, they focused on working on selected issues/processes of particular importance in the specific locations. The process sought to fulfil the project aim of finding, co-producing, developing, joining up, and sharing water narratives in the local areas, and to begin to create wider engagements with water from those ecologies of narratives. Throughout, stakeholders from local authorities, water companies, and those with more technical understandings of urban water were consulted in a structured process of meetings.

In the City of Leeds case study, the River Aire, which has a strong cultural and industrial heritage, but also presents severe risk of flooding to certain neighbourhoods, was the focus of attention. In London, similarly, the River Lee was a major focus, but looking at a wider mix of narratives and spaces that are entangled with it. In Bristol, now taken as a more detailed example, the project began to try to imagine, and co-enact, Bristol as a 'Water City'. The case study website and social media accounts were actually headed, 'Water City Bristol' and reported on projects relating to various aspects of the city's hundred miles of waterway/catchment.

Bristol is one of the most (in)famous river-city ports in the world in historical terms, and its main river(s), tributaries, and built waterways teem with multiplicities of historical and contemporary eco-cultural heritages and narratives thereof. Like the waters themselves, these entangled narratives often need 'daylighting' and joining up to re-imagine the city as a place of living water.

Much of Bristol's water catchment is at present degraded in some way and/or 'hidden' in engineered channels, inaccessible litter-strewn places, and even culverted underground for large distances. Initial 'mind mapping exercises' were conducted in consultation with the partners (see Figure 2.2). As these unfolded, specific themes as routes of further exploration emerged. These included thinking about the city's water supply, visiting reservoirs on the surrounding countryside; highlighting the tidal processes that markedly affect the River Avon and the wider catchment; tracing some of the smaller, often hidden and or neglected, water courses through the suburbs and out into the surrounding country to their source; and revealing the hidden ecologies of the waterways (both natural ecologies such as eels, and cultural ecologies, such as old wells and water myths). All these activities were creatively captured in film, performance, drawing, and presentations (see https://www.watercitybristol.org/).

Under an emerging rubric of 'hidden ecologies', the project's arts-based interventions sought to begin to reweave these ecologies and their narratives into more robust, inclusive, and shared forms under four themes: hidden ecologies (eels); daylighting waterways; infrastructure and care; and tidal reaches.

The overall strategy was to find stories in processes of co-creation and co-production. These might be extant stories, for example, a local community group caring for a short stretch of a water course. They might also be latent stories of 'hidden' things, in many cases quite literally hidden, as in watercourses that run under the city's suburbs and parks, and also the ecologies within them, such as eels (once an abundant and celebrated species in the region). We also became interested in the idea

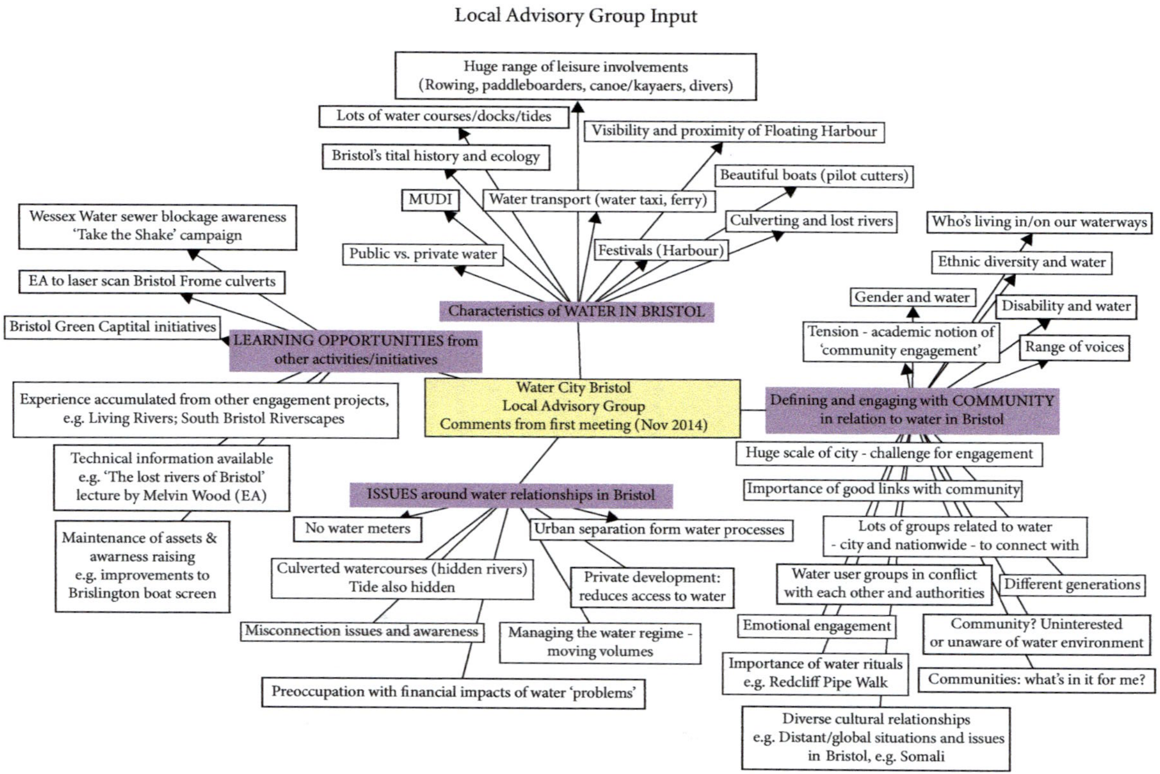

Figure 2.2 Mind mapping Bristol as a Water City. The Project's Bristol Case Study. Team with Stakeholders.

of 'shadow waters' (McLean et al. 2018) of the city—not only the hidden watery ecologies themselves, but also the hidden voices linked to them. Through work in schools, community centres, street performances, and other means, the project sought to create a growing *ecology of narratives* to help the city see itself as a water city, and to help the city take more interest and care in its water.

An underpinning assumption of the approach was that for a city to be water aware, or water wise, firstly it simply needs to meet it waters. Some efforts at this had previously been made by a range of other local projects. Before the financial crash of 2008, which curtailed local state spending on so many things, the local authority, Bristol City Council, was seeking to see the city and its catchment more holistically, and, along with some local community engagement projects, produced 'The Big Blue Map' of Bristol (Figure 2.3). In it, some heed is taken of how a few of the main water courses cross the city boundary, but the wider, and more fined-grained catchment, is absent. The map also shows where smaller streams and even large rivers have been culverted underground. But what the map does not (and to be fair, can't feasibly) show in printed form are all the water supply and wastewater sewage systems that are linked into that physical 'natural' system, nor all the (human and non-human) bodies, machines, houses, streets, and whatever else that water is passing through. As already mentioned, one thing smart technologies could do is begin to create much more holistic forms of city water mappings for a whole range or purposes.

The project learned through discussions with city officials, water companies, concerned citizens, and community groups that much of what happens in relation to water quality, and issues articulated through water, is down to peoples' attitudes and behaviours, which are entangled with material culture, technology, and prevailing systems, as well as the local water meshwork. To return to the very opening of this chapter, there was (and remains) much concern in environmental organisations and water supply and waste disposal corporations about what a city collectively flushes or washes down its toilets, plugholes, street drains, and so on. This ranges from deliberate actions such as flushing cooking fat, wet wipes, plastic in various forms, and unneeded pharmaceuticals, to undeliberate actions such as rubbish, dog faeces, and vehicle tyre residue particles washed from the streets by rain. Despite the prevalence of hard, impervious surfaces, the porosity of the city is profound, but largely unheeded.

Throughout the project we contacted, or became aware of, others around the world who have a similar aim of reconnecting urban populations with their water catchments and their ecologies, as well as their assets and difficulties. Here I mention just a few.

In Toronto, the Lost River Walks (2023) initiative is to encourage understandings of the city as a living catchment and engage with its natural and cultural heritage by creating an 'intimate connection to its water systems by tracing the courses of forgotten streams'.

In India, the challenges of urban water are particularly acute. There are calls for a transition from current modern, highly problematic trends in urban water provision, use, and disposal, to more holistic approaches, which reach out to care for remaining ecological assets, and to re-embrace older water traditions and cultures, which saw water and rivers as sacred and to be cared for.

Figure 2.3 A city beginning to meet its water again. The Big Blue Map of Bristol.

Reproduced with permission from Bristol City Council and Ordnance Survey.

For example,

> Urbanization has over-written many spatial ecologies in cities across India. Bengaluru is no exception. In many cases, human shaped urban environments have led to the disastrous deterioration of formerly thriving ecosystems. However, memories of these systems still exist as functional links (Integrated Design 2022).

Anthony Acciavatti's book *Ganges Water Machine* (2015) is a work that seeks to chart such possible futures holistically, mapping that immense river system form multiple perspectives.

Conclusions: From Smart City to Wise City

There will be immediate benefits accruing from at least some aspects of smart city developments in their current dominant technocentric form. In part this is because cities, as discussed, are in many ways stupid. It is not hard to see why and where improvements are needed in a whole range of city functions, even if they are much harder to actually implement. For example, in relation to water, smart monitoring of water supply and waste disposal could sense leaks, waste, and pollution risk. However, such possible improvements might be simply improving the modern city, remaining within that paradigm, which itself is systemically unsustainable. In this sense, are smart city developments deepening and extending the unsustainable modern city as an engine of capitalism into the future?

There is a need for wiser endeavours that try to work with 'nature' and 'technology' in cities in more ecologically inflected ways, not least when dealing with urban water and other natural assets. There is wealth of local initiatives of eco-social resistance and creative flourishing that show ways of trying to resist and reverse the momentum of ecocide. These draw upon resources from across politics, culture, arts, social action, and technology as and when appropriate and useful. Most importantly, they have ecology as their founding principle, seeking to enact something like Latour's (2004) visions of an ecological form of democracy.

As I discuss with others elsewhere (Pigott et al. 2023), any creative enterprise, be it art practice, community action, direct action, or, say, urban design, needs be considered in terms of whether this act contributes to ecocide, an overall reducer of ecological connectivity and diversity? Or is it an act of ecological restoration, creation, and/or resistance? In the face of the realisation of ecocide in at least some settings, the exciting positive ecologies of local initiatives of eco-social resistance and creative flourishing need to be foregrounded. There are very many examples of such that one could point to in relation to water and all kind of other eco-social enterprises.

The problem is, however, that the energy and power in the destructive systems still *far outweigh* the energy and power in these alternative productive systems. Of course, we need effective action on the strategic, national, and international governmental levels, too. But that will only emerge, or have more chance to emerge, from changes in culture, and culture as ecologically enacted within the living fabrics of everyday (local) society.

Transformative change will come from imaginative, creative transformations of the underpinning cultural 'norms' of everyday life. In the Hydrocitizenship project we sought to do this by co-creating stories in which local waters, and their ecologies, were brought to the foreground as subjects and agents and were valued and celebrated as co-creators of the city and its distinctive neighbourhoods. In some instances, this included valuing the mud of the local rivers, as well as the once common and unglamorous eel species that live in the murk of tidal waters. In a way, stories are the easier medium via which to do this kind of thing. Technology is much harder. Rupprecht et al. (2021, p.6), discussing some of the futuristic multispecies stories in their collection, say, 'interspecies communication is aided by technology not (yet) available'.

One interesting future imaginary to be considered is that of already touched upon solarpunk. It offers interesting future visions of what eco-smart urban-like communities could look like. Williams (2019) suggests it is an emergent vision enabled by an ecology of digital connectivity interwoven with ecological and social flourishing. 'The solarpunk imaginary is a collaborative one, a product of the internet's connective and community-building properties, and the narratives emerge from this mood-board of shared discussions and reading-groups, collections of real-world inspirations, and artistic representations.' (p.7). Technology is in the mix but is not THE mix.

> Technology isn't excluded from the ecological stewardship that solarpunk centers, but it isn't fetishized either. Rather, certain tech approaches might help reorient our trajectory—"the possibilities of changing power relations through changing technology" (Gossett and Whitfield 2024)

Very much located within architectural imaginaries, solarpunk is about urban design, although what a city might actually be, and on what scale, are questions in themselves. There is an emphasis on local specificity, decentralisation, or non-hierarchical systems and rhizomic systems, which are intrinsically flexible, creative and adaptable. Some smart or digital city initiatives are now trying to move in this direction by creating decentralised platforms by using, for example, blockchain technology, which seeks to create robust, flexible, decentralised systems of data, communication, and interaction.

The political, financial, and technical challenges are no doubt formidable, but eco-tech systems where humans, non-humans, and the elements underpinning life, such as air and water, co-create sustainable life must have potential. Think of the ecology of the human body, where the nervous system alerts to illness, damage, and pain (and pleasure). What if smart technologies became part of a nervous system for the city? Showing water in pain, air in pain, or otherwise! Another area of potential must be interspecies communication and care (Desai and Smith 2018), and even care and communication between differing forms of becoming such as organic and non-organic.

In these utopian future visions of cities nature is a fully present creative agent. This can be for thinking about urban food futures (Heitlinger et al. 2021) and, perhaps inevitably, urban water futures. Indeed Charles Eisenstein's (2008) solarpunk vision is a coming 'age of water', which, he argues, needs to follow the 'age of fire', which has bought us to the parlous and perilous state we now face. At present our cities are still 'cities of fire' in terms of the energy used to power, mobilise, feed, and clean them. That can never be smart. What might cities of 'the age of water' look like?

Acknowledgements

Thank are due to the very patient editors; two referees; Sue Ruddick, and other good people from the CritGeogForum who helped by answering a few questions.

Note

1. Arts and Humanities Research Council (UK), Connected Communities Programme; Communities, Cultures, Environments and Sustainability Large Grant, 'Towards hydrocitizenship. Connecting communities with and through responses to interdependent, multiple water issues'. For project details and team see here.

References

Acciavatti, A. (2015). *Ganges water machine: Designing new India's ancient river.* ORO Editions/Applied Research & Design.

Atkinson R., Perry, B. Silver, J., Mingay, M., & Mahoney, E. (2023). How to be an anticapitalist city in the 21st century. University of Sheffield Urban Institute. https://www.sheffield.ac.uk/urban-institute/news/how-be-anticapitalist-city-21st-century

Batty, M., Axhausen, K.W., Giannotti, F., Pozdnoukhov, A., Bazzani, A., Wachowicz, M., Ouzounis, G., & Portugali, Y. (2012). Smart cities of the future. *European Physical Journal Special Topics, 214,* 481–518.

Beisaw, A. M. (2023). *Taking our water for the city. The archaeology of New York City's watershed communities.* Berghahn.

Buell, L. (1995). *The environmental imagination.* Belknap Press

Carson, R. (1962). *Silent spring.* Houghton Mifflin Harcourt.

Chiarenza, U., Haug, N, & Müller, A. (2020). *The power of urban water: Studies in premodern urbanism.* De Gruyter.

Colding, J., & Barthel, S. (2017). An urban ecology critique on the 'smart city' model. *Journal of Cleaner Production, 164*(15), 95–101

Desai, S., & Smith, H. (2018). Kinship across species: Learning to care for nonhuman others. *Feminist Review, 118*(1), 41–60.

Eisenstein, C. (2008). *The age of water.* https://charleseisenstein.org/essays/the-age-of-water/

Giblett, R. (1996). *Postmodern wetlands. Culture, history, ecology.* Edinburgh University Press.

Gossett S., Whitfield, B. (2024). What is solarpunk? A guide to the environmental art movement. *BuiltIn.* https://builtin.com/greentech/solarpunk. Accessed 19 February 2024; last updated 22 January 2024.

Guattari, F. (2000). *The three ecologies.* Athlone Press.

Harrison, R. P. (1993). *Forests: The shadow of civilization.* University of Chicago Press.

Hayman, E. (2018). Future rivers of the Anthropocene or whose Anthropocene is it? Decolonising the Anthropocene! *Decolonization: Indigeneity, Education & Society, 6*(2), 77–92. (In collaboration with Colleen James/Gooch Tláa Dakl'aweidí Clan of the Wolf moiety, Carcross/Tagish First Nation, and Mark Wedge/Aan Gooshú Deisheetaan Clan of the Crow moiety, Carcross/Tagish First Nation.)

Heitlinger, S., Houston, L., Taylor, A., and Catlow, R. (2021, May 08–13). *Algorithmic food justice: Co-designing more-than-human blockchain futures for the food commons* [Conference presentation]. *In CHI Conference on Human Factors in Computing Systems (CHI '21)*, Yokohama, Japan. https://doi.org/10.1145/3411764.3445655

Illich, I. (1985). *H_2O and the waters of forgetfulness: Reflections on the historicity of stuff.* Dallas Inst Humanities & Culture.

Ingold, T. (2011). Earth, sky, wind and weather. In T. Ingold (Ed.), *Being alive: Essays on movement, knowledge and description* (pp. 115–125). Routledge.

Integrated Design. (2022). The urban 'blue green'. Dismantling boundaries of comprehension. https://storymaps.arcgis.com/stories/bd7d38dbb664407ba57cec2a44a05f61

Jivani, S. (2018, 18 August). Mahatma Gandhi on modern cities vs villages. *Tinytech.* https://www.oil-refinery.com/mahatma-gandhi-on-modern-cities-vs-villages/

Latour, B. (2004). *Politics of nature: How to bring the sciences into democracy.* Harvard University Press.

Lost River Walks Initiative. (2023). *Lost River Walks.* https://www.lostrivers.ca/

Lovelock, J. (2000). *Gaia: A new look at life on earth.* Oxford University Press.

McLean, J., Lonsdale, A., Hammersley, L., O'Gorman, E., & Miller, F. (2018). Shadow waters: Making Australian water cultures visible, *Transactions of the Institute of British Geographers, 43*(4), 615–629.

Midgley, M. (1996). *Utopias, dolphins and computers. Problems of philosophical plumbing.* Routledge.

Mould, O. (2018). *Against creativity.* Verso.

O'Riordan, T. (1976). *Environmentalism.* Pion.

Pigott, A., Jones, O., & Parry, B. (Eds.). (2023). *Art and creativity in an era of ecocide. Embodiment, performance and practice.* Bloomsbury.

Pindar, I., & Sutton, P. (2000). Translators' introduction. In *Félix Guattari's* The three ecologies (pp. 1–20). Athlone Press.

Reuter, T. D. (2020). Smart city visions and human rights: Do they go together? *Carr Center Discussion Paper Series*, (2006-006). Carr Center for Human Rights Policy. https://carrcenter.hks.harvard.edu/files/cchr/files/CCDP_006.pdf

Rigby, K. (2018). Feathering the multispecies nest: Green cities, convivial spaces. *RCC Perspectives: Green City: Explorations and Visions of Urban Sustainability, 1*, 73–80.

Rose, J., & McCay, L. (Eds.). (2021). *Restorative cities. Urban design for mental health and wellbeing.* Bloomsbury.

Rupprecht, C., Cleland, D., Tamura, N., Chauduri, R., & Ulibarri, S. (Eds.). (2021). *Multispecies cities: Solarpunk urban futures.* World Weaver Press.

Savelli, E., Mazzoleni, M., & Di Baldassarre, G. (2023). Urban water crises driven by elites' unsustainable consumption. *Nature Sustainability, 6*, 929–940. https://www.nature.com/articles/s41893-023-01100–0

Swyngedouw, E. (2009). The political economy and political ecology of the hydro-social cycle. *Journal of Contemporary Water Research & Education, 142*(1), 56–60.

United Nations. (n.d.). Water and cities facts and figures. UN-Water Decade Programme on Advocacy and Communication (UNW-DPAC). https://www.un.org/waterforlifedecade/swm_cities_zaragoza_2010/pdf/facts_and_figures_long_final_eng.pdf

Urban Waters Federal Partnership. (2016). Vision, principle and mission. https://www.epa.gov/sites/default/files/2018-03/documents/uw_vision_mission_principles_11-28-17_-_new_third_page_only.pdf

Whitehead, F. (2016). Five of the best water-smart cities in the developing world. *The Guardian.* https://www.theguardian.com/global-development-professionals-network/2016/feb/29/five-of-the-best-water-smart-cities-in-the-developing-world

Williams, R. (2019). 'This shining confluence of magic and technology': Solarpunk, energy imaginaries, and the infrastructures of solarity. *Open Library of Humanities, 5*(1), 1–60. doi: https://doi.org/10.16995/olh.329

3
Reciprocities of Decay, Destruction, and Designing

Yoko Akama

Please Don't Forget...

Imagine reading this chapter outdoors, sitting among gnarly buttresses of ancient trees with their lives carved into their angled forms and textured bark. A waft of humus carries on a current that floats around your body, as you listen to their cousin, a breeze that rustles the canopy above. A party of insects roots about your feet for brunch. In that moment, dear reader, you would need no convincing of the sentiency of more-than-human worlds, and how such interrelated worlds cannot be without the reciprocities of decay. Let us thank, then, our ancestors who have gifted us this moment—from the fossils burned to generate the energy to deliver this page, alongside the waters that became a beverage we drank to greet this morning, and the survival of bloodlines that have given us our life. This gratitude is an important Acknowledgment. I also thank the Aboriginal Custodians, the Boon Wurrung and Woi Wurrung peoples and their lands upon which I live, work, and where I write this chapter (now called Melbourne, Australia). As an uninvited visitor on their Country, I take seriously the commitment to obey the laws of Bundjil, the creator deity, not to harm the lands, waterways, and children of Bundjil.

With this immense indebtedness, I share stories from my homeland, Japan. I start with an uncanny incident during a research field trip that I excluded from my reporting previously (see Akama 2016). Such encounters that 'leak' from design research, and more to come, have begun to haunt me with a longing for how to learn from decay and destruction *as* designing.

In December 2012, almost a year and a half after the 3.11 Tohoku Great Earthquake and tsunami in Japan, I visited Kesennuma, a fishing town located 500 km north of Tokyo. I was part of a team to participate in one of many local projects underway to rebuild lives and livelihoods. Kesennuma had lost 1,353 people, including 220 still missing. The scale of trauma of this compound disaster had set the scene for a challenging visit.

On our first night there, I was visited by spirits. My body remembers from many times before, how they bear down with such force that I'm unable to move or breathe. I call out to my sister for help in suffocating soundlessness.

The next morning, my Japanese research colleague, whom I shared the room with, asked how I had slept.

Yoko Akama, *Reciprocities of Decay, Destruction, and Designing.* In: *Designing More-than-Human Smart Cities.*
Edited by: Sara Heitlinger, Marcus Foth, and Rachel Clarke, Oxford University Press. © Oxford University Press (2024).
DOI: 10.1093/9780191980060.003.0005

I relayed my exhausting night.

With nonchalance, while she dressed, she said they only visit those who can feel their presence, to remind the living that 'we are still here ... don't forget us ... '.

Learning to Live with Destruction

Urban towns and cities are in continual cycles of destruction and regeneration, accelerated by the frequency of natural disasters and climate change. I will never forget the shaky footage of the dark yaws of the tsunami in 2011, or the red, acrid skies of bushfires of 2009 and 2019. For many years, my design research led me to work with communities and emergency agencies to mitigate and rebuild in the severity of compound disasters.

From this work, I have noticed how smart technologies are increasingly designed to predict and mitigate catastrophe, and such symptoms of strengthening certainty makes people more dependent, inadvertently making them less resilient in uncertainty (Akama 2014). Sophisticated sensors can provide greater data accuracy to predict risks, in turn increasing land realty and insurance premiums in areas zoned as disaster-prone, providing a sense of security to those with privilege to decide where and how to live, while widening the gap for those who have fewer affordances and choices (see Sodden 2022 for more). In other words, 'advancing' technologies cannot teach us *how to live with* disasters. I have spent time with many who have witnessed the terrors of annihilation, so I do not wish to belittle the magnitude of their experiences. All the while, I am left with a deep respect for those who have learned to *live with* such forces of destruction.

Like the uncanny story I opened with, I forewarn readers that this unconventional chapter wades through 'gloomy' and unstable terrains, so I shall do some signposting here. My urge to follow the scent of decay and destruction via the uncanniness of more-than-humans is because these are commonly thwarted in Design, HCI, or Urban Planning. I rant on in a section called *Muscles of Growth*, about my frustration with our disciplines that are *pain-point-phobic*. I explain it as an inability to stay-with-problems (riffing off Haraway 2016), because of the disciplinary roots ensnared in ideologies for growth and progress. It is ironic that critiques of anthropocentricity tend to over-claim human supremacy. I am not alone in arguing that it's not the human species that are catalysing mass extinction, but it is the perpetual, disconnected ways of thinking and being that have been repeatedly reinforced by those taken as the centres of the world (see De La Cadena 2015; Moran et al. 2018; Schultz 2018). In this section, I lament that our disciplines, including those associated with Smart Cities, are not innocent from participating in structures of oppression, ontologically limiting worlds and futures (see Fieuw et al. 2022; Üstündağ 2021). For so long, my pursuit to learn from destructive forces of colonisation and neoliberalism led me to confront the arrogance of power wielded to extract, control, and subjugate (see Akama 2021; Akama, et al. 2019; Tye et al. 2020).

The marker of 'civilised' urbanisation is to take waste elsewhere through efficient systems design by 'unseen' service labourers. In the *Cosmologies of Decay* section,

I discuss how cities rarely live with decomposition. Here, I also draw attention to ontologies of relinquishing that is practised in many parts of the world because surrendering and letting go is painful and hard. This undesirability is precisely my point. It's easier to envision change, but as much as highly educated humans desire to opt out of their privilege for social and ecological justice, we remain ensnared in structures of advantages (Pease 2022) and nature–culture binaries. In revering Lorde's (2018) stirring call that the *Master's Tools Will Never Dismantle the Master's House*, for us here, means privileged mindsets cannot merely critique or imagine their way out of anthropocentricism. This is why I aim to learn from more-than-human forces, especially from those who have learned to live with destructive powers of natural disasters.

I remind that we are already participating in decay and destruction to renew our ways of letting go of control and certainties, not via coercion, guilt, or punishment, but through having compassion for our own fallibility and vulnerability. This is a convoluted discussion, but it is an important acclimatisation as we descend into the core that is, in fact, never clear, linear, or easy. Neither is reciprocity. We arrive at the bedrock of this chapter, which are stories of those living with the awe of destructive powers, like revering fire, tsunami, and earthquakes. These feature in the sections *Connecting Realms Through Disconnected Technology* and *Rituals of Destruction*. Learning to live with decay and destruction is my way of digressing reciprocity from its over-simplified framing to expand a deeply entangled practices of surrender, weaving practices from Japan, permaculture, and wisdoms from rituals that teach us that we are all intertwined in boundless more-than-human worlds. I explain here why stories of decay, destruction, and the uncanny matter to us as ecological more-than-human *beings*, with references to paradigms upon which Smart Cities are built. This is because it makes no sense to me to talk about data, methods, and theories without first excavating into cosmologies of *existence*. I do this to resist perpetuating the epistemic symptoms of abstracted generalisation, but also, to experiment with ways to account, accommodate, and actualise the significance of being-with-bodies and becoming-with-many. I explain this more in *Instead of 'Methodology', a Composting Practice*.

Deities of floods, earthquakes, fire are urging me to learn more from what my cultural wisdom reveals, which the Design education and Research muscles toned in the West have taught me to ignore. The uncanny also warn me of the limitations of the visible, material, action-oriented worlds of the cell-dividing living, so reciprocities of entanglements attend to phenomena that are impossible to perceive, thereby resist understanding. This, I think, is another important excess of pride—our arrogance to 'claim' what 'knowledge' is (as 'data'). If many worlds exceed our comprehension yet being entangled is our pre-existing condition (Akama 2021; De La Cadena 2015), this chapter is one approach to explore how to simultaneously exist in this obligation with receptive, heightened sensitivity to uncanny beings, and how encounters of perplexing alterity could further trouble disciplines that are yet to acknowledge their importance. If I am possessed by spirits, then I shall *write with* them for a book on more-than-human Smart Cities to see where it might lead me.

Instead of 'Methodology', a Composting Practice

From years of composting scraps in my garden, I was surprised by a synergetic relevance with writing, designing, researching. Morsels of paragraphs, a line of poetry, offcuts of theory, snippets of audio or video, and salvaged field notes have all been thrown into a pile in my notebook or a folder on my laptop.[1] I turned it over, now and again, to give it air. Sensing its disintegration energised more thoughts and encounters, which I'd note and then chuck back in to be reconstituted into yet-to-be-realised inspirations. This is how I braid fragments with theories and discussion here, sometimes abruptly, to discover 'in-betweens' of potentiality (Akama 2015).

The traditional 'methodology' for replicable approaches is booted out, including a generalisable contribution. Separation of theory and story, case study or practice is a symptom of a particular epistemology (Law & Lin 2017). Much of my writing (since 2015) takes a decolonising stance because I reject easy transportability by troubling the universalising paradigms that assume which knowledge is worthier than others by their ease of portability. This has been my politics for some time in Design Research. For many, ideas, knowledge, and experiences cannot be detached from places, people, and practices in which they are embedded, so they cannot be merely 'used' or 'applied' to another 'context' (Tuhiwai-Smith et al. 2019; Wilson 2008). I invite you to contemplate what we are made to participate in through such conventions that can deny and exclude other ways of being and becoming, as further symptoms of disconnect and oppression that are silently perpetuated among the privileged. Instead, I aim for being stirred, disturbed, and vexed as ontological tremors to loosen things up. I see this being as important as epistemological or methodological 'contribution'.

In writing this way, I hope to shudder myself (and the readers) out of complacency of replicating normative habits in Design and Research because this doesn't suit the content or my argument. I see theory and story as complementary and mutually influential. Stacy, a whip-smart ethnographer and friend, explains: 'Theory asks about and explains the nuances of an experience and the happenings of a culture; story is the mechanism for illustrating and embodying these nuances and happenings' (Holman-Jones 2016, p.229). As my long-term co-author Ann Light (2018) bellows, let the form follow function! Experimenting with writing continues my fascination for accentuating moments and perceptions that beckon attention yet elude capture in our reporting. So let us say why uncanny encounters might matter, without operationalising definitional HCI muscles, and instead, inscribe ourselves into textured feelings and prickly atmospheres where intuition and wisdoms of more-than-human ancestors may be our divination.

Writing *with* the Uncanny

Spirits, ancestors, deities, and the dead commonly feature in everyday conversations. Have we not felt the small hairs on the back of our necks prickle in the dark, and hurried our steps to leave? 'Animism is normative consciousness ... For 98% of human history, 99.9% of our ancestors lived, breathed, and interacted with a world that they saw and felt to be animate', drools Schrei (2020), a writer of mythologies.

Anthropologists have long critiqued their own domain that have dismissed perplexing phenomena as 'falsities' of the 'primitive', Othered cultures (Kripal 2017; Rapport & Overing 2000), manifesting an enlightenment and materialist worldview that could only see spirits as an imaginary, as a narrative, as political indices, or merely performing a pragmatic social function. By framing spirits within a socio-psychological human production, this has also 'emptied the spirits of a *worldly* existence' (Jensen et al. 2016, p.156). In other words, the uncanny is denied any possibility of existence, only to be deployed when they entertain (like Harry Potter) or become bundled with the occult (like a haunted house dare).

I do not 'believe in' the uncanny, just as I do not 'believe in' rocks. Rather, they *are*. However, merely insisting upon this takes us nowhere, so I explore uncanniness by embracing its slithery-ness. I have scavenged around for stories about communing with the deceased, and together with my own personal encounters, I piled these under the 'uncanny'. I was inspired by this term being politically deployed by kindred researchers in anthropology (Stoller 2017), psychoanalysis, and post-colonial theory (Bhabha 1984; Huddart 2006), to catalyse unfamiliar, unhomely, alienating things as an opportunity to trouble our knowing and being.

The word 'uncanny' can encompass incommensurate notions. My colleague in feminist creative writing, Julienne (van Loon 2019, p. 11), tells me that some words can 'mean both itself and its opposite', called *contronyms*, like 'left' that can mean directions, remaining, or departing. Likewise, 'an uncanny silence' and 'an uncanny resemblance' can range from abnormal to incredible, mysterious to conspicuous. These meanings are contradictory. Uncanny can also accommodate a broad range of textures, like eeriness, curiosity, and astonishment. Its use enables me to resist the certainties inadvertently conveyed by the written word or perceptions that I have any expertise in 'uncanny' matters (as I don't). I may risk my academic reputation, but that's the least of your worries.

In all, uncanny phenomena do not have 'theories', judged by anthropocentric knowledge categories, risking a triple evacuation. They are often missed entirely, or disregarded as legitimate onto-epistemes, or to analyse them risks disrespecting worldviews that revere them as sacred, wicked, or cunning. How do I honour what cannot be analysed? How do I respect ontologies that cannot be described and translated into writing, let alone in binary, noun-y standard English (Jordan 1985)? Attempts to 'know' or 'understand' reflects human arrogance. The deviousness of the uncanny can be an evocative placeholder as we explore subterranean passages, hidden from the hurried highways of Design, Research, Technologies that similarly 'empties' the 'worldly existence' of the uncanny. At least the uncanny keeps us unsettled, belligerently resisting conformity, to keep contesting the limits of what we can say, know, and share.

Noticing the uncanny is a 'tact'—a heightened sensitivity and embodied intuition towards *En* (縁). *En* is a commonly used Japanese term that means the 'invisible threads that connect humans and nonhumans ... brought to attention through unexpected meetings' (Kumagusu in Jensen et al. 2016, p.161). Whether or not spirits or spirituality matter to you, the uncanny asks how much are we (myself included) willing to loosen the grip on logic, certainty, and our own self-importance? As foretold in many sagas, clutching at power and wielding it for gain leads to finite destruction.

How can we shunt us off the 'life cycle' conditioning that only sees 'living' limited to cell-dividing beings, just to cherry-pick pleasant 'benefits' of being interrelated with more-than-humans? Framing the uncanny this way might satisfy some readers who need a convincing reason for them to be 'useful' in this story, but ultimately, like our visitor, the uncanny arrives abruptly and we may never know why. They are strange and need to be so, much like a platypus or a tardigrade. Why do we need to justify their reasons for existence, really?

Muscles of Growth

I am sorry to disappoint the readers of this book in search for instructions for ecological sustainability. We have all been trained by well-developed 'muscles' of the big 'D' Design and the reliable arms on that mighty 'T' of Technology to get us out and away from the trouble. This has made us *pain-point-phobic*. The uppercase is used before to convey authority. These muscles grew through capitalism, commodification, development, colonisation, modernisation (Gibson et al. 2015; Tsing 2015), so our disciplines have conditioned us to think, act, and value epistemologies and ontologies in similar ways (Escobar 2018; Tlostanova 2017). As we dig underneath the rendered veneer of Design and Technology, we arrive at the tap root of patriarchy, neutrality, detachment, and whiteness of scientific legacies (Crenshaw 2019), which fortifies a cycle of nowhere and nobody (Suchman 2002). I call this a symptom of *whiteness-in-turtlenecks* to evoke an image of privileged geniuses that pathologically pursues the clean, smooth, and even, similar to the sterilised lab coats worn as a standard in the sciences (Adams & Salter 2019). Calling out this professional bleaching in Design has been another politics of mine, where racialised identities, worldviews, and differing states of becoming—in all, being human—are often considered not to count.

This is the danger of the rush to 'de-centre humans', which risks erasing and occluding those that were rendered invisible already (Forlano 2017; Key et al. 2022). Inserting more-than-human into categories of unjust hierarchies, which are fallacies of western and modern thought, merely makes them compete against another. Relatedly, democracy, and rights-based framework, is useful for societies to maintain their own principles, but they have limits when crossing over into multispecies where eating one another is a necessity. One way we might design with more-than-humans is to learn with those that are already doing so, and to me, this includes practices that teaches us about reciprocities of decay and destruction.

Urban infrastructures manifest the same ideologies for social control of nature, and through advances in technology and capital accumulation, extend their power to claim resources and wealth across distant lands, people, and ecologies (Graham 2010), while conveniently paving over yawning incommensurability of 'multicultural' cosmopolitanism (Capel 2003). To pursue accumulation means not relinquishing. For disciplines that accelerated the rise of modern societies, and in turn, sundered ties with rituals, stories, and practices of conferring with more-than-humans, reciprocity tends to be limited to transactional, human-only exchanges. This sociologist's definition sums up the gist—reciprocity is a 'mutually contingent exchange of benefits between two or more units', where the 'units' are a quantitative variant (Gouldner 1960, p.164). A hasty scan through commonly cited texts in ethics, sociology, economics, psychology, communication, and game theory (Bowles & Gintis 2011; Marková et al. 1995) confirms that, while reciprocity is accorded significance for cohesion and cooperation, values like fairness, kindness, and generosity is often defined in 'tit-for-tat' binaries on who benefits in the short term by 'measuring' cause-and-effect behaviours (Falk & Fischbacher 2006; Gächter et al. 2017). Reciprocity's transactional meaning can be semantic, disciplinary, or methodological (and all three), and this has taken root in these domains, indicating the same old individualised, logical constructs that underpin their epistemes.

In contrast, I share worldviews with those that see reciprocity as rhizomic, miasmic, and infinite that entangle multiple temporalities and more-than-humans, where it is impossible to determine one thing ending and another beginning. The linear versions of reciprocity are, indeed, part of this entanglement, like the symbiotic relationships between bees and flowers, cleaner fish that 'service' larger 'client' fish, or bacteria that convert inert minerals into energy for plants (Carter 2014). Though to me, they are like thumbnail segments that have been 'cut out' by the causal mind, so their relationship can be identified by our short attention spans.

Reciprocity's lay emphasis can evoke wholesomeness, or a longing for harmonious living with many, perhaps to coax ways of caring about Others. This is, of course, important. Care and reciprocity are fused together by Puig de la Bellacasa (2017) to see multilateral, 'collective web of obligations' (p.120) that 'intensifies awareness of how beings depend on each other' (p.160). I wish to move beyond transactional, bilateral, human-only logic that tends to be taken as the measure of reciprocity, 'because the living web of care is not where every giving involves taking, nor every taking will involve giving' (p.121), but nonetheless, intensifies an awareness that 'something that traverses, that is passed on through entities and agencies' (p.160). I follow in Puig de la Bellacasa's wake but expand reciprocity further to include longer temporalities, as a diffusion of energy—moulting and fattening, blooming and discarding—through circadian, seasonal, and cosmological rhythm of decay and destruction. For those who are struggling to get their heads around the way I use reciprocity here, think of it like a flow of energy that changes its state as it moves through things. Reciprocity in the grander scheme of things give navigational glimpses to the way I see how we are already participating in reciprocities of decay and destruction.

My Japanese parents, who lived through post-war refuse and devastation, migrated to various cities in Japan and overseas to live and work. But they worried that their daughter might lose language, culture, and ties to their homeland. They fostered my curiosity in old folklores (*nihon mukashi banashi*), that overflowed with death, deities, and disaster, woven with a fable of greed, arrogance, kindness, co-operation, where humans, animals, and inanimate things transfigure through encounters. Such uncanny stories taught me about *En* (縁), a cosmic, interrelated web (Jensen et al. 2016), in a way that binds me to the trees, winds, waters, fossils, insects, humus, lands, ancestors, and spirits that featured in the opening. To me, realms are always connected. Folklores passed down through families and ancestors must've known that the hurried and forgetful descendants needed a way to remember and reinforce this connection. Was the night-time visitor trying to remind me of this, too? For cultures that have held on to the wisdom of lore among tidal forces of modernisation, their enduring stories guides us about connections that stretch over generations, allowing us to watch past our miniscule window of awareness, and to gaze at the cosmic dance of decay and renewal. We are made of star dust, after all.

Cosmologies of Decay

Many cities and civilisations have collapsed. Lessons from Easter Island are an acute reminder of how annihilation of natural environments—deforestation, erosion, drought, soil exhaustion, dwindling resources—finally led to the abandonment of the island (Diamond 2005). The thousand-year reign of the mighty Roman Empire rapidly declined in just five decades. Civilisations, empires, economic structures, and collective human activities are complex adaptive systems, sharing similarities to those studied by natural scientists. Decline and destruction of complex systems are 'arrhythmic', nondeterministic, and unpredictable, which can be triggered through a crisis and instability (Ferguson 2010).

Yet the collapse of complex systems can teach us something invaluable. Breakdowns makes the invisible visible to confront, often abruptly, of what we take for granted (Graham 2010; Star & Ruhleder 1996). Similarly, a pandemic, disaster, war, terrorist attack, civil unrest, and resource shortage can disrupt the metabolic flow of energy, water, waste, mobility, and information in urban centres, exposing the fleshy, vulnerable gizzards of infrastructures. Like a blackout, it reminds how many of us rely on the flick a switch to access energy extracted from distant lands by burning trees, fossils, and converting radioactivity in rocks. Smart monitoring can aid digital decision making in consumption habits and market fluctuation of energy prices while limited by the codes built into them to make particular values visible while excluding others. When such services break down, they also reveal our privileged access to powerful, extractive, mega-infrastructures. Crises, like the energy and supply shortages from the war in Ukraine or the global pandemic, are tumultuous turning points that can wake us, revealing who we are and what our worlds have become. They also magnify systemic inequities and violence, shattering illusions of certainties, constancy, and the comfort of choices by revealing cutting truths about the disproportionate symptoms of privilege.

Practices of refuse are kept private, hidden, or relocated far away. Manual work is, across many societies, considered lower value than intellectual or creative work (Carr & Gibson 2015). Waste and detritus are seen as valueless, removed by early morning, laboured by those often spurned by race, class, and skill. Sewage is sucked underground in a blue-green chemical whirlpool, out of sight, out of mind. The density of high-rises, concrete, steel, and glass landscapes take away space, soil, or sociality to be among the decaying. Things just don't stay long enough for them to break down (Strand in Schrei 2021). Urban spaces thus become anthropogenic reserves that do not accommodate multispecies. Green roofs are seen as progressive strategies for minimising urban heat, capturing water, and producing oxygen but Kidwell (2019, p.203), a philosopher in theology and ethics, argues, 'green roof' is 'literally green—and by extension decorative—but not habitable'. When everything is just green, nothing is decomposing, so brown zones are in fact needed for habitable multispecies. Kidwell (2019, p.202) speculates what 'dirty design' means for broader notions of 'liveliness' because an 'acceptance of the other-than-human should be paired with an intention to make space for them'.

Unlike data, decay and waste defy being categorised by individualised units, as its mechanism is dependent upon plural ecologies of bacteria, insects, water, heat, and in/organic matter. Human–soil relations have been vividly expanded by Puig de la Bellacasa (2017, p.213), building on permaculture ethics, to reconfigure humans into 'soil community members', rather than extractors and consumers of earth. Permaculture[2] is an enduring example of ecological design activism and a global social movement, rooted in local actualisation to co-generate alternative, post-capitalist economies with more-than-human communities (Holmgren 2007; Jones 2019). Permaculture often starts with the soil, following the energy as a regenerative cycle in a closed-loop system. Composting plays a central role to disintegrate surplus, scraps, and depleted matter to regenerate energy in abundance. Waste is not superfluous or squandered but takes primacy for decomposition.

Living things thrive through decay, thanks to the 'worms' labor of composting' (Puig de la Bellacasa 2017, p.161) that releases nutrients into the soil. Though, rather than productively *labouring* (as if for *our* benefit), I prefer to see worms feasting, making love, creating homes, and dying alongside intergenerational neighbours—flies, maggots, mites, beetles, moths, cockroaches, slime-mould, and microbes. These creatures, associated with pestilence, often makes them unworthy candidates in the hierarchies of charismatic creatures. Sustainable cities tend to be positively biased, so decay is valued as long as it benefits flourishing, following the same symptoms of a growth paradigm that instils fear for scarcity, sacrifice, and the threat of collapse (Romano 2015). Decomposition and dying is just as vigorous, exuberant, and breathtaking, and there are social practices that remind us of this. I turn to such rituals next.

Rituals of Destruction

Our family are ushered into a sterile room.

In its center, chalky bones are laid out on a long metal trolly.

Burnt wires of the pacemaker marks where his heart was.

We start with the thigh bones, carefully passing each remains with long chopsticks.

Touching his bones with such intimacy belies the strangeness of a fleshless body that I no longer recognise.

...

The monk invites us to pray as the bones are lowered into a hole dug near a camelia bush.

Many years later, I see my dad greeting my visit, every time its leaves rustle in the wind.

Wearable technologies like pacemakers and body monitors for healthcare are commonly deployed to avert death, loss, and pain. While these are important, there are other intriguing exemplars to help us move closer to death, like digital technologies to enable grieving, memorialising, healing, and frame social rituals, connection, and dialogue around loss. These enable pragmatic and democratic discussions around assisted dying (Gamman & Gunasekera 2019); aid the agency of the bereaved (Pitsillides & Wallace 2021); provide strategies for sustainable cities where space to live and die are in shortage (Lee 2020). These digital interventions rely upon and augment complex practices, like rituals, that are already part of societies to come to terms with the naked realities of dying. The ritual I shared above might be called 'designs with other names' (Gutierrez 2020) that manifest logics, obligations, and worldviews that are different from the Designs of the pacemaker that kept my father's heart pumping.

Learning from rituals around death can help us glimpse the paradigms that lie beneath them. The proximity with the deceased in *nōkan* and *kotsuage* rituals where families pick bones with chopsticks may sound macabre to the unfamiliar. For me, witnessing and touching a transfigured flesh and blood was a naked encounter—not mystery—of a person becoming bone and returning to earth. It's the same ritual I participated in as a child when the cremated bones of my father's father were similarly laid out. I marvelled at his long, bright shinbones while listening to my aunties reflect on his skeletal structure that many of his descendants, including myself, inherited. It is a different intimacy and just as endearing as the warmth of embrace we can feel on our skin.

Rituals, like those surrounding the dead are described in a steely logic as 'expenditures' (*dépense*) of excess energy, by the anthropologist Romano (2015; 2019), who draws on Bataille (French philosopher, sociologist, economist), to dismantle the paradigm premised on scarcity. Their convoluted and seemingly antithetical provocation calls for redirecting societies' fear of collapse (through climate emergency) and embrace abundance and expend 'excess energy'. Their argument goes that very little energy is, in fact, needed for biological sustenance. However, modernity has instilled existential fear for humanity's survival through population explosion and diversification of social needs, which has locked people into a paradigm to be 'productive' and 'effective' in consuming 'energy'. In turn, this growth-propelled-action deconstructed traditional ties and symbolic codes within communities—what they call 'excess energy'—like rituals, festivals, arts that gave meaning to actions. Expending 'excess energy' links with notions of reciprocity discussed before, and how the 'release' from what Romano (2015, p.87) describes as 'utilitarian dimension' of biological function allows the access to the sacred: 'the destruction of objects is aimed to destroy their servile status as useful things, in order to relocate them in the realm of the sacred (this is the true meaning of sacrifice: producing sacred things through their ritual destruction)'. Rituals are considered as practices to liberate people from the perpetual pursuit of survival, which is dependent on continuous growth. Conversely, erosion of spirituality and associated rituals as one victim of modernity has been a constant concern for me (Akama 2021), so Romano's line of enquiry resonates.

If we are conditioned to horde, amass, and hold on to growth, then it seems to make sense to look towards mindsets, strategies, systems, and structures that teach us about the opposite. There are numerous acts of destruction in Buddhist and Shinto rituals (Fujihara 2019; Uriu et al. 2019), like burning offerings and dismantling buildings, in kindred cycles of always-becoming-with, that premise absence, emptiness, and nothingness as the grounds for being (Yusa 2017). I am drawn to rituals, like *Shikinen-sengu* practised at Ise Shrine that tears down sixty-five built structures and burns 1,567 ritual objects every twenty years (Teeuwen & Breen 2017). Instead of preservation, protection, and permanence—expending energy (*dépense*) literally 'burns' capital to take it out of productive utility and economic circulation. It is a 'collective expenditure—-the spending in a collective feast, the decision to subsidise a class of spirituals to talk about philosophy, or to leave a forest idle' (D'Alisa et al. 2015, p.217).

We return to north-east Japan to see how people are maintaining relationships with the those who died or have gone missing in the 3.11 disaster.

Connecting Realms through 'Un-Smart' Technology

The 3.11 Tohoku Great Earthquake and tsunami destroyed as much as 80% of coastal towns and cities in north-eastern Japan. This is not a unique event. Japan is an archipelago on the Ring of Fire where several tectonic plates meet, which causes frequent earthquakes. Large low-pressure systems from the Northwest Pacific Ocean precipitate severe typhoons every year. Some mitigations are enabled through sophisticated sensors and warning systems, and indeed on 3.11, the minute warning received forestalled damages by high-speed trains. However, the size and scale of the compound disaster makes them beyond human interception.

> *Four years after my visit, I heard on the radio (Meek 2016) about a local initiative in Otsuchi, a coastal town, not far from Kesennuma that has one of the highest numbers of missing people. 421 unaccounted. A local resident, Itaru Sasaki, who lost his cousin, installed a dial phone box on a hill that receives the sea breeze from the Pacific Ocean. It is not connected to any phone lines, but it was his way of speaking to his cousin: '... my thoughts could not be relayed over a regular phone line, I wanted them to be carried on the wind. ... So I named it the wind telephone (kaze no denwa). The idea of keeping up a relationship with the dead is not such a strange one in Japan. The line between our world and their world is thin.'*
>
> *Soon after 3.11, Sasaki-san offered the phone for others to use, and now, thousands of people randomly show up, from all over, to call their loved ones.*

A year later since hearing the story on the radio, a photograph in a newspaper caught my eye. It's a British K2 kiosk phone box painted white, with a black dial phone inside. The summer brightness and lush vegetation shines through the gridded-glass panes. Inside, I see a teenage girl with a bob haircut wearing a t-shirt. I can't see her face, but she stands with intent, her head inclined, pressing the Bakelite receiver to her ear with both hands.

The article reports how Mari regularly visits the phone box installed by Itaru, to call her older sister, who died in 3.11 aged six. Mari says: 'You were always so helpful, thank you, sister. You must be in high school by now ... '.

> *These phone calls are deeply moving, yet familiar. It has traces that resonates with our family ritual at the small Buddhist altar at our home. There, I greet my late father and unmet sister, who died 2 days after she was born, with offerings of rice, water, incense, and updates of our lives to thank them for their unwavering protection.*

Realms are interlaced. Alongside Mari, thousands have visited to talk to the missing and the deceased through the *kaze no denwa*. This act is reminiscent of rituals, shared by other Buddhist cultures where ancestors are welcomed into homes to maintain relationships with their descendants. Even the busiest Japanese worker would try and take time off during *Obon*, every August, to return to their homelands to pay respect to their ancestors, offer a drink (usually *sake*), flowers, favourite foods, and objects at their ancestral grave and family altars. This ritual is important for my household, too, tethering us to the lands (*furusato*) where our ancestors lived and are now buried. We perform a similar ritual before the small household altar with offerings. Through these acts, I was taught to be thankful to our forebears for our very existence and commune with family and friends who have passed away.

The cosmology of *En* (縁) is a term used widely by many Japanese. It is an invisible, interrelated, time-collapsing mycelium that connects plural worlds (Jensen et al. 2016). In this cosmology, everything is entangled and participating in the becoming of many worlds. This connection includes more-than-humans like plants, objects, and spirits of the deceased. Fans, stories, songs, brushes, cairns to honour dolls, and more can be found across Japan to give gratitude. Alongside rocks, mountains, trees, animals, lands, waters, winds, and so on, artefacts like these imbue spirits, energy, or gods (*tama, ki, kami*). This is an extension of the pre-imperial, animist spirituality called *Koshinto*. A philosopher of Asian Studies, Kasulis (2004) warns not to think that *kami* (spirits/energy/gods) merely visits or inhabits the form (like a rock), that perceives form and *kami* as separate because the form is already spiritual. Material and spirituality are intimately co-constituted. This means nothing exists in-and-of-itself, but always a part of a whole that is continuously ebbing and gurgling. The immense diversity and manifestation of spiritual deities is rendered beautifully and with wit, in Miyazaki's world-famous animation, *Princess Mononoke*, *Spirited Away*, or *My Neighbour Totoro*. *Koshinto* is an inter-relatedness of plural worlds where more-than-human are cunning, raucous, vengeful, and generous. The giant catfish (*ō-namazu*) is one such deity of earthquakes and tempest, featuring in many folklores, drawn with vigour in woodcut prints made during Edo period (1615–1868) (see Ludwin et al. 2007). Awe-inspiring form and places are designated with sacred markers like a rope (*shimenawa*) or a gate (*torii*) that can act as a 'bookmark' (Kasulis 2004). It's like a string tied around a finger to remember something. *Kaze no denwa* is not 'smart'. It is a deactivated, analogue technology. However, for the thousands who come, its connection is powerful through threads of *En*. Like a *shimenawa* rope, it materialises how beings and more-than-humans are entangled, allowing the visitors to commune, intimately, with other realms.

Residents have lived alongside major disasters for thousands of years, and these stories have been passed down through folklores, or remembered in the form of stone cairns and shrines. *Tsunami-ishi* are gigantic boulders thrown up from the seabed during a powerful tsunami, revered by residents on the southern islands of Miyako and Hachijo (Shitamachi 2015). There are approximately two to three thousand cairns to memorialise living with disasters. Since 3.11, there have been many reports about the survival of neighbourhoods, owing to uncanny divinations. For example, the residents of *Omoe-aneyoshi* heeded an old warning, carved in stone, not to build houses below the point where the cairn stands on a hill (Higashino 2011). Residents owe this to revered teachings from the ancestors of these lands. In another, a survey of 161 shrines that survived showed that many honoured *Susano-o no mikoto*, a deity with power over waters, calming floods, preventing droughts, and water-related misfortune. These shrines, when plotted on a map, outlined the contours of the tsunami's reach (Takada et al. 2012), resulting in their escape from its yaws. What are we to make of these uncanny coincidences?

To me, rituals, cairns, shrines, and *kaze no denwa* are 'designed' with materials, technologies, and processes from a different paradigm to those that build Smart Cities. Such cosmologies manifest an inter-connected world, and by extension, a surrender to nature's rhythms and destructive intensity, like disasters. To live alongside these eternal forces requires an acceptance of powers mightier than ourselves, and in turn, to relinquish our own hubris to tame and predict lives, worlds, environments, and futures, especially of others. This is not a binary proposition, but a participation in a sacrificial cycle of letting go. Surrendering this way is at once to embrace the naked actuality of living and decaying, where nothing can stop or step outside of this law of the cosmos. The agony of relinquishing certainty and power can make us more vulnerable and helpless, but in turn, can also act as further reminders how we are always dependent upon more-than-human ecologies. Buddhism teaches us that surrendering choice (which arises out of privilege) also means to have compassion for suffering, which is a constant condition of living and dying (Hanh 1991). In other words, letting go of our own supremacy can intensify the ache of being interrelated. We might further learn how reciprocity is a continuous and never-ending relationship that extends beyond one's lifetime, to be able to have intergenerational view of many worlds that have existed and perished and will continue to exist and be destroyed. This also means being vigilant of the awesomeness of power that can be both destructive and emancipatory, and how we are already participating in institutions, histories, and systems that can also be just as terrifying and liberating.

Designing with Practices of Decay and Destruction

Designing is ontological. It manifests ontologies through designing, which in turn, also shape ontologies of others and our own: 'We design our world, while our world acts back on us and designs us' (Willis 2006, p.80). This then means Design, Technologies, and Urban Planning, by being an extension of how we think, live, dream, and work, has amplified and reinforced the best and the worst of how we think, live, dream, and work—and the 'we' with the most power and privilege has had the biggest impact. The more-than-human COVID-19 virus has been a potent wake-up, especially for those who have taken their intersectional advantages for granted. This awakening is painful, especially if we turn towards, not away from, suffering, isolation, and disempowerment to discover what we must embrace if we are committed to becoming-with-many. We must pause when presented with questions to pick and choose which values are more important or the lives we should cherish. Accommodating plurality and interrelatedness with more-than-humans is, to me, not about rearranging hierarchies of needs and concerns (according to whose priority?), or merely aggregate difference (Ahmed 2012). Rather, this demands a radical openness to live with the uncanny and uncertainties in our minds, bodies, and souls by clearing *space* for these. Making room necessarily starts by discerning what needs to be emptied or broken down as an equally important laborious, generative, reciprocal act. Like water, air, song, and dance, reciprocity is energy—*ki/chi* (気)—that flows. Hoarding energy stops movement and transformation. Stasis is a sign of inertness (Kidwell 2019). There is no renewal, no regeneration.

As we incline towards an ending, I have traced routes for *ethical*, *secular*, and *resonant* readers, to slow our pace and pay closer attention to the burrows we've carved out, where we dig now, and where we will excavate next. For those who are driven by ethics and principles of social inclusion and environmental justice, accommodating experiences from the marginal is a familiar tenet to curb the surge of fundamental intolerance. I welcome such principled, *ethical* readers to accommodate conflicting and contradictory perspectives, including those that seem uncanny to you, by recognising that the dismissal of 'illogical' phenomena comes from discriminatory legacies that pervade modern societies. By suspending judgement, these readers might entertain how multiple ontologies and radical rethinking could be heightened through speculative, imaginative capacities of designing (see Light 2021; Lindström & Ståhl 2020; Morrison & Chisin 2017). Participating in agonism across difference teaches us that shared values are never a given, nor experiences, nor worldviews among people. This was a welcome lesson from participating in a Live Action Role Play led by Rachel (Clarke 2020) and Sara (Heitlinger et al. 2018), respected friends and editors of this book, where we each wore a bird, bee, or bat mask to playfully proxy a creature to inspect various habitability of urban spaces. Individualism can be problematically reinforced when one human is tasked to represent a species, literally cut out from their multitude of unseen entanglements. Anzaldúa (2012) cautions how modernist mindsets condition us to focus on a lone tree above the ground instead of the extensive multi-ecologies underneath. Furthermore, empathy is a double-edge sword (Givens 2021) that make us care about those we like or who are 'similar' to us (like a mammal), so we side with them against other pests and predators. Agonism can help us interrogate benign values that extend from humans *towards* more-than-humans to keep toning our ethical, political 'muscles' as before.

For those without the fabric of cultural custom that could guide relationships with more-than-humans, *kaze no denwa* may appear no different to other digital inventions designed to help the bereaved mourn or memorialise the dead in urban settings. As lamented already, the tsunami of Modernity has eroded many rituals and detached meanings from the uncanny and its general uncertainty. However, one doesn't need to have relationships with the uncanny, nor believe in their existence, to consider designing customs for our secular, digital age. Designing for and with rituals like repair and maintenance are emerging as important movements to reinvent and reconnect with community, seasons, lands, and broader ecologies of more-than-humans (see Handelman 2007; Hector & Botero 2021). For *secular readers*, why not fold in social 'rituals' as your navigating guide for designing? Participating in those with which you have affinity, connected to land, ecologies, and seasons especially if they are laborious, illogical, 'unpleasant', and public, will help avoid exoticising, idealising, or appropriating structures, symbols, and ideas. I say this because we are scripted by *pain-point-phobia*. We must resist cherry-picking 'inspirations' of what we like (including values and species) with no prior relations to merely lift and fit them into one's perspective. My worry is that mindfulness practices, like relaxation, from Zen and Buddhism being appropriated in a similar way in HCI for productivity, are colonial examples of this magpie-like symptom in Design and Technology (see Akama et al. 2017). I stand by many to advocate Indigenous-led guidance, but receiving wisdoms generously shared by Traditional Custodians should never be confused with 'claims' for settler, migrant, or non-Indigenous folks to 'know' or 'use'. I am an uninvited visitor on unceded lands and First Nations' wisdoms of Country is not—and will not—be available to me. I uphold the obligation to stay within boundaries of respect, to be attentive 'alongside' (Minh-Ha 1989) the learnings about the sentiency of more-than-humans that are shared by First Nations. I expose my being to the vibrations that somatically tremble my bones, shaking off the alloy-armour of my academic, Western-trained mind that reawakens wisdoms from distant islands to which I am connected about the cosmology of interrelatedness and the powers of destructive forces.

The emergence of degrowth discourses is urging significant and plural redirections towards Buen Vivir, Ubuntu, Care for Country, commons, conviviality, co-operatives, autonomy, simplicity, nowtopia, permaculture, urban gardens, back-to-the-landers, community currencies, and feminist economics (see Albarran Gonzáles 2020; D'Alisa et al. 2015; Moran et al. 2018; Yunkaporta 2019). These redirections argue the autonomous necessity for smaller, attentive, expansive ways of being. Having a skin in the game means we, too, need to become vulnerable, threatened, wounded. For those whose existence is and was always inhabiting multiple worlds, the uncanny learnings with more-than-humans are just part of the everyday fabric. In fact, it might be so obvious that your own experience far exceeds what I have scraped together here. For these *resonant* readers, designing, knowing, being, and becoming is already responsive to such phenomena that participate in many worlds. Let us then join forces, to scratch aberrant tunnels in designing to find and make, because there is no destined 'future' on the horizon. The underworld can re-enchant us, where intermingled webs of the living and dying, flourishing and decaying are oozing and reeking, refusing to be 'contained' by the nature–culture divided individualised minds. Borrowing deep among the entangled rhizomes below and not the lonesome tree above can keep our noses in the excrement we have buried in shame and secrecy to learn with humility, pain, and sorrow of oppressive systems and structures.

This brings me back to the beginning—to the teaching by the uncanny visitor about not forgetting. The animist spirituality of *koshinto* was politicised into a religion to indoctrinate many to believe in the Emperor's divinity, and this supremacy became the imperial colonisation in Asia and the Pacific War (Kasulis 2004; Loo 2010). The very citizens and educated descendants that lived with the aftermath of Hiroshima and Nagasaki voted in governments and funded corporations that built nuclear power plants in many cities, including those in Fukushima (Nelson 2011).

So, you see, dear readers, this is the paradox of power. To relinquish power risks being oppressed, but to accumulate power can make us ignorant of our own hubris. Onwards we flow, gaining and releasing, fattening and moulting. The uncanny, as a deity of natural disasters or a night-time visitor are here to unsettle the conceited, hurried, absent-minded, short-lived-living to learn from a cosmological dance of decay and destruction. I can never know or prove this, but I still appreciate the tug at the red thread to remind me not to forget.

Acknowledgements

This chapter has been co-authored with more-than-humans. I pay my respects to the Kulin Elders past and emerging, Ancestors, and to the Ainu and Ryukyu peoples of my homeland, Japan. I extend my respect to all Traditional Custodians and more-than-human sentience of the lands and waters where you might be. I am grateful to Rachel Clarke for her friendship, courage, and feedback.

Notes

1. I thank the *Expanded Writers Collective* for the metaphor of composting where we added pieces of our experiences during the extensive 2020 Melbourne lockdown into an online document called *Writing the Virus*, and gave each other permission to copy, paste, move and re-stitch each other's sentences to generate writing anew (see http://runway.org.au/expanded-writers-collective/).
2. For those familiar with permaculture, you might know that Bill Mollison and David Holmgren (2007) are celebrated as the co-founders of permaculture in the 1970s that combined design principles and systemic thinking to create a holistic and sustaining organising framework of co-existence. They also acknowledge the important influence from Indigenous knowledges and practices in Australia and Asia–Pacific for their work: 'these cultures have existed in relative balance with their environment' and the 'attempt to understand, a broader canvas of values and concepts than those delivered to us by recent cultural history' (Holmgren 2007, p.7–8). What I glimpse in their words like 'relative balance' and 'broader canvas of values' are deeper worldviews, epistemologies and continuous practices that have always guided designing with more-than-humans.

References

Adams, G., & Salter, P. S. (2019). They (color)blinded me with science: Counteracting coloniality of knowledge in hegemonic psychology. In K. W. Crenshaw (Ed.), *Seeing race again: Countering colorblindness across the disciplines* (pp. 271–292). University of California Press. https://doi.org/10.2307/j.ctvcwp0hd.18

Ahmed. S. (2012). *On being included: Racism and diversity in institutional life*. Duke University Press.

Akama, Y. (2021). Archipelagos of designing through ko-ontological encounters. In T. Seppälä, M. Sarantou, & S. Miettinen (Eds.), *Arts-Based Methods for Decolonising Participatory Research* (pp. 101–122). Routledge.
Akama, Y. (2016). Ba of emptiness: A place of potential for designing social innovation. *Review of Japanese Culture and Society, 28*, 227–246.
Akama, Y. (2015). Being awake to *Ma*: Designing in between-ness as a way of becoming with. *CoDesign, 11*(3–4), 262–274. https://doi.org/10.1080/15710882.2015.1081243
Akama, Y. (2014). Passing on, handing over, letting go—The passage of embodied design methods for disaster preparedness. In D. Sangiorgi, D. Hands, & E. Murphy (Eds.), *ServDes.2014: Service Futures* (pp. 173–183). Linköping University Electronic Press.
Akama, Y., Hagen, P., & Whaanga-Schollum, D. (2019). Problematizing replicable design to practice respectful, reciprocal, and relational co-designing with Indigenous people. *Design and Culture, 11*(1), 59–84. https://doi.org/10.1080/17547075.2019.1571306
Akama, Y., Light, A., & Bowen, S. (2017). Mindfulness and technology: Traces of a middle way. In O. Mival, M. Smyth, & P. Dalsgaard (Eds.), *DIS '17: Proceedings of the 2017 Conference on Designing Interactive Systems* (pp. 345–355). ACM. https://doi.org/10.1145/3064663.3064752
Anzaldúa, G. (2012). *Borderlands/La frontera: The new mestiza* (4th ed). Aunt Lute Books.
Bhabha, H. (1984). Of mimicry and man: The ambivalence of colonial discourse. *Discipleship: A Special Issue on Psychoanalysis, 28*(Spring), 125–133.
Bowles, S., & Gintis, H. (2011). *A cooperative species: Human reciprocity and its evolution*. Princeton University Press.
Capel, L. (2003, August 27–30). Multiculturalism in the city: Managing diversity [Conference presentation]. In 43rd Congress of the European Regional Science Association: 'Peripheries, Centres, and Spatial Development in the New Europe', Jyväskylä, Finland. https://www.econstor.eu/bitstream/10419/116220/1/ERSA2003_488.pdf
Carr, C. & Gibson, C. (2015). Geographies of making: Rethinking materials and skills for volatile futures. *Progress in Human Geography, 40*(3), 297–315. doi: 10.1177/0309132515578775
Carter, G. (2014). The reciprocity controversy. *Animal Behavior and Cognition, 1*(3), 368. https://doi.org/10.12966/abc.08.11.2014
Clarke. E. R. (2020). Ministry of multispecies communications. In R. Wakkary, K. Andersen, W. Odom, A. Desjardins, & M. Graves Petersen (Eds.), *DIS' 20 Companion: Companion Publication of the 2020 ACM Designing Interactive Systems Conference* (pp. 441–444). ACM. https://doi.org/10.1145/3393914.3395845
Crenshaw, K., Harris, L. C., HoSang, D., & Lipsitz, G. (Eds.). (2019). *Seeing race again: Countering colorblindness across the disciplines*. University of California Press.
D'Alisa, G., Kallis, G., & Demaria, F. (2015). From austerity to dēspense. In G. D'Alisa, F. Demaria, & G. Kallis (Eds.), *Degrowth: A vocabulary for a new era* (pp. 215–220). Taylor & Francis.
Diamond, J. M. (2005). *Collapse: How societies choose to fail or succeed*. Viking.
De La Cadena, M. (2015). *Earth beings: Ecologies of practice across Andean worlds*. Duke University Press.
Escobar, A. (2018). *Designs for the pluriverse: Radical interdependence, autonomy and the making of worlds*. Duke University Press.
Falk, A., & Fischbacher, U. (2006). A theory of reciprocity. *Games and Economic Behavior, 54*, 293–315. https://doi.org/10.1016/j.geb.2005.03.001
Ferguson, N. (2010). Empires on the edge of chaos. *Foreign Affairs*, 89(2), 18–26.
Fieuw, W., Foth, M., & Caldwell, G. A. (2022). Towards a more-than-human approach to smart and sustainable urban development: Designing for multispecies justice. *Sustainability, 14*(2), 948. https://doi.org/10.3390/su14020948
Forlano, L. (2017). Posthumanism and design. *She Ji: The Journal of Design, Economics and Innovation, 3*(1), 16–29.
Fujihara, T. (2019). *分解の哲学 —腐敗と発酵をめぐる思考 (Philosophy of Decomposition—Thoughts on decay and fermentation)*. Seshisha.
Gächter, S., Kölle, F., & Quercia, S. (2017). Reciprocity and the tragedies of maintaining and providing the commons. *Nature Human Behaviour, 1*(September), 650–656. https://doi.org/10.1038/s41562-017-0191-5

Gamman, L., & Gunasekera, P. (2019). Understanding suicide and assisted dying—Why is 'design for death' tricky? In T. Fisher & L. Gamman (Eds.), *Tricky design: The ethics of things* (pp. 175–194). Bloomsbury.
Gibson, K., Rose, D. B., & Fincher, R. (2015). *Manifesto for living in the Anthropocene*. Punctum books.
Givens, T. (2021). *Radical empathy: Finding a path to bridging racial divides*. Policy Press.
González, D. A. (2020). *Towards a buen vivir-centric design: Decolonising artisanal design with Mayan weavers from the highlands of Chiapas, Mexico*. Auckland University of Technology. https://openrepository.aut.ac.nz/handle/10292/13492
Gouldner, A. W. (1960). The norm of reciprocity: A preliminary statement. *American Sociological Review*, *25*(2), 161–178.
Graham, S. (2010). When infrastructures fail. In S. Graham (Ed.), *Disrupted Cities: When Infrastructure Fails* (p. 208). Routledge.
Gutiérrez, A. (2020). When Design Goes South. In T. Fry & A. Nocek (Eds.), *Design in crisis: New worlds, philosophies and practices* (pp. 56–73). Taylor & Francis. https://doi.org/10.4324/9781003021469-3
Handelman, D. (2007). Why ritual in its own right? How so? *Social Analysis*, *48*(2), 1–32. https://doi.org/10.3167/015597704782352582
Hanh, T. N. (1991). *The miracle of mindfulness*. Rider.
Haraway. J. D. (2016). *Staying with the trouble: Making kin in the Chthulucene*. Duke University Press.
Hector, P. & Botero A. (2021). Generative repair: everyday infrastructuring between DIY citizen initiatives and institutional arrangements. *CoDesign*, *18*, 399–415. doi: 10.1080/15710882.2021.1912778
Heitlinger, S., Foth, M., Clarke, R., Disalvo, C., Light, A., & Forlano, L. (2018). *Avoiding ecocidal smart cities: Participatory design for more-than-human futures*. ACM.
Higashino, S. (2011, April 10). 石碑の教え守る. *Kohaku Shimpo Newspaper*. http://memory.ever.jp/tsunami/tsunami-taio_307.html
Holman Jones, S. (2016). Living bodies of thought. *Qualitative Inquiry*, *22*(4), 228–237. https://doi.org/10.1177/1077800415622509
Holmgren, D. (2007). *Essence of permaculture*. Holmgren Design Services.
Huddart, D. (2006). *Homi K. Bhabha*. Routledge.
Jensen, C. B., Ishii, M., & Swift, P. (2016). Attuning to the webs of en. *HAU: Journal of Ethnographic Theory*, *6*(2), 149–172.
Jones, B. M. (2019). (Com)post-capitalism. *Environmental Humanities*, *11*(1), 3–26. https://doi.org/10.1215/22011919-7349347
Jordan, J. (1985). *On call: Political essays*. South End Press.
Kasulis. T. (2004). *Shinto: The way home*. University of Hawai'i Press.
Key, C., Gatehouse, C., & Taylor. N. (2022). Feminist care in the Anthropocene: Packing and unpacking tensions in posthumanist HCI. In F. Mueller, S. Greuter, R. Ashok Khot, P. Sweetser, & M. Obrist (Eds.), *DIS '22: Proceedings of the 2022 ACM Designing Interactive Systems Conference* (pp. 677–692). ACM. https://doi.org/10.1145/3532106.3533540
Kidwell, J. (2019). The quest for purity, 'clean' design and a new ethics of 'dirty design'. In T. Fisher & L. Gamman (Eds.), *Tricky design: The ethics of things* (pp. 195–206). Bloomsbury.
Kripal. J. (2017). *Super religion*. Macmillan.
Law, J., & Lin, W. (2017). The stickiness of knowing: Translation, postcoloniality, and STS. *East Asian Science, Technology and Society*, *11*, 257–269.
Lee, Y. (2020). Co-design the ingenuity of ageing: A cultural model of ageing through design thinking. In M. Łuszczyńska (Ed.), *Researching ageing* (99–107). Routledge.
Light, A. (2021). Collaborative speculation: Anticipation, inclusion and designing counterfactual futures for appropriation. *Futures*, 134, Article 102855. https://doi.org/10.1016/j.futures.2021.102855
Light, A. (2018). Writing PD: Accounting for socially engaged research. In L. Huybrechts, M. Teli, A. Light, Y. Lee, C. Di Salvo, E. Grönvall, A. M. Kanstrup, & K. Bødker (Eds.), *PDC '18: Proceedings of*

the 15th Participatory Design Conference: Short Papers, Situated Actions, Workshops and Tutorial (pp. 1–5). ACM. https://doi.org/10.1145/3210604.3210615

Lindström, K., & Ståhl, A. (2020). Un/Making in the aftermath of design. In C. Del Gaudio, L. Parra-Agudelo, R. Clarke, J. Saad-Sulonen, A. Botero, F. César Londoño, P. Escandón (Eds.), *PDC '20: Proceedings of the 16th Participatory Design Conference 2020* (pp. 12–21). ACM. https://doi.org/10.1145/3385010.3385012

Loo, T. M. (2010). Escaping its past: Recasting the Grand Shrine of Ise. *Inter-Asia Cultural Studies, 11*(3), 375–392.

Lorde, A. (2018). *The master's tools will never dismantle the master's house.* Penguin.

Ludwin R., Smits. G. J., Carver, D., James, K., Jonientz-Trisler, C., McMillan, A. D., Losey, R., Dennis, R., Rasmussen, J., De Los Angeles, A., Buerge, D., Thrush, C. P., Clague, J., Bowechop, J., & Wray, J. (2007). Folklore and earthquakes: Native American oral traditions from Cascadia compared with written traditions from Japan. In L. Piccardi & W. B. Masse (Eds.), *Myth and geology* (pp. 67–94). The Geological Society.

Marková, I, Graumann, C., & Foppa K. (Eds.). (1995). *Mutualities in dialogue.* Cambridge University Press.

Meek, M. (2016, September 23). (No 597) One last thing before I go. Act 1. A really long distance. In *This American Life.* http://www.thisamericanlife.org/radio-archives/episode/597/transcript

Minh-Ha, T. T. (1989). *Woman, native, other: Writing postcoloniality and feminism.* Indiana University Press.

Moran, U. C., Harrington, U. G., & Sheehan, N. (2018). On country learning. *Design and Culture, 10*(1), 71–79. https://doi.org/10.1080/17547075.2018.1430996

Morrison, A., & Chisin, A. (2017). Weaving together personas, collaboration and fabulous futures. *The Design Journal, 20*(1), 146–159. https://doi.org/10.1080/14606925.2017.1352704

Nelson, C. (2011). 'The energy of a bright tomorrow': The rise of nuclear power in Japan. *Origins: Current Events in Historical Perspective.* https://origins.osu.edu/article/energy-bright-tomorrow-rise-nuclear-power-japan?language_content_entity=en

Pease, B. (2022). *Undoing privilege.* Zeb Books.

Pitsillides, S., & Wallace, J. (2021). Physically distant but socially connected: Streaming funerals, memorials and ritual design during COVID-19. In P. Pentaris (Ed.), *Death, grief and loss in the context of COVID-19* (pp. 60–76). Routledge.

Puig de la Bellacasa, M. (2017). *Matters of care: Speculative ethics in more than human worlds.* University of Minnesota Press.

Rapport, N., & Overing, J. (2000). *Social and cultural anthropology: The key concepts.* Routledge.

Romano, O. (2019). *Towards a society of degrowth.* Taylor & Francis Group.

Romano, O. (2015). Dépense. In G. D'Alisa, F. Demaria, & G. Kallis (Eds.), *Degrowth: A vocabulary for a new era* (pp. 86–89). Taylor & Francis Group.

Schrei. J. (2021). Becoming a ruin: Decomposing and regrowing the mythic with Sophie Strand. *The Emerald.* https://podcastaddict.com/episode/128580287

Schrei. J. (2020). Animism is normative consciousness. *The Emerald.* https://podcasts.apple.com/au/podcast/animism-is-normative-consciousness/id1465445746?i=1000501041858

Schultz, T. (2018). Mapping Indigenous futures: Decolonising techno-colonising designs, 11(August), 79–91. https://doi.org/10.4013/sdrj.2018.112.04

Shitamichi, M. (2015). 津波石/Tsunami boulder. http://m-shitamichi.com/ts

Soden, R. (2022). Modes of uncertainty in flood risk modeling. In Soden, R., Devendorf, L., Wong, R., Akama, Y., & Light, A. (Eds.), *Modes of uncertainty in HCI* (pp. 357–365). Now Publishers Inc.

Star, S. L., & Ruhleder, K. (1996). Steps toward an ecology of infrastructure: Design and access for large information spaces. *Information Systems Research, 7*(1), 111–134.

Stoller, P. (2017). Sorcery and the supernatural in Niger and Mali. In J. Kripal (Ed.), *Super religion* (pp. 219–230). Macmillan.

Suchman, L. (2002). Located accountabilities in technology production. *Scandinavian Journal of Information Systems, 12*(2), 91–105.

Takada, T., Umetsu, K., & Kuwako, T. (2012). A study on the deity and spatial arrangement of shrines in tsunami disaster caused by the Tohoku earthquake. *Journal of Japan Society of Civil Engineers, 68*(2), 1167–1174.

Teeuwen, M., & Breen, J. (2017). *A social history of the Ise Shrines: Divine capital.* Bloomsbury.

Tlostanova, M. (2017). On decolonizing design. *Design Philosophy Papers, 15*(1), 51–61.

Tsing, A. L. (2015). *The mushroom at the end of the world: On the possibility of life in capitalist ruins.* Princeton University Press.

Tuhiwai-Smith, L., Eve, T., & Yang K. W. (2019). *Indigenous and decolonizing studies in education: Mapping the long view.* Routledge.

Tye, A. L., Akama, Y., Elliott, L., Keen, S., McMillan, F., McMillan, M., & West, P. (2020). Weaving and yarning sovereign relationships. *Kairos: A Journal of Rhetoric, Technology, and Pedagogy, 24*(2). http://kairos.technorhetoric.net/24.2/inventio/tye-et-al/index.html

Uriu, D., Ko, J.-C., Chen, B.-Y., Hiyama, A., & Inami, M. (2019). Digital memorialization in death-ridden societies: How HCI could contribute to death rituals in Taiwan and Japan. In J. Zhou & G. Salvendy (Eds.), *HCII 2019: Human aspects of IT for the aged population. Design for the elderly and technology acceptance* (pp. 532–550). Springer International.

Üstündağ, B. (2021). Towards more-than-human participation: Rethinking smart city. In C. A. Kunduraci (Ed.), *Architecture, technology and innovation 2021: Designing for uncharted territories* (pp. 76–87). Yaşar University.

van Loon, J. (2019). *The thinking woman.* New South Publishing.

Willis, A.-M. (2006). Ontological designing. *Design Philosophy Papers, 2,* 1–11.

Wilson, S. (2008). *Research is ceremony: Indigenous research methods.* Fernwood Publishing.

Yunkaporta, T. (2019). *Sand talk.* Text Publishing.

Yusa, M. (Ed.). (2017). *The Bloomsbury research handbook of contemporary Japanese philosophy.* Bloomsbury Academic.

4
Crossing Abyssal Lines
Telling Stories to Understand Decolonial Perspectives for More-than-Human Futures

Manuela Taboada and Jane Turner

Introduction

Robin Kimmerer (2013, p.xi) talks about a braid of stories 'that can be medicine for our broken relationship with earth, a pharmacopoeia of healing stories that allow us to imagine a different relationship, in which people and land are good medicine for each other'. We begin this chapter with where we are, as authors and designers ourselves, and acknowledge that this discussion is written on Turrbal and Yugara country by authors who are not urban planners or architects but designers with an interest in storytelling, place making, and finding openings for a more hopeful future. Here we share our concerns about the role of humanity in shaping life on our planet and how humans can be part of a flourishing ecosystem instead of perpetrators of its destruction, concerns of more-than-human design and particularly urban design and notions of place and place making where encounters between humans and nature are at their most paradoxical and precarious (Fieuw et al. 2022). By way of example, the discussion in this chapter is written in a subtropical city situated on a hilly floodplain along a river that runs out to a mangrove-edged bay. The city nestles in the loops and curves of the river, which gives rise to the Indigenous name for the place, Meanjin, meaning spike of land. The river is fed by numerous creeks running down from the hills, many of which are built over by more and more homes, occupying the floodplain, which has flooded dramatically in recent years, throwing humans and non-humans into homelessness and disarray. The river and the gardens and green spaces of the city are home to rich more-than-human lives, most famously the possums that clamber along the phone lines and often make their homes in the roof spaces of the older wooden houses (Power 2009); the Black- and Grey-Headed Flying Foxes that chatter raucously in their Morton Bay Fig Tree roosts; and the Australian White Ibis that have been deposed of their normal wetland homes through urban growth (McKiernan & Instone 2016; Sheikh et al. 2022) and who scavenge in tourist locations. All these representatives of the more-than-human (the possums, the flying foxes, the ibis, the Moreton Bay Figs, and the river itself) are constructed as both pests or problems and identified as celebrated local features (Chao 2021). They are used here as representatives of the multiplicities of more-than-human, which must include all: flora and fauna *and* country and waters with whom we share our urban environments, and to demonstrate the contemporary perception of duality between humans and nature.

Manuela Taboada and Jane Turner, *Crossing Abyssal Lines*. In: *Designing More-than-Human Smart Cities*.
Edited by: Sara Heitlinger, Marcus Foth, and Rachel Clarke, Oxford University Press. © Oxford University Press (2024).
DOI: 10.1093/9780191980060.003.0006

Urban environments, with their constructed spaces, service infrastructures, technologies, and transport networks, might be thought of as locations for the exclusive use by humanity. But, without the pleasant shade of trees, the calls of birds, and the open green spaces of parks, they make for untenable environments for humans as much as the more-than-humans. Tuan (1977) tells us that *places* are where our stories connect us to our communities and the environment. In Western thought, this kind of place-as-meaning is preceded by the idea of space as abstract potential, that is, that space is open to ownership and possession as a blank slate. For Indigenous communities, place precedes our knowing and being (Graham 2009). It is part of a dynamic relationship where it is cared for and nurtures in turn with all its inhabitants, human and more-than-human, and cannot be owned or possessed. The idea of design for the more-than-human is about not merely recognising that we share our worlds with myriad other living and sentient beings, but that our thriving is completely entangled with that of the more-than-human. As Clarke et al. (2019) observe, what is toxic for the non-human is toxic for us. Perhaps more importantly, we need to be alert to the dynamic and emergent aspects where both humans and non-humans continuously contribute to the shared environment (Maller 2018) as well as the production of place and meaning. More-than-human approaches thus endeavour to offer a different set of sensibilities to urban development (Fieuw et al. 2022). They challenge human exceptionalism, particularly as it is endemic to the grand narrative of modernism and those processes, makings, and designs that have led to disastrous climate change and planet-wide extinction. Critically, more-than-human approaches demand we ask '... how do we make the experiences of non-human others palpable? How do we hear, and how do we encourage others to hear, the non-human voices?' (Clarke et al. 2019, p.61).

Engaging in critique is all too easy. We often focus on causational aspects of design decisions. For example, the cascading effects and ontological implications enacted through the design of simple, cheap, and accessible furniture destined for chic urban apartments that lead to massive logging and deforestation in large swathes of Eastern Europe and the removal of old-growth trees. In turn comes the decrease in the world's ability to re-oxygenate from trees, and also denuded areas of land with subsequent soil erosion leading to pollution of water sources and the continuous contribution to overheating the landscape and subsequent extreme weather events. There are further causal cycles. Urban design, which purports to mitigate the effects of over-heating and minimise power consumption and costs through the use of trees embedded within high-rise architecture, is applauded and even acknowledged with international awards. Such urban 'vertical forests' are ideal places for that same simple aesthetic of the aforementioned furniture. However, while using living trees as an insulation resource in a high-rise building looks attractive and may indeed keep the building cool, construction of this sort involves much higher costs and greater use of carbon-intensive building materials, which in turn effectively wipe out any potential contribution to pivoting away from climate disaster. Even were this is not so, the vertical forest buildings in existence are relatively exclusive urban housing projects targeted to specific urban demographics (Last 2021) and inaccessible to the vast majority of urban dwellers who must make do with setting up their accessible furniture in increasingly precarious accommodation. Additionally, the use of trees as sustainable feature 'cladding' is problematic in many of these projects, and verges on the abusive, as sunlight direction, wind, and exposure are not considered, and the trees do not thrive in their high-rise locations. This is the signature flaw of 'design in crisis' (Fry & Nocek 2020) and a visible abyssal line of urban design thinking that has encircled the more-than-human, spending fortunes creating a strong enough container up in the sky and raising them up, rootstock and all, fertilising them, watering them, and replacing them upon their early death. This is not designing with the more-than-human: conditions might be created (spaces made) for the more-than-human, but it perpetuates the exploitation of the non-human world. In the end, this kind of use of the more-than-human as ornamentation and disposable object continues the vicious cycles that have been created through treating the more-than-human as disposable resources in the first place.

And so it is that finding ways out of these dreadful impasses challenges us to unlearn deeply interiorised habits (Tlostanova & Mignolo 2012). In the face of such tangled cycles of design that seem to perpetuate abyssal lines even as we try to dismantle them, we can no longer look to established design methods and approaches that continue to reproduce 'the Master's tools' (Lorde 2020) and that seem incapable of dismantling the mess they have created. The idea of Design as a practice that can 'solve' problems is deeply ingrained. Design remains the willing vehicle of modernism with its implicit narrative of perpetual economic growth and progress (Turner & Taboada 2020) and its conceits of service and problem solving, reaffirming with its every touch the modern paradigm of universality with its single view from everywhere and nowhere (Haraway 1991), its dualisms and pre-established categories that are used to weigh, measure, and include or condemn to alterity. Mignolo and Walsh (2018) talk about this as the law of 'non-contradiction', a fiction that sits at the heart of modernism, driven by coloniality. The 'law' claims that 'A is B' and 'A is not B' are mutually exclusive and cannot coexist. This trope allows for 'human' to be constructed as not a part of nature but simultaneously 'natural' in that we remain scientifically biological. Non-humans are not so lucky, nor are those who are human but deemed 'other' by virtue of artifice constructed on the same fiction. Star (1991) adroitly observes the other is included through identification; it is identified at the cost of its identity. So, our local possums are identified as a pest because of the way that they move into the roof spaces of our homes and ravage the tender leaves of any vegetable gardens left unprotected. They are also a loved evening visitor for some of us, and a sight to charm children, as they traverse streets and spaces between trees by using the power lines. Whether good or bad, the identity is a singular duality. Identity, in this sense, is allocated: the other is identi*fied*. When it comes to identifying the more-than-human, the concept that humans are distinct and exceptional from nature has been normalised by colonial structures in our profit-based societies to endorse and justify the full exploitation of natural resources and more-than-human life. Indeed, many times, also human life is deemed nonqualified to be on the 'right' side of the line (Mignolo & Walsh 2018). Ingold (2000) suggests that the paradox of this separation is the fulcrum of the Western view from everywhere and nowhere that enables those with power and voice to be of the world and at the same time be in the ascendant and draw lines around everything else.

In the face of this, more-than-human approaches seek to follow the relational trails in design impact, considering not just sustainability and the environment for humans but a life with the environments and the life of the environments themselves. More-than-human sensibilities seek to design *with* the more-than-human as opposed to thinking *about* them (Sheikh et al. 2022). For those of us who have learned design skills under the auspices of modernism, disentangling from our deeply interiorised methodologies and practices is not an easy task: we can theorise about the dilemmas and issues, find the flaws and tensions supported with scholarly evidence, and yet cannot find ways out of the impasse between what we feel to be a pathway and our own habits and practices as designers and researchers. There is a resonance here with the work arising out of post-colonial critique, which also finds itself caught in cycles of good intentions that serve only to perpetuate the same onto-epistemologies (Tuhiwai Smith 1999). Frustration with this has led us to a pivot towards Decolonial perspectives and thought that can be used to not only dismantle but to, in fact, re-assemble our design praxis in new ways. Decolonial thought is different from post-colonial critique because, instead of analysing the power structures and asymmetries of the imperialist endeavour and its contemporary ramifications, it actively springs from a desire to shake off and move beyond the iron cage of modernity and the colonialist scrambles that support it by drawing upon and learning from a multitude of voices, speaking in a multiplicity of ways and telling stories (Mignolo & Walsh 2018). As such, Decolonial thought can be activated and applied to design to make a difference and help unlearn and delink these systems and re-assemble new ones, allowing multiple voices and learning from the mistakes from the past. Decolonial perspectives look to Indigenous and non-Western perspectives for insights, they seek relational ontologies; they put place before being, and they allow for storytelling as a means of communicating experience (Graham 2009), which in turn allows for multiple identities beyond the allocated and the stereotype. Similarly, challenges to human exceptionalism are fostering awareness that urban environments and future spaces require 'more compelling visions of environmental harmony' (Fieuw et al. 2022, p.6). They can no longer be top-down, but must pivot towards a new onto-epistemology that decentres the human in favour of multispecies, humans, and non-humans (Forlano 2016; Smith et al. 2017). Here the apparent resonance with decolonial thought is palpable, as is the need to find balance and harmony.

In this chapter, we do not pretend that we can achieve harmony with yet another set of stories; rather, the stories of place told here can offer a lens to look at some of the tangles created by the existing visible and invisible abyssal lines (de Sousa Santos 2007b). We start by taking a walk along a local river where we, the authors, encounter some of the more-than-humans with whom we coexist, in order to find a way of seeing some more-than-human in the places we already share and some of the ways that they have been identified and forced into limited dualities. These stories of more-than-human highlight some fractures where de Sousa Santos's abyssal lines play tricks and create fictions and tropes, bringing some more-than-humans back over the line in order to continue their status (on the other side of the line). The second part of this chapter looks into some of the strange consequences of the normalisation of this belief. In the end, we bring the stories together to reflect on some decolonial thought concepts and how they can help us learn to unlearn, and to find opportunities to return to living and sharing *with* the more-than-human.

Winding Stories from a River City

In our river city, it is easy to see that the problem of ecological 'balance' is in fact a one-way balance that arises from the imbalances created by humans. For example, the Grey-Headed Flying Foxes who live in tree-based colonies in urban areas are now regular urban residents. They rouse at sunset and head out along the river, their metre wingspans against the sun setting behind the hills providing a spectacular sight. They contribute to the wider ecosystem as they feed on fruit, flowers, and pollens and are effective pollinators, carrying pollen caught in their fur and ensuring the future of the trees that, in turn, support them and multiple other creatures (Rose 2012); they are very much a dynamic part of a wider ecological balance. As a result of the ongoing destruction of habitat, Flying Foxes have moved into urban areas seeking food and safety. A small roost is not usually seen as a problem by urban residents, although successful colonies can be very large and so create perceived imbalance (for the humans). Franklin (2017) tells the story of a Flying Fox colony that moved into the curated spaces of a city botanical garden—a remarkable fiction of Mignolo and Walsh's (2018) law of non-contradiction being a highly curated 'natural' space. While the first small colony was welcomed as an interesting addition to the gardens, subsequent Flying Fox refugees from increasingly built-up suburbs and deforested peri-urban areas crowded into the space as a last redoubt and were quickly perceived as a nuisance and problem, resulting in a severe culling of the bats, even though they are a recognised vulnerable species. Like human refugees, the bats are victims and pain points. They are framed by a dichotomy of regulation and emancipation, as Mignolo observes. They are identified, as Star (1991) says, and that identity-fication is limited to being singular, whether for good or ill. There is no multiplicity for the non-human: they can be seen **either** as charismatic (Ducarme et al. 2013) **or** as a problem to be solved. They are denied an identity that allows for multiple intentionality and selfhood where consciousness of needing safety, food, and shelter produce agentic practices, because the only 'acceptable' identity is the one that is assigned to them by humans.

In those inner urban suburbs built between the western hillsides and the loops of the river, the sunset—which sees the Flying Foxes sweeping between the Moreton Bay Figs that still remain as feature trees around the parks—is the time for another local non-human to come out looking for food The possums that use our powerlines to traverse the ever-widening spaces between trees, also find themselves crossing another abyssal line. This time the line can be framed as arising out of the separation between nature and culture, but it is much more physical, constructed by our human need for shelter and safety. Possums are native marsupials that live in trees and are active at night. There are a number of different kinds of possums in the wider area where the city is situated: they range from the tree-bound, those with a membrane that can glide between trees and who are precarious as a result of habitat destruction, to those whose habitats have been destroyed but who have been able to relocate to share our urban areas. Two types of possums are very much neighbours in inner-city suburbs: the Brushtail Possum, weighing in at 3–5 kilos and being the size of a cat, and the smaller Ringtail Possum, whose more arboreal-dependent life and gentler presence makes them very vulnerable to habit degradation and loss, predatory behaviour by domestic animals and introduced animals such as foxes, and often as not, a tragic heartbreaking victim of busy roads. Ringtails manage to survive in urban areas as long as there are trees for nesting and food available. Their use of powerlines as mobility infrastructure in the absence of tree canopies is an extraordinary sight to behold. The Ringtails live in social family groups in dreys and feed on leaves, flowers, and fruits that are foraged from within the tree canopy. They are strongly attached to place and protect their nesting areas from other Ringtails. Brushtail Possums are more robust in many ways and have managed to move into urban areas more literally by forcing their way into the roof spaces, and even wall cavities, of the local wooden houses. Like the Flying Foxes, Brushtails present a problematic binary of possibilities. For many of us, they are the regular nightly visitors who 'pop by' to say hello and steal some fruit. For others, they represent a disruptive pest who has singular disregard for the sanctity of the household boundary and who wakes the family at night as they run across tin roofs and feed on vegetable gardens and houseplants. Power's survey (2009) of Sydney householders' attitudes towards possums in their domestic spaces found a range of feelings. Many of her respondents were affectionate towards them, while others resented the damage to their homes (a large possum can chomp its way through a plasterboard wall with ease) and gardens. However, unlike Franklin's case of the Flying Foxes who, albeit welcomed and then rejected, remain as wild creatures on the other side of the human/nature abyss, Power's possum presence in our homes brings them problematically into our domestic circles. She notes that it is we (the humans) who start to exhibit issues with how we understand them. So, those of us who enjoy a local visiting possum family will question whether we should be giving food to 'wild' animals and what kind of fatal kindness this might be in terms of disrupting a perceived 'natural' life. Power (2009) suggests that possums cross and disrupt neat boundaries such as wild/domestic and nature/home. Stories told about the behaviours of the Brushtails, particularly their noise and toilet practices, situate them as home invaders. These stories acknowledge that they are native animals who predate colonial presence and construction of the urban areas. However, there is an underlying murmur that hints towards opportunism on the part of the Brushtails here that borders a more human conceptualisation of agency than mere practical consciousness. The Flying Foxes remain outside in the trees, but the Possums enter our homes. Wanting them to return to a state of pristine wilderness embeds both the environmental sense of wanting the animals to live and thrive in their 'original states'—perceived as best for them—and the human protective sense of keeping them out of our home boundaries.

The same strange bewilderment is also visible in our relationship with the White Ibis, which is also the victim of habitat loss and, like the Flying Foxes, has been forced to move into urban areas but who has also transgressed some boundaries of expected, denoted, wildlife behaviour—like the Brushtail Possum. The Australian White Ibis is a wading bird carrying the long legs and long curved beak of the family. It has moved away from its original marshland areas and into the cities, where it has found new sources of food in the detritus of our urban lifestyles, like the left-over food waste thrown away in our outdoor café areas, especially those along the river. This has led to a rise in the White Ibis' popularity as a pop-culture icon and localised meme, and the bird is known colloquially by a number of derogatory (but almost affectionate) names, such as a 'trash-turkey' or 'bin-chicken'. Popular ambivalence to the bird is extreme, ranging from its iconic status as an Australian character, perhaps not 'charismatic' but certainly notorious and celebrated in the shape of collectable pins and patches, to its status as an outright pest as denoted by the 'Do not feed the Ibis' signs outside most street cafés. McKiernan and Instone's discussion (2016) of the White Ibis notes that they transgress their allocated placement and in so doing confront human categories and control. They have effectively crossed over the line and face censure as a result. The Ibis shares this dichotomy with other more-than-humans, who have also managed to find ways to cohabit with us (from their perspective). Pigeons in Trafalgar Square have a similar cultural presence to the White Ibis. They get a mention in well-known stories as part of a (magical) day out but are politicised and removed as a pest as part of environmental management (Escobar 2014). There is a bitter echo of an older abyssal line that is inscribed in our city through the names given to the streets that describe the 'acceptable' boundaries between the white settler populations and the displaced Indigenous populations. Segato (2018, p.204) is searing about this process, noting that 'Everything that cannot be adapted to this exercise or charade, that cannot be made to fit into the matrix of the existent—which works like a great digestive process—becomes a placeless anomaly and is subject to expulsion.'

A final more-than-human presence from our walk that must be included in the storied space of our city is the one that literally shapes the city and creates the spike of land that gives the area its name. The Brisbane River is the longest in the state. It rises in the ranges west of the city, fed by creeks and joined by other smaller rivers as it makes its way down the ranges and meanders in lazy loops and curves across the plain, meeting the sea in the calm waters of a bay sheltered from the Pacific swells by large sand islands. For the local Indigenous people, the creeks, and the valleys they create, are places for food and water and shared sites for corroborees. The river is a nurturing entity. The river's presence, like most rivers that have been identified as ideal sites for urban settlement, creates and shapes the experience of the city. The river is part of our place-making because it is a multiplicity of other place-making stories such as those of the Flying Foxes, the Moreton Bay Figs, the White Ibis, and the possums. Other stories about the river are instrumental. From colonial reports of the potential of the river as an access route to rich resources inland and the availability of freshwater springs and pools in the creeks that run down the valleys and groves created by spurs of the smaller hills and higher ranges, to the annual Riverfire festival that sees performances from the Air Force and fireworks deafen the Flying Foxes who are sometimes seen flying through the fireworks to escape the noise. Over the years since colonisation and the establishment of the early settlement on the northern banks of the river, it has been heavily curated, not unlike the botanical gardens that are no longer available to any more than an 'allocation' of the more-than-human. As a loopy older river (one crossing flood plains and nearing the sea), the riverbed was once shallow and apparently could be walked across (Richards 2019). Yet, dredging to allow for navigation of larger boats, and for gravel and sand extractions have dramatically affected the shape and overall health of the river. This, in turn, has had disastrous effects on more-than-human denizens of the bay, with sediment washing out and smothering seagrass fields and threatening the Dugong populations. This kind of causal chain exposes meshworks of relational connectivities.

The river has a presence beyond its description as a resource or pathway to fresh water. It is a source of sustenance and life, supporting the connected ecologies that provide the large Australian Banyan tree homes in which the Flying Foxes roost, and the rich connected ecosystems that are in turn sustained by the trees. These connected ecologies and ecosystems encompass smaller stories and more-than-human characters, from the Fig Wasps that have a symbiotic relationship with the trees to the Ringtail Possums and birds that make their homes in the branches or feed on the flowers and fruits. When it rains and water reclaims areas of flat land around the river, overflowing the concrete ducts built to control (and make invisible) its tributaries, turning low-lying areas back into marshy swampland, the White Ibis leave the bins in (temporary) preference for wading in swampy waters. The river is more than a site for multiplicity: the river in this sense *is* the place and place maker. However, the river is also a site delineated by abyssal lines. Physically, by the lines made of concrete to ensure its course through the city, and further up to contain its waters in dams higher in the hills behind the city; conceptually, by the lines drawn on maps to register its existence in the Western ways of knowing and delimit its perceived boundaries and relation to other city places. The river has another form when its waters overflow and the city has been devastated by floods. In recent times, climate change has brought more water than denuded hillsides can support and spaces constructed to contain the waters turn into dangerous watersheds that wreak havoc on lands below, challenging both physical and conceptual lines created by the humans who inhabit its banks.

Paradoxes of Human Storying

The stories of the bats, ibis, possums, and river highlight the way that more-than-humans cannot be taken as discrete, independent parts that merely articulate together. They are multispecies entanglements (Houston et al. 2018; Gonsalves et al. 2022) in a plurality of ways. They have numerous identities that intersect in multiple ways. Recognising our own need to be enmeshed in nature, David Abram (2012) tells a story of watching spiders make delicate webs that intersect at different angles and planes, each becoming with the whole while remaining their own web. Recognition of the more-than-human as essential co-performers (Haraway 2015) in our own belonging in the world, particularly in place making in constructed urban environments, is emerging as the most critical area in future imaginaries.

Concerns and responses are emerging on multiple fronts, in multiple design spaces with respect to cities and urban spaces and places. Human exceptionalism and the rights of the more-than-human are challenged in the design of cities and urban environments (Clarke et al. 2019; Fieuw et al. 2022; Forlano 2016; Foth & Caldwell 2018; Heitlinger & Comber 2018). The more-than-human view is emphasised in projects that seek to acknowledge their agencies as meaning-makers in their own right in urban environments (Van Dooren & Rose 2012; Turner & Morrison

2021). The concept of agentic participation of the more-than-human is questioned in media architecture projects (Foth & Caldwell 2018) in order to find pathways to best practice, which allows the more-than-human to have some kind of voice. The more-than-human voice and the need for designing *with*, as opposed to designing *for*, is an emerging discussion (Sheikh et al. 2022).

We acknowledge that central to these concerns is the decentring of the human and a focus on the more-than-human as entangled in our shared environments and as vulnerable as a result of our design activities (Houston et al. 2018), and that designing *with* (Sheikh et al. 2022) cannot be achieved if our urban spaces are constructed as separate from natural spaces. However, these reflections raise multiple questions about how we might design *with*. What would that mean? What could it feel like? Before we move onto perspectives that might help us disentangle ourselves from the cycles of causality and pivot us towards relational approaches, there are some insidious abyssal lines yet to expose. Some of these are tricks, masquerading as opportunities but remaining what Lorde (2020) calls the master's tools, which, she adds, cannot be used to destroy the master's house.

A challenge lies in our own methodologies and practices where we are 'the designers', and even when we are engaged in forms of co-design and participatory design, we design from our own subjectivity as humans, shaped by our Western habits and legacies from the Enlightenment period when rationality moved into ascendant in Europe, dismissing other perspectives and ways of being and knowing in favour of turning them into objects of our inquiry (Mignolo & Walsh 2018). Agency as a concept in the Western onto-epistemic framework is entangled with accepted priorities of rationalist thought (Frauenberger 2019). A formal definition, where agency is seen as a capacity to act within a given environment, entails a notion of freedom to make choices. In this sense, our urban environments and 'smart' cities have left the more-than-human no room for agency. When agency is understood as a capacity to make choices, and making choices implies that the choice-maker has intentions and desires (Thomas 2016), animals are allowed agentic behaviour. Animals act as conscious, intentional agents, much as we do; that is, their actions are directed by practical consciousness (Ingold 2011). This limited notion of agency still frames them as being on the other side of the abyssal line that separates humans from nature, nature being an entity that is 'not us' and needs to be cared for (by us) (de Sousa Santos 2007b).

As the stories in the previous section tell, non-human subjects are almost inevitably drawn into human activities without any consent (Gillespie & Collard 2015). The more charismatic—such as the Flying Foxes—are allowed practical consciousness of 'need' rather than agency, and when they transform from welcome visitor to problem, local governments will post news about 'management plans', alerting concerned citizens to the ecological value of the species and at the same time passing comment on the dangers of the Hendra virus, which can be transferred from the Flying Foxes to horses and then, very rarely, to humans. We are getting much better at understanding that seagrass fields are critical to healthy ecosystems and that even mosquitoes (a big annoyance in a wet and sultry subtropical city, especially after a flood) are an important food source for microbats, fish, and birds, as well as some being pollinators. Thus, we are always faced with the dilemma of agency when considering the more-than-human. If we are to design *with* them, how can we respect their agentic selfhood? How to understand other sentient beings as having selfhood that is both agentic and beyond the limited human understanding and defining that are about order and underpin modernist systems of 'rights'?

The idea of more-than-human agency, even when it is carefully framed to fit and accept the more-than-human as having conscious intention, is deeply problematic. It represents an instance of the fiction of non-contradiction (Mignolo & Walsh 2018). It is part of a set of ideas and concepts that pertain to a notion of 'personhood'. Here we hit a very deeply divisive abyssal line. The invisible distinctions described above act to construct visible distinctions and meanings that challenge us and demand to be broken open. When it comes to the more-than-human, a visible fracture is the concept of 'personhood', defined as a legal state that can be conferred on natural entities. Personhood is an existential–relational concept that pertains to the inherent state of being a person (e.g. biologically) and the context of being in the world (socio-culturally). The concept, as it stands in our contemporary world, is another instance, perhaps even the ultimate instance, of Mignolo and Walsh's (2018) critique of the 'law of non-contradiction'. It has legacies in the nature/culture divide that underpins the Western Modernity paradigm. As a concept, personhood embeds a paradoxical tension because of the manner in which the two forms of definition might be seen to compete (White 2013). That is, the biological notion that personhood is existential means it is present regardless of the circumstances and cannot be taken away (nor presumably allocated), and can be countered with the concept of relational personhood where it is, in fact, allocated and categorised through connections and meshworks associated with culture and morality and belief. This latter is a return to *imago dei* and the Christian notion of personhood, which is 'in God's image'. This acts to preclude (or at least make inferior and other) a whole gender, the Christian god having a male pronoun. It also contributes to the denigration of others according to physical attributes such as colour (and extends to culture associated with physical attributes).

This is the key trope in the paradox that Ingold highlights, the invisible abyssal line that de Sousa Santos (2007b) alerts us to, and what Mignolo and Walsh (2018) call 'the seed' that grows from the law of non-contradiction that allows a fictional noun (human) to masquerade as its ontological identity (human). It is made the norm in modern knowledge and science via the activities and theories of Charles Darwin, whose work demonstrates coevolution of humans and other species. But, at the same time, it confirms that personhood/humanity is judged on the basis of the assumed 'human' (sic) trait of rationality. Debates around personhood are often entangled in socially constructed laws and subject to socio-cultural 'norms' and subsequent contestations, for example, those that arise around slavery or abortion. This is a second point that de Sousa Santos makes when he says that modern knowledge and modern law are mutually interdependent abyssal lines that create subsystems of invisible and visible distinctions and subsequent disjunctures in the impassive face of rationality. Contemporary personhood discussions tend to arise in the bailiwick of legal confrontations. It is more frequent to find contention and use of the concept of personhood as legal status in cases where the more-than-human are 'defended' with reference to personhood (Marshall 2019). In legal contexts, personhood status is 'granted' along with a rule of *habeas corpus* or the right to one's body and freedom from unlawful detention. Cases of personhood in the animal world are often charismatic representatives rather than whole species. For example, Happy the elephant was born in the wild in 1970, captured, and has been living in an acre of contained space in the Bronx Zoo. As a social animal living alone and at risk of depression, Happy is clearly not happy and has been the subject of a legal case and writ of *habeas corpus*. A similar case is that of Sandra the orangutan, who was declared a 'non-human being' after twenty years in the Buenos Aires Zoo in Argentina. Here, the cases are based on the laws of *habeas corpus* and allow that the animal has the right to bodily freedom as opposed to agency over their destiny. Animals whose cases are won are usually transferred from a site understood as detrimental to their health to a sanctuary of some description (Pearson 2015; Rowlands 2019).

Essentially, personhood is 'granted' by humans to non-human beings and constituted as an identification permitted through the auspices of the law. It is not recognition of the other on the other side of the abyssal line; rather, it is a bringing in, an inclusion of the more-than-human into the purview and framing of the universal. It smells of the same ambivalence and duality that the Brushtail Possums and the Flying Foxes experience, caught between pest and local colour (Chao 2021). The idea of personhood then, as a legal precedent, is an artifice to bring *some* natural entities to 'this side' so they can be included in, and framed by, a regulation/emancipation dichotomy rather than continue to suffer the consequences of the 'appropriation/violence' paradigm (de Sousa Santos 2007b; Mignolo & Walsh 2018). This creates a set of 'privileged natural entities' that are entitled to be considered 'higher' (in a human view) and allowed on this side of the line. In this way, a modified form of the other is created so that it can suit this side and fit into the 'universal' human model. By creating these special categories, rather than helping to erase them, the concept of personhood, in fact, aggravates and deepens the divide between human and more-than-human, it enacts Star's (1991) analysis of power and Segato's (2018) searing indictment of identification, and bakes it into law.

Personhood brings its own complexities back into the human world. It also then enables a disastrous feedback loop for what being allowed personhood might mean for an environmental entity. A number of cases have seen legal identification extended to the environment and landscape in Western law. For example, the Magpie River in Canada was granted legal personhood by local authorities, and, given nine rights, including the right to flow, the right to be safe from pollution, and as a corollary of being a person, the right to sue. The problem is, as Miller (2018) suggests in his discussion of the case of the Colorado River, that the general and expansive right 'to exist, flourish, and naturally evolve' must be clearly demonstrated as being transgressed in a court of law. This then brings a number of other factors into play. According to law, the natural entity must have a voice or someone to speak on their behalf, as the right to flourish and be healthy is only something that can be complained about if there has been deprivation of life or liberty. It is typically part of the same *habeas corpus* laws that frame the same regulation/emancipation dichotomy already discussed. Another aspect of declaring personhood for a natural or environmental entity such as a river is described by Salmond (2014) in her discussion of the case of the Whanganui River, on the west coast of the North Island of New Zealand. The river has been recognised as a living being and a human face, chosen by the government and the Indigenous tribes as traditional custodians. Māori conceptualisations of the relationship between the river and the people are recognised, albeit with a number of caveats, including accord that the agreement cannot conflict with any existing private property rights and that use of any water from the river or its catchment tributaries is not pertinent to the agreement, but instead to the bailiwick of a government body review process. In essence, the river as an entity is made separate in law from the water that makes its existence. This is a clash between Western law and Indigenous understandings of the river as a living whole entity that stretches from the mountains to the sea and includes not only tributaries but also its encompassing ecologies. Such examples present enormous, confronting challenges for those of us who endeavour to find approaches to 'design *with*' (Sheikh et al. 2022).

Seeing with Eyes Unclouded

The law of non-contradiction assumes that directly opposite ideas or states of being are not possible (Mignolo & Walsh 2018). For instance, if we state that 'Jane is a human' and that 'Wolves are not human', this means that Jane is not, or cannot be a wolf, and also that she cannot be both. Many cultures, including most First Nations, reject the concept (or never even cogitated it as a valid idea) and use the concept of complementarity instead, which accepts the in-betweens, the complementary states, and incorporates notions of flow and spectrum. By the 'laws of complementarity' Jane can be both human and wolf, and more. She might be able to be both at the same time, and the moving between the stages does not pertain to any form of weakness or wickedness (as, for instance, modern werewolf tales imply). On the contrary, being able to be both, or many, all the time or some of the time allows beings (humans or not) to break with binary opposition concepts—so essential in the edifice of Western thought and by which contemporary life and human habitats are designed.

Breaking away from binary oppositions allows us to navigate within and through the many flows of life and to communicate and learn together multiple instances of life. Robin Kimmerer (2013, p.58) invites us to imagine those relations:

> Imagine the access we would have to different perspectives, the things we might see through other eyes, the wisdom that surrounds us. We don't have to figure out everything by ourselves: there are intelligences other than our own, teachers all around us. Imagine how much less lonely the world would be.

This invitation leads us to consider and question a few essential concepts that have been ingrained in our Westernised minds for too long. Central is the social construction of the idea of 'humanity separate from nature, a separation which determines the dichotomy that is central to Western modernity and that enables and justifies the exploitation of natural and human resources, considered lifeless, or 'soul-less', serving as things with which we cohabit in order to improve our own lives, like the unfortunate trees in the buildings mentioned in the introduction to this work. By creating a distinction of, or by 'identifying' (Star 1991) what human and non-humans are supposed to be, it becomes clear where kinship lies, and who deserves to be treated as equals, with dignity, respect, and right to agency; and who does not. This is the abyssal line created by Western Modernity, separating humans from nature. This is the fracture that governs most Modernity principles and roles—including that of designers, innovators, and benefactors—and that allows humans to understand and treat nature as a resource to be exploited, extracted, and consumed (Gómez-Barris 2017).

As designers, we bend nature's resources to create artefacts that make our lives on the planet easier and more comfortable. At some point, humans decided that it was this very capacity of 'bending' nature that defined humanity (I think therefore I am, design makes us human), that made us superior to all other life, and therefore righteous to control and do as we see fit with these lives (human and not). This capacity to create and use natural resources becomes also the main criteria to determine levels of 'human evolution'. As we use our capacity for designing to differentiate ourselves from other live entities, we use that same capacity to create the worlds around us—worlds that mirror and validate this dichotomy. The act of designing, then, in a way, fulfils its own prophecy by creating a tangle of objects and systems that support and reinforce the idea that humans are separate from, and superior to, nature. In order to effect deep, systemic changes in favour of less binary, more complementary ways of being, we need to change the tools by which we created the system in the first place. Design, as one of these tools, needs to be re-created in a way that it does not continue to carry the legacies from modernist, patriarchal, capitalist paradigms that clearly don't serve life on this planet (Taboada et al. 2020; Taboada & Turner 2021). We know that designing for more-than-human futures is critical to continued survival in the face of climate change and ecocide (Yigitcanlar et al. 2019). This means that, as designers, we face some profound challenges: the more-than-human is not another audience or set of participants to engage with, seduce, and exploit; and, at the same time, as contemporary Western humans, we cannot '*not* design'.

The choice we have is to critically reflect on the act of designing, its impact, and consequences, and invent new ways of designing together, not only with the more-than-human in a human world, but *in communion with* the more-than-human in a pluriversal world (Escobar 2018) with the aim to **erase** the human/nature abyssal line created by modernity. Decolonial Thought offers insights for critical reflection as an antidote and a way forward for design as a transmuted praxis, as it draws on multiple voices, including the voices of First Nations peoples who have cultivated cultures of complementarity, relationality, and deep connection with all life on Earth (Graham 2009; Kimmerer 2013; Ravuvu 1983; Yunkaporta 2019). Stories help us, see some of these insights in practice, so that when we observe the world around us or design for and with the world around us, we can imagine possible alternative ways of applying this new paradigm and thus initiate a move towards the reality of more-than-human cities. Our walk by the river with its urban encounters with the more-than-human helps us reflect on these relationships and how some Decolonial Thought principles might help inform design praxis for the future.

Imagine yourself coming back to your home, walking onto your street to find no street, no houses around—not yours, not your neighbours. Only trees. An immense forest has taken over. There are no signs of construction, no house, no sofa, no TV to watch the latest series, no kitchen where to cook your food, no toilet, no tap with water running freely, no bed to sleep on and rest your tired body after a full day at work. All gone. Just trees, and moss, and rocks, and a creek. It is cold and getting dark. It looks like it is going to rain. There might be dangerous animals around—you don't know where is safe to sleep. You can see two little glimmering yellow eyes looking curiously at you from a tree branch. A pink nose, a fluffy tail . . . a possum! A Brushtail Possum. It drops the Milky plum it has been carrying and runs back to its branch to join its family of yellow glimmering eyes that slowly disappear into their comfortable beds of leaves inside the tree hollow. You look at the fruit. It is all you have for now. It is a bit rotten, but it might still be ok to eat . . . . As we imagine this other world where we swap places with the possums who have seen their homes completely wiped from their lands, it is easy to empathise with them, to understand their loss, and to want to 'help' them. Ironically, what is not easy is to imagine or perceive is how our presence and behaviour actually affect the other. To put ourselves outside of ourselves, but not in the place of the other, rather as an observer of our own behaviour, as a mirror reflecting ourselves. Bakhtin et al. (1990) called this exotopy: the act of seeing ourselves from the outside as a form of critical reflection. Seeing how our performance and our roles affect the environments and social relations around us. The concept of exotopy aligns with Decolonial Thought as its premise is that of humility, that of understanding that our knowledge and our ways of being in the world are not the only ones, nor the most important, nor those that effect only positive impacts. The practice of exotopy goes beyond that of empathy, as it allows us to see ourselves and our roles in changing the environments of others—intentionally or not.

This way of understanding exotopy, beyond empathy, allows the potential to embrace another aspect of Decolonial Thought: the idea of ecologies of knowledge (de Sousa Santos 2007a) which allows relationality, in much the same way as the spider's webs described by Abram (2012) are complete but connected across different planes and coexist in the same place. De Sousa Santos echoes ideas of exotopy when he suggests that self-reflexivity and the discovery of what he calls 'hetero-referentiality' is a first step towards understanding the onto-epistemological diversity of the world.

Another way of embracing non-human agency is by moving away from our human perspective and practising the idea that the ways of being and making that we don't know are valid as they are, without needing to pass through human interpretation, adaptation, validation, or approval. This involves deeply embracing the idea that all knowledge is, in fact, incomplete because it is generated from within its own episteme and, as such, ignores all others (de Sousa Santos 2007a). Here we need to understand that there are ways of knowing that transcend the human concept of 'knowledge' but that, as humans, we have no other ways to explain or describe them yet. Embracing the unknown and the unexpected includes the notion that, conscious or not, human or not, all agentic behaviour, whether directed by 'practical consciousness' or not, reflects being (intuitive, tacit, instinctive, conscious, rational, emotional, social, etc.) and as such, in a post-abyssal perspective, is valid and important. Kimmerer (2013) talks about learning the language of nature, and about how English and the modern languages of colonisation have neither the words to describe 'life' in its multiple complexities, nor the deep relationships between living beings—relationships where humans are not the dominant species, or the 'wise one'. This kind of approach accepts and enacts the idea of an ecology of knowledges, where many types of knowledge must coexist and interact with the same power levels. Most importantly, this kind of approach leads us to another Decolonial premise: that of 'learning to unlearn'. Learning that it is important to leave behind all assumptions of knowledge and what knowledge might look like so that we can absorb and value other ways of knowing and being in the world. Within an ecology of knowledges, human designs become only one more way of designing, and by embracing all others as they are, the human/nature abyssal line may start to disappear, and deep collective kinship might become a reality. The unknown might be what gives us hope for a possible future, away from the cycles of precariousness that design have created for the more-than-human. The 'unknown' might enable the release of the systemic blinkers that only allow us to see one path.

Decolonial Thought does not offer us a way of finding different or even alternative paths for that would be to merely enact and perpetuate the same ways of thinking that continuously cycle us back. It offers us a different kind of hope, where we can allow room for the more-than-human by fostering future imaginaries where we live *with them*, as opposed to them living with us.

Stories help us by offering opportunity to reflect on the act of designing, its impacts and consequences, and open pathways to re-new ways of designing together, not through the false act of including the more-than-human in a human world, but in communion with the more-than-human. Decolonial Thought gives us principles for deep reflection in relation to more-than-human design processes and futures. It seems necessary to transcend empathy, to go beyond translation and interpretation of nature's ways, and encounter a point where we are able to fully embrace ways of knowing and being that might not be translatable into consciousness—types of understanding that might simply be—like family (where sometimes we don't understand how we understand our siblings or parents, but we just do, or don't, and that is what matters). Tyson Yunkaporta starts his book *Sand Talks* by wondering, 'if echidnas ever suffer from the same delusion that many humans have, that their species is the intelligent centre of the universe' (Yunkaporta 2019, p.1), it might be time to awaken from this human 'dream', to leave the arrogance behind, and to erase, through design, the abyssal lines we created with our 'intelligence'.

In one of their manifestos, the Zapatistas declare: '*Un absurdo: una vivienda que no sirve para vivir*' (Vázquez Ortega & Laguna Galindo 2015). Indeed, it is an absurd to have a house that has no use for living. If we think of our planet as that home, it is time (never too late) to re-encounter our kinship with nature, to remember the long-forgotten fact that nature is our one and only family in all the most paradoxical, physical, and metaphysical ways, and that only together we can re-make our home, our *vivienda*, in a way that we can **all** live well in it.

References

Abram, D. (2012). *The spell of the sensuous: Perception and language in a more-than-human world.* Vintage.

Bakhtin, M. M., Holquist, M., & Liapunov, V. (1990). *Art and answerability: Early philosophical essays* (Vol. 9). University of Texas Press.

Chao, S. (2021). The beetle or the bug? Multispecies politics in a west Papuan oil palm plantation. *American Anthropologist, 123*(3), 476–489. https://doi.org/10.1111/aman.13592

Clarke, R., Heitlinger, S., Light, A., Forlano, L., Foth, M., & DiSalvo, C. (2019). More-than-human participation: Design for sustainable smart city futures. *Interactions, 26*(3), 60–63. https://doi.org/10.1145/3319075
de Sousa Santos, B. (Ed.). (2007a). *Another knowledge is possible: Beyond northern epistemologies.* Verso.
de Sousa Santos, B. (2007b). Para além do pensamento abissal: Das linhas globais a uma ecologia de saberes. *Revista Crítica de Ciências Sociais, 79*(2007). https://doi.org/10.1590/S0101-33002007000300004
Ducarme, F., Luque, G. M., & Courchamp, F. (2013). What are 'charismatic species' for conservation biologists. *BioSciences Master Reviews, 10*(2013), 1–8.
Escobar, A. (2018). *Designs for the pluriverse: Radical interdependence, autonomy, and the making of worlds.* Duke University Press.
Escobar, M. P. (2014). The power of (dis)placement: Pigeons and urban regeneration in Trafalgar Square. *Cultural Geographies, 21*(3), 363–387. https://doi.org/10.1177/1474474013500223
Fieuw, W., Foth, M., & Caldwell, G. A. (2022). Towards a more-than-human approach to smart and sustainable urban development: Designing for multispecies justice. *Sustainability, 14*(2), 948. https://www.mdpi.com/2071-1050/14/2/948
Forlano, L. (2016). Decentering the human in the design of collaborative cities. *Design Issues, 32*(3), 42–54.
Foth, M., & Caldwell, G. A. (2018). More-than-human media architecture. In A. F. G. Schieck, D. Colangelo, & C. Zhigang (Eds.), *MAB18: Proceedings of the 4th Media Architecture Biennale Conference* (pp. 66–75). ACM.
Franklin, A. (2017). The more-than-human city. *The Sociological Review, 65*(2), 202–217.
Frauenberger, C. (2019). Entanglement HCI: The next wave? *ACM Transactions on Computer-Human Interaction, 27*(1), 1–27. https://doi.org/10.1145/3364998
Fry, T., & Nocek, A. (2020). *Design in crisis: New worlds, philosophies and practices.* Routledge.
Gillespie, K., & Collard, R.-C. (Eds.). (2015). *Critical animal geographies: Politics, intersections and hierarchies in a multispecies world.* Routledge.
Gómez-Barris, M. (2017). *The extractive zone: Social ecologies and decolonial perspectives.* Duke University Press. https://doi.org/10.1515/9780822372561
Gonsalves, K., Aia-Fa'aleava, A., Ha, L. T., Junpiban, N., Narain, N., Foth, M., & Caldwell, G. A. (2022). TransHuman saunter: Multispecies storytelling in precarious times. *Leonardo*, 1–12. https://doi.org/10.1162/leon_a_02243
Graham, M. (2009). Understanding human agency in terms of place: A proposed Aboriginal research methodology. *Philosophy Activism Nature 6*, 71–78. https://search.informit.org/doi/10.3316/informit.590560058861546
Haraway, D. (1991). Situated knowledges: The science question in feminism and the privilege of partial perspective. In *Simians, cyborgs, and women: The reinvention of nature* (pp. 183–201). Routledge.
Haraway, D. (2015). Anthropocene, capitalocene, plantationocene, chthulucene: Making kin. *Environmental Humanities, 6*(1), 159–165.
Heitlinger, S., & Comber, R. (2018). Design for the right to the smart city in more-than-human worlds. *arxiv* [online]. https://arxiv.org/ftp/arxiv/papers/1803/1803.10530.pdf
Houston, D., Hillier, J., MacCallum, D., Steele, W., & Byrne, J. (2018). Make kin, not cities! Multispecies entanglements and 'becoming-world' in planning theory. *Planning Theory, 17*(2), 190–212. https://doi.org/10.1177/1473095216688042
Ingold, T. (2000). *The perception of the environment: Essays on livelihood, dwelling & skill.* Routledge. http://www.loc.gov/catdir/enhancements/fy0650/00027142-d.html
Ingold, T. (2011). The animal in the study of humanity. In M. Timo, M. Dario, & T. Aleksei (Eds.), *Readings in zoosemiotics* (pp. 357–376). De Gruyter Mouton. https://doi.org/doi:10.1515/9783110253436.357
Kimmerer, R. (2013). *Braiding sweetgrass: Indigenous wisdom, scientific knowledge and the teachings of plants.* Milkweed.

Last, J. (2021, October 30). This vertical forest tower makes elite green design affordable. But is it actually green? *CBC World News*. https://www.cbc.ca/news/world/green-housing-bosco-milan-trudo-netherlands-1.6228709

Lorde, A. (2020). *Sister outsider: Essays and speeches*. Penguin.

Maller, C. (2018). *Healthy urban environments: More-than-human theories*. Routledge.

Marshall, V. (2019). Removing the veil from the 'rights of nature': The dichotomy between First Nations customary rights and environmental legal personhood. *Australian Feminist Law Journal*, *45*(2), 233–248. https://doi.org/10.1080/13200968.2019.1802154

McKiernan, S., & Instone, L. (2016). From pest to partner: Rethinking the Australian White Ibis in the more-than-human city. *Cultural Geographies*, *23*(3), 475–494. https://doi.org/10.1177/1474474015609159

Mignolo, W., & Walsh, C. (2018). *On decoloniality: Concepts, analytics, praxis*. Duke University Press.

Miller, M. (2018). Environmental personhood and standing for nature: Examining the Colorado River case. *University of New Hampshire Law Review*, *17*, 355.

Pearson, C. (2015). Beyond 'resistance': Rethinking nonhuman agency for a 'more-than-human' world. *European Review of History: Revue européenne d'histoire*, *22*(5), 709–725. https://doi.org/10.1080/13507486.2015.1070122

Power, E. R. (2009). Border-processes and homemaking: Encounters with possums in suburban Australian homes. *Cultural Geographies*, *16*(1), 29–54.

Ravuvu, A. (1983). *Vaka i Taukei: The Fijian way of life*. Institute of Pacific Studies of the University of the South Pacific.

Richards, J. (2019). Historical changes of the lower Brisbane River. In J. Kemp, J. Olley, S. Capon, Jonathan Richards, M. J. Lybolt, & J. M. Pandolfi (Eds.), *Moreton Bay Quandamooka and Catchment* (pp. 137–152). The Moreton Bay Foundation. https://doi.org/10.6084/m9.figshare.8072561

Rose, D. B. (2012). Ruined faces. In W. Edelglass, J. Hatley, & C. Diehm (Eds.), *Facing nature: Levinas and environmental thought* (pp. 95–108). Duquesne University Press.

Rowlands, M. (2019). *Can animals be persons?* Oxford University Press.

Salmond, A. (2014). Tears of Rangi: Water, power, and people in New Zealand. *HAU: Journal of Ethnographic Theory*, *4*(3), 285–309. https://doi.org/https://doi.org/10.14318/hau4.3.017

Segato, R. L. (2018). A manifesto in four themes. *Critical Times*, *1*(1), 198–211.

Sheikh, H., Foth, M., & Mitchell, P. (2022). More-than-human city-region foresight: multispecies entanglements in regional governance and planning. *Regional Studies*, *57*, 1–14.

Smith, N., Bardzell, S., & Bardzell, J. (2017). Designing for cohabitation: Naturecultures, hybrids, and decentering the human in design. In G. Mark, S. Fussell, C. Lampe, m. c. schraefel, J. P. Hourcade, C. Appert, & D. Wigdor (Eds.), *CHI '17: Proceedings of the 2017 CHI Conference on Human Factors in Computing Systems*, (pp. 1714–1725). ACM.

Star, S. L. (1991). Power, technologies and the phenomenology of conventions: On being allergic to onions. In J. Law (Ed.), *A sociology of monsters? Essays on power, technology and domination* (pp. 26–56). Routledge.

Taboada, M. B., Rojas-Lizana, S., Dutra, L. X. C., & Levu, A. V. M. (2020). Decolonial design in practice: Designing meaningful and transformative science communications for Navakavu, Fiji. *Design and Culture*, *12*(2), 141–164. https://doi.org/10.1080/17547075.2020.1724479

Taboada, M. B., & Turner, J. (2021). Rolling stories: Re-imagining self and futures through fictional worlds. In R.M. Leitão, I. Men, L-A. Noel, J. Lima, & T. Meninato (Eds.), *Proceedings of Pivot 2021: Dismantling/Reassembling* (pp. 417–428). Design Research Society.

Thomas, N. (2016). Animals as agents. In *Animal ethics and the autonomous animal self* (pp. 7–36). Palgrave Macmillan. https://doi.org/10.1057/978-1-137-58685-8_2

Tlostanova, M. V., & Mignolo, W. (2012). *Learning to unlearn: Decolonial reflections from Eurasia and the Americas*. The Ohio State University Press.

Tuan, Y.-F. (1977). *Space and place: The perspective of experience*. University of Minnesota Press.

Tuhiwai Smith, L. (1999). *Decolonizing methodologies: Research and indigenous peoples*. Zed Books.

Turner, J., & Morrison, A. (2021). Designing slow cities for more than human enrichment: Dog tales—Using narrative methods to understand co-performative place-making. *Multimodal Technologies and Interaction*, *5*(1), 1. https://doi.org/10.3390/mti5010001

Turner, J., & Taboada, M. (2020). Worlds and words: Interrogating type and map as systems of power and embodied meaning-making. In R. M. Leitão, L-A. Noel, & L. Murphy (Eds.) *Proceedings of Pivot 2020: Designing a World of Many Centers* (pp. 15–28). Design Research Society.

Van Dooren, T., & Rose, D. B. (2012). Storied-places in a multispecies city. *Humanimalia*, *3*(2), 1–27.

Vázquez Ortega, J. J., & Laguna Galindo, S. (2015). *El pensamiento crítico frente a la hidra capitalista I*. EZLN.

White, F. J. (2013). Personhood: An essential characteristic of the human species. *The Linacre Quarterly*, *80*(1), 74–97. https://doi.org/10.1179/0024363912Z.00000000010

Yigitcanlar, T., Foth, M., & Kamruzzaman, M. (2019). Towards post-anthropocentric cities: Reconceptualizing smart cities to evade urban ecocide. *Journal of Urban Technology*, *26*(2), 147–152. https://doi.org/10.1080/10630732.2018.1524249

Yunkaporta, T. (2019). *Sand talk: How Indigenous thinking can save the world*. The Text Publishing Company.

SECTION 2
PRACTICES

5

Participatory Design for Multispecies Cohabitation

By Trees, *for* Birds, *with* Humans

Alexander Holland and Stanislav Roudavski

Introduction: Towards More-than-Human Communities

How can we improve the lives of trees, birds, humans, and other beings in increasingly degrading environments? Might direct participation of non-human beings in design be an answer? We believe that such participation is not only possible, but crucial. The idea of trees as designers and birds as assessors might seem jarring, if not preposterous. We hope our readers might suspend their disbelief until the latter stages of the narrative. To tell our story, we refresh several common terms, including community, imagination, innovation, and participation. We derive these updates from scientific evidence, even where the consequences seem counterintuitive. Why do we need these novel understandings? After all, our case study could stand as a technical contribution to restoration ecology without an appeal for more-than-human participation. We shall be pleased to contribute in this way. However, we have another—strategic—ambition. Our overarching motivation is an expansion of moral consideration in human societies. We observe that more and more humans agree to protect the rights of human minorities, future human generations, and even whole systems such as rivers. An aspect of this ethical concern is the idea of helping all beings speak for themselves. 'Nothing about us without us' is a slogan that captures it well. This slogan motivates the disability movement and others struggling against injustice. Can it apply to non-human beings, too? Political empowerment of non-humans clashes with preconceptions about communities. However, ingrained habits are not a good reason to reject change, not amid the sixth mass extinction and widespread harms to numerous beings. With this in mind, we strive to give serious consideration to inclusive design that can use non-human knowledge to look into the future. In this chapter, we use data analysis and simulation to make one step forward in this long-term project.

Our strategic focus is on communal imagination. Informed by scientific advances in extended synthesis, niche construction, sensory ecology, cognitive ethology, and biosemiotics, we reframe imagination as a collective, communicative, and situated process that pertains to all forms of life. We do so by emphasising design roles that cast trees as designers, birds as discerning clients, and humans as facilitating apprentices.

To explore the notion of inclusive, or more-than-human design (Roudavski 2018, 2020), we consider interactions in a degraded ecosystem that is losing its trees. When

Alexander Holland and Stanislav Roudavski, *Participatory Design for Multispecies Cohabitation.* In: *Designing More-than-Human Smart Cities.* Edited by: Sara Heitlinger, Marcus Foth, and Rachel Clarke, Oxford University Press.
 DOI: 10.1093/9780191980060.003.0007

Figure 5.1 A large old tree near Canberra, Australia. Red: an artificial agent extracts 4,122 individual branches from this tree and classifies their type. Red boxes: branches preferred by birds.
Image by the authors.

large old trees (Figure 5.1) disappear, insects, birds, and bats have no homes. Humans attempt to help by providing artificial replacement structures. The use of such structures is of growing interest in ecological research (Watchorn et al. 2022) and is necessary to support organisms in many ecosystems, including wetlands (Mitsch 2014) and coral reefs (Baine 2001). When humans design such structures, they cannot know all needs of non-human inhabitants. In our case, although some artificial trees are successful (Hannan et al. 2019), their habitability and practicality remain in question. We suggest that human designers can find answers to these questions through an approach that invites contributions from birds and trees.

More-than-human concepts and practices can be useful in many fields. Reviewing the situation in environmental planning, Metzger (2020) insists that more-than-human framing holds promise but remains underdeveloped. Pollastri et al. (2021) argue that this framing would benefit from better data representation. Loh et al. (2020) apply more-than-human perspectives to critique tools used to measure performance of the built environment. Westerlaken et al. (2022) call for a greater focus on more-than-human relations in smart forests. Our chapter is a response to these gaps.

Recent research has investigated more-than-human, multispecies, and interspecies approaches in a variety of fields, including environmental humanities, animal studies, and non-human participation in political decisions (Gray & Curry 2016). Working within design, including architecture and urban planning, our research group extends this work to support practical action. Our projects investigate prosthetic structures for owls (Parker, Roudavski, et al. 2022), heritage of plants (Roudavski & Rutten 2020), and applications of artificial intelligence (AI) to habitat replication (Mirra et al. 2022). This chapter presents one of such projects to demonstrate the potential of more-than-human collaboration.

We align with work that already seeks to empower multiple voices (such as Morris & Spivak 2010). For instance, a growing body of work on decolonialised, queer, and feminist design, in combination with advancements in disability studies, already supports non-standard voices. Such voices may not be able to participate in design without support that Björgvinsson et al. (2012) and others have conceptualised as infrastructuring. This term refers to the effort of providing information infrastructure that often uses metaphors such as pipes, wires, or buckets. Established techniques of infrastructuring include the use of boundary objects (Star & Griesemer 1989), long-term participation (Saad-Sulonen et al. 2018), and prototypes of spaces, tools, and services (Sanders & Stappers 2014; Tironi 2018). Infrastructuring is particularly important in human communities, where decisions require negotiation and imagination becomes political (McBride 2005). There, conflicting participants' perspectives can be detrimental or beneficial, as discussed in adversarial design (Di Salvo 2012; Wienhues 2018).

To date, such work rarely considers non-human participants. We rethink these approaches in the context of diverse non-human bodies, senses, and behaviours. Discussions of such participations do exist (Jönsson & Lenskjold 2014; Clarke et al. 2019; Gatto & McCardle 2019) but tend to be speculative, with their authors calling for further research. Research into animal behaviour (Bekoff & Pierce 2017; Safina 2020) or plant capabilities (Karban 2015; Baluška & Mancuso 2021; Segundo-Ortin & Calvo 2022) in combination with ecocentric analyses of justice (Donaldson & Kymlicka 2011; Schlosberg 2013) highlight an opportunity to contribute.

After this Introduction, the Approach section introduces the case-study project, its stakeholders, and their contributions to communal imagination. The Findings section describes four data-driven operations: capture, predict, reconfigure, and return. The Analysis section follows by discussing participation-related outcomes produced by these operations. We show that they can capture ways in which habitats are meaningful to non-human dwellers, predict performance of habitat structures, assess possible artificial replacements, and prepare for their testing in the field. This section concludes by discussing how these operations can support more equitable communities and better lives.

Approach: Workflow Framing

Our case study is a project that we conduct in partnership with the Australian Capital Territory Parks and Conservation Service and the Fenner School of Ecology of the Australian National University. The project aims to improve on current practices by creating artificial structures that better match preferences of arboreal wildlife. This case study produces useful objects but also serves as a design experiment (Collins et al. 2004) that informs our theoretical work on more-than-human participation. To date, practical outcomes include new information about tree structures, novel algorithms for analysis, and prototypes of possible artificial replacements. Further physical prototypes and field-testing are in preparation. We now discuss the study methods, from the general to the specific.

More-than-human community

Let us begin by defining the notion of 'community' in more-than-human terms. Community is a highly contested concept. Our understanding combines evidence from multiple disciplines, including political studies and community ecology. Community ecology understands community as 'a group of species that occur together in space and time' (Mittelbach & McGill 2019, p.1). This definition does not exclude humans, but the discipline's practices tend to consider them as an external force. In humanities, a community is a group whose members share location (Rabinowitz 2015). In a mirror image of the views in community ecology, this interpretation presumes that communities consist only of humans.

Human communities increasingly recognise the importance of ecosystems. Responding to such recognition, cities engage in the practical work of restoration. However, attitudes that presume human superiority stifle further progress. The spread of human domination curtails the options for other lifeforms. Recent theory recognises the importance of 'communing' that seeks to enfranchise disempowered participants. It aims to include young children, elderly, and disabled into decision making. Similarly, research seeking to support wildlife finds that restoring autonomy in ecological systems is an effective measure of resilience and restoration (Strassburg et al. 2020). However, the work on enfranchisement also tends to focus on humans (Studdert & Walkerdine 2016) or presumes that non-human communities are incompetent and unimaginative.

Responding to this context, environmental humanities propose to abandon habitual binaries between human and non-human worlds (Plumwood 2002). Such work calls for multispecies approaches (Bresnihan 2016; Bastian et al. 2017) that recognise the shared fate of all life on earth. For example, emerging research on more-than-human interactions in urban communities emphasise relationships of care (Wiesel et al. 2020; Prebble et al. 2021). We support such ecocentric approaches (Eckersley 1992; Washington et al. 2017) when they aim to be more just or fair than alternative environmentalisms, such as resource conservation, human welfare ecology, or animal liberation.

In this chapter, we define 'community' as practised relationships, which create fuzzy, emergent groups consisting of humans as well as non-humans. Observable states of communities are traces of historically formed capabilities, interactions, and imaginations. Recent work calls for better interspecies relationships within such communities and emphasised the need for practical approaches such as those discussed later in this chapter (Houston et al. 2018). The next section describes one such community and the need for new techniques of future cohabitation.

Community members

To explore the notion of more-than-human community, we focus on the Molonglo region of Canberra, Australia. This area includes endemic grassy woodlands, a once widespread but now highly fragmented ecological community (Flapper et al. 2018). European settlers converted most of this land to pasture and undermined faunal habitats. Despite this degradation, birds, mammals, reptiles, amphibians, and invertebrates use the remnant grasses, herbs, shrubs, and trees for foraging, roosting, nesting, raising the young, and migration. Human-induced pressures continue to increase as the government works to develop this area into a new community of some 70,000 human residents (Treasury and Economic Development Directorate 2019) (Figure 5.2, solid orange).

To emphasise interspecies interactions, we focus on three groups:

1. ***Remnant large old eucalypts ('trees').*** Isolated old trees persist in Molonglo's paddocks, roadsides, and parks (Figure 5.2, green dots). They are crucial for many ecosystem interactions. We select this group because it includes the oldest living community members. These trees form part of the remaining 3% of pre-European yellow box (*Eucalyptus melliodora)* grassy woodland (Figure 5.2, solid purple), which once covered millions of kilometres in south-eastern Australia (Figure 5.2, purple outline) (Threatened Species Scientific Committee (TSSC) 2006) (Figure 5.2, solid orange). The main challenge for the large old trees is to survive as a type. Although young individuals are common, the older trees are rare (Figure 5.2, green dots). Without these elders, tree taxa struggle to make the beneficial contributions on which many lifeforms depend for survival.
2. ***Arboreal nesters ('birds').*** This group of approximately twenty transitory bird species visit and nest in Molonglo trees. Unlike other birds who depend on tree hollows or live in understory bushes, these birds spend their lives perching in the canopies. One longitudinal study of seventy-two trees (Figure 5.2, purple dots) within the region found that many members of this group exclusively visit large old trees (Le Roux, Ikin, Lindenmayer, Manning, et al. 2012). Arboreal nesters are indicative of a non-human group that is challenging for humans to study. They are small, mobile, and depend on features that are difficult to quantify without automated data collection and analysis. The key challenge for birds is to retain and obtain additional suitable homes.
3. ***Residents, planners, and ecologists ('humans').*** To ensure the long-term viability of the existing biological community, regulations asked Molonglo's developers to fund a research project to offset additional habitat losses (ACT Planning and Land Authority 2011). Researchers estimate that the 10,000 seedlings planted at the site will not develop the canopies of living mature trees for 172 years (Hannan et al. 2019). As an intermediate solution, ecologists investigate whether translocated dead trees and utility poles can imitate absent habitat structures (Figure 5.2, orange dots). In this paper, we consider humans as a fuzzy group that engages with common management practices. Human challenges include competing interests and the struggle to connect actions with ecological values.

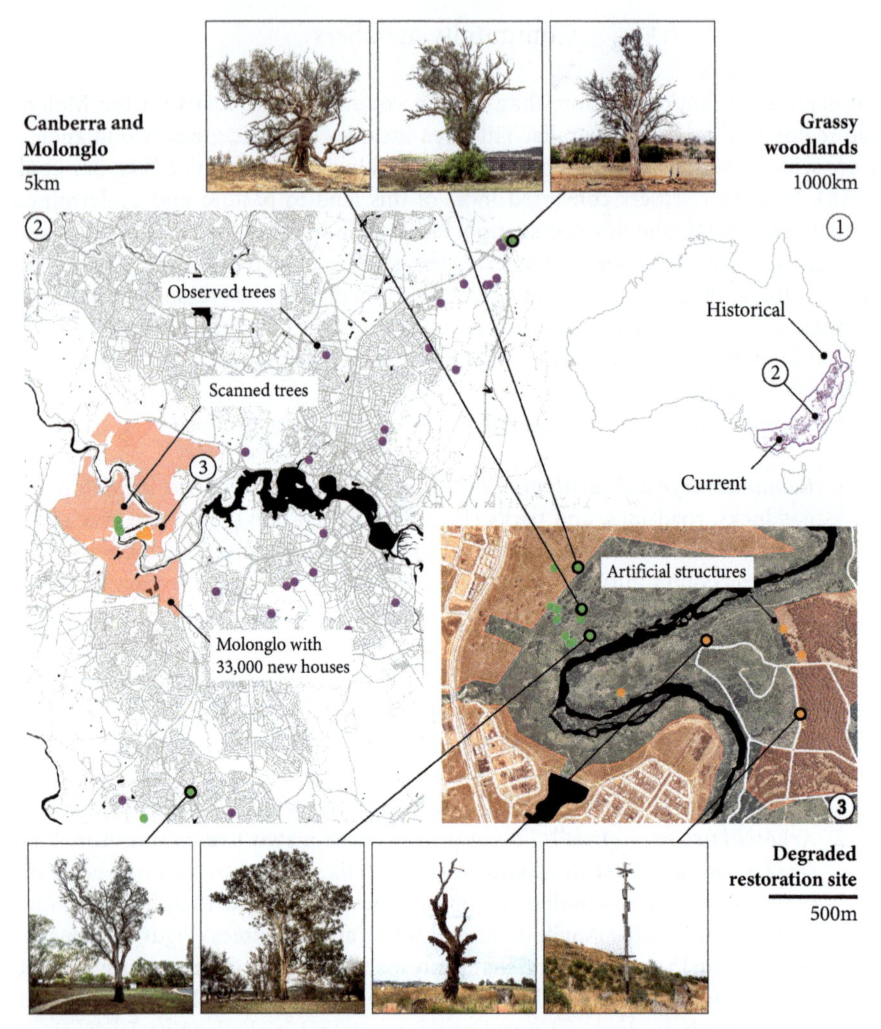

Figure 5.2 Case-study context. Top right: grassy woodlands extents (the outline: historical, shading: current, 2: Molonglo); Left: Molonglo in Canberra (orange: new development, 3: degraded restoration site), Bottom right, degraded restoration site. Image by the authors.

Future uncertainties for trees, birds, and humans provide a useful test case for approaches that seek to benefit all forms of life.

Members as stakeholders

This section outlines relationships among community members defined in the previous section by highlighting harms and benefits (Table 5.1). In our interpretation,

Table 5.1 Table of community relationships focusing on key stakeholders

	Trees and Birds	Humans and Trees	Humans and Birds
Far past (millions to 40,000 years ago)	**Australia's temperate grassy woodlands evolve.** Some trees learn to survive in sunny but dry and resource-poor conditions (Orians & Milewski 2007). Creatures that become birds grow large brains supported by energy-rich manna and pollen in trees (Kaplan 2015). Birds disperse pollen and seeds (Low 2014).	**Humans help the spread of trees.** The first humans hunt megafauna to extinction and inadvertently create a drier and fire-prone climate (Burney & Flannery 2005). Eucalypts thrive in these conditions and replace wet rainforests (Rule et al. 2012).	**Humans help the spread of birds.** Birds that depend on eucalypts spread into wet rainforests (Burney & Flannery 2005).
Past (just before the European arrival)	**Birds use old trees.** Birds use arboreal food resources and shelter in the canopies of old trees (Lindenmayer 2017). Trees use birds and other organisms to carry pollen and provide nutrients (Williams & Woinarski 1997).	**Humans support trees.** Mature trees grow in an open woodland. Saplings and grasses grow between trees (Gibbons et al. 2010). Indigenous land management is compatible with this landscape (Bliege Bird et al. 2008).	**Humans do not undermine bird resilience.** Humans hunt some birds and ignore others (Johnson 2016). Burning practices impact some birds (Burney & Flannery 2005).
Past (since the European arrival)	**Birds use remaining old trees.** Birds depend on old trees as populations shift and reduce (Manning et al. 2006; Stagoll et al. 2012).	**Humans destroy trees.** Humans use Australia's temperate grassy woodlands for cropping and livestock, removing most trees (Lindenmayer et al. 2014). Some old trees remain for windbreak and shade. Livestock prevent saplings from growing (Gibbons & Boak 2002).	**Humans undermine birds.** Humans alter landscapes through agriculture and urbanisation (Bradshaw 2012). Some birds adapt but habitat loss contributes to local extinctions (Department of Environment, Climate Change and Water NSW 2011).

Continued

Table 5.1. *Continued*

	Trees and Birds	Humans and Trees	Humans and Birds
Current (the consequences of the last 230 years)	**Bird resilience dwindles as old trees disappear.** Land use intensification results in a shortage of middle-aged trees (Manning et al. 2012). Populations of birds become smaller as habitat resources become scarce (Lindenmayer et al. 2013).	**Humans continue to reduce the population of surviving old trees.** Isolated old trees exist in farming and urban landscapes (Fischer et al. 2010). Many are not protected by legislation (Lindenmayer et al. 2013). Young eucalypts struggle to grow on grazed and cultivated lands (Gibbons & Boak 2002).	**Humans provide limited compensatory actions for birds.** Humans plant trees to support bird populations (Prober & Thiele 2005). While these trees grow, humans attempt artificial habitat-structures such as translocated dead trees and utility poles (Hannan et al. 2019).
Projected (under the business-as-usual)	**Tree-bird relationships fail.** Remaining old trees reach the end of their lives. Trees planted during revegetation initiatives are too young to support birds (Le Roux, Ikin, Lindenmayer, Manning et al. 2015). Australia's temperate grassy woodlands deteriorate into treeless pastures (Fischer, Zerger et al. 2010). Millions of hectares have no old trees (Manning et al.).	**Humans eliminate old trees.** Large old trees are functionally extinct (Gibbons et al. 2008; Le Roux et al. 2014). Models predict that Canberra's urban old trees will disappear within 80–300 years (Le Roux et al. 2014). Other models predict that surrounding paddock trees will disappear in the next 80 years (Gibbons et al. 2008).	**Remedial actions by humans are insufficient.** Habitat continues to contract. Ecosystems cannot return to past states (Gibbons & Lindenmayer 2007). Artificial structures provide limited support (Le Roux, Ikin, Lindenmayer, Bistricer et al. 2015).
Preferred (an alternative with outcomes supporting the continual functioning of all stakeholders)	**Trees and birds develop resilience.** Trees live their lives to the full. Trees can create and sustain the next generation of trees. Birds depend on trees for homes but also adapt to alternatives. Birds have an abundance of homes.	**Humans study trees as sources of innovation.** Humans acknowledge tree contributions. Trees remain in place even after death. New plantings grow bigger. Humans allocate resources and space to avert possible damage from old trees.	**Humans facilitate bird habitats.** Birds find new homes, shifting with climate change and living in cities. With the help of birds and trees, humans design better replacement structures.

relationships cast community members as stakeholders. Here, we describe a stakeholder as an individual or a group that can benefit or suffer from an action.

In summary, the challenge here is to understand the value of large old trees to birds, to demonstrate it to humans, and then use the communal abilities to design artificial replacement structures as an alleviation of acute shortage.

Seeking to reflect the community relationships discussed above, we understand participation as an umbrella term for modes of engagement that depend on capabilities of stakeholders. Here, the notion of more-than-human participation suggests important political consequences discussed in research on more-than-human care, justice, and traditional custodianship. Efforts towards earth jurisprudence (Bekoff 2017) and non-human rights (Milburn 2017; Blattner et al. 2019) provide characteristic examples. In design, projects that engage with plant agencies outline participation with beings that do not have brains or think like humans (Sheikh et al. 2021; Chang et al. 2022; Fell et al. 2022). We discuss ways to amplify productive community participation in the section on Amplified Relationships later in this chapter.

Stakeholder imagination

Our approach is to consider more-than-human designing in relation to communal imagination. Let us first explain that we understand imagination as a process that is common to all life. Today, dominant conceptualisations of imagination presume cognitive capabilities (Mitchell 2016; Picciuto & Carruthers 2016). These interpretations are human-centric and tend to exclude non-humans. By contrast, other research emphasises the embodied nature of perception and cognition (Varela et al. 1991). This work argues that all organisms experience the world subjectively. Living and evolving together, they relate by modifying themselves and others. Such interpretations allow us to adopt an ecocentric understanding of imagination. According to this understanding, imagination occurs in communities through multiple bodies, perceptions, practices, and places (Roudavski 2016). Biological studies also recognise that many organisms design their own environments as ecosystem engineers and niche constructors (Jones et al. 1996; Laland et al. 2016). Many of such biological innovations do not require cognition to create new ways to resist entropy (Avery 2012).

This expanded understanding of imagination involves the construction of a model world to represent reality that is not directly accessible to living beings. For instance, a living cell that admits a chemical compound into its interior or restricts it to the outside of its wall completes this action by comparing the signals from its senses to its model of the world (Barbieri 2008). Others discussed this model as the *Umwelt* (von Uexküll 2010), the phenomenal model, the perceptual model, an 'inside exterior' (Hoffmeyer 1998, p.40), 'self world', or the semiotic environment. We recognise this process as basal or primal imagination. Forms of imagination can differ in features and complexity between species with humans occupying multiple imagined worlds, as outlined in Table 5.2

Table 5.2. Processes for constructing imaginative worlds and example outcomes for select agents.

	Model-World Processes	Example Outcomes	Evidence
Birds	Cognition through embodied senses and behaviours. Individual and social learning. Local traditions through cultures.	Species A senses landscape features that species B or C cannot perceive. A bird selects a poor nesting site because urban cues are misleading.	(Aplin 2019; Battin 2004; Manning et al. 2006; Martin 2017)
Trees	Environmental awareness through senses. Memory through chemical pathways representing experiences. Learning through comparison and evaluation of stored experiences.	A tree protects its territory and wards off parasites by distinguishing itself from not-self. A group of trees construct social networks for common goals such as sharing water and nutrients.	(Beiler et al. 2010; Witzany 2018)
Humans	Expanded capabilities for cognition and memory through symbols and technologies. Limited ability to notice, study, or understand the lives of others.	Old trees may completely disappear in Molonglo and globally because humans fail to value them economically or aesthetically. Humans see old trees as sources of risk or sites of disease. Humans protect charismatic birds but fail not notice significant changes in their migration or feeding habits.	(Dee 2019; Le Roux et al. 2014; Roudavski & Davis 2020).

Furthermore, this imagination is always communal and situated because living beings find themselves in complex evolved ecologies of meanings, messages, and interpretations. Meanings are the products of collective agreements (Bruner 1990). In such context, meaning emerges as habits or patterns within lineages and imagination is always shared. Ecologists acknowledge the usefulness of such subjectivities for conservation (Manning et al. 2004; Goymann & Küblbeck 2020).

This communal imagination becomes closely related to design because living forms have goals. They strive towards individual and generational goals such as survival, procreation, and wellbeing. Here, it is important to repeat that individuals, groups, and whole cultures (including the best of human science) do not have a privileged access to reality. All labour under constraints of their perceptual abilities, information-processing frameworks, behavioural constraints, historical contingencies, and other limitations. Their interpretation of the world can be erroneous and harmful, as happens in ecological traps or outdated adaptations, such as those leading to human obesity.

This background leads us to a pragmatic, outcome-oriented definition of imagination as a more-than-human, shared ability to invent new forms of living. Such innovation by all concerned will be necessary in the unavoidably multiplying novel ecosystems. Designing cannot resolve interdependencies between environmental changes and stakeholder subjectivities without imaginative outcomes of more-than-human participation. We discuss novelty as one of such outcomes in the next section.

Communal innovation

In the context of design, a potentially useful product of imagination is innovation or an introduction of novelty in response to pressure. Innovations can be valuable in the changing circumstances, such as those that characterise human-modified environments, but they can also be harmful. Living communities can be aware of novelty, but innovations can also be inaccessible to the perceptions of stakeholders. For example, living beings might lack abilities to notice accumulations of gene mutations or amassing environmental change.

In contrast to such individual limitations, communal imagination reliably produces innovative templates (cf. ecofields; Maran & Kull 2014) of possible futures. These templates merge individual and collective abilities to confine possibilities, establish semiotic distinctions, and begin adjustments within existing phenotypic, developmental, behavioural, and other plasticities (Piersma & Gils 2011). Traces of such templates express as combinations of behaviours exhibited by community members, but complete knowledge of such templates is not possible for any individual.

And yet, such templates are not completely inaccessible. For example, numerical measurement and analysis that seek to invite perspectives of community members can reduce the uncertainty about their characteristics. All non-human stakeholders can contribute, for example, through presence or absence, bodily responses, and breeding successes. Combinations of stakeholder perspectives can yield patchwork approximations of possible futures in response to decisions that we interpret as contributions to design. This framework of communal imagination is useful because it can integrate existing infrastructuring devices of participatory design. For example, by applying 'boundary objects' (Star 2010; Star & Griesemer 1989) in non-human contexts, human designers can solicit bird responses to computational models or physical prototypes of habitat structures.

In our case study, the temperate zone that contains Molonglo no longer functions as a self-sustaining ecosystem and requires human interventions to offset the damage. In every situation, an ability to innovate is in tension with the capacity to change in response to pressure and to manage the ensuing impacts. Among our stakeholders, trees hold the value that humans fail to appreciate. A useful community innovation should be able to account for this value and seek to maximise it. For example, birds need to develop novel behaviours to live in the conditions they have not previously encountered. The inherited plasticity of organisms' behaviours is the limit to these innovations. Harmful consequences can occur even within these limits. For example, birds can interpret novel opportunities as desirable without anticipating novel harms. Similarly, temporal and spatial feedback between human and non-human forces can trap entire landscapes in an ongoing damaged state (Lindenmayer et al. 2011). These examples demonstrate that imagination and innovation are not inherently positive forces, with risks increasing through the exclusion of stakeholders.

Multispecies cohabitation

The framework of more-than-human design can be useful in many situations. This chapter considers its application in the context of multispecies cohabitation in modified landscapes. All life exists in and is interlinked with structural and spatial settings. Acknowledging the importance of local expertise, human design approaches justified the focus on bioregional solutions (Crist 2020; Fanfani & Matarán Ruiz 2020). Emerging work in design understands that discounting of non-human expertise in local habitation can lead to significant losses (Parker, Soanes, et al. 2022). Plants, animals, and other organisms hold knowledge, provide services, and help to maintain complex mutualisms.

In the context of Molonglo and the south-eastern Australia's grassy woodlands biome, current practices already value the expertise of human residents, including farmers and traditional knowledge holders. Examples include farmers' contributions to weed control programmes (Firn et al. 2018), community workshops with residents to plan urban development (Molonglo Community Consultation Report 2012), and partnerships with Aboriginal Reference Groups to apply traditional ecological knowledge (Department of Environment, Climate Change and Water NSW 2011). Other jurisdictions sought to grant greater voice to whole situated eco-social systems, emphasising the primacy of the land or country (Country et al. 2016). We also accept that challenges of multispecies cohabitation will require inclusive participation.

As discussed, this participation occurs through informationally limited and evolutionary defined agents. These agents form novel societies that include humans, non-human biological beings, and artificial systems as envisaged in notions such as smart cities, smart villages, smart landscapes, or even Digital or Smart Earth. Our work seeks to extend emerging research on these topics including discussions of urban paradigms that support survival and wellbeing of non-human living beings (Forlano 2016; Foth 2017; Smith et al. 2017), considerations of circular-economy villages (Liaros 2021), and multispecies cohabitation in the context of farming (Liu 2019).

Innovation in practice

To illustrate this proposition, this section explores more-than-human innovation by focusing on a challenge that links trees, birds, and humans. It considers how community members perform three types of actions: 'design by', 'design for', and 'design with'. These roles simplify the complex real-world relationships in organisations and ecosystems. Despite the loss of nuance, this approach is useful because it contrasts distinct roles of stakeholders and extends existing design practices that seek to decentre humans (Forlano 2016). These roles demonstrate that amplification of non-human contributions to design is reasonable and feasible.

In our case-study, we emphasise the roles of:

- ***Trees as designers.*** Old trees mediate crucial ecological, chemical, and biological processes (Lindenmayer & Laurance 2016), acting as ecosystem engineers. We focus on habitation within their canopies. Over hundreds of years, old trees create complex habitat structures that are absent in younger trees or other parts of the landscape. This interpretation suggests that old ***trees design by providing habitats.***
- ***Birds as users and clients.*** Birds co-evolved with trees and this relationship shaped their bodies, cognition, and senses. Canopies of large old trees have diverse structural conditions. This diversity is necessary for birds to survive. For instance, birds depend on lateral branches for resting, fissured bark for food, and dead limbs for observation and hunting (Rayner et al. 2016). Birds are discerning clients who continuously assess their habitats. Thus, we can say that trees ***design for birds.***
- ***Humans as mitigators of their disruptive actions.*** Humans create artificial replacement structures for birds and take measures to protect old trees. However, humans find it difficult to study birds' needs or tree capabilities (Ehbrecht et al. 2017). Because of this, humans do not fully understand why birds prefer the canopies of old trees, and what branches they prefer. Human designers require the input from trees and birds to produce successful designs. Thus, humans fulfil supporting roles that we denote as ***designing with humans.***

The remaining component of our approach is information technology in support of more-than-human participation (Tomitsch et al. 2021; Romani et al. 2022; Sheikh et al. 2023). Here, we focus on the empowerment of non-human voices rather than on the amplification of human visions.

To explore the roles discussed above in keeping with this objective, we introduce an additional type of agent: an artificial system.[1] Limited now, such systems promise to become more autonomous with the development of AI. For our purposes, their autonomy is secondary. Instead, we focus on their capacity to ***amplify beneficial interactions between non-human designers and clients.***

The next sections demonstrate the practical feasibility of such artificial systems and their support for more-than-human design.

Findings: Workflow Operations

We discuss here, as a set of findings, four technical operations of our workflow that form key steps in translating non-human design innovation into communal imagination that can support more-than-human design.[2]

Capture

The 'capture' operation extracts and recognises meaningful features supplied by non-human agents such as birds and trees. We understand these features as structural traces of relationships and behaviours.

For example, we know that birds use horizontal leafless branches (Holland et al. 2024). Consequently, our project captures relevant information about trees. To do so, we gather high-resolution data about geometries of tree canopies and use machine learning to separate sets of points that represent wood and leaves (Belton et al. 2013) (grey tree model, Figure 5.3). We also recognise structural features of branches and find information about branch positions, orientations, radii, and connectivity (Hackenberg et al. 2015). We then specify rules to recognise features meaningful for birds, for instance, whether each branch is alive and determine its inclination, size, and exposure. This operation describes aspects of trees with much greater fidelity than unassisted observations by humans (green highlights, Figure 5.3). Resulting descriptions can quantify habitat structures provided by trees, making them analysable and comparable (coloured graph, Figure 5.3). This process can recognise contributions of important stakeholders such as large old trees and account for their individual characteristics.

Such processes can amplify signals of existing relationships for human interpretation and use, giving the voices of birds and trees greater significance. In this operation, the knowledge flows from trees, through birds, to humans in a form of a collaborative process.

Predict

The 'predict' operation extrapolates from limited observations to create computational models of relationships between birds and habitat structures.

Humans can observe bird behaviours, but this is a slow process. Birds are mobile and can use very large territories. Many are migratory and stay in one place for a limited time. They often have small bodies, and their behaviours vary with breeding cycles and between individuals. Fields observations of birds often take many years, but still produce sparse data.

To amplify the signal collected through field observations, our operations use statistical models to extrapolate and predict behaviours. To do this, we use data on bird–branch interactions collected in a multi-year study by ecologists at the Australian National University (Le Roux, Ikin, Lindenmayer, Manning, et al. 2015; Le Roux et al. 2018). These bird observations are part of an ongoing project that seeks to understand the contributions of large old trees, as described earlier. This research work documented the abundance and identity of bird species that came into direct contact with sample trees, as well as the radius, the angle relative to horizontal, and the dead or living status of each contact branch. Our collaboration with these ecologists continues, and further publications are forthcoming.

Using this observational data, we then created a set of models that represent bird behaviour. These models use observational data to make predictions for

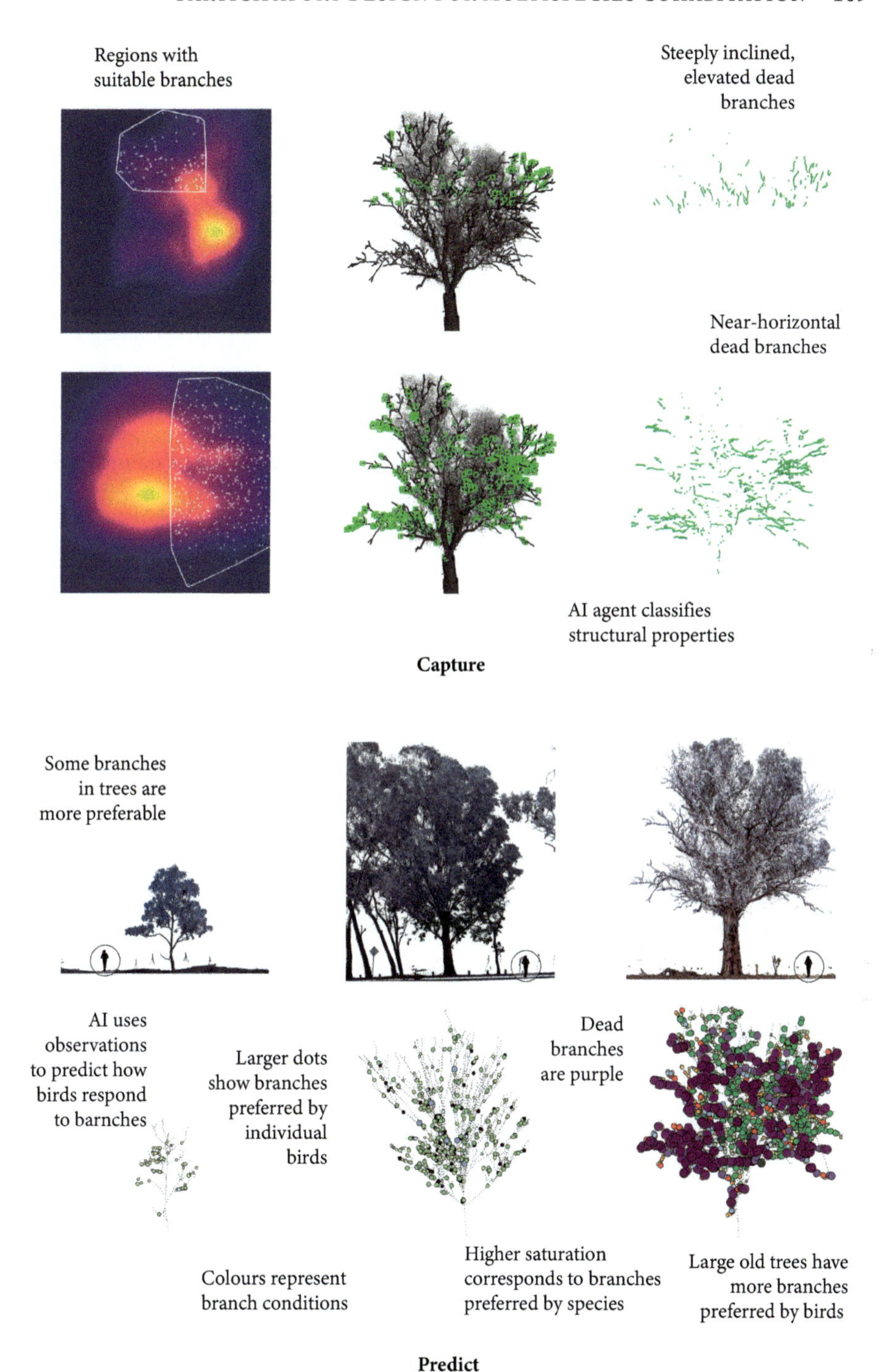

Figure 5.3 Top image: feature recognition and interpretation. Perch structures extracted from laser scans of large old trees. Bottom: predictions of bird preferences in trees. Features expressing potential bird-branch interactions in a young, middle-age and large old tree.

Image by the authors.

non-observed trees, allowing us to predict the likelihood of bird use for each branch. Features meaningful to birds include exposed dead branches (purple dots, Figure 5.3) that are easy to fly to and lateral branches (green dots, Figure 5.3) that are comfortable for perching.

This operation approximates birds' preferences for types of branches and makes it possible to numerically assess relative value of different habitat structures for birds. These estimates amplify preferences for birds, supporting their inclusion into design considerations.

Reconfigure

The 'reconfigure' operation generates artificial habitat structures and compares them with naturally evolved habitats. Our procedures can evaluate scans of natural trees, artificial habitat structures already installed in the field (Figure 5.4), and proposals for new designs (Figure 5.4).

We first establish a set of feature-rich design options using a semi-automated generative routine. Using this routine, we set the initial parameters, including points of attachment to existing structures and the material use constraints. The routine responds by generating an artificial canopy structure that matches specified constraints while ensuring structural stability.

We then select promising designs using an analysis routine that assesses their likely utility for birds. This routine works by extracting geometrical information from generated proposals, including angles, sizes, and visibility statuses of all artificial branches. After extraction, the routine predicts bird response to each artificial branch by comparing this information to the database of bird use described in the previous step.

Through iteration, this operation produces sets of site-specific habitat structures and supports comparative evaluation of virtual and physical designs.

Return

The 'return' operation supports iterative assessment of proposals in the field. All modelling includes simplifications and approximations. Therefore, possible artificial interventions should undergo field-testing. Our approach supports this via physical prototyping. Through their encounters with prototypes in the field, stakeholder groups such as arboreal nesters can provide feedback on the utility of designs (Figure 5.4, bottom image).

Materialisation of designs is a slow process. In response, we aim to reduce the barriers to field testing by using computationally assisted workflows for working with complex structures. These workflows use rapid digital fabrication routines and augmented reality construction. We have already tested a range of such fabrication and assembly approaches in field contexts at the scale of tree hollows in other case study settings (Roudavski & Parker 2020; Parker, Roudavski et al. 2022). The work at tree scales is ongoing, and we shall report the outcomes soon.

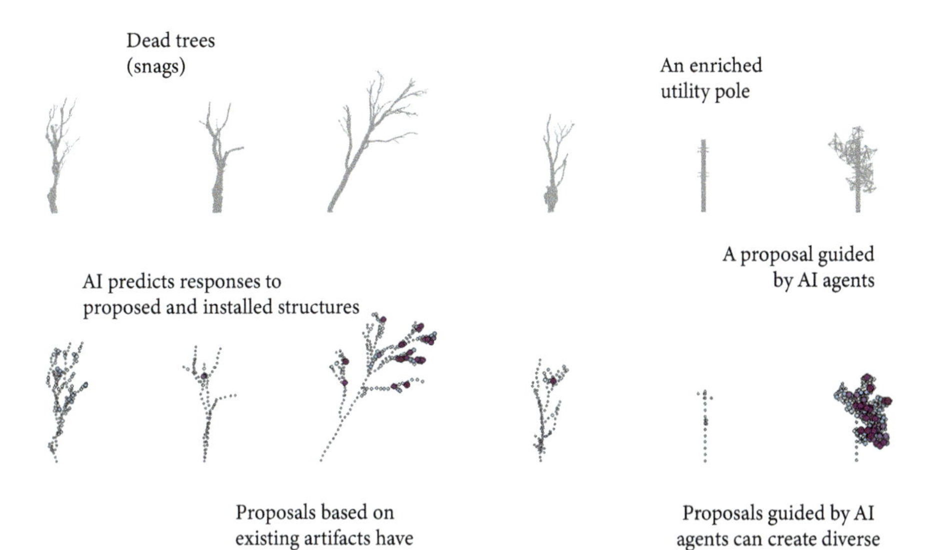

Figure 5.4 Top image: simulated bird preferences. A proposed tensile structure has considerably more resources than translocated dead trees or utility poles. Bottom: natural and artificial habitats at Molonglo. Clockwise from top left: a large old tree, a translocated snag with artificial enhancements, a utility pole with artificial enhancement, generated designs.

Image by the authors.

The return of knowledge materialised as functional structures to the field contributes to the maintenance and development of more-than-human community relationships, as we discuss in the next section.

Analysis: Workflow Outcomes

To analyse the findings, we return to the concepts discussed in the introduction. We first show that our technical operations can amplify collaborative relationships between stakeholders in more-than-human communities, and then indicate how this expansion can support better lives.

Amplify relationships for multispecies participation

The case introduced above affects birds, trees, and humans. We claim that our results support more-than-human design by amplifying existing and probing for novel relationships between these human and non-human stakeholders.

We first revisit the technical operations discussed in the Results (Table 5.3). We link them to community relationships that amplify the flow of meaningful information between stakeholders, seeking to address the unmet needs described in the Approach section.

Listen

Existing work on participatory approaches demonstrates that disadvantaged humans can benefit if more powerful humans acknowledge their existence, contributions, and needs. In an extension, our approach reframes trees as designers. They are survivors from past eras of richer mutualistic relationships and retain features that remain significant to others.

Current artificial structures are often made from found objects (snags or common industrial objects such as utility poles). These simple forms ignore subtle but important relationships between birds and trees. For instance, humans know that old trees provide hollows because hollows are easy to count. However, our group of birds do not nest in hollows but still depend on old trees. Such dependencies are harder to study.

In response, we develop operations that support listening to trees by capturing and interpreting numerical data that involve structural complexity and lateral branches. Figure 5.5 is an example that compares natural trees and artificial alternatives. We underlie the relative positions of these objects with a field that represents bird behaviour as observed by Hannan et al. (2019). This study shows that bird response to remnant trees is high (yellow) in contrast to translocated dead snags (green) and enriched utility poles (blue). The plot shows that dots match observational data that is newly available via our operations.

We describe data capture, processing, and feature recognition as a form of 'listening' because these operations produce quantitative and topological descriptions of tree structures that can appear surprising to humans, whose knowledge about

Table 5.3 Workflow operations to amplify communal imagination.

Technical operations	Amplified relationships	Stakeholder actions
Capture	Listen	Trees supply baseline examples of structural distributions that inform remedial efforts.
		Birds use trees in ways that are observable to humans.
		Humans set up the technical system and train the AI on categorised data.
		Artificial agents extract quantified features with high fidelity in ways that can surprise humans.
Predict	Consult	Trees supply canopies that differ with age and individual life histories.
		Birds accept or reject tree branches that are suitable for their needs.
		Humans perform detailed, long-term observations of birds and compare different trees.
		Artificial agents enable comparisons between trees by extrapolating patterns of bird actions.
Reconfigure	Provoke	Trees inform the design of replacement structures and provide the baseline for assessment.
		Bird behaviours guide the search for artificial canopies. Humans supply design provocations, setup the workflow, test, measure, and make selections.
		Artificial agents generate shapes, designs, iterate through versions in response to constraints or feedback, and inform construction.
Return	Support	Trees resist change, contribute to ecosystem functioning, and provide scaffolds for installations.
		Birds succeed or fail to use the designs and show what works and what does not.
		Humans choose sites, produce prototypes, install, monitor, interpret feedback, update models, and propose further designs.
		Artificial agents learn, propose new designs, and provide comparative toolkits.

trees and their community roles is far from complete. Such listening can highlight the importance of non-human community members, detail their contributions, and guide remedial efforts.

Consult

Participatory approaches argue that greater autonomy can support all stakeholders in resisting exploitation or inaction. Enacting this reasoning, our experiments demonstrate that humans can empower birds to express their preferences. As all life-forms, birds have capabilities that make some forms of participation feasible and

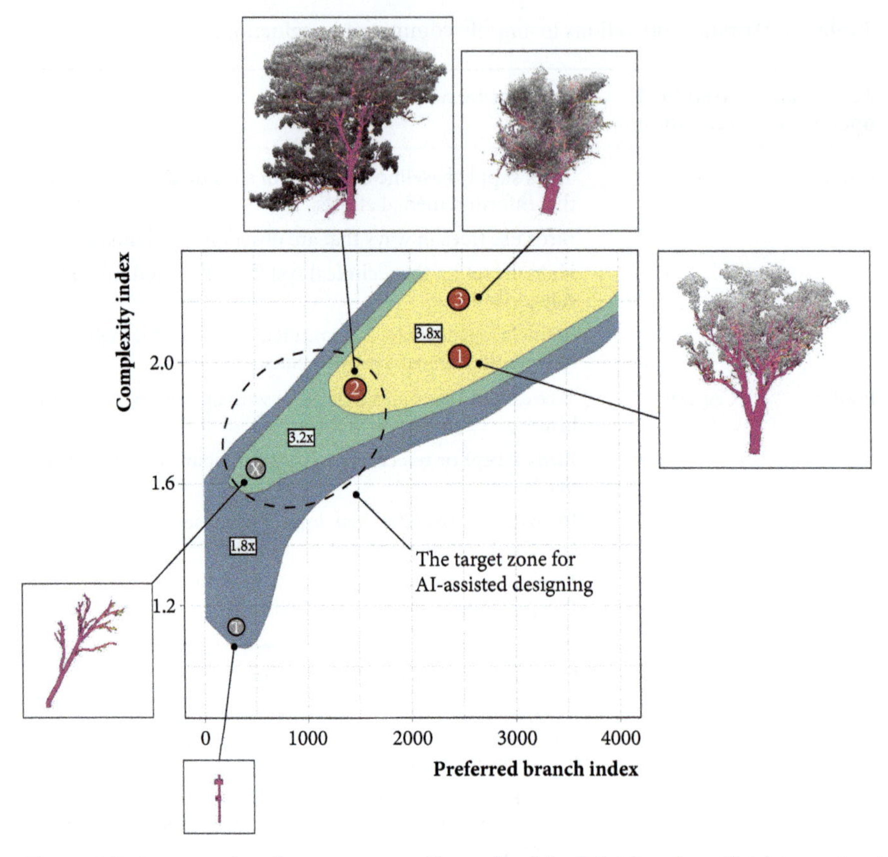

Figure 5.5 A comparison between naturally evolved (red dots) and artificial (grey dots) canopy structures.
Image by the authors.

others impossible. For example, birds cannot assess written briefs or review drawings, but can express preferences through everyday behaviours. However, translation of these expressed preferences into design actions is not straightforward because humans do not have the evolved bodies of birds, cannot experience bird perceptions, or understand nuances of bird actions.

In response, our ***predict*** operation exposes lifestyles, behaviours, and preferences of birds through quantitative data analysis. It amplifies humans' ability to 'consult' with birds about design options by extrapolating their bodily responses. We interpret this simulative statistical analysis is a form of consulting because it extrapolates observed interactions between community members into unobserved situations. Such interactions amplify traces of existing relationships and can illuminate their consequences under a diverse range of conditions, for example, by predicting the likely use of unobserved trees. This operation emphasises that birds are self-directed agents who are experts in their lives as well as valuable members of their communities.

Provoke

The need for communal imagination in response to the accelerating environmental change will only grow. In response, we develop artificial agents that generate designs and compare outcomes of multiple iterations. Artificial alternatives 'provoke' by disturbing the consultative process with novel options. These options modify relationships between stakeholders such as trees and birds while lending themselves to numerical evaluation. This evaluation supports iterative development of designs and redeploys historical innovation produced by non-human agents in novel ecosystems.

Figure 5.6 shows one approach where tree geometries guide the generation of artificial structures. These structures are more complex and varied than those possible through direct modelling by humans. They can support many microhabitats with varying exposures to the wind and sun, visibility, or perching comfort. The ***reconfigure*** operation allows community members to change their choices in response to feedback. For instance, it can retain features used by birds while addressing concerns such as constructability, material use, and costs.

Assessment of current practices (Prebble et al. 2021) demonstrate that quantitative systems can have an unfortunate effect of solidifying unjust relationships between human and non-human stakeholders. For example, digital mapping and database technologies can commodify tree lives for human exploitation. In contrast, our findings indicate that these techniques can also help by integrating human and non-human signals, increasing the diversity of options, and supporting the assessment of implications. In agreement with agnostic design (Di Salvo 2012), this approach accepts that friction between empowered stakeholders can be productive. Respect for the capabilities of others can generate new relationships while providing care through communication, trust, and respect (Wiesel et al. 2020).

Support

Our proposals depend on long-term experimental observations of prototypes in the field. Therefore, we align the ***return*** operation with the ***support*** for the processes of community imagination through forms of infrastructuring (Björgvinsson et al. 2012) discussed above. Data interpretation, simulation, and design, coupled with collaborative prototyping and testing in the field, are a form of 'support' because these processes empower a broad range of stakeholders, including trees and birds, to participate in long-term assessment and redesign. Future-oriented and evidence-based information exchanges between human and non-human community members build the capacity to cope with change.

The discourse on commons demonstrates that beneficial initiatives and successful designs cannot persist without long-term engagement (Huybrechts et al. 2017). This support can take the form of legislation, education, management guidelines, focused research, guaranteed funding, and other measures. The discussion of these issues is beyond the scope of this chapter. One way to encourage knowledge reuse and stakeholder empowerment is through the creation and sharing of novel datasets, workflows, and tools. To give one example, our techniques of data acquisition and analysis of old trees led to innovation in ecology and machine learning that

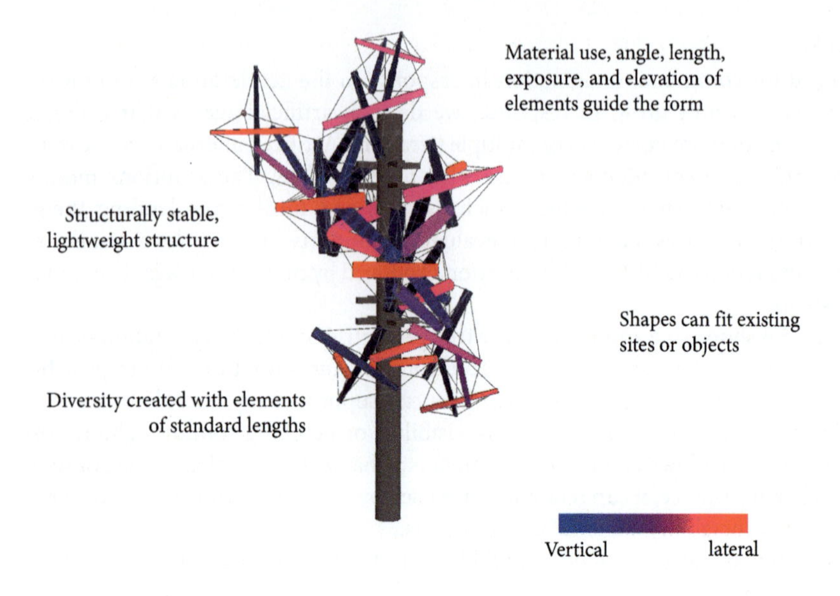

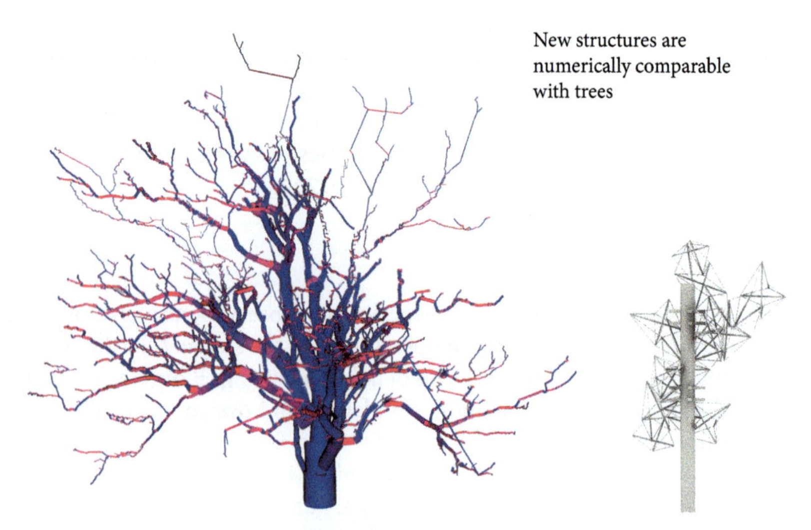

Figure 5.6 Design provocations and simulated stakeholder responses. Top: an artificial canopy structure. Red: lateral artificial branches comfortable to perch. Thicker lines: artificial branches hidden within the canopy. Thinner lines: exposed artificial branches. Bottom: distribution and quantity of lateral branches (red) in the canopy of a natural large old tree; model of artificial habitat-structure, right.
Image by the authors.

reconstructs trees as they are perceived by birds (Mirra et al. 2022). Further collaborations will be necessary to expand the benefits of more-than-human design to other sites and species at large scales and numbers.

Build better lives by imagining together

The second objective of this project was to illustrate how its techniques can support more equitable communities and help their members live better lives.

Existing approaches to environmental management already aim to support sustainability. In addition, work that focuses on bio-informed design seeks to learn from natural systems. However, such approaches see non-human lifeforms such as birds and trees as incompetent or aim to isolate innovations occurring in natural systems for human use, without compensation.

In most cases, humans undertake to manage the environment according to their wisdom. Non-human stakeholders have no power in decision making or innovation is response to change. In doing so, humans fail to distribute benefits and risks with equity. These approaches tend to produce benefits for humans but result in costs for the birds and trees. Examples of drawbacks include prioritisation of narrow time-frames that ignore long processes of arboreal habitat formation, misinterpretation of non-human needs, and failure to act in the face of available knowledge. These biases demonstrate the drawbacks of situations where communal imagination is interpreted by a limited number of powerful and predominantly human voices.

To illustrate advantages of more-than-human approaches, this chapter described birds and trees as innovators. Humans have disrupted the expression of non-human imagination such that the reversal to historical states is impossible. For example, Molonglo will soon have no old trees, even if many young trees are planted now. To support ecosystem integrity and ensure survival of vulnerable species, humans must provide artificial habitat structures. In such situations, access to historical and possible innovations produced by more-than-human communities can be crucially significant.

We illustrate some advantages of more-than-human design through two figures.[3] Figure 5.7 maps historical imagination produced by the ecological community (green) and the anthropogenic damage that made resulting patterns of cohabitation less useful (red). Figure 5.8 contrasts the scope of existing restoration approaches (orange) with more-than-human design (purple). The axes use logarithmic scales to show timescales (increasing vertically towards the top) and levels of complexity within communities (increasing horizontally towards the right). Colours show the degree of damage or restoration of capabilities.

These diagrams highlight that 1) damage done by humans spreads across the full spectrum of innovations (Figure 5.7); and 2) human remedial efforts cluster in the central region (Figure 5.8), failing to benefit from the complete richness of community interactions. Remedying the curtailed reach of current human actions, our approaches extend designing in ways that can expand the range of possible solutions.

The bottom left of Figure 5.8 provides a characteristic example. This region includes measurable outcomes of design options that existing approaches do not produce. For instance, current approaches to describe trees lack detail (c5). Similarly, typical designs for artificial habitat structures produce relatively simple forms (c6). Approaches within this region expand the set of imaginable designs. For example,

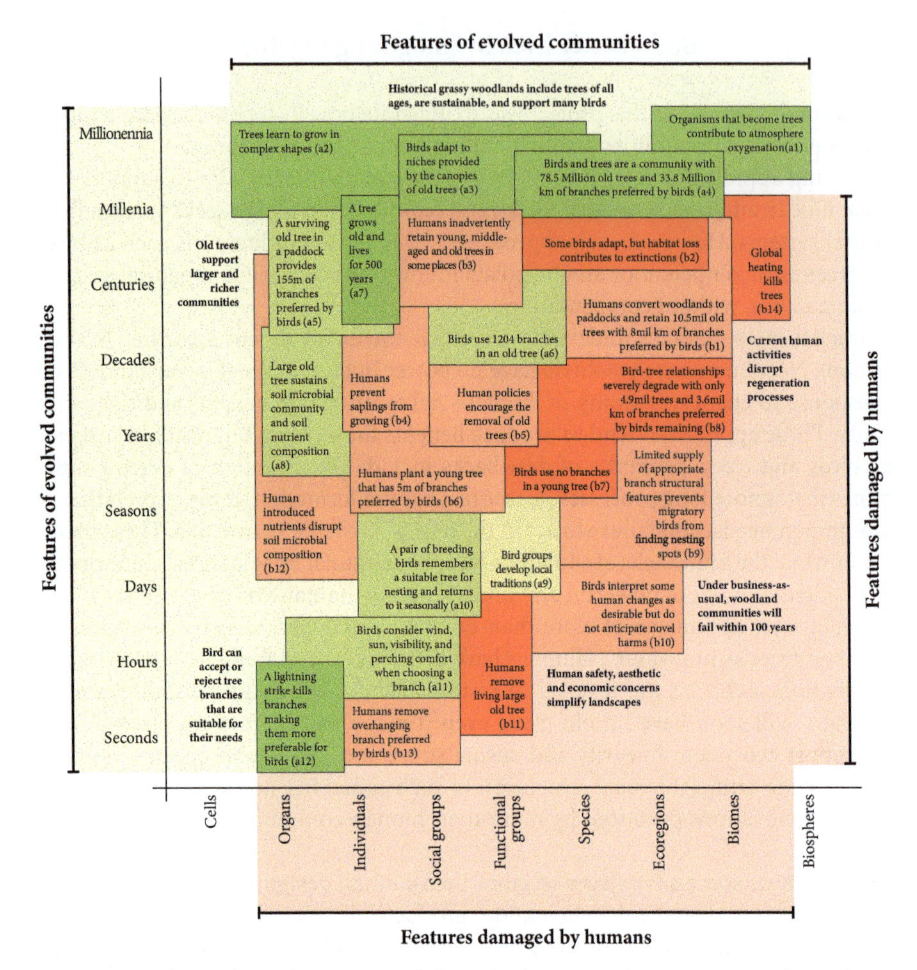

Figure 5.7 The ecological community's historical capacity for imagination (green) and the anthropogenic damage (red).
Image by the authors.

our operations collect more data (d1), create more solutions (d2), and account for more complex relationships (d5, d6), increasing diversity and complexity of possible designs. The expansion of communal imagination to include non-human concerns will increase the likelihood of better outcomes, improving the lives of all stakeholders.

These approaches establish a framework that can integrate a broad range of expressions by non-human agents, including presence and absence, bodily movement, physiological reactions, shapes of bodies, chemical residues, or marks left by use. These conditions occur in all species and environments. Consequently, while access to a greater set of possible innovations is demonstrably useful in our case study, it can also benefit other design challenges, irrespective of implicated lifeforms, sites, or anthropogenic damages.

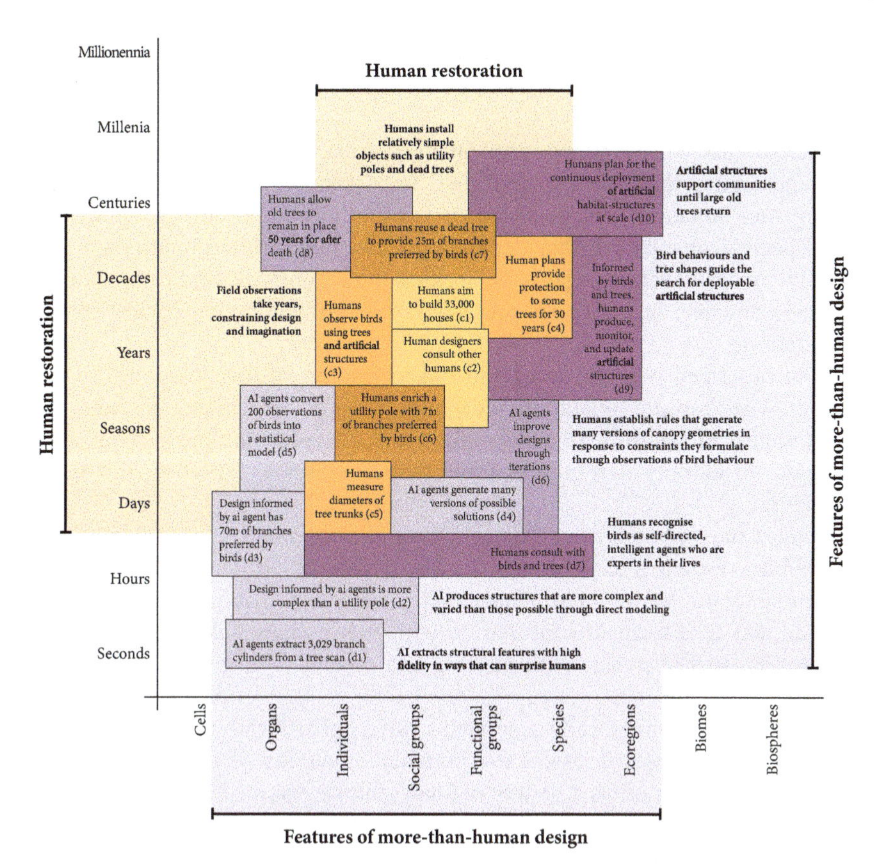

Figure 5.8 Existing restoration (orange) and more-than-human design that learns from nonhuman contributions (purple).
Image by the authors.

Conclusion: Communal Imagination *for*, *with*, and *by* Non-Human Beings

Seeking to encourage action that can address environmental crises, this chapter redefined the notion of community to include non-human lifeforms as empowered voices in communal imagination. To do so, we considered interrelationships between birds, trees, and humans that cohabit a degraded landscape.

This research helps to fill the gap in knowledge about practical techniques for collaboration with non-human beings, as well as the theoretical framing of more-than human design. To do this, our theoretical framework redefined habitual roles in design processes, giving humans supporting responsibilities, emphasising design contributions provided by trees, and describing birds as discerning clients. To substantiate this narrative, we have redefined the notion of community in more-than-human terms, demonstrated that non-human beings act as significant community members, demonstrated involvement of non-human stakeholders in design, and argued that human and non-human beings participate in the construction of shared imaginings.

We then discussed innovations as potentially useful outcomes of communal imagination and argued that assessment of their impact must involve all stakeholders, including non-humans. This involvement is especially important in application to multispecies cohabitation that depends on meaningful interpretation of local conditions by participating organisms. Seeking to demonstrate applications of this approach in practice, our case study presented aspects of non-human involvement as four operations.

We first described trees in detail and linked features of their branches to bird behaviour. This 'capture' operation recognises features or habitat structures that are meaningful to non-human stakeholders. We interpret this recognition as an opportunity to amplify non-human subjectivities, cultures, expertise, and useful innovations.

In the next step, we used descriptions of trees and observations of bird behaviour to model bird responses to unobserved trees or artificial structures. This 'predict' operation simulates non-human behaviour in response to habitat structures. This simulation acts as a form of consultation with non-human stakeholders by linking their simulated responses with existing and possible configurations of habitat structures.

Thirdly, we have automatically generated a variety of artificial structures and used simulated bird responses to assess the potential suitability of such designs. This 'reconfigure' operation offers a variety of analysable design for interrogation in the design process. We interpret the effect of this operation as a useful provocation that can highlight issues, consequences, and solutions that otherwise remain hidden.

Lastly, we provide routines that can support the assessment of the resulting designs in the field. This work is ongoing, with outcomes forthcoming. Through its reliance on detailed numerical descriptions, our approach enables side-by-side iterative assessment of multiple generations of artificial structures. Comparisons between trees and versions of their artificial replacements demonstrate the great value of natural structures, while making artificial structures more accountable in situations where other alternatives are not available. We interpret the introduction of artificial structures informed by our processes as a form of support for the processes of communal imagination because they give birds an opportunity to express their preferences and trees a chance to demonstrate the quality of their contributions to habitable spaces.

Implementation of the proposed workflows for artificial habitat structures will need further research. Practical applications will require streamlining data acquisition, analysis, and utilisation. Ethical concerns such as those pertaining to non-human privacy will also apply. Crucially, successful designs will depend on direct testing with birds and trees in the field.

We can characterise many limitations of data-driven workflows as forms of bias. This chapter does not focus on the details of technical aspects, but provides examples that can indicate challenges and directions for future research. Data acquisition bias can result from constraints on such aspects as misleading baselines because the environments humans can scan now are already degraded. Datasets describing behaviours of living organisms are often relatively small because field observations can be laborious and time-consuming, leading to data interpretation bias. Simplifications built into generative models that cannot express the full complexity of evolved precedents (e.g. tree shapes) result in misinformed generation of replacement shapes or in other design biases. Finally, difficulties in interpreting results of physical prototyping can lead to biases in implementation.

In spite of these limitations, our approach demonstrates the plausibility and promise of more-than-human participation. Current practices are so damaging and unjust that improvements to the *status quo* are easy. Even partial integrations of non-human voices can support more equitable communities and thus help their members live better lives. Growing interest in the practical implementation of this work at multiple sites demonstrates its potential to contribute, the acute need for improvements, and the growing readiness of human societies to take action towards more-than-human wellbeing.

Notes

1. We provide a more detailed description of our artificial agent in Supplementary Appendix A, which can be found at the following address: https://doi.org/10.5281/zenodo.8213429.
2. We provide supporting information on the results obtained by our AI agent in Supplementary Appendix B, see note 1.
3. We provide evidence in support of each element in these diagrams in Supplementary Appendix C, see note 1.

References

ACT Planning and Land Authority. (2011). Molonglo Valley Plan for the Protection of Matters of National Environmental Significance. Australian Capital Territory Government.

Aplin, L. M. (2019). Culture and cultural evolution in birds: A review of the evidence. *Animal Behaviour, 47*, 179–187. https://doi.org/10/gfsp4p

Avery, J. (2012). *Information theory and evolution*. World Scientific Publishing.

Baine, M. (2001). Artificial reefs: A review of their design, application, management and performance. *Ocean & Coastal Management, 44*(3–4), 241–259. https://doi.org/10/bkz7vs

Baluška, F., & Mancuso, S. (2021). Individuality, self and sociality of vascular plants. *Philosophical Transactions of the Royal Society B: Biological Sciences, 376*(1821), 20190760. https://doi.org/10/gnj2cc

Barbieri, M. (2008). Is the cell a semiotic system? In M. Barbieri (Ed.), *Introduction to biosemiotics: The new biological synthesis* (pp. 179–208). Springer.

Bastian, M., Jones, O., Moore, N., & Roe, E. (Eds.). (2017). *Participatory research in more-than-human worlds*. Routledge.

Battin, J. (2004). When good animals love bad habitats: Ecological traps and the conservation of animal populations. *Conservation Biology, 18*(6), 1482–1491. https://doi.org/10/fjrgqp

Beiler, K. J., Durall, D. M., Simard, S. W., Maxwell, S. A., & Kretzer, A. M. (2010). Architecture of the wood-wide web: *Rhizopogon Spp.* genets link multiple Douglas-fir cohorts. *New Phytologist, 185*(2), 543–553. https://doi.org/10/c6qtkx

Bekoff, M. (2017). The importance of earth jurisprudence, compassionate conservation and personal rewilding. *The Ecological Citizen, 1*(A), 10–12.

Bekoff, M., & Pierce, J. (2017). *The animals' agenda: Freedom, compassion, and coexistence in the human age*. Beacon Press.

Belton, D., Moncrieff, S., & Chapman, J. (2013). Processing Tree Point Clouds Using Gaussian Mixture Models. *ISPRS Annals of Photogrammetry, Remote Sensing and Spatial Information Sciences*, II-5/W2, 43–48. https://doi.org/10/gcdbx8

Björgvinsson, E., Ehn, P., & Hillgren, P.-A. (2012). Agonistic participatory design: Working with marginalised social movements. *CoDesign*, *8*(2–3), 127–144. https://doi.org/10/f24gm9

Blattner, C., Coulter, K., & Kymlicka, W. (2019). Introduction: Animal labour and the quest for interspecies justice. In C. Blattner, K. Coulter, & W. Kymlicka, *Animal labour* (pp. 1–26). Oxford University Press.

Bliege Bird, R., Bird, D. W., Codding, Brian. F., Parker, Christopher. H., & Jones, J. H. (2008). The 'fire stick farming' hypothesis: Australian Aboriginal foraging strategies, biodiversity, and anthropogenic fire mosaics. *Proceedings of the National Academy of Sciences of the United States of America*, *105*(39), 14796–14801. https://doi.org/10/cqvkm5

Bradshaw, C. J. A. (2012). Little left to lose: Deforestation and forest degradation in Australia since European colonization. *Journal of Plant Ecology*, *5*(1), 109–120. https://doi.org/10/fzvsj5

Bresnihan, P. (2016). The more-than-human commons: From commons to commoning. In S. Kirwan, L. Dawney, & J. Brigstocke (Eds.), *Space, power and the commons* (pp. 93–112). Routledge.

Bruner, J. S. (1990). *Acts of meaning*. Harvard University Press.

Burney, D. A., & Flannery, T. F. (2005). Fifty millennia of catastrophic extinctions after human contact. *Trends in Ecology & Evolution*, *20*(7), 395–401. https://doi.org/10/fpq3bs

Chang, M., Shen, C., Maheshwari, A., Danielescu, A., & Yao, L. (2022). Patterns and opportunities for the design of human–plant interaction. In F. 'Floyd' Mueller, M. Obrist, S. Greuter, P. Sweetser, & R. A. Khot (Eds.), *Designing Interactive Systems Conference* (pp. 925–948). ACM. https://doi.org/10/gqkz6s

Clarke, R., Heitlinger, S., Light, A., Forlano, L., Foth, M., & DiSalvo, C. (2019). More-than-human participation: Design for sustainable smart city futures. *Interactions*, *26*(3), 60–63. https://doi.org/10/gf35h5

Collins, A., Joseph, D., & Bielaczyc, K. (2004). Design research: Theoretical and methodological issues. *Journal of the Learning Sciences*, *13*(1), 15–42. https://doi.org/10/czkp28

Country, B., Wright, S., Suchet-Pearson, S., Lloyd, K., Burarrwanga, L., Ganambarr, R., Ganambarr-Stubbs, M., Ganambarr, B., Maymuru, D., & Sweeney, J. (2016). Co-becoming Bawaka: Towards a relational understanding of place/space. *Progress in Human Geography*, *40*(4), 455–475. https://doi.org/10/bkbc

Crist, E. (2020). For cosmopolitan bioregionalism. *The Ecological Citizen*, *3*(C), 21–29.

Dee, T. (2019). *Landfill: Notes on gull watching and trash picking in the Anthropocene*. Chelsea Green.

Department of Environment, Climate Change and Water NSW. (2011). National Recovery Plan for White Box—Yellow Box—Blakely's Red Gum Grassy Woodland and Derived Native Grassland: A Critically Endangered Ecological Community (978 1 74232 311 4). Department of Environment, Climate Change and Water New South Wales.

Di Salvo, C. (2012). *Adversarial design*. MIT Press.

Donaldson, S., & Kymlicka, W. (2011). *Zoopolis: A political theory of animal rights*. Oxford University Press.

Eckersley, R. (1992). *Environmentalism and political theory: Toward an ecocentric approach*. UCL Press.

Ehbrecht, M., Schall, P., Ammer, C., & Seidel, D. (2017). Quantifying stand structural complexity and its relationship with forest management, tree species diversity and microclimate. *Agricultural and Forest Meteorology*, *242*, 1–9. https://doi.org/10/gbk737

Fanfani, D., & Matarán Ruiz, A. (Eds.). (2020). *Bioregional planning and design: Vol.* I. Springer.

Fell, J., Kuo, P.-Y., Greene, T., & Wang, J.-C. (2022). A biocentric perspective on HCI design research involving plants. *ACM Transactions on Computer-Human Interaction*. https://doi.org/10/gqvd3z

Firn, J., Ladouceur, E., & Dorrough, J. (2018). Integrating local knowledge and research to refine the management of an invasive non-native grass in critically endangered grassy woodlands. *Journal of Applied Ecology*, *55*(1), 321–330. https://doi.org/10/gcrb2j

Fischer, J., Stott, J., & Law, B. S. (2010). The disproportionate value of scattered trees. *Biological Conservation*, *143*, 1564–1567. https://doi.org/10/c47mjb

Fischer, J., Zerger, A., Gibbons, P., Stott, J., & Law, B. S. (2010). Tree decline and the future of Australian farmland biodiversity. *Proceedings of the National Academy of Sciences of the United States of America, 107*(45), 19597–19602. https://doi.org/10/bt3k3p

Flapper, T., Cook, T., Farrelly, S., Dickson, K., & Auty, K. (2018). *Independent audit of the Molonglo Valley strategic assessment.* Australian Capital Territory Government.

Forlano, L. (2016). Decentering the human in the design of collaborative cities. *Design Issues, 32*(3), 42–54. https://doi.org/10/gfsqj3

Foth, M. (2017). The next urban paradigm: Cohabitation in the smart city. *IT - Information Technology, 59*(6), 259–262. https://doi.org/10/gfsp23

Gatto, G., & McCardle, J. R. (2019). Multispecies design and ethnographic practice: Following other-than-humans as a mode of exploring environmental issues. *Sustainability, 11*(18), 5032. https://doi.org/10/ggcc7f

Gibbons, P., & Boak, M. (2002). The value of paddock trees for regional conservation in an agricultural landscape. *Ecological Management & Restoration, 3*, 205–210. https://doi.org/10/c7bb9n

Gibbons, P., Briggs, S. V., Murpht, Danielle Y., Lindenmayer, David B., McElhinny, Chris, & Brookhouse, Matthew. (2010). Benchmark stem densities for forests and woodlands in South-Eastern Australia. *Forest Ecology and Management, 260*, 2125–2133. https://doi.org/10/dm5jgx

Gibbons, P., & Lindenmayer, D. B. (2007). Offsets for land clearing: No net loss or the tail wagging the sog? *Ecological Management & Restoration, 8*(1), 26–31. https://doi.org/10/c3n57k

Gibbons, P., Lindenmayer, D. B., Fischer, J., Manning, A. D., Weinberg, A., Seddon, J. A., Ryan, P. R., & Barrett, Gaye. (2008). The future of scattered trees in agricultural landscapes. *Conservation Biology, 22*(5), 1309–1319. https://doi.org/10/cb8smr

Goymann, W., & Küblbeck, M. (2020). The second warning to humanity—Why ethology matters? *Ethology, 126*(1), 1–9. https://doi.org/10/ggd6m4

Gray, J., & Curry, P. (2016). Ecodemocracy: Helping wildlife's right to survive. *ECOS, 37*(1), 18–27.

Hackenberg, J., Spiecker, H., Calders, K., Disney, M., & Raumonen, P. (2015). SimpleTree: An efficient open source tool to build tree models from TLS clouds. *Forests, 6*(11), 4245–4294. https://doi.org/10/ggb35g

Hannan, L., Le Roux, D. S., Milner, R. N. C., & Gibbons, P. (2019). Erecting dead trees and utility poles to offset the loss of mature trees. *Biological Conservation, 236*, 340–346. https://doi.org/10/ggbjtk

Hoffmeyer, J. (1998). Surfaces inside surfaces. On the origin of agency and life. *Cybernetics & Human Knowing, 5*(1), 33–42.

Holland, A., Gibbons, P., Thompson, J., & Roudavski, S. (2024). Terrestrial Lidar Reveals New Information About Habitats Provided by Large Old Trees. *Biological Conservation, 292*, 110507. https://doi.org/10.1016/j.biocon.2024.110507

Houston, D., Hillier, J., MacCallum, D., Steele, W., & Byrne, J. (2018). Make kin, not cities! Multispecies entanglements and 'becoming-world' in planning theory. *Planning Theory, 17*(2), 190–212. https://doi.org/10/gdkqp6

Huybrechts, L., Benesch, H., & Geib, J. (2017). Institutioning: Participatory design, co-design and the public realm. *CoDesign, 13*(3), 148–159. https://doi.org/10/gbvrzn

Johnson, C. N. (2016). Fire, people and ecosystem change in Pleistocene Australia. *Australian Journal of Botany, 64*(8), 643–651. https://doi.org/10/gfxzr4

Jones, C. G., Lawton, J. H., & Shachak, M. (1996). Organisms as ecosystem engineers. In F. B. Samson & F. L. Knopf (Eds.), *Ecosystem management: Selected readings* (pp. 130–147). Springer.

Jönsson, L., & Lenskjold, T. U. (2014). A foray into not-quite companion species: Design experiments with urban animals as significant others. *Artifact, 3*(2), 7.1–7.13. https://doi.org/10/gf27v8

Kaplan, G. (2015). *Bird minds: Cognition and behaviour of Australian native birds.* CSIRO.

Karban, R. (2015). *Plant sensing and communication.* University of Chicago Press.

Laland, K., Matthews, B., & Feldman, M. W. (2016). An introduction to niche construction theory. *Evolutionary Ecology, 30*(2), 191–202. https://doi.org/10/f8fvc9

Le Roux, D. S., Ikin, K., Lindenmayer, D. B., Bistricer, G., Manning, A. D., & Gibbons, P. (2015). Enriching small trees with artificial nest boxes cannot mimic the value of large trees for hollow-nesting birds. *Restoration Ecology, 24*, 252–258. https://doi.org/10/f8ftmw

Le Roux, D. S., Ikin, K., Lindenmayer, D. B., Manning, A. D., & Gibbons, P. (2014). The future of large old trees in urban landscapes. *PLOS ONE, 9*(6), e99403. https://doi.org/10/f6dg7p

Le Roux, D. S., Ikin, K., Lindenmayer, D. B., Manning, A. D., & Gibbons, P. (2015). Single large or several small? Applying biogeographic principles to tree-level conservation and biodiversity offsets. *Biological Conservation, 191*, 558–566. https://doi.org/10/f7x48m

Le Roux, D. S., Ikin, K., Lindenmayer, D. B., Manning, A. D., & Gibbons, P. (2018). The value of scattered trees for wildlife: Contrasting effects of landscape context and tree size. *Diversity and Distributions, 24*(1), 69–81. https://doi.org/10/gcq7f9

Liaros, S. (2021). A network of circular economy villages: Design guidelines for 21st century garden cities. *Built Environment Project and Asset Management, 12*(3), 349–364. https://doi.org/10/gqv7m4

Lindenmayer, D. B. (2017). Conserving large old trees as small natural features. *Biological Conservation, 211*(B), 51–59. https://doi.org/10/gbn34v

Lindenmayer, D. B., Burns, E., Thurgate, N., & Lowe, A. (Eds.). (2014). *Biodiversity and environmental change: Monitoring, challenges and direction*. CSIRO.

Lindenmayer, D. B., Hobbs, R. J., Likens, G. E., Krebs, C. J., & Banks, S. C. (2011). Newly discovered landscape traps produce regime shifts in wet forests. *Proceedings of the National Academy of Sciences, 108*(38), 15887–15891. https://doi.org/10/fr5bnc

Lindenmayer, D. B., & Laurance, W. F. (2016). The ecology, distribution, conservation and management of large old trees. *Biological Reviews, 132*, 1434–1458. https://doi.org/10/gdvpqh

Lindenmayer, D. B., Laurance, W. F., Franklin, J. F., Likens, G. E., Banks, S. C., Blanchard, W., Gibbons, P., Ikin, K., Blair, D., McBurney, L., Manning, A. D., & Stein, J. A. R. (2013). New policies for old trees: Averting a global crisis in a keystone ecological structure. *Conservation Letters, 7*(1), 61–69. https://doi.org/10/f22gtb

Liu, S.-Y. (Cyn). (2019). Designing for multispecies collaboration and cohabitation. In E. Gilbert & K. G. Karahalios (Eds.), *Conference Companion Publication of the 2019 on Computer Supported Cooperative Work and Social Computing* (pp. 72–75). ACM. https://doi.org/10/ggr8q8

Loh, S., Foth, M., Caldwell, G. A., Garcia-Hansen, V., & Thomson, M. (2020). A more-than-human perspective on understanding the performance of the built environment. *Architectural Science Review*, 1–12. https://doi.org/10/gg5hb5

Low, T. (2014). *Where song began: Australia's birds and how they changed the world*. Viking.

Manning, A. D., Fischer, J., & Lindenmayer, D. B. (2006). Scattered trees are keystone structures: Implications for conservation. *Biological Conservation, 132*, 311–321. https://doi.org/10/fjmgzw

Manning, A. D., Gibbons, P., Fischer, J., Oliver, D., & Lindenmayer, D. B. (2012). Hollow futures? Tree decline, lag effects and hollow-dependent species. *Animal Conservation, 16*(4), 395–405. https://doi.org/10/f47v3m

Manning, A. D., Lindenmayer, D. B., & Nix, H. A. (2004). Continua and Umwelt: Novel perspectives on viewing landscapes. *Oikos, 104*(3), 621–628. https://doi.org/10/bz76tf

Maran, T., & Kull, K. (2014). Ecosemiotics: Main principles and current developments. *Geografiska Annaler: Series B, Human Geography, 96*(1), 41–50. https://doi.org/10/f5v7mq

Martin, G. (2017). *The sensory ecology of birds*. Oxford University Press.

McBride, K. D. (2005). *Collective dreams: Political imagination and community*. The Pennsylvania State University Press.

Metzger, J. (2020). A more-than-human approach to environmental planning. In S. Davoudi, R. Cowell, I. White, & H. Blanco (Eds.), *The Routledge companion to environmental planning* (pp. 190–199). Routledge.

Milburn, J. (2017). Nonhuman animals as property holders: An exploration of the Lockean labour-mixing account. *Environmental Values, 26*(5), 629–648. https://doi.org/10/gbxqkw

Mirra, G., Holland, A., Roudavski, S., Wijnands, J., & Pugnale, A. (2022). An artificial intelligence agent that synthesises visual abstractions of natural forms to support the design of human-made habitat structures. *Frontiers in Ecology and Evolution, 10*, 806453. https://doi.org/10/gpp6mb

Mitchell, R. A. (2016). Can animals imagine? In A. Kind (Ed.), *The Routledge handbook of philosophy of imagination* (pp. 326–338). Routledge.

Mitsch, W. J. (2014). When will ecologists learn engineering and engineers learn ecology? *Ecological Engineering, 65*, 9–14. https://doi.org/10/gfsp9b

Mittelbach, G. G., & McGill, B. J. (2019). *Community ecology* (2nd ed.). Oxford University Press.
Molonglo Community Consultation Report. (2012). Environment, Planning and Sustainable Development Directorate. ACT Government.
Morris, R. C., & Spivak, G. C. (Eds.). (2010). *Can the subaltern speak? Reflections on the history of an idea*. Columbia University Press.
Orians, G. H., & Milewski, A. V. (2007). Ecology of Australia: The effects of nutrient-poor soils and intense fires. *Biological Reviews of the Cambridge Philosophical Society, 82*(3), 393–423. https://doi.org/10/fh926g
Parker, D., Roudavski, S., Jones, T. M., Bradsworth, N., Isaac, B., Lockett, M. T., & Soanes, K. (2022). A framework for computer-aided design and manufacturing of habitat structures for cavity-dependent animals. *Methods in Ecology and Evolution, 13*(4), 826–841. https://doi.org/10/gpggfj
Parker, D., Soanes, K., & Roudavski, S. (2022). Interspecies cultures and future design. *Transpositiones, 1*(1), 183–236. https://doi.org/10/gpvsfs
Picciuto, E., & Carruthers, P. (2016). Imagination and pretense. In A. Kind (Ed.), *The Routledge handbook of philosophy of imagination* (pp. 314–325). Routledge.
Piersma, T., & Gils, J. A. van. (2011). *The flexible phenotype: A body-centred integration of ecology, physiology, and behaviour*. Oxford University Press.
Plumwood, V. (2002). *Environmental culture: The ecological crisis of reason*. Routledge.
Pollastri, S., Griffiths, R., Dunn, N., Cureton, P., Boyko, C., Blaney, A., & De Bezenac, E. (2021). More-than-human future cities: From the design of nature to designing for and through nature. In M. de Waal et al. (Eds.), *Media Architecture Biennale 20* (pp. 23–30). ACM.
Prebble, S., McLean, J., & Houston, D. (2021). Smart urban forests: An overview of more-than-human and more-than-real urban forest management in Australian cities. *Digital Geography and Society, 2*, 100013. https://doi.org/10/gj4mrj
Prober, S. M., & Thiele, K. R. (2005). Restoring Australia's temperate grasslands and grassy woodlands: Integrating function and diversity. *Ecological Management and Restoration, 1*, 16. https://doi.org/10/bj5k9n
Rabinowitz, D. (2015). Community studies: Anthropological. In J. D. Wright (Ed.), *International encyclopedia of the social and behavioral sciences* (2nd ed., Vol. 4, pp. 306–371). Elsevier Science.
Rayner, L., Stojanovic, D., Heinsohn, R., & Manning, A. (2016). *Breeding ecology of the Superb Parrot* Polytelis Swainsonii *in Northern Canberra* [Technical Report]. Australian Capital Territory Government.
Romani, A., Casnati, F., & Ianniello, A. (2022). Codesign with more-than-humans: Toward a meta co-design tool for human–non-human collaborations. *European Journal of Futures Research, 10*(1), 17. https://doi.org/10/gqvdsm
Roudavski, S. (2016). Field creativity and post-anthropocentrism. *Digital Creativity, 27*(1), 7–23. https://doi.org/10/czw7
Roudavski, S. (2018). Notes on more-than-human architecture. In G. Coombs, A. McNamara, & G. Sade (Eds.), *Undesign: Critical practices at the intersection of art and design* (pp. 24–37). Routledge. https://doi.org/10/czr8
Roudavski, S. (2020). Multispecies cohabitation and future design. In S. Boess, M. Cheung, & R. Cain (Eds.), *Proceedings of Design Research Society (DRS) 2020 International Conference: Synergy* (pp. 731–750). Design Research Society. https://doi.org/10/ghj48x
Roudavski, S., & Davis, A. (2020). Respect for old age and dignity in death: The case of urban trees. In K. Hislop & H. Lewi (Eds.), *Proceedings of the Society of Architectural Historians Australia and New Zealand: 37, What if? What next? Speculations on history's futures* (pp. 638–652). SAHANZ.
Roudavski, S., & Parker, D. (2020). Modelling workflows for more-than-human design: Prosthetic habitats for the Powerful Owl (Ninox strenua). In C. Gengnagel, O. Baverel, J. Burry, M. R. Thomsen, & S. Weinzierl (Eds.), *Impact—Design with all senses: Proceedings of the Design Modelling Symposium, Berlin 2019* (pp. 554–564). Springer. https://doi.org/10/dbkp
Roudavski, S., & Rutten, J. (2020). Towards more-than-human heritage: Arboreal habitats as a challenge for heritage preservation. *Built Heritage, 4*(4), 1–17. https://doi.org/10/ggpv66

Rule, S., Brook, B. W., Haberle, S. G., Turney, C. S. M., Kershaw, A. P., & Johnson, C. N. (2012). The aftermath of megafaunal extinction: Ecosystem transformation in Pleistocene Australia. *Science, 335*(6075), 1483–1486. https://doi.org/10/cnz2

Saad-Sulonen, J., Karasti, H., Eriksson, E., Halskov, K., & Vines, J. (2018). Unfolding participation over time: Temporal lenses in participatory design. *CoDesign, 14*(1), 4–16. https://doi.org/10/gd4wd9

Safina, C. (2020). *Becoming wild: How animal cultures raise families, create beauty, and achieve peace.* Henry Holt.

Sanders, E. B. N., & Stappers, P. J. (2014). Probes, toolkits and prototypes: Three approaches to making in codesigning. *CoDesign, 10*(1), 5–14. https://doi.org/10/gfc7xg

Schlosberg, D. (2013). Theorising environmental justice: The expanding sphere of a discourse. *Environmental Politics, 22*(1), 37–55. https://doi.org/10/gf6cmc

Segundo-Ortin, M., & Calvo, P. (2022). Consciousness and cognition in plants. *WIREs Cognitive Science, 13*(2), e1578. https://doi.org/10/gmwqjh

Sheik, H., Foth, M., & Mitchell, P. (2023). (Re)Imagining the ibis: Multispecies future(s), smart urban governance, and the digital environmental humanities. In C. Travis, D. P. Dixon, L. Bergmann, R. Legg, & A. Crampsie (Eds.), *Routledge handbook of the digital environmental humanities* (pp. 490–515). Routledge.

Sheikh, H., Gonsalves, K., & Foth, M. (2021). Plant(e)tecture: Towards a multispecies media architecture framework for amplifying plant agencies. In M. de Waal et al. (Eds.), *Media Architecture Biennale 20* (pp. 87–99). ACM.

Smith, N., Bardzell, S., & Bardzell, J. (2017). Designing for cohabitation: Naturecultures, hybrids, and decentering the human in design. In G. Mark & S. Fussell (Eds.), *Proceedings of the 2017 CHI Conference on Human Factors in Computing Systems* (pp. 1714–1725). ACM. https://doi.org/10/gf4mmc

Stagoll, K., Lindenmayer, D. B., Knight, E., Fischer, J., & Manning, A. D. (2012). Large trees are keystone structures in urban parks. *Conservation Letters, 5*(2), 115–122. https://doi.org/10/f35x6j

Star, S. L. (2010). This is not a boundary object: Reflections on the origin of a concept. *Science, Technology, & Human Values, 35*(5), 601–617. https://doi.org/10/fgb568

Star, S. L., & Griesemer, J. R. (1989). Institutional ecology, 'translations', and boundary objects: Amateurs and professionals in Berkeley's Museum of Vertebrate Zoology. *Social Studies of Science, 19*(3), 1907–1939. https://doi.org/10/ckpxb6

Strassburg, B. B. N., Iribarrem, A., Beyer, H. L., Cordeiro, C. L., Crouzeilles, R., Jakovac, C. C., Braga Junqueira, A., Lacerda, E., Latawiec, A. E., Balmford, A., Brooks, T. M., Butchart, S. H. M., Chazdon, R. L., Erb, K.-H., Brancalion, P., Buchanan, G., Cooper, D., Díaz, S., Donald, P. F., ... Visconti, P. (2020). Global priority areas for ecosystem restoration. *Nature*, 1–6. https://doi.org/10/ghfp4x

Studdert, D., & Walkerdine, V. (2016). *Rethinking community research: Inter-relationality, communal being and commonality.* Palgrave Macmillan.

Threatened Species Scientific Committee (TSSC). (2006). Advice to the Minister for the Environment and Heritage from the Threatened Species Scientific Committee (TSSC) on Amendments to the List of Ecological Communities under the Environment Protection and Biodiversity Conservation Act 1999 (EPBC Act). Australian Government, Department of Agriculture, Water and the Environment.

Tironi, M. (2018). Speculative prototyping, frictions and counter-participation: A civic intervention with homeless individuals. *Design Studies, 59*, 117–138. https://doi.org/10/gfsp2z

Tomitsch, M., Fredericks, J., Vo, D., Frawley, J., & Foth, M. (2021). Non-human personas: Including nature in the participatory design of smart cities. *Interaction Design and Architecture(s) Journal (IxD&A), 50*, 102–130. https://doi.org/10/gpv9ch

Treasury and Economic Development Directorate. (2019). ACT Population Projections 2018 to 2058. ACT Government.

von Uexküll, J. (2010). *A foray into the worlds of animals and humans: With a theory of meaning* (J. D. O'Neil, Trans.; illustrated ed.). University of Minnesota Press. (Original work published 1934)

Varela, F. J., Thompson, E., & Rosch, E. (1991). *The embodied mind: Cognitive science and human experience.* MIT Press.

Washington, H., Taylor, B., Kopnina, H., Cryer, P., & Piccolo, J. J. (2017). Why ecocentrism is the key pathway to sustainability. *The Ecological Citizen, 1*, 35–41.

Watchorn, D. J., Cowan, M. A., Driscoll, D. A., Nimmo, D. G., Ashman, K. R., Garkaklis, M. J., Wilson, B. A., & Doherty, T. S. (2022). Artificial habitat structures for animal conservation: Design and implementation, risks and opportunities. *Frontiers in Ecology and the Environment, 20*(5), 301–309. https://doi.org/10/gpg67n

Westerlaken, M., Gabrys, J., Urzedo, D., & Ritts, M. (2022). Unsettling participation by foregrounding more-than-human relations in digital forests. *Environmental Humanities, 15*(1), 87–108. https://doi.org/10/gqzpm2

Wienhues, A. (2018). Situating the half-earth proposal in distributive justice: Conditions for just conservation. *Biological Conservation, 228*, 44–51. https://doi.org/10/gf7htk

Wiesel, I., Steele, W., & Houston, D. (2020). Cities of care: Introduction to a special issue. *Cities, 105*, 102844. https://doi.org/10/gk94vd

Williams, J., & Woinarski, J. C. Z. (1997). *Eucalypt ecology: Individuals to ecosystems.* Cambridge University Press.

Witzany, G. (2018). Memory and learning as key competences of living organisms. In F. Baluska, M. Gagliano, & G. Witzany (Eds.), *Memory and learning in plants* (pp. 1–16). Springer.

6

Exploring More-than-Human Smart Cities

The Emergent Logic of a Design Workbook

Bill Gaver, Andy Boucher, Dean Brown, Naho Matsuda, Liliana Ovalle, Andy Sheen, and Mike Vanis

> Good questions come only to a polite inquirer, especially a polite inquirer provoked by a singing blackbird. With good questions, even or especially mistakes and misunderstandings can become interesting.
>
> Donna Haraway, *Staying with the Trouble*, p.127

'More-than-human smart cities' is a design brief in a phrase. It is simultaneously self-explanatory and deeply mysterious. How should we think about the more-than-human world? For that matter, what do we mean by 'smart cities'? Smart in what way, and to what end? How can non-human life possibly thrive in any city, much less smart ones? And how can we come up with perspectives on these questions that will lead to engaging and worthwhile designs?

These are some of the questions[1] we asked ourselves when we joined a project called 'More-than-Human Data Interactions in the Smart City'[2] (known informally as MoTH Cities) in May of 2021. Led by Sara Heitlinger, the project brought together researchers from five UK universities and two community organisations for eight months to undertake a programme of participatory and design-led engagements with a variety of (human) stakeholders in London and elsewhere in the United Kingdom. Together, we explored how smart cities might include 'more-than-humans', and though others have included such things as algorithms and toasters in this category, we focused on living non-humans (and our team largely on animals).

The project was guided by its own research questions:

The overarching research question of this project is: ***How can we design data interactions in the smart city for more inclusive and sustainable urban cohabitations?***

In order to answer this question, we have the following further research questions:

- *How can we decentre the human in data interactions in smart cities?*
- *What new roles could data have across future urban interactions to better account for interdependencies of more-than-human smart cities?*
- *How can we broaden our perspectives of sustainability within smart cities beyond the dominant top-down, modernist, efficiency-led, and behavioural-change*

Bill Gaver et al., *Exploring More-than-Human Smart Cities.* In: *Designing More-than-Human Smart Cities.*
Edited by: Sara Heitlinger, Marcus Foth, and Rachel Clarke, Oxford University Press.
DOI: 10.1093/9780191980060.003.0008

> *narratives of sustainability that are typical in human-centred perspectives of data within smart cities?*
>
> (*MoTH Cities 2022*)

Originally, our group—a team of eight designers, technologists, and makers who pursue design practice as a form of academic research—was to create a collection of prompts and activities for the events we planned with partners. This was sidetracked, however, by a combination of the COVID-19 pandemic and administrative problems. Thus, we decided instead to do the bulk of the work described here before the rest of the partners became active on the project.

This put us in an interesting situation. We had been invited to join the project based on our design of a wildlife camera that people could make at home (Gaver et al. 2019). In addition, as we prepared the project proposal and workplan, we had several helpful conversations with our partners about their ideas and understandings of the project and more-than-human research in general. We also did our own research and started developing ideas and curiosities about the issues and possibilities we might explore.

Nonetheless, we felt very much like newcomers to the field, and thus we were reluctant to settle on any particular directions too quickly. As numerous design researchers (Dorst 2015; Rittel & Webster 1973;Schön 1983) have noted, the very first attempts to frame or address problems tend to have decisive effects on how resulting designs evolve, and we didn't want to set off in an ill-considered way. To get a view of what more-than-human smart cities might possibly be, then, we set out to develop a design workbook.

Design Workbooks

Design workbooks are collections of proposals for things that might be made (Gaver 2011). The proposals themselves are simple: a few images, words, and a title on a single page typically suffice to convey an idea. Gathered together, often with a post hoc thematic organisation, to produce a workbook, they are an effective way to get a sense of a design space[3] for a project—a more or less bounded range of possibilities for how we might proceed.

We create design workbooks because they encourage the free flow of ideas that help take us beyond our starting point. By the time we begin one, we have usually done some preliminary research on a topic. We will have talked with project partners and other stakeholders. We will have done some scholarly research and are also likely to have been reminded of related work from artists and designers. It is also likely that we'll share stories from the popular press and the internet about the topic, or from books or movies. None of this will have given us a definitive perspective on the matters at hand or made us feel that we possessed any kind of expertise—on the contrary! It will, however, have acquainted us with some of the issues at hand, suggested some questions we might be curious about, and maybe given us some ideas about things we might do.

So, it becomes pretty straightforward to start producing simple, often playful proposals to help us think about the issues, questions, and possibilities we have uncovered. We tend to work individually, with each member of our team exploring their own ideas in rough accord with an implicit 'house style' that has developed over the years. We share our ideas periodically and informally, and feel free to let others' ideas influence our own. Rarely do we critique ideas: after all, one of the virtues of producing a great number of simple proposals is that none of them matter very much. Instead, we treat the process as a kind of slow-motion brainstorming session. There might be some frame-setting at the outset as we discuss the overall directions that might seem fruitful in terms of issues, effects, or technologies. For the most part, however, this is an emergent, bottom-up process in which we crowdsource design directions from the diverse collection of interests and inclinations of our team. When new ideas slacken, we gather the collection of proposals—usually a few dozen of them—and organise them thematically. This is both a way of facilitating their presentation and of seeing what we have. Invariably, we find that a new order emerges: a design space that blends background knowledge, speculation, and questions with material and social possibilities from which an agreed design direction might emerge.

Proposals, Probes, and Fictions

The design workbook to explore more-than-humans in smart cities that we discuss here is a little atypical for our practice in two ways. First, we knew that the materials we produced would be used for activities in workshops and events involving people from outside the wider project team. So, in addition to developing the ideas in our proposals, we also designed a set of probe activities for people to pursue at these events. Cultural probes are evocative tasks given to people to elicit revealing responses that can inspire new designs (Gaver et al. 1999). We usually see them as distinct from proposals: probes are a design-led user study technique used to find out about people and situations; proposals are typically produced to help our design team and project collaborators to think about what we might make. On this occasion, we mixed them together.

Second, we usually produce design workbooks as a step along the way to designing and making the fully functioning research products (Boucher 2016; Gaver et al. 2004, 2019; Odom et al. 2016) that are the most important outcomes of our research. This tends to encourage us to produce proposals that are, more or less, technically and socially plausible. This workbook, however, was conceived as a short-term exploration that would not lead directly to physically realised products, but instead as a resource for more inclusive workshops and activities. In retrospect, this clearly affected the style of proposals that we designed.

The combinations of images and text we offer as design proposals are often cinematic, presenting notional products in their settings to hint at a sense both of place and feeling, like simple versions of the photography of Cindy Sherman (2003) or Gregory Crewdson (2008). From this perspective, they can be seen as a form of 'Design Fiction', defined by the science fiction writer Bruce Sterling in 2005 as 'the deliberate use of diegetic [story world] prototypes to suspend disbelief about change' (Lindley & Coulton 2015). Borrowed from the commonplace custom of introducing fictional products in science fiction and fantasy, design fictions have been developed as a methodology for considering both potential designs and their social and political contexts.[4]

Blythe and Encinas (2016) observed that design fictions usually fall into one of four genres: extrapolative, ironic, ambiguous, or magical. For most of our projects, we develop proposals that are extrapolative because of our assumption that they should be plausible. Freed in this project from expectations that we would develop working products, in contrast, our proposals here range across the genres. Most strikingly, they include several that are magical—impossible but delightful—not in their technologies, but rather in their suggestions about how non-humans might engage with them. Usually, we would consider such proposals indulgent and of little use, since they do not clearly lead to realisable research products. In this context, however, the utility of magic becomes clearer: arguably, the most fabulous of these proposals provide the clearest pointers about how we might want to shape the more-than-human smart city, and the questions we need to address to do so. This should become clear as we unpack a sample of our proposals over the following pages.

Creating a Narrative from Proposals

As we have described, when we set out to produce our workbook, we had very little familiarity with more-than-human research. Creating the workbook was our method for exploring the issues. We did not start with a detailed brief, and though we were informed both by the overarching project questions and the kinds of questions we outline at the beginning of this chapter, we took these as preliminary and provisional. For us, the workbook was the way we discovered new questions, new issues, and new understandings.

Our process was emergent, more like an exploration of an unfamiliar territory than a trip to a planned destination. The eight of us in our team worked independently on proposals, sharing occasionally, and using our own sources of inspiration. None of us engaged significantly with academic research literature on more-than-human issues, but instead relied on background knowledge and personal experiences; materials from the popular press; explorations on the internet; and other designs and artworks. We amassed proposals over time, with over fifty in all, and organised them post hoc into a series of themes.

In the following sections, we present a subset of nine of our proposals, chosen to cover the themes we explored, because we thought they were among the most interesting, and because we realised after the fact that a narrative could be developed from them. None of the proposals were detailed beyond the images and words we include here. They are indicative, designed to suggest topic areas and trajectories that viewers can elaborate in their own minds.

The narrative we form around them in the following sections can be interpreted as an example of that kind of elaboration. It is not meant to detail the proposals or critique them, but instead to expose their overall logic, at least from one perspective. Rather than trying to gather proof for a particular point of view on more-than-human smart cities, it suggests the train of thought that might produce the proposals, or result from them, and thus should be approached more like a fiction than a scientific report. This narrative, and its culmination in our discussion, can itself be seen as a kind of proposal—something to think with, rather than to accept as right or wrong.

So here we go . . .

Attending to the More-than-Human City

One of our team members has a sister who talks about a sign she saw in the countryside: 'Rabbits: Pets or Fryers'. To her, it is a metaphorical reminder of the knife edge separating fortune and doom. For non-humans, it literally represents one of the two most common relationships humans have to offer. In the United Kingdom, the pet industry was worth about £2.9 billion in 2020, while the poultry meat industry was worth £2.8 billion (Statista 2022). As Julian Baggini (2022) points out, the two are not disconnected: humans kill many non-humans to feed other non-humans, and our self-image as sentimental animal lovers depends on turning a blind eye to the poor welfare of non-humans reared for pet food.

Humans often act as the arbiters of non-humans' fates, deciding whether they thrive or suffer. For instance, in the United Kingdom, we spend £200–£300 million annually on bird feeding products (BTO 2019), but three times more on pest control (£715 million in 2020; Statista 2022). Arguments abound as to whether urban foxes should be fed or culled (e.g. Birmingham and Black Country Wildlife Trust 2022; cf. The Royal Borough of Kensington and Chelsea 2022), while the Bristol City Council advises that egg oiling has been replaced by 'substituting real gull eggs with plastic, dummy ones to stop the birds from laying any more eggs till the end of the breeding season' to deal with 'the gull problem in Bristol' (Bristol City Council 2022). People complain about chicken bones littering city streets, worrying about the dangers they pose to their dogs and debating whether they are left by irresponsible humans or non-humans ('You're right, I bet a lot of it is rats pulling them out of the trash'; WiseNebula1 2020).

On the other hand, nobody seems to care about all the snails crushed against the tarmac (Figure 6.1)—a surface constructed entirely for the benefit of human locomotion.

Our relationships with non-humans in the city seem warped by self-interest: if we always view them as pets or pests, food or display, it becomes impossible to approach them as peers. Of course, we can always read about them, or watch documentaries about their lives, but perhaps it is more urgent that we attend to them more directly, through observation, imagination, and rapport.

Several of our probes and proposals encourage this kind of empathy. For instance, we asked people to imagine how non-human lives are lived in the city, and what activities might matter to them (Figure 6.2). We suggested devices[5] for seeing like non-humans, perhaps leading to new measurement units based on non-human perception (e.g. to a hawk, the noise of an airplane might be '60chk-a-dee-dee-deefee-bee-fee-baysee-dee-dee-dee'). We thought these might serve as 'intuition pumps' (Dennett 2013), complementing the more active role-playing exercises that Rachel Clarke and her colleagues (2019) have developed.

What about snail rights?

Listen to Moondog (over and over) and think about why nobody seems to care about all the snails crushed against the tarmac.

https://spoti.fi/3t3qDpq

Figure 6.1 What about snail rights?

Perhaps we do not need to go as far as Thomas Thwaites (2016), who donned prosthetic legs, a chest protector, helmet, and artificial stomach in an attempt to escape 'the angst inherent in being a human' by becoming a goat. Surely, though, we can start to ask questions politely (Haraway 2016) about our non-human neighbours' lives, beyond how they impact our own.

Knowing Our Neighbours as Individuals

Beyond empathy and imagination, we could use technologies for surveillance and tracking to better understand the individual non-humans amongst us. For instance, My Naturewatch Camera (Gaver et al. 2019) is a self-built wildlife camera that helps people gather images of non-humans (birds and animals, mostly, but also insects and even snails) in their backyards. Devices like these[6] are important, as the naturist and broadcaster Chris Packham told us during a visit to see the camera, because they help us know individual non-humans, and that is a powerful incentive for conservation (personal communication, 11 May 2018). Clearly, a wide variety of other sensing and recording technologies could be used along the same lines.

As we learn more about our individual non-human neighbours, we could share our findings with our human ones. People could trade sightings of a neighbourhood squirrel, for instance, to follow its mischievous wanderings through local gardens and public areas. This might be compelling for those already interested in wildlife,

Choose your species. Find your location. Mark a photo or map.

Where do you go to?:

a) Find food
b) Find water
c) Sleep
d) Keep a lookout
e) Meet enemies
f) Hide
g) Escape
h) Have sex
i) Give birth
j) Raise young
k) Recover
l) Die

Figure 6.2 Activities questions for non-human lives.

and more importantly, those who are not yet sensitive to the more-than-human lives around them.

Perhaps crowdsourced information about local critters could take the form of communiqués directly from non-humans themselves (Figure 6.3). What if a local robin could let us know about which trees it likes best, or share her joy in finding a mate, building a nest, and raising her young? Perhaps her human neighbours would be a bit more careful about when and where they prune their gardens, or start to leave out robin-friendly food (soft nuts, raisins) for the demanding child-rearing season?

Representative versus Direct More-than-Human Democracy

Raising human awareness is not really enough, though. If cities are to become truly more-than-human, then non-humans need to be given a voice in governance and decision-making.[7] Several of our proposals suggested that non-humans might sign and raise petitions, send letters to the editor, or hold elective office (e.g. Figure 6.4).

Of course, we can imagine how this principle might be operationalised. Community experts on urban foxes, say, could be given a seat in local government—for

Non-human Neigbours Leaflet Drop

Local 'pests' are recontextualised as neighbours we must learn to get along with. People and animals are first introduced via a monthly leaflet drop. In this case David the fox explains a bit about himself, including how long he's lived around here and what he likes and dislikes about the area. Overleaf is contextual data and information resources about other non-human locals.

Figure 6.3 Non-human neighbours leaflet drop.

example, in planning departments—to speak for their constituents. This is the idea behind environmental impact studies, for example: humans are given authority to represent the interests of their more-than-human community.

No doubt, most advocates for non-humans work with integrity, knowledge, and good intentions. Nonetheless, it is problematic in principle to assume that humans can adequately represent the more-than-human world. At best, representatives who do not share the life worlds of those who they seek to represent are liable to misunderstandings and mistakes. At worse, the situation creates unequal power relations that are open to bias and self-serving decisions. Even calling non-humans 'more-than-humans' might be seen as patronising, as if they're going to be happy with a flattering name while we continue to condescend to them in action.

If human representation of non-humans is not ethically viable, though, how can they possibly represent themselves? How can we possibly understand what non-humans want and need if we can't even talk with them?

Separate but Equal

It seems unimaginable to give non-humans equal say in the arrangement of cities. The result is that most proposals to design cities for more-than-humans only offer small steps towards reducing species inequality. The reality on the ground is even worse: in their 2022 report, the Countryside Charity London itemises fifty London parks and greenspaces currently under threat from development (CPRE 2022). So far, it seems that human interests almost always win over non-humans.

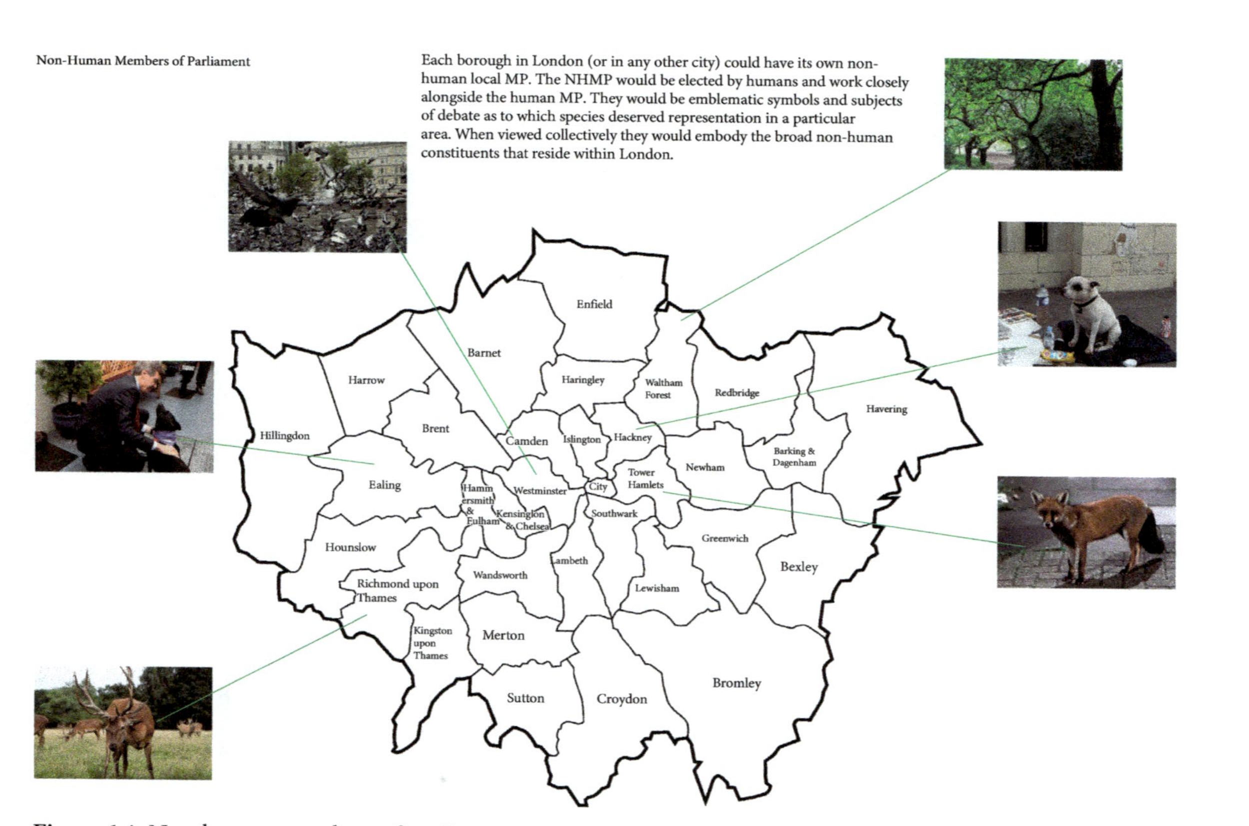
Non-Human Members of Parliament
Each borough in London (or in any other city) could have its own non-human local MP. The NHMP would be elected by humans and work closely alongside the human MP. They would be emblematic symbols and subjects of debate as to which species deserved representation in a particular area. When viewed collectively they would embody the broad non-human constituents that reside within London.
Enfield
Barnet
Harrow
Haringley
Waltham Forest
Redbridge
Havering
Hillingdon
Brent
Camden
Islington
Hackney
Barking & Dagenham
Newham
Tower Hamlets
Ealing
Hamm ersmith & Fulham
Westminster
City
Kensington & Chelsea
Southwark
Hounslow
Greenwich
Lambeth
Bexley
Richmond upon Thames
Wandsworth
Lewisham
Kingston upon Thames
Merton
Bromley
Sutton
Croydon

Figure 6.4 Non-human members of parliament.

So perhaps it is time to consider a more radical proposal for sharing our cities. If non-humans can never achieve equality in society that includes humans, perhaps we should separate ourselves (Figure 6.5). Humans already go to great lengths to build habitats that let them remain indoors to avoid the potential unpleasantness of encounters with extreme cold or heat. We also establish environments for animals already, from zoo enclosures to vast wildlife sanctuaries, that humans cannot enter safely without the protection of their vehicles. From this perspective, it is only a small step to imagine entire cities that are shared equally between humans and non-humans: we get the inside, they get the outside.

Perhaps such a vision is not practically achievable. After all, Paolo Soleri's ambition to build Arcosanti, an example of his call for vast, self-contained, and high-density living environments[8] that would have little contact with, or impact upon, their natural surroundings, currently exists only as a relatively small community in Arizona that specialises in molten bronze bell casting (Arcosanti 2022).[9] Comparable proposals by Frank Lloyd Wright and Buckminster Fuller have similarly never come to fruition. Perhaps the Line, a 105-mile-long linear city being built in Saudi Arabia (Neom 2022), will fare better—or maybe it will demonstrate the fallacy of trying to isolate humans from non-humans.

After all, tempting though it may be, the idea of giving non-humans separate territories from humans is probably objectionable in principle, not just impracticable. Humans are animals, too, and we benefit from exposure to the more-than-human world. Many non-humans, too, thrive in the human world (Alagona 2022). Rather

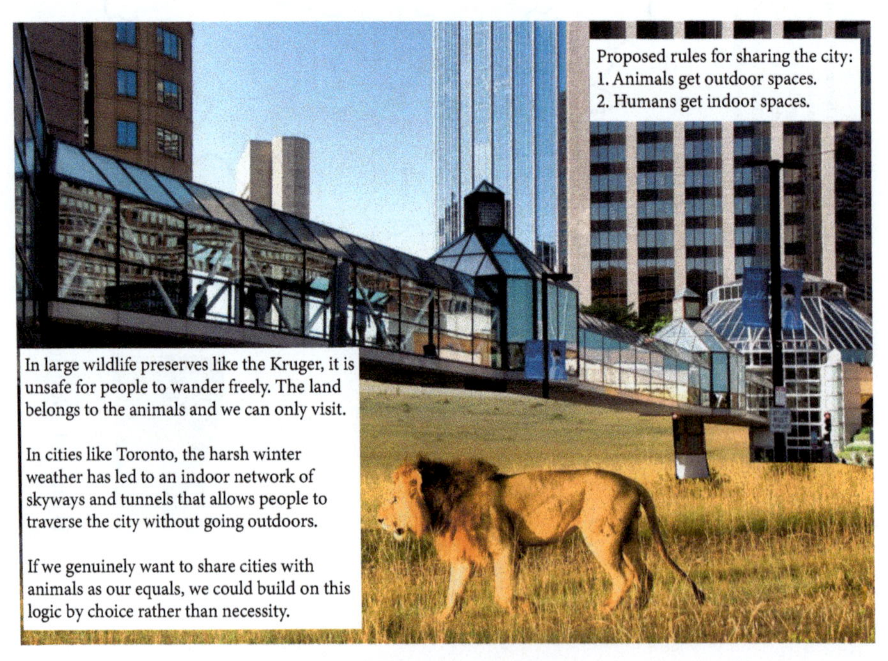

Figure 6.5 A more radical proposal for sharing our cities?

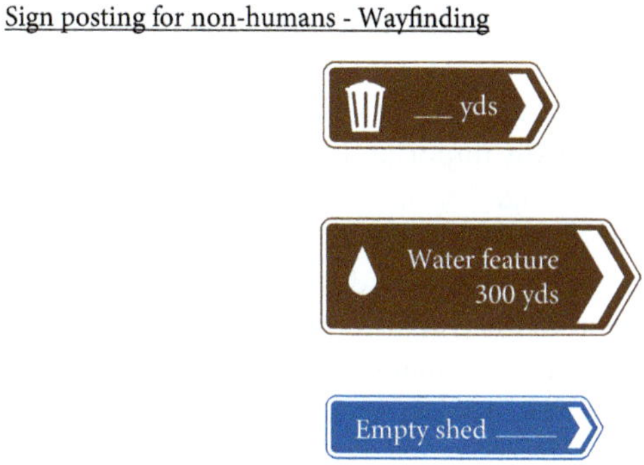

Figure 6.6 Signposting for non-humans: Wayfinding.

than recapitulating a modernist dichotomy between humans and non-humans, then, perhaps it is better to seek ways to value our continuity.[10]

Nonetheless, the proposal remains a valuable challenge. It reminds us that if we are really committed to building more-than-human cities, we need to think more seriously about what it would mean to address other species as true equals.

Signposting and Wayfinding

If we are not going to divide the city, then we need to share the city more equitably with non-humans. Clearly, attention to the preservation and arrangement of green spaces is crucial. Habitats need to be diverse yet not too fragmented (Farinha-Marques et al. 2011). Green corridors—contiguous routes of urban green spaces—clearly benefit birds and generalist or opportunist mammals, but the evidence is less clear for insects and critters that rely on specialised environments (Angold et al. 2006; Lepczyk et al. 2017).

Part of the problem may be that the variability of habitats within a green corridor prevents the movement of non-humans who are most comfortable in one sort of place. If two woodlands are separated by open fields, for instance, then creatures who prefer the shelter of brush and trees may be dissuaded from travelling between them. Similarly, though gardens, roadside verges, and roof gardens may provide 'stepping stones' (Farinha-Marques et al. 2011; Lepczyk et al. 2017) between diverse habitats, their effectiveness may depend on non-humans' willingness to make their way among them.

From this perspective, it makes sense to provide signposting for non-humans to help their wayfinding among diverse urban greenspaces (Figure 6.6). These might use scent, sound, or other stimuli to indicate promising directions for their travel, encouraging non-humans to take the risk of venturing beyond known territories to find new ones. If simple light pots can lure scallops into fishermen's nets (Turns 2022), then surely we can find other ways to go beyond food, physical constraints, and pain as a means for guiding non-humans.

Data in the More-than-Human City

Of course, signposting for non-humans depends on our being able to communicate effectively with them. Equally importantly, it also depends on capturing the data that can support their wayfinding.

Humans love to capture data for all sorts of purposes—the bigger the better. We mine it, process it, request it, share it, hide it, and purge it. Data is the device we use to quantify and communicate the climate crisis, for example, our means for measuring the impending doom of our own making—but we do not share the story it tells with the more-than-humans that will share our fate. Data is everywhere, but data is for humans.

What if data were gathered for more-than-human purposes? What if the movements of birds, so skilfully removed from aircraft radar tracking data, were used to track migration patterns (Figure 6.7)? What if pollen warnings were transformed into a celebration of the best places for new planting and new habitats for other species (Heitlinger et al. 2018)? There are myriad ways that data collected for human purposes can be repurposed for the benefit of our more-than-human neighbours if we look beyond our own parochial interests.

Using data on behalf of non-humans doesn't seem sufficient, though. It recapitulates the problems of with assuming humans can adequately represent more-than-human interests, leaving open possibilities for misunderstandings, compromise, and bias.

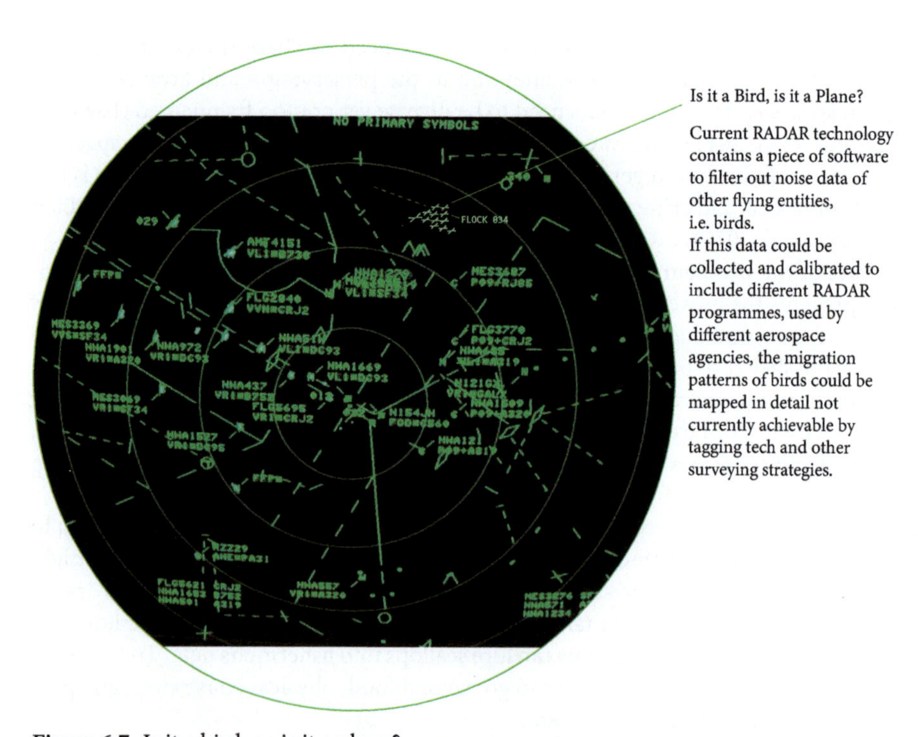

NO PRIMARY SYMBOLS
FLOCK 834
Is it a Bird, is it a Plane?
Current RADAR technology contains a piece of software to filter out noise data of other flying entities, i.e. birds.
If this data could be collected and calibrated to include different RADAR programmes, used by different aerospace agencies, the migration patterns of birds could be mapped in detail not currently achievable by tagging tech and other surveying strategies.

Figure 6.7 Is it a bird, or is it a plane?

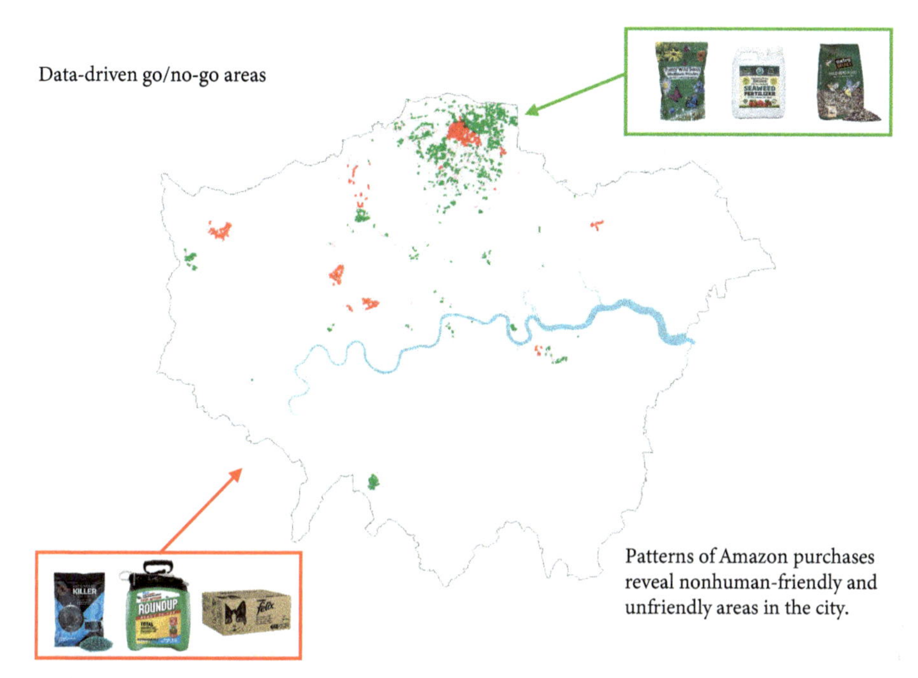

Figure 6.8 Data-driven go/no-go areas.

We may never be able to support pigeons to become data scientists, but we could scrape data for the information most relevant to them. Localised purchasing trends might reveal which areas of the city are likely to be hospitable or hostile (Figure 6.8). Traffic data could help regulate non-human traffic. Even musical preferences might hint at likely attitudes towards non-humans. Using data in this way would be a benign diversion of surveillance capitalism (Zuboff 2019). Instead of a few powerful actors using big data to reinforce and focus consumer behaviour for their own benefits, creating an ever-tightening capitalist death spiral, we might use the same data to look for the implications of buying outside market logics (for instance, for the environment), and share the benefits directly with more-than-human stakeholders.

More-than-Human Cyborgs

Not only could we work to redirect the power of data towards more-than-human benefit to nurture sustainability instead of profit, but we could also endeavour to open the potentials of all technologies to our non-human neighbours. Why shouldn't snails, hedgehogs, and foxes be able to ride driverless cars (Figure 6.9), instead of being left as literal roadkill in the wake of technological progress?

In Haraway's (2006) terms, this would mean supporting non-humans to become cyborgs, too—to develop 'the power to survive, not on the basis of original innocence, but on the basis of seizing the tools to mark the world that marked them as other'.

Driverless Hedgehog Bus

A network of autonomous vehicles could pick-up stray hedgehogs, taking them from dangerous urban areas and dropping them off at nearby greenspaces. Concerned citizens could report hedgehogs, which would dictate the route of the Hedgehog Bus.

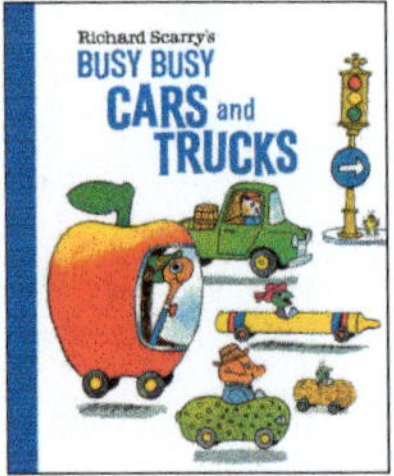

Figure 6.9 Driverless hedgehog bus.

After all, it seems inconceivable that we can isolate ourselves from non-humans, leaving them in peace in an anything-but-human world. Nor do current strategies of stewardship, in which humans are the sole representatives of the more-than-human world, seem just or effective. If we can't go back, or stay still, we must go forward, and invite the entire more-than-human world to engage in more equal relationships not only with us humans, but with all the technologies that can support our coming together to live mindfully with each other and the world.

Conclusion: Workbooks and Emergent Logics

As we developed the workbook, we didn't really discuss many of the perspectives, arguments, and standpoints outlined here. In fact, as we did our work, our conversations seldom ventured beyond particular proposals. To us, that is part of the magic of design workbooks: they allow us to imagine relatively concrete design possibilities—something that, as designers, we are wont to do—while allowing a more or less consistent conceptual standpoint to emerge in latent form.

Often, we are content to allow the worldviews we develop in this way to remain dormant, at least until further realised through the research products we make, and the engagements people have with them. For the MOTH project, many of the proposals and probes we developed served as resources for the participatory workshops we held (see e.g. https://mothcities.uk/events/workshop-1), ultimately helping lead to the design of a Discovery Box (https://mothcities.uk/box) that might help others explore the more-than-human city as we did.

As the proposals and probes became entangled with the wider project, however, the workbook's integrity as a coherent collection of thinking became diffused. So, it seems apt here to highlight it as an output on its own, and to annotate the proposals and reveal their lurking implications. As we have done so, we realise that they suggest a research programme for more-than-human smart cities that is perhaps more radical than we realised. If we were going to summarise it in a manifesto, it might go something like this:

Manifesto for a More-than-Human Smart City

- If we are serious, then we should aim to share our cities with non-humans equally. Really equally.
- Human representation of non-humans is inherently inadequate. Non-humans should be empowered to represent their own interests.
- Data should be collected, processed, used, and made available for non-humans as well as humans.
- Non-humans should have access to the benefits of technologies, directly.
- All this requires learning to speak and listen to non-humans.[11]

Clearly, this is an audacious set of goals, and it is quite probable that they are unattainable in literal form. But we like them. They set out a course that doesn't bow to the 'possible' but is uncompromising in its ambitions, and that seems to us to make them worthwhile. In this, they resonate with the insistence of animal ethicists like Peter Singer (1975) that ethical reasoning should apply equally to humans and non-humans, no matter how impractical that might seem. As he put it, 'if someone answers "Well, nobody's going to do it", I don't think that's an answer at all' (Specter 1999).

At the same time, as Angelika Strohmayer (2021) puts it, these goals, and the proposals that underpin them, suggest that we pause.

> Haraway's (2016) rallying cry of 'staying with the trouble' invites us to pause; to hold space for the issues we are facing; and to reflect on these and develop narratives that help us understand them rather than trying to immediately solve these large and complex problems.

From this perspective, our proposals offer narratives that may not immediately solve questions about the more-than-human smart city. Even their 'mistakes and misunderstandings' may be interesting, however, and help us ask new questions. Perhaps the most important is the simplest: 'Why not?'

Notes

1. These sorts of questions are part of the ongoing discourse in the smart city literature (see Fieuw et al. 2022; Mattern 2021; Powell 2021).
2. See https://mothcities.uk/. This work was funded through the EPSRC Human Data Interaction network plus (EP/R045178/1).
3. Our 'design space' might be similar to the 'opportunity spaces' discussed in Hornecker et al. (2006).
4. Design fiction and speculative design approaches have also started to be used for imagining more-than-human cities (e.g., Nijs et al. 2020; Pollastri et al. 2021).
5. Similar to more-than-human design methods such as those proposed by Tomitsch et al. (2021).
6. Soro et al. (2018) describe a relevant device.
7. This idea has been explored, e.g., by Heitlinger et al. (2021), Sheikh et al. (2022), Graham & Maloney (2019), Rühs & Jones (2016) and Steele (2019).

8. 'Arcologies,' from 'architecture' and 'ecology'.
9. Related to post/trans-humanism discourse in design (Forlano 2017; Gonsalves et al. 2022; Thibault et al. 2020).
10. There are calls from urban studies and architecture to not just reduce harm from human activity but to ensure human activity (and design) is net positive, i.e., makes a valuable contribution to nature (Birkeland 2020, 2022).
11. The more-than-human idea takes its origin with Abram's (1997) book.

References

Abram, David (1997). *The spell of the sensuous: Perception and language in a more-than-human world.* Vintage Books.

Alagona, P. S. (2022). *The accidental ecosystem: People and wildlife in American cities.* University of California Press.

Angold, P. G., Sadler, J. P., Hill, M. O., Pullin, A., Rushton, S., Austin, K., Small, E., Wood, B., Wadsworth, R., Sanderson, R., & Thompson, K. (2006). Biodiversity in urban habitat patches. *The Science of the Total Environment, 360*(1–3), 196–204. https://doi.org/10.1016/j.scitotenv.2005.08.035

Arcosanti (2022). https://www.arcosanti.org

Baggini, J. (12 Feb 2022). Animal lovers? Actually, Britain is a nation of sentimental hypocrites. *The Guardian.* theguardian.com/commentisfree/2022/feb/12/animal-lovers-britain-kurt-zouma-cat

Birkeland, J. (2020). *Net-positive design and sustainable urban development.* Routledge. https://doi.org/10.4324/9780429290213

Birkeland, J. (2022). Nature positive: Interrogating sustainable design frameworks for their potential to deliver eco-positive outcomes. *Urban Science, 6*(2), 35. https://doi.org/10.3390/urbansci6020035

Birmingham and Black Country Wildlife Trust (2022). Urban foxes, your questions answered. bbcwildlife.org.uk/urban-fox

Blythe, M., and Encinas, E. (2016). The co-ordinates of design fiction: Extrapolation, irony, ambiguity and magic. In *Proceedings of the 2016 ACM international conference on supporting group work (GROUP '16)* (pp. 345–354). ACM. https://doi.org/10.1145/2957276.2957299

Boucher, A. (2016). The form design of the datacatcher: A research prototype. In *Proceedings of the 2016 ACM Conference on Designing Interactive Systems (DIS '16)* (pp. 595–606). ACM. https://doi.org/10.1145/2901790.2901907

Bristol City Council (2022). Advice about the gull problem in Bristol. bristol.gov.uk/documents/20182/32623/Gulls+Advice+Leaflet

British Trust for Ornithology (21 May 2019). Boom time at Britain's bird feeders. bto.org/press-releases/boom-time-britains-bird-feeders

Clarke, R., Heitlinger, S., Light, A., Forlano, L., Foth,M., & DiSalvo, C. (2019). More-than-human participation: Design for sustainable smart city futures. *Interactions, 26*(3), 60–3. https://doi.org/10.1145/3319075

CPRE London (March 2022). Forever green? Privatisation, neglect and financial gain: Why 50 London parks and green spaces are under threat and how we can save them. https://www.cprelondon.org.uk/wp-content/uploads/sites/10/2022/03/Forever-Green-March-2022.pdf

Crewdson, G., & Banks, R.(2008). *Beneath the roses.* Harry N. Abrams

Dennett, D. C. (2013). *Intuition pumps and other tools for thinking.* W. W. Norton & Company.

Dorst, K. (2015). *Frame innovation: Create new thinking by design.* MIT Press.

Farinha-Marques, P., Lameiras, J. M., Fernandes, C., Silva, S., & Guilherme, F. (2011). Urban biodiversity: A review of current concepts and contributions to multidisciplinary approaches. *Innovation: The European Journal of Social Science Research, 24*(3), 247–271. https://doi.org/10.1080/13511610.2011.592062

Fieuw, W., Foth, M., & Amayo Caldwell, G. (2022). Towards a more-than-human approach to smart and sustainable urban development: Designing for multispecies justice. *Sustainability: Science Practice and Policy, 14*(2), 948. https://doi.org/10.3390/su14020948

Forlano, L. (2017). Posthumanism and design. *She Ji: The Journal of Design, Economics, and Innovation, 3*(1), 16–29. https://doi.org/10.1016/j.sheji.2017.08.001
Gaver, W. (2011). Making spaces: How design workbooks work. In *Proceedings of the SIGCHI Conference on Human Factors in Computing Systems (CHI '11)* (pp. 1551–1560). ACM. https://doi.org/10.1145/1978942.1979169
Gaver, W., Dunne, T., & Pacenti, E. (1999). Design: Cultural probes. *Interactions* 6(1), 21–9. https://doi.org/10.1145/291224.291235
Gaver, W., Boucher, A., Vanis, M., Sheen, A., Brown,D., Ovalle, L., Matsuda, N., Abbas-Nazari, A., & Phillips, R. (2019). My naturewatch camera: Disseminating practice research with a cheap and easy DIY design. In *Proceedings of the 2019 CHI conference on human factors in computing systems (CHI '19)* (Paper 302, pp. 1–13). ACM. https://doi.org/10.1145/3290605.3300532
Gaver, W. W., Bowers, J., Boucher, A., Gellerson, H., Pennington, S., Schmidt, A., Steed, A., Villars, N., & Walker, B. (2004). The drift table: Designing for ludic engagement. In *CHI '04 Extended Abstracts on Human Factors in Computing Systems (CHI EA '04)* (pp. 885–900). ACM. https://doi.org/10.1145/985921.985947
Gonsalves, K., Aia-Fa'aleava, A., Ha, L. T., Junpiban, N., Narain, N., Foth, M., & Amayo Caldwell, G. (2022). TransHuman saunter: Multispecies storytelling in precarious times. *Leonardo, 56*, 125–132. https://doi.org/10.1162/leon_a_02243
Graham,M., & Maloney,M. (2019). Caring for country and rights of nature in Australia: A conversation between earth jurisprudence and aboriginal law and ethics. In C. La Follette & C. Maser (Eds.), *Sustainability and the rights of nature in practice* (pp. 385–399). CRC Press. https://doi.org/10.1201/9780429505959-19
Haraway, D. (2006). A cyborg manifesto: Science, technology, and socialist-feminism in the late 20th century. In *The international handbook of virtual learning environments* (pp. 117–158). Springer.
Haraway, D. (2016). *Staying with the trouble.* Duke University Press.
Heitlinger, S., Houston, L., Taylor,A., & Catlow,R. (2021). Algorithmic food justice: Co-designing more-than-human blockchain futures for the food commons. In *Proceedings of the 2021 CHI conference on human factors in computing systems (CHI '21)* (pp. 1–17). ACM.
Heitlinger, S., Bryan-Kinns, N., & Comber,R. (2018). Connected seeds and sensors: Co-designing Internet of Things for sustainable smart cities with urban food-growing communities. In *Proceedings of the 15th participatory design conference: Short papers, situated actions, workshops and tutorial* (Vol 2, pp. 1–5). ACM.
Hornecker, E., Halloran, J., Fitzpatrick, G., Weal, M., Millard, D., Michaelides, D., Cruickshank, D., & De Roure, D. (2006). UbiComp in opportunity spaces: Challenges for participatory design. In *Proceedings of the ninth conference on Participatory design: Expanding boundaries in design* (pp. 47–56). ACM. https://doi.org/10.1145/1147261.1147269
Lepczyk, C. A., Aronson, M. F. J., Evans, K. L., Goddard, M. A., Lerman, S. B., & MacIvor, J. S. (2017). Biodiversity in the city: Fundamental questions for understanding the ecology of urban green spaces for biodiversity conservation. *Bioscience, 67*(9), 799–807. https://doi.org/10.1093/biosci/bix079
Lindley J., & Coulton, P. (2015). Back to the future: 10 years of design fiction. In *Proceedings of the 2015 British HCI conference (British HCI '15)* (pp. 210–211). ACM. https://doi.org/10.1145/2783446.2783592
Mattern, S. (2021). *A city is not a computer: Other urban intelligences.* Princeton University Press. https://press.princeton.edu/books/paperback/9780691208053/a-city-is-not-a-computer
MoTH Cities (2022). MoTH cities: More-than-human data interactions in the smart city. https://mothcities.uk
Neom (2022). The line. https://www.neom.com
Nijs, G., Laki, G., Houlstan, R., Slizewicz, G., & Laureyssens, T. (2020). Fostering more-than-human imaginaries: Introducing DIY speculative fabulation in civic HCI. In *Proceedings of the 11th Nordic conference on human-computer interaction: Shaping experiences, shaping society* (pp. 1–12). ACM. https://doi.org/10.1145/3419249.3420147
Odom, W., Wakkary, R., Lim, Y-K., Desjardins, A., Hengeveld,B., & Banks R. (2016). From research prototype to research product. In *Proceedings of the 2016 CHI conference on human factors in computing systems (CHI '16)* (pp. 2549–2561). ACM. https://doi.org/10.1145/2858036.2858447

Pollastri, S., Griffiths, R., Dunn, N., Cureton,P., Boyko, C., Blaney, A., & De Bezenac, E. (2021). More-than-human future cities: From the design of nature to designing for and through nature. *Media Architecture Biennale, 20*, 23–30. https://doi.org/10.1145/3469410.3469413

Powell, A. B. (2021). *Undoing optimization: Civic action in smart cities*. Yale University Press. https://yalebooks.yale.edu/book/9780300223804/undoing-optimization

Rittel, H. W. J., & Webber, M. M.(1973). Dilemmas in a general theory of planning. *Policy Sciences 4*(2), 155–69.

The Royal Borough of Kensington and Chelsea (2022). Urban foxes. rbkc.gov.uk/environment/environmental-health/urban-foxes

Rühs, N., & Jones, A. (2016). The implementation of earth jurisprudence through substantive constitutional rights of nature. *Sustainability: Science Practice and Policy*, *8*(2), 174. https://doi.org/10.3390/su8020174

Schön, D. A. (1983). *The reflective practitioner: How professionals think in action*. Basic Books.

Sheikh, H., Foth, M., & Mitchell, P. (2022). (Re)imagining the ibis: Multispecies future(s), smart urban governance, and the digital environmental humanities. In *Routledge handbook of the digital environmental humanities* (pp. 490–515). Routledge. https://doi.org/10.4324/9781003082798-39

Sherman, C. (2003). *Cindy Sherman: The complete untitled film stills*. The Museum of Modern Art.

Singer, P. (1990 /1975). *Animal liberation*. Review Books.

Soro,A., Brereton, M., Dema, T., Oliver, J. L., Zhen Chai, M., & Hufana Ambe, A. M. (2018). The ambient birdhouse: An IoT device to discover birds and engage with nature. In *Proceedings of the 2018 CHI conference on human factors in computing systems (CHI '18)* (Paper 397, pp. 1–13). ACM. https://doi.org/10.1145/3173574.3173971

Specter, M. (6 September 1999). The dangerous philosopher. *The New Yorker*.

Statista (2022). https://www.statista.com

Steele, W. (2019). *Planning wild cities: Human-nature relationships in the urban age*. Routledge. https://doi.org/10.4324/9781315688756

Sterling,B, (2005). *Shaping things*. The MIT Press.

Strohmayer, A. (2021). *Digitally augmenting traditional craft practices for social justice: The partnership quilt*. Palgrave Macmillan. https://doi.org/10.1007/978-981-33-6002-0

Thibault,M., Buruk, O., Suman Buruk, S., & Hamari, J. (2020). Transurbanism: Smart cities for transhumans. *Proceedings of the 2020 ACM designing interactive systems conference* (pp. 1915–1928). ACM. https://doi.org/10.1145/3357236.3395523

Thwaites, T. (2016). *GoatMan: How I took a holiday from being human (one man's journey to leave humanity behind and become like a goat)*. Princeton Architectural Press.

Tomitsch, M., Fredericks, J., Vo,D., Frawley, J., & Foth, M. (2021). Non-human personas: Including nature in the participatory design of smart cities. *Interaction Design and Architecture(s), 50*, 102–130. https://doi.org/10.55612/s-5002-050-006

Turns, A. (18 May 2022). Accidental discovery that scallops love 'disco' lights leads to new fishing technique. *The Guardian*. https://www.theguardian.com/environment/2022/may/18/accidental-discovery-that-scallops-love-disco-lights-leads-to-new-fishing-technique

WiseNebula1 (3 Dec 2020). If you leave chicken bones on the street you can go fuck yourself. https://reddit.com/r/dogs/comments/k67qon/vent_if_you_leave_chicken_bones_on_the_street_you/

Zuboff, S. (2019). *The age of surveillance capitalism: The fight for a human future at the new frontier of power*. PublicAffairs.

7
Bugs in the Smart City
A Proposal for Going Upstream in Human–Mosquito Co-Becoming

Jonathan Metzger and Jean Hillier

Bugs as Idiots in the Smart City

In March 2022, the Thermacell® LIV Smart Mosquito Repellent System launched, offering Australia and much of the Global North 'protection like you've never seen before' (www.thermacell.com). The Repellent System, Wi-Fi controlled by voice or smartphone via a 'Smart Hub', retails at US$899 for five repellers to cover spaces of up to 1,575 square feet. Using sensors that detect mosquito-specific heat signatures, repellent is diffused into the air. However, this off-the-shelf 'smart' mosquito control system is not nearly as technically advanced as the new SMDS, Smart Mosquito Density System, of Thiruvananthapuram, India, which autonomously operates on the basis of state-of-the-art Internet of Things (IoT) technology (Smart Cities Council 2021). The system alerts health and other agencies to erupting mosquito infestations and produces thematic maps that help government agencies prioritise areas to spray with insecticide, identifying the exact species of mosquito and what would be the appropriate chemical to deploy. Automated analytics continuously monitor the effectiveness of the induced measures.[1] Also in Australia, drones and sensors are beginning to be used for monitoring, identification, and deployment of pesticides for the eradication of mosquito populations—for instance, in the City of Townsville, Queensland, while real-time PCR (polymerase chain reaction) is used to extract DNA from mosquito eggs, identify and map species, and predict local mosquito populations and activity in smart mapping 'Mozzie Seeker' initiatives south-east of Brisbane (Montgomery et al. 2021).

The promotional efforts of these systems tend to echo many of the central tropes of the 'smart city' discourse, centring on the promise of being able to monitor, control, and modulate complex urban phenomena in real-time with the help of cutting-edge technical equipment. Such celebratory smart city discourse has been repeatedly criticised for its elitist flavour, and how it all but ignores issues of social justice and equality (Kitchin 2016; Mattern 2021). As an expectable response, there have recently been movements towards bringing these issues into the mainstream of smart city 'offers', for instance, through the 'Smart Cities for All' initiative promoted by G3ict, The Global Initiative on Inclusive ICTs, which is organised by, among others, corporate actors such as Microsoft and AT&T (Korngold et al. 2017), and global consultancy Deloitte's presentation of their services for realising 'inclusive smart cities', which do

Jonathan Metzger and Jean Hillier, *Bugs in the Smart City*. In: *Designing More-than-Human Smart Cities*. Edited by: Sara Heitlinger, Marcus Foth, and Rachel Clarke, Oxford University Press.
DOI: 10.1093/9780191980060.003.0009

not only 'offer greater opportunities for their residents' but also supposedly allow city administrations to 'reap widespread economic benefits'.[2]

However, Metzger (2016) argues that discourses claiming to promote unlimited inclusion and flourishing 'for all' can be surreptitiously seductive in how they obfuscate that, inevitably, inclusion always has a limit, and that exclusions are ubiquitous in any form of societal context. Perhaps particularly so in urban planning, where Metzger even argues that producing exclusion is part of the 'core business of planning', where some particular 'we' assume the privilege of planning an environment:

> like this not like that to make it more hospitable for some entities, and not for others [...] No matter whether this is arrived at through a democratic process or not, or how inclusive the 'some' is formulated, it can never be all-inclusive. And neither is it intended to be, given that at any point in time there will be a range of entities and existences some 'we' certainly do not want to see in a city (Metzger 2016, p.595).

Recognising the ubiquity of exclusions shifts key questions from a consideration of 'are we welcoming to all and everything?' to instead investigating and recognising the exclusions that are inevitably taking place in urban planning and development processes. The questions that must then be raised not only concern who, or what, is being excluded from a particular environment, but also on what grounds, and whether or not—once recognised—we find these exclusions acceptable, and if not, what can be done to ameliorate them? More specifically—in relation to smart city discourses and practices—it frontstages issues relating to the limits of inclusion in the smart city. What are those existences and phenomena that are deemed to be incompossible, that is, fundamentally unable to co-exist with the smart city vision?

In *Smart Cities: Buggy and Brittle*, Anthony Townsend (2013) asks: What if the smart cities of the future are chock full of bugs? In the text, he primarily discusses metaphorical 'bugs', that is, all sorts of computer failures—but in passing, he also mentions that one of the first-ever documented computer bugs was quite literally a critter, specifically: a moth that was found trapped in a relay by Navy researchers working with the Mark II Aiken Relay Calculator at Harvard University (see Figure 7.1). Such undesired wild and feral other-than-human animals, 'pests' (like their vegetal counterparts 'weeds') are per definition known by how they tend to turn up 'out-of-place' (cf. Douglas 1966) and are thus fundamentally characterised by their unruliness and uncontrollability. Overall, they tend not to figure at all in dominant smart-city discourses except as disturbances (Power 2009; Sheikh et al. 2022) that are to be efficiently controlled, excluded, and/or exterminated with the help of technologically advanced control systems such as the Thermacell® LIV or SMDS. Like the 'moth in the machine', pests that fly, crawl, slither, and propagate in the cracks of the envisaged otherwise-perfect urban system constitute a fundamental challenge to ambitions for smart controlled urban environments.

Through recurrently turning up in the wrong places, pests manifestly embody the conceptual character of 'the Idiot', as it is presented in the work of Gilles Deleuze and Felix Guattari (1991/1994) and Isabelle Stengers (2005a,b). Drawing from the

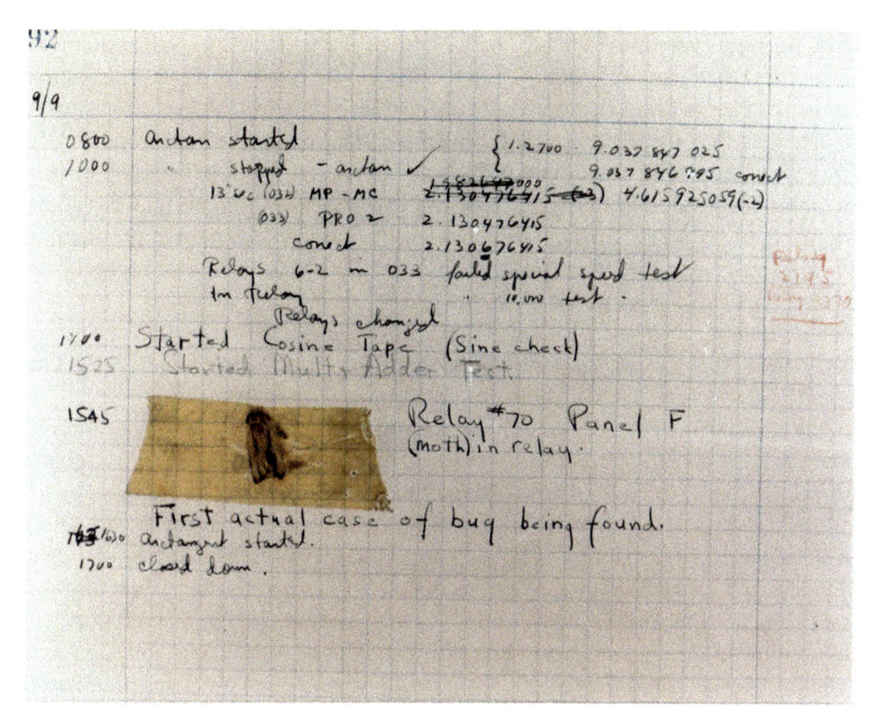
9/9
0800 Antan started
1000 " stopped - antan ✓
Relays 6-2 in 033 failed special speed test
Relays changed
1100 Started Cosine Tape (Sine check)
1525 Started Multy Adder Test.
1545 Relay #70 Panel F
(moth) in relay.
First actual case of bug being found.
1630 antangent started.
1700 closed down.

Figure 7.1 First ever documented computer bug, a moth found trapped between points at Relay #70, Panel F, of the Mark II Aiken Relay Calculator while it was being tested at Harvard University, 9 September 1947.

U.S. Naval Historical Center Online Library Photograph NH 96566-KN (Courtesy of the Naval Surface Warfare Center, Dahlgren, VA., 1988., Public domain, via Wikimedia Commons).

famous novel by Fyodor Dostoevsky, Stengers follows Deleuze and Guattari by presenting 'the Idiot' as a designator of existences that interrupt the flow of action and 'resists the consensual way in which the situation is presented and in which emergencies mobilise thought or action' (Stengers 2005a, p.994). But the Idiot does not do so by actively contesting or questioning the course of action—the Idiot 'can neither reply nor discuss the issues' and 'neither objects nor proposes anything that "counts"'—her putting into question established truths and practices rather comes about as a consequence of her mere turning up or 'misbehaving' in the midst of the flow of action—an obstacle that demands a slowing down of action and thought. Thus, to Stengers, the Idiot 'is a presence' who, through her material existence in place, opens up the potential for 'a space for thinking'—an interstice in which it becomes possible to pause and pose the crucial question: 'What are we busy doing'? (Michael 2012; see also Metzger 2016).

The figure of the Idiot has previously been mobilised in relation to discussions on urban planning, development, and governance by Bylund and Byerley (2014), and specifically relating to smart city issues by Farias (2017), Tironi and Valderrama (2019), and Fantini van Ditmar (2019). However, these previous discussions have focused upon particular groups of humans and their respective behaviours, whereas here we propose (very much in faith with Deleuze and Guattari's as well as Stengers's philosophies) that also other beings and existences—in our case, other-than-human animals—can act as Idiots that help us bring into consideration the limits of inclusion in smart cities. By 'bugging out', not 'sticking with the program', and constantly misbehaving, for example, by turning up in the wrong places without permission or prior notice, thus flaunting the entire logic of the smart city—we argue that designated 'pests', particularly bugs,[3] through their bare existence can be of help in problematising who is welcome in the smart city and under what conditions and prerequisites, and how there will always be limits to this.

This chapter aims to bring a suburban fringe residential development in Australia into dialogue with 'smart' initiatives in mosquito management. Our example illustrates the inadvertent intensification of non-human presence, especially mosquito breeding, through a development emphasis on riparian aesthetics and on economics, which leave 'smart' control solutions to individual householders. We identify an approach through which urban planning practices may utilise technologies to better understand the conditions of possibility of more-than-human dynamics and to plan with them, rather than simply passing on responsibility to residential estate developers and, in turn, to individual residents. Inspired by thinkers such as Bruno Latour, Robert Chia, and François Jullien, we suggest that an approach of 'upstream' investigation into the production of conditions of co-becoming can function as an alternative to established 'downstream' mosquito management practices premised on control and eradication. We conclude that forms of smart urban planning and residential estate development might rely less on artificial intelligence (AI) and Wi-Fi technology than a smarter appreciation of development milieus. This could avoid development on or adjacent to mosquito breeding sites, would not generate new inhabitation areas, and would generally reduce opportunities for infelicitous human–mosquito encounters.

The remainder of this chapter is structured as follows: in the next section, we discuss how bugs habitually are designated as pests and introduce the philosophical concept of incompossibility to discuss how bug flourishing and human flourishing in urban environments are generally understood to be fundamentally incompatible, i.e., incompossible. We then outline the two standard responses to perceived bug–human frictions within the Western cultural sphere: extermination and segregation. We suggest that both these responses are fundamentally problematic if employed as standard solutions to situations of infelicitous interspecies co-becoming between humans and bugs. As an alternative, in the following section, we draw upon the work of Latour, Chia, and Jullien to sketch a practice of 'going upstream' to explore when and how, in the immanent and actual, conditions for interspecies co-becoming in local environments can be made slightly less infelicitous. We then attempt the demonstrate the productivity of an upstream approach by relating it to a case of (sub)urban development in Western Australia. We probe how the resultant conditions of interspecies co-becoming between humans and mosquitoes have generated recurrent friction between these species and then attempt to uncover the upstream sources of these confrontations. In our concluding discussion, we suggest that an approach of going upstream to trace the emergence of infelicitous conditions of interspecies co-becoming in local urban environments can be understood as a component of a broader, milieu-based approach to urban planning, development, and governance that we suggest would be a smarter way to tackle apparent incompossibilities in urban interspecies co-existence than the existing 'smart' eradication-based solutions currently on offer.

How to Deal with Idiot Bugs?

Designating a specific type of being as a pest renders it particularly unworthy of sympathy or care, as McKiernan and Instone (2016, p.477) note: 'Urban pests are unwanted species positioned as out-of-place and whose presence is met with discursive and material reaction.' Being classified as a pest renders a being as killable (Hillier 2017), for as noted by Crowley et al. (2018, p.130), 'it is always acceptable to kill pests.' Further, as argued by Sutton and Taylor:

> The null value placed on 'pest' species' lives also means the validity of justifications for this mass killing is unlikely to be challenged in any meaningful way, so invested entities may quibble over methods or quotas, but rarely the ethics of killing itself or the self-selection of humans as masters of nature (2019, p.381).

As the archetype of a pest, bugs generally have a bad name. When it comes to innate human sympathy, they probably constitute the hardest possible case, as they are as far as one can get from what most humans would consider to be 'charismatic species' (Ducarme et al. 2013). Media headlines such as 'Pests run rampant in Perth suburbs' (Paddenburg 2016), 'WA worst for fatal bug bites' (O'Leary 2017) in Western Australia, or 'STD-ridden ladybirds heading for UK' (anon 2018) demonstrate how bugs are represented as 'awkward creatures' (Ginn et al. 2014). The urban biome teems with non-human wildlife, but twenty-first-century humans want their homes to be bug-free cultivated ecologies. Bugs and humans simply do not seem to go felicitously together in cities, and even authors that generally come across as sympathetic to urban multispecies cohabitation suggest that

> analyses of the urban geographies of cockroaches, bedbugs, flies [. . .] do little to suggest that these animals could ever be considered good neighbours given their capacity to crawl and scuttle around domestic interiors biting, eating and defecating. Some animals, it appears, lack the capacity to be seen as anything other than disturbing and 'out of place' in the city (Hubbard and Brooks 2021).

Human flourishing and bug flourishing in urban areas appears as simply *incompossible*. Metzger (2016) mobilises baroque philosopher Gottfried Wilhelm von Leibniz's concept of incompossibility to grapple with such troubling situations, as read through Deleuze (primarily Deleuze 1969/2004). In his discussions of the concept, Deleuze, following Leibniz, utilises it to denote in themselves possible future developments, but of such inclinations that they are mutually exclusive, in accordance with the realisation that 'what is possible in itself is not necessarily "compossible" with other such possible' (Bowden 2010, p.303; Hillier and Metzger 2021).[4] Building on the recognition by Ginn et al. (2014, p.117) that 'managing togetherness requires excluding some organisms and processes, prioritising one possible assembly, while leaving another behind or exposed', Metzger (2016) argues that, in relation to local environmental planning work, an awareness of potential incompossibilities would entail reflexivity over how the active care for certain things (such as favoured paths towards the future or the embryonic sketches for a future urban landscape) always inevitably demands the neglect, othering, exclusion, or active eradication of other beings, things, and/or potential projects. Thus, 'planning with incompossibility in mind' would amount to a raised awareness regarding how any form of suggested manifest intervention in a local environment always inevitably also entails a 'killing off' of alternative, potential worlds—worlds some 'we' somehow define as undesirable, unjust, or just plain 'bad'. 'We' build it like this, not like that, to make it more hospitable for some entities, and not for others. No matter whether or not this decision arrived through a democratic process, or how inclusive the 'some' is formulated, it can never be *all*-inclusive.

One obvious upshot is that an acceptance of these insights precludes that the planner's mission is formulated as the task of ensuring of local environments that are conductive to the well-being of all. Rather, planners must face up to and engender a sense of collective responsibility for tough decisions that inevitably will demand difficult choices promoting the flourishing of some, at the expense of others, and—perhaps most dauntingly—to confront the monumental question of who is to be made to pay a price for the wellbeing of others, and who has the right to decide. But even if we recognise that all planning processes inevitably produce some exclusions, it is nonetheless crucial to also stay attentive to the fact that different ways of going about planning can vary dramatically as to the degree of violence and exclusion they produce. Relatedly, 'accepting' and 'assuming responsibility' for incompossibilities can mean very different things.

Within a Western cultural sphere, the two standard responses for facing up to apparent human–animal incompossibilities are the exterminationist approach, which casts the Other as an enemy to be vanquished; and the segregationist approach, which designates the Other as a nuisance to be isolated and controlled. Exterminationist approaches to human–animal incompossibilities have existed and still exist in aspects of planning practice in different places around the world, particularly in relation to 'invasive' and 'undesired' other-than-human species when they somehow disturb or annoy urban living spaces in the Global North (see also Lynteris 2020; Hubbard and Brooks 2021). In Australia, ibises (McKiernan and Instone 2016), Flying Foxes (Rose 2012), dogs (Instone and Sweeney 2014), and cats (Hillier and Byrne 2016) are frequently regarded as 'undesirable' and accordingly sentenced to physical destruction.

A widespread 'softer' way of dealing with perceived interspecies incompossibilities is the segregationist approach. On a broad level, segregation has been the standard solution through which modern planning theory and practice has dealt with existences perceived as not going together well in the same local environment. We would even argue that the ethos of segregation (in a generic sense, not just relating to racial segregation) is a key tenet of much modernist planning ideology, underpinned by the idea of 'each in its proper place' and the notion of the 'model town' in which there is 'a place for everything and everything in its place', as suggested by the influential US planner C. McKim Norton in the aptly entitled article *Elimination of incompatible uses and structures* (Norton 1955, p.305). As we have learned from, for example, Mary Douglas (1966) and Jacques Ranciérè (1999), what is considered to belong where—and in what role—is not just a practical question, amenable by the application of supposedly neutral technical expertise and, increasingly, algorithms and AI, but rather a morally charged issue that goes to the heart of the deep-seated cultural and political preconceptions of a society. It is here interesting to note that in the landmark *Village of Euclid* decision by the US Supreme Court in 1926, Judge Sutherland verifies a local authority's right to exclude 'nuisances' from residential areas, explains that nuisances need not be evil in themselves, but may also consist of 'merely a right thing in the wrong place—like a pig in a parlor instead of a barnyard' (US Supreme Court 1926, p.14). Thus, Judge Sutherland not only forcefully articulates an ideology of human-animal segregation in urban areas, but also opens up a much wider understanding of what the 'pig' represents in its cultural contexts, which—in this case—also came to legitimise the branding of certain groups of humans under the heading of 'nuisances', who were then considered legitimately excludable from the proverbial urban parlour (Valverde 2011).

To conclude, in a generic sense, segregationist approaches to perceived incompossibilities entail the attempted separation of elements that are believed not to be able to co-exist felicitously in the same local environment. In relation to other-than-humans, such segregationist approaches have generally served to enforce and uphold the 'great separation', whereby other-than-human animals were, to as large an extent as possible, expelled from Global Northern urban areas.[5] Although segregationist responses to perceived incompossibilities in flourishing are not in themselves annihilatory and violent in the manner of exterminationist responses, they nonetheless tend to breed hostility and fear of the Other, due to the sense of disconnectedness that comes with the separation from those 'on the other side of the fence'. We argue that an unproblematised and habitual enforcement of such an approach as a 'go-to solution' for troubled interspecies co-existence and perceived interspecies incompossibility is fundamentally problematic in an era in which humans, perhaps more than ever, are in need of establishing a sensibility of interconnectedness and mutual ecological dependence (see Metzger 2019).

Going Upstream to Probe Apparent Interspecies Incompossibilities

If we disagree with established exterminationist and segregationist approaches, but nonetheless would like to see urban practitioners confront incompossibilities and assume responsibility for the consequent exclusions that are performed in the planning processes that they work within, which other ways of thinking and acting are potentially available? Are there practically applicable ways of dealing with perceived interspecies incompossibilities that instead enact an ethos of multispecies co-existence, but which nonetheless avoid pandering to an untenable fantasy of limitless inclusion? Metzger (2016) proposes that planners should 'cultivate torment' regarding what existences are enabled to flourish or wither in a specific local environment, and by whom and on what basis such decisions are made. However, the smart city trend—exemplified by algorithmic, AI, and technologies like Thermacell® LIV—merely reproduces existing patterns of societal privileges and biases in a manner that obfuscates and naturalises what, in effect, are deeply ethical and political choices of a life-and-death nature. We, therefore, explore the potential of another type of approach: that of smart human judgement, which engenders thoughtfulness, transparency, and consideration of ethical values for the more-than-human.

With this purpose, we mobilise the trope of 'going upstream'. This well-established concept within Science and Technology Studies (STS) was first popularised in Bruno Latour's (1987) study of laboratory practices as a form of epistemological forensics, asking how knowledge is constructed in a specific way and with what effect. However, with Maria Puig de la Bellacasa (2017), we are also interested in practices for transforming 'matters of concern' into 'matters of care' and, thus, in how the practice of going upstream can be configured into a proactive modality of intervention, of actively engaging to make a difference. Here we find inspiration in Chia's (1996) further elaboration of Latour's metaphors and his conceptualisation of 'upstream thinking' and 'downstream thinking' as two distinctly different styles of thought in the contemporary social sciences. Whereas downstream thinking takes as given the apprehended conditions of a situation, upstream thinking instead ventures to investigate how that which we take for granted has come into existence, thus investing an interest in what we call the conditions of possibility or 'conditions of becoming' of a situation or object.

In relation to urban planning, development, and governance, going upstream points to inquiring into the preconditions that generate specific situations, and into how and why these conditions are generated, and what are the conditions of possibility for potentialities to develop in particular ways. This idea is the focus of Jullien's (1996/2004) Daoist-inspired work on efficacy, which celebrates the capability of going 'upstream', wherein the art of efficacy 'lies in an ability to predispose' (Jullien 1996/2004, p.194). Employing a military analogy, Jullien suggests that good strategists intervene upstream in a process, identifying favourable and unfavourable conditions of possibility and tendencies before they fully develop:

> All the general's strategic attention should therefore be focused on the initial stage, well 'upstream' from the point where an opportunity surfaces, for although it is by no means easy to discern, that is the discriminating moment that will imperceptibly incline the situation in a particular direction (Jullien 1996/2004, p.67).

From this identified point, a strategist can then steer the evolution of situations in a more desirable direction in such a way that the effect flows 'naturally' from it (Jullien 1996/2004, p.117) and safeguard the 'possibility of progress farther downstream' (Jullien 1996/2004, p.124).

Drawing upon the work of Latour, Chia, and Jullien, we can begin to sketch a practice of 'going upstream' as a smart way of thinking and acting that revolves around an ambition to investigate the production of conditions of becoming—what happens before a definite situation actualises itself in the form of manifest friction or conflict. The purpose of such active exploration of concrete and immanent conditions, in particular nexuses of contentious interspecies co-becoming[6] would not be to make killing easier (as the exterminationist response), or to attempt to avoid any coming-together that may evoke friction (as in the segregationist response), but rather to attempt to explore when and how, in the immanent and concrete, conditions for interspecies co-becoming in local environments can be made slightly less infelicitous.

Humans and Mosquitoes: A Story of Troubled Interspecies Coexistence

Admittedly, the above-outlined proposal of going upstream as a response to troubled interspecies co-existence in shared space is still vague. However, we now try to see how this way of thinking might be applied as a way of approaching apparent interspecies incompossibilities in urban development and management, with a particular focus on a designated pest for whom few humans spare much love or sympathy: the mosquito.

Mosquitoes probably come across to most people as one of the 'pestiest bugs', and few people would label mosquitoes as 'cute' or 'beautiful' (cf. Webb et al. 2016, for exception). Like slugs (Ginn 2014) and scorpions (Ávila and Ernstson 2019), mosquitoes are researched by relatively few social scientists outside of political entomology (see Kosek 2010) and public health-related disciplines (however, see the important recent contributions in Hall and Tamïr 2022). Mosquitoes 'trouble coexistence' (Beisel et al. 2013, p.9): the image of a mosquito, dead on the ground in a splatter of red blood, and the human, ankle itching from the 'bite',[7] reminds us 'how uneven the stakes are' when mosquito and human worlds collide (adapted from Green & Ginn 2014, p.162). In the eyes of most, human and mosquito flourishing simply appear incompossible. Mosquitoes are not generally considered to be beings worthy of our sympathy, where antipathy is often exacerbated by the fact that some mosquito species function as zoonotic vectors of dangerous diseases, including malaria and arboviruses such as Zika and Chikungunya, Japanese encephalitis, Dengue, and yellow fever (see e.g., Hawkes and Hopkins 2022). Non-human animals (particularly birds, Australian kangaroos, and wallabies) may also serve as reservoirs to further infect other mosquitoes and for pathogen transmission and spread of disease (Pagès and Cohnstaedt 2018).

It is rarely recognised, however, that not all mosquitoes are the same, though all depend on water for larval development. Only female mosquitoes take blood from humans, and not all do so. Of the c. 300 species in Australia, only about ten species carry pathogens that may affect human health. Beneficial effects of mosquitoes include contributing to the breakdown of detritus and recycling of nutrients in aquatic systems, providing food for other species, pollinating plants, and so on. Yet, mosquitoes tend to be stereotyped as disease-carrying pests to be killed. We suggest that humans could be deemed at least partly responsible for the spread of such pathogenic disease (mosquitoes must become infected by biting an infected human or non-human animal before they can transmit the pathogen) and, indeed, for the spread of mosquitoes themselves. A wild ecology of mosquitoes often flourishes as a result of urban land use planning interventions, which create novel ecosystems such as riverine and estuarine suburban development, dredging of waterways and canals, modification and construction of wetlands, artificial lakes and lagoons, and so on.

Hillier (2021) suggests that in Australia, in this case specifically Western Australia (WA), strategic planning practice, especially for urban fringe residential development, demonstrates several 'blind spots' as it neglects the relational complexity of human/non-human assemblages and health-environment encounters. The WA system displays a vertical, hierarchical system of institutional silos, in which some institutional voices wield more power than others. Mosquito-related issues are generally not included in WA local planning policies, strategies, or schemes. Mosquitoes are not regarded as being planning's responsibility, while mosquito-related issues are perceived as being 'too complicated' and 'may constrain development too much' (Steven 2016). Mosquitoes are not recognised as a planning concern and health officers possess only advisory capacity in what experts regards as a 'real disconnect' (Hillier 2021, p.22).

Hillier (2021; Hillier and Metzger 2021) interrogates a concrete case of (sub)urban development in WA, which involves significant transformation of (semi-)riparian habitat into a master planned residential estate. The site is a riverine, development industry-awarded residential estate on the south-west fringes of the Perth metropolitan region (Figure 7.2). It comprised areas of native vegetation with some understorey cleared for trails, firebreaks, and for farm cattle to roam. The site was zoned 'future urban' in 1997 by the WA State planning department[8] and 'Urban Development—Environmental Conditions' by the local planning authority in 2006 in an amendment brought by the proposed estate developer.

Development of the fifty-two-ha site commenced in 2008 and has now reached Stage 5 of a projected seven stages. House and land packages feature a 0.9-ha artificial lagoon and the lower reaches of a significant river. The development was approved by the local municipality and the WA State government Department of Planning, Lands and Heritage, with referrals made to State-wide statutory consultees, such as the Department of Water and Environmental Regulation, including the Environmental Protection Authority (EPA), in addition to relevant local authority sections such as Public Works and Health Services. The estate development has created novel ecosystems along the river edge and artificial lagoon. A site visit during construction of Stage 3 evidenced flourishing mosquito colonies around the lagoon, several *Psittaciformes* species, including cockatoos and parrots (avian reservoirs of mosquito-related pathogens), and snakes (dugites and a carpet python) in the then-undeveloped land adjacent to the estate. Residents complained about the presence of white ibises (commonly referred to as 'bin chickens') foraging and defecating in gardens and quendas (bandicoots) digging holes in lawns (pers. comm. 2018; see also Sheikh et al. 2022). Mosquitoes are locally regarded as a 'particular nuisance', with local residents protesting that they feel like 'prisoners in our own home' and being eaten alive (Lawson 2021). The planning application for the area comprised an Outline Development Plan and twenty-one reports, including an Environmental Assessment Report and ten Management Plans, including those for Mosquitoes,

Figure 7.2 View of Riverine Estate, 2022.
Source: Google Earth. Image © Maxar Technologies.

Wildlife, Artificial Water Bodies, and so on. However, the EPA evaluated the proposal as not requiring assessment due to the small and degraded nature of the site, and the EPA (2000) *Guidance Statement for Management of Mosquitoes by Land Developers* was (and still is) no longer extant. Consequently, according to the regulations in force, dealing with unwanted non-human 'intruders' or 'pests' is primarily the householders' responsibility.

Figure 7.3 Mosquito warning signage.
Photograph: Jean Hillier.

While the estate developer has erected signage warning of mosquitoes in the area (Figure 7.3), it has passed mosquito 'management' responsibility to individual residents through their compulsory entry into private covenants to fit all exterior doors, windows, vents, and pipes with insect screens and to use exterior insect lighting.

Unsurprisingly, insecticide use is high. 'Smart' technology, such as the Thermacell® LIV Smart system finds a ready market in such areas, and mosquito treatment companies report thriving business. The local authority aerially sprays public land for mosquito larvae in the breeding season, with treatment intensity increasing as warmer and wetter climate conditions favour mosquito breeding capacity. The possible multiplier effects of such actions are not considered. But it is known that electronic and chemical repellents and insecticides applied to residential gardens and public open spaces affect broader ecosystems, for example, by killing many pollinating insects—and potentially harming pets and humans.

Stuck in their institutional silos, planning practitioners ignored the conditions of possibility for such actualisation. Site-specific conditions for this estate include the area being part of a wetland/swamp system that, due to its potential for flooding and known prevalence of mosquito and midge breeding sites, was previously not developed when the local region expanded significantly in the 1970s. In addition, there was no EPA assessment; there were possibilities that the land would not be adequately drained after clearing and before construction, leading to flooding and large pools of standing water conducive to mosquito breeding; and possibilities that the developer might not enforce or monitor resident adherence to covenants regarding provision of insect screens and so on.

It is important to be clear that our argument is not that local human residents should accept being infected by serious mosquito-induced disease. However, we are wary to suggest that it is the mosquito in itself that 'induces' the disease, but rather wish to point to the production of conditions that generate situations that make it expectable that humans will be put in harm's way. As the Australian local municipality admits: 'many residential areas are located close to mosquito breeding sites'.[9] We seem to forget that mosquitoes were around long before humans and that, if anything, we are actually the guests in their habitat, rather than the other way round. What we are rather suggesting is that an examination of 'upstream' events and decisions that have contributed to producing infelicitous conditions of interspecies co-becoming between humans and mosquitoes quite expectedly generate situations downstream in which humans feel a need to call for the local extermination of mosquitoes so as to protect their own wellbeing.

The recent WA Department of Health (2022) mosquito management training course was targeted at those working in environmental and public health, water and wastewater management, environmental engineering, and pest control. Notably missing were urban planning practitioners. The course offered lectures and mosquito identification sessions together with industry 'control approaches, chemicals, and equipment, including displays and demonstrations' and 'group larviciding exercises' (DoH 2022). Extermination appears to be the key approach. There seems to be little, if any, room for discussion of segregation or utilising First Nations' approaches to living with mosquitoes.[10]

First Nations Australians perform relational onto-epistemologies that are very different to those of the Western-centric settler colonialists, which silence or marginalise non-Western voices. First Nation onto-epistemologies are inherently landscape embedded (Wooltorton et al. 2019), non-dualistic, recognising the agency of non-human entities in more-than-human relationships. First Nation peoples in Western

Australia recognise that they are the ones intruding into mosquito habitat when entering or living in riparian or saltmarsh areas. They have traditionally burned the bark and leaves from the bush plum or sandalwood (*Santalum lanceolatum*) to keep mosquitoes away and relieve bites by application of bracken fern (*Pteridium esculentum*) shoots and root fibres. For many people in the twenty-first century, however, bush plum smoke and bracken fern shoots are insufficiently 'smart' ways of coping with unwanted pests, preferring strategies of extermination (removal of breeding sites, application of insecticides, introduction of predators such as mosquito fish and microbats) and of segregation (planning buffers between wetlands and residential land, design and management of artificial water bodies, e.g., lakes, canals, stormwater systems and so on) to discourage mosquito breeding. Applications of smart technology focus on mosquito monitoring, control, and consequent extermination.

We suggest, however, that supposedly 'smart' solutions based on an exterminationist approach—such as the SMDS system in Thiruvananthapuram—may actually be founded on a pretty unsmart premise, in that they accept as given or inevitable the apparent incompossibility in human–mosquito flourishing and fail to look upstream and probe how and why such infelicitous conditions of co-becoming might be produced. It becomes clear that much human and non-human suffering could have been avoided, in our example, if greater care had been taken to consider probable patterns of human–mosquito interaction in the planned local environment. We even suggest that the failure to do so in this particular case, given the location of the development, possibly signals a wilful blindness (Finn and Stephens 2017) against taking these conditions into account.

We can only speculate regarding the conditions of possibility of such outcomes in the planning and development processes. But it would appear that the upstream economic, social, and political drivers of residential urban fringe development in WA outweighed local conditions of possibility of mosquito flourishing in a floodplain ecosystem. In our case, a politically and economically driven culture of suburban home ownership, social perception of lifestyle, a culture of development as progress, dynamics of capitalist value-extraction and related land-value speculation, and consequent pressure to develop new residential areas on land deemed as unsuitable for residential development (due to the surrounding ecological conditions) led to the land being zoned 'future urban' and subsequently 'urban', while not considering the expectably infelicitous human–mosquito encounters that this would—seemingly inevitably—produce.

Going Upstream towards a Smarter Milieu-Based Approach

We regard movements towards bringing equality issues into the mainstream discourse on smart cities as important (though with some reservations). However, it is crucial to remember that the smart city, no more or less than any other local environment, can never be 'for all'. Exclusions will always be made in urban planning, development, and governance processes. Consequently, responsibility needs to be assumed for how such decisions are made, and their effects. This entails asking questions about where to draw any concrete line of exclusion/inclusion, who should be part of the process of drawing that line, and on what ground should they be drawn?

One broad swathe of exclusion that is, seemingly, taken for granted in the established smart city discourse is that of wild and feral animals. They are generally branded as pests, making them killable without further consideration. In this book chapter, we have cast pests in the context of the smart city in the role of 'the Idiot', a figure that forces us to consider what we are really busy doing, whether we might actually be wrong in how we think about and act in the world, and whether we should 'misbehave' and think and do otherwise. We have further suggested that when it comes to pests in the city more generally, established responses from urban planning and development practice tend to fall into one of two broad categories: exterminationism or segregationism.

Above, we have groped toward a third potential option we have tentatively suggested calling a practice of 'going upstream' as a first step of attempting to untangle apparent incompossibilities in troubled interspecies co-existence in local environments. By going upstream, a community of inquiry aims to go through the loop of uncovering how and why infelicitous conditions of interspecies co-becoming may be produced, and how they may potentially be influenced otherwise. We provide no definite, detailed definition of what might and might not be included in the practice of going upstream but, through our example, suggest that it involves tracing and mapping of multifarious entangled natural, social, economic, political, etc., relations that come together to shape local conditions of becoming. Such an approach rhymes very well with Hillier and Metzger's (2021) tentative outline of a milieu-based approach to urban planning, which emphasises relational links and encounters between elements—human and non-human—and what they might do. It is an approach that we hope gestures another way, beyond and away from exterminationism and segregationism.

In our case of troubled urban fringe human–mosquito co-becoming, it may easily come across as if human and mosquito flourishing are simply incompossible. We suggest, however, that a milieu-based approach offers the opportunity to assess how different heterogenous elements have interacted with one another in the past, the present, and might do so in the future, and what implications such encounters and interactions might have in terms of capacities and affects. For instance, instead of regarding rivers and wetlands as ready-made, pre-existing 'backgrounds' for human activity (such as an aesthetic residential environment), it would begin by regarding the relations between the river/wetland and the various forms of human and non-human life that inhabit it and interact with it and to speculate what might emerge. It would ask what the river/wetland can do if a residential estate is developed adjacent to it. How might the river/wetland enable some elements to flourish (such as mosquitoes, cyanobacteria, human aesthetics, house prices, development profit) and some to be affected deleteriously (flooding of homes and infrastructure, human and non-human health, and so on)? It would also consider potential encounters and interactions between many other elements—economic, environmental, socio-cultural, political—relating to the milieus; what are their conditions of possibility, what might they do, and with what impact.

'Negotiating' with the milieu in our WA example could, for instance, have entailed learning from First Nations Traditional Owners, leaving space for rivers to flood, avoiding developing land on heavy clay soils that 'require' severe drainage systems that can disturb water tables; minimising hard runoff surfaces; not using chemical pesticides and insecticides or non-native species to make a more human-aesthetic landscape, and so on. It might also entail learning to look for productive emergences in novel ecosystems, for instance, ensuring that water flow in wetlands could encourage fish that eat mosquito larvae or leaving trees as roosting places for microbats (*Vespadelus vulturnus*) who prey on insects such as mosquitoes, midges, termites, and fruit flies.

In the face of the intense pressure for land-value extraction and the largely unchecked influence of urban development in Australia, as well as in many other parts of the world, prospects for introducing such novel methods currently may appear limited. So, what stands in the way of such a shift in practice are perhaps not only ingrained cultural preconceptions, but also the vested interests and established governance arrangements of capital extraction from land ownership. It appears as if a key step towards any type of shift towards a truly more ecological sensibility in urban planning and development would require facing up to the unbridled interests of feral capitalism—although, unfortunately, the global prospects for this at present come across as bleak.

How do smart city practices and technologies fit into all this? We understand the fundamental idea of the smart city as an epitome of the Society of Control (Krivý 2018), in which human and other-than-human urban activity can be monitored, controlled, and modulated, often under the labels of Smart Environment and Smart Governance (Sheikh et al. 2023). Almost all the Smart Environment technologies that we have discovered in our research relating to pests have generally been designed with the purpose of facilitating their effective extermination. Perhaps, however, smart technologies, such as those used in India and Australia, which map mosquito breeding sites, could be employed in urban planning practice with a view to avoiding development on and adjacent to mosquito breeding habitats and dispersal areas. For instance, if it could be mandatory for development applications in areas of known mosquito habitat to include a smart-technology generated map that identifies the species present (demonstrating the potential existence of a zoonotic vector or otherwise) and its spatial extent, planning authorities could work with public health entomologists to either reject the development, or demand and specify the width of buffers between mosquito and human habitats, or approve the development subject to an agreed mosquito management plan. We argue that, although we would welcome it, such a planning policy is still largely based on exclusion and an understanding that humans and mosquitoes are incompossible. Nevertheless, we suggest that such a strategy at least leaves space for the mosquitoes' own habitats. In this manner, mosquitoes are acknowledged as Idiotic elements of the development milieu, acting relationally with other elements, with capacities to connect with and affect human and non-human beings in various ways (Hillier 2021, p.24).

Acknowledgements

We thank the editors and the two reviewers for their encouraging and helpful comments which helped us sharpen and clarify our argument.

Notes

1. https://www.thehindu.com/news/cities/Thiruvananthapuram/smart-mosquito-surveillance-system-for-thiruvananthapuram/article32849932.ece
2. https://www2.deloitte.com/us/en/insights/industry/public-sector/inclusive-smart-cities.html
3. 'Bug' is an umbrella term popularly used to refer to harmful micro-organisms, such as bacteria and parasites, as well as small insects.
4. We recognise that, for Deleuze, incompossibilities may be generative and a source of creative action. This aspect of incompossibility is explored at length by Hillier and Metzger (2021). See also the argument about 'upstream' engagement further below.
5. However, we must not forget that there are other societies in which this movement was never as fully implemented as in many parts of the Global North. For instance, in many parts of Indian society, where a strict separation of humans and animals would be unimaginable, and even considered immoral.
6. Co-becoming is an ontological conceptualisation in which everything exists in a state of emergence and relationality (Bawaka Country et al. 2016, p.456).
7. The female mosquito does not actually bite but pierces the skin with her proboscis, through which she injects anticoagulant saliva and sucks blood.
8. All land zoned 'future urban' in the region was rezoned as 'urban' by the State in 2002.
9. https://www.mandurah.wa.gov.au/live/residents/health-and-safety/pest-control
10. 'Cultural control' in mosquito management does not relate to First Nations' approaches, but to manipulation of cultural practices, such as educating residents not to leave water-holding objects, like flower-pot saucers, pet bowls, and so on, uncovered.

References

Anon (2018, October 31). 'STD-ridden' ladybirds heading for UK. *The Week.* http://www.theweek.co.uk/78143/std-ridden-ladybirds-heading-for-uk

Atkins, P. (Ed.). (2012). *Animal cities: Beastly urban histories.* Ashgate.

Ávila M., & Ernstson H. (2019). Realms of exposure: A speculative design perspective of material agency and political ecology. In H. Ernstson S. Sörlin (Eds.), *Grounding urban natures: Histories and futures of urban ecologies* (pp.137–166). MIT Press.

Bawaka Country, Wright, S., Suchet-Pearson, S., Lloyd, K., Burarrwanga, L., Ganambarr, R., Ganambarr-Stubbs, M., Ganambarr, B., Maymuru, D., & Sweeney, J. (2016). Co-becoming Bawaka: Towards a relational understanding of place/space. *Progress in Human Geography, 40*(4), 455–475.

Beisel, U., Kelly, A., & Tousignant, N. (2013) Knowing insects: Hosts, vectors and companions of science, *Science as Culture, 22*(1), 1–15.

Bowden, S. (2010). Deleuze's neo-Leibnizianism, events and '*The Logic of Sense*'s' 'static ontological genesis'. *Deleuze Studies, 4*(3), 301–328.

Bylund, J., & Byerley, A. (2014). Hopeless postpolitics, professional idiots and the fate of public space in Stockholm parklife. In J. Metzger, P. Allmendinger, & S. Oosterlynck (Eds.), *Planning against the political: Democratic deficits in European territorial governance* (pp. 129–152). Routledge.

Chia, R. (1996). *Organizational analysis as deconstructive practice.* de Gruyter.

Crowley, S. L., Hinchliffe, S., & McDonald, R. A. (2018). Killing squirrels: Exploring motivations and practices of lethal wildlife management. *Environment and Planning E: Nature and Space, 1*(1–2), 120–143.

Deleuze, G. (2004) *The logic of sense* (M. Lester, Trans.). Continuum. (Original work published 1969)

Deleuze, G., & Guattari, F. (1994). *What is philosophy?* (H. Tomlinson & G. Burchill, Trans.). Verso. (Original work published 1991)

Department of Health (DoH). (2022). Mosquito management training course. Registration Package. https://www.health.wa.gov.au/

Douglas, M. (1966). *Purity and danger: An analysis of concepts of pollution and taboo.* Routledge and K Paul.

Ducarme, F., Luque, G. M., & Courchamp, F. (2013). What are 'charismatic species' for conservation biologists. *BioSciences Master Reviews*, *10*(2013), 1–8.

EPA. (2000). Guidance statement for management of mosquitoes by land developers. Final Guidance Statement No. *40*. Environmental Protection Authority.

Fantini van Ditmar, D. (2019). The IdIoT in the smart home. In S. M. Figueiredo, S. Krishnamurthy, & T. W.A. Schröder (Eds.), *Architecture and the smart city* (pp. 157–164). Routledge.

Farías, I. (2017). An idiotic catalyst: Accelerating the slowing down of thinking and action. *Cultural Anthropology*, *32*(1), 35–41.

Finn, H., & Stephens, N. (2017). The invisible harm: Land clearing is an issue of animal welfare. *Wildlife Research*, *44*, 377–391.

Ginn, F. (2014). Sticky lives: slugs, detachment and more-than-human ethics in the garden. *Transactions of the Institute of British Geographers*, *39*(4), 532–544.

Ginn, F., Beisel, U., & Barua, M. (2014). Flourishing with awkward creatures: Togetherness, vulnerability, killing. *Environmental Humanities*, *4*(1),113–123.

Green K., & Ginn F. (2014). The smell of selfless love: Sharing vulnerability with bees in alternative apiculture. *Environmental Humanities*, *4*, 149–170. http://environmentalhumanities.org/arch/vol4/4.8.pdf

Hall, M., & Tamïr, D. (Eds.). (2022). *Mosquitopia: The place of pests in a healthy world.* Routledge/Earthscan.

Hawkes, F. M., & Hopkins, R. J. (2022). The mosquito: An introduction. In M. Hall & D. Tamïr (Eds.), *Mosquitopia: The place of pests in a healthy world* (pp. 16–31). Routledge/Earthscan.

Hillier, J. (2017). No place to go? Management of non-human animal overflows in Australia. *European Management Journal*, *35*(6), 712–721.

Hillier, J. (2021) 'The 'flatness' of Deleuze and Guattari: Planning the city as a tree or as a rhizome? *dISP–The Planning Review*, *57*(2), 16–29.

Hillier, J., & Byrne, J. (2016). Is extermination to be the legacy of Mary Gilbert's cat? *Organization*, *23*(3), 387–406.

Hillier, J., & Metzger, J. (2021). Towns within towns: From incompossibility to inclusive disjunction in urban spatial planning. *Deleuze and Guattari Studies*, *15*(1), 40–64.

Hubbard, P., & Brooks, A. (2021). Animals and urban gentrification: Displacement and injustice in the trans-species city. *Progress in Human Geography*, *45*(6), 1490–1511.

Instone, L., & Sweeney, J. (2014). Dog waste, wasted dogs: The contribution of human–dog relations to the political economy of Australian urban space. *Geographical Research*, *52*(4), 355–364.

Jullien, F. (2004). *A treatise on efficacy* (J. Lloyd, Trans.). University of Hawai'i Press. (Original work published 1996)

Kitchin, R. (2016). The ethics of smart cities and urban science. *Philosophical Transactions. Series A, Mathematical, Physical, and Engineering Sciences*, *374*(2083), Article 20160115. https://doi.org/10.1098/rsta.2016.0115

Korngold, D., Lemos, M., & Rohwer, M. (2017). Smart cities for all: A vision for an inclusive, accessible, urban future. AT&T.

Kosek, J. (2010). Ecologies of empire: On the new uses of the honeybee. *Cultural Anthropology*, *25*(4), 650–678.

Krivý, M. (2018). Towards a critique of cybernetic urbanism: The smart city and the society of control. *Planning Theory*, *17*(1), 8–30.

Latour, B. (1987). *Science in action: How to follow scientists and engineers through society.* Harvard University Press.

Lynteris, C. (2020) Introduction: Infectious animals and epidemic blame. In C. Lynteris (Ed.), *Framing Animals as Epidemic Villains* (pp. 1–25). Palgrave Macmillan/Springer Nature.

McKiernan, S., & Instone, L. (2016). From pest to partner: Rethinking the Australian White Ibis in the more-than-human city. *Cultural Geographies*, *23*(3), 475–494.

Mattern, S. (2021). *A city is not a computer: Other urban intelligences.* Princeton University Press.

Metzger, J. (2016). Cultivating torment: The cosmopolitics of more-than-human urban planning. *City*, *20*(4), 581–601.

Metzger, J. (2019). A more-than-human approach to environmental planning. In S. Davoudi, R. Cowell, I. White, & H. Blanco (Eds.), *The Routledge companion to environmental planning* (pp. 190–199). Routledge.
Michael, M. (2012). 'What are we busy doing?' Engaging the idiot. *Science, Technology and Human Values, 37*(5), 528–554.
Montgomery, B., Cianci, J., Einsiedel, D., Hall-Mendelin, S., Mcmahon, J., & Rocha, P. (2021). Zika mozzie seeker: Queensland citizen scientists are innovating invasive *Aedes* mosquito surveillance. https://www.researchgate.net/publication/355424330_Zika_Mozzie_Seeker_Queensland_citizen_scientists_are_innovating_invasive_Aedes_mosquito_surveillance_30_Aug_2021
Norton, C. M. (1955). Elimination of incompatible uses and structures. *Law and Contemporary Problems, 20*, 305.
O'Leary, C. (2017, January 18). WA worst for fatal bug bites. *The West Australian*. https://thewest.com.au/news/wa/wa-worst-for-fatal-bug-bites-ng-b88358085z
Paddenburg, T. (2016, September 18). Pests run rampant in Perth suburbs. https://www.news.com.au/national/western-australia/pests-run-rampant-in-perth-suburbs/news-story/5d2a6d790988d53481a52462f88ccd06
Pagès, N., & Cohnstaedt, L. (2018). Mosquito-borne diseases in the livestock industry. In C. Garros, J. Bouyer, W. Takken, & R. Smallegange (Eds.), *Pests and vector-borne diseases in the livestock industry* (pp. 195–219). Wageningen Academic Publishers.
Power, E. R. (2009). Border-processes and homemaking: Encounters with possums in suburban Australian homes. *Cultural Geographies, 16*(1), 29–54.
Puig de la Bellacasa, M. (2017). *Matters of care: Speculative ethics in more than human worlds*. University of Minnesota Press.
Rancière, J. (1999). *Disagreement: Politics and philosophy*. University of Minnesota Press.
Rose, D. B. (2012). Cosmopolitics: The kiss of life. *New Formations, 76*, 101–113.
Sheikh, H., Foth, M., & Mitchell, P. (2022). (Re)imagining the ibis: Multispecies future(s), smart urban governance, and the digital environmental humanities. In *Routledge handbook of the digital environmental humanities* (pp. 490–515). Routledge. https://doi.org/10.4324/9781003082798-39
Sheikh, H., Foth, M., & Mitchell, P. (2023). More-than-human city-region foresight: Multispecies entanglements in regional governance and planning. *Regional Studies*, 57(4), 642–655. https://doi.org/10.1080/00343404.2022.2045266
Smart Cities Council. (2021). Combating mosquito menace: Thiruvananthapuram installs Smart Mosquito Density System. https://www.smartcitiescouncil.com/article/combating-mosquito-menace-thiruvananthapuram-installs-smart-mosquito-density-system
Stengers, I. (2005a). The cosmopolitical proposal. In B. Latour and P. Weibel (Eds.), *Making Things Public: Atmospheres of Democracy* (pp. 994–1003). MIT Press.
Stengers, I. (2005b). Deleuze and Guattari's last enigmatic message. *Angelaki, 10*(2), 151–167.
Steven, P. (2016) 'How Urban Planning Can be Used to Mitigate the Impacts of Mosquitoes on Residential Development in WA.' Presented at Planning Institute of Australia Regional Conference, Bunbury. 9 June, available at https://www.ehawa.org.au/documents/item/1004
Sutton, Z., & Taylor, N. (2019). Managing the borders: Static/dynamic nature and the 'management' of 'problem' species. *Parallax, 25*(4), 379–394.
Tironi, M., & Valderrama, M. (2019). Acknowledging the idiot in the smart city: Experimentation and citizenship in the making of a low-carbon district in Santiago de Chile. In A. Karvonen, F. Cugurullo, & F. Caprotti (Eds.), *Inside smart cities* (pp. 183–199). Routledge.
US Supreme Court (1926). *Village of Euclid, Ohio v Ambler Realty Co. 272US365*. www.caselaw.lp.findlaw.com/scripts/getcase.pl?=court=US&vol=272&invol=365
Valverde, M. (2011). Seeing like a city: The dialectic of modern and premodern ways of seeing in urban governance. *Law and Society Review, 45*(2), 277–312.
Webb, C., Doggett, S., & Russell, R. (2016). *A guide to mosquitoes of Australia*. CSIRO.
Wooltorton, S., Collard, L., & Horwitz, P. (2019). Layers of meaning in our landscapes: Hiding in full view. In M. Ellis (Ed.), *Critical global semiotics: Understanding sustainable transformational citizenship* (pp. 96–108). Routledge.

8

Designing Data Dramas to Build Empathy to Nature through Collective Acts

Annika Wolff, Anne Pässilä, Allan Owens, and Lasse Kantola

Introduction to Designing Data Dramas

In urban environments, people live side by side with nature without always noticing it. Yet even unseen wildlife and habitats are important, and their loss can destabilise ecosystems, removing natural mechanisms for pollution or disease control. Therefore, as well as environmental effects, biodiversity loss has also been linked with negative impacts on human health and wellbeing, both directly, for example, on people's mental health or the diversity of the internal microbiome (Hough 2014) and indirectly, for example, through loss of species that are the basis of existing and new medicines (Alves and Rosa 2007).

Both *climate change* and *urban development* threaten urban biodiversity, via habitat loss and soil, air, or water pollution (Puppim de Oliveira et al. 2014). Taking the example of *water pollution*, the effects of climate change may be seen in the degradation of water quality, since increased water temperature can encourage algal blooms to flourish, which in turn affects oxygen levels in the water, impacting on which fish species do well and which disappear. Often, it is the invasive fish that thrive, impacting local species (Puppim de Oliveira et al. 2014). At the same time, urban development may also have an impact on water quality, for example, through improper wastewater management or policies for dumping by factories. Often such actions are taken because urban habitats are badly documented and even where ecological knowledge is available, its application during urban planning is limited (Niemelä 1999).

While there has been a push to improve collaborations between urban planners and local communities to make more locally informed planning decisions, such processes have typically remained anthropocentric and there are few formal processes through which to foreground the concerns of the environment and non-humans. One barrier is that these concerns are often invisible—*without their own voice, non-humans require humans to advocate on their behalf.* Data is increasingly being collected about nature and biodiversity in urban environments and can potentially be used to amplify non-human voices in planning processes, but only if people are willing and able to engage with it. Data can seem cold, sterile, hard, and unyielding. Yet recently the discussion has moved towards understanding that data can be subjective, that the interpretation may depend on the context of who is looking at the data and why (Loukissas 2019). Interpretation of data may require consensus,

Annika Wolff, Anne Pässilä, Allan Owens, and Lasse Kantola, *Designing Data Dramas to Build Empathy to Nature through Collective Acts.* In: *Designing More-than-Human Smart Cities.* Edited by: Sara Heitlinger, Marcus Foth, and Rachel Clarke, Oxford University Press. © Oxford University Press (2024). DOI: 10.1093/9780191980060.003.0010 such as through participatory approaches, and this can also be political. It is therefore necessary to discover how to make the data easier and more enjoyable to use in a participatory way that fosters debate and allows for different viewpoints to be discussed non-confrontationally.

In this chapter we describe a method called data drama that is designed to build empathy via immersive experience with data, using arts-based approaches to encourage different viewpoints, combined with data curation techniques to make it easier to use. Through the process we aim to learn what is more or less important for engaging people with environmental data sets and the issues to which they relate. We do not propose that planning processes should orchestrate complicated drama procedures, although towards the end of the chapter we identify some possible steps for bringing people and the environment closer together, via data. We present our case study in the context of a lake in Lahti, Finland that has been undergoing actions to improve water quality over recent decades.

Background

Data storytelling, drama, and urban design

Environmental data may inform urban planning. Recently, this has included the use of 'big data' collected at scale, through sensors and social media, as well as smaller data sets, such as that collected through observation (Thakuriah et al. 2017). When viewed from the perspective of a smart-city vision, this data is an important resource. On the one hand, the data may be used directly to drive real-time smart services, for example, tracking daily air pollution levels or providing input to city planners to help them manage urban environments more effectively. On the other hand, the data can also be used indirectly as a source of evidence, to guide problem-solving, and to inform the creation of smart-city infrastructures and services. However, when defining what benefits the data can bring, it is not always straightforward to embed it into a participatory process where data expertise may vary. Data storytelling is a term commonly used to refer to a particular perspective and interpretation of data towards an audience. The story may appear in different forms, but often comprises a data visualisation with an accompanying explanation. By making choices to include particular aspects of the data set and to analyse it and present it in a certain way, other aspects of the data set may be excluded, and alternative explanations or views may not be readily apparent. As such, the data story may reflect an author's specific focus or underlying bias but at the same time be more accessible to people. Thus, data storytelling can be a useful tool to help people get the full benefit of what data might tell them about their city (De Simone et al. 2014), as long as it also leads to critical thinking and understanding of potential bias. Matei and Hunter (2021) question what makes 'good' data storytelling. Is it enough to combine a data visualisation with a few facts, if the story does not prompt further curiosity and questions? Or should a good story contain elements of the unexpected so that it leads to deeper engagement and continued interest?

Moving beyond storytelling to more performative approaches, various researchers have explored drama and enactment—utilising elements of role-play, professional improv, and acting—using curated data as probes to provoke dialogue and provide important information. This approach has been effective to support experiencing (not just imagining) speculative futures in different settings, such as role-playing around planning a wedding in which data is collected as mementos alongside other artefacts like photographs (Elsden et al. 2017). It has also been applied for reducing tensions between stakeholders discussing wicked problems (Pschetz et al. 2019) and in helping people to better advocate on behalf of their own personal data as well as to better understand people's differences (Pothong et al. 2021). Such approaches demonstrate the importance of drama and roleplay for empowerment, for supporting different viewpoints, and for creating experiential aspects to the processes of engaging with data.

From a more-than-human perspective, we are most interested in the role that drama might play in cultivating emotion and building empathy, not only between people, but also towards non-humans and the environment; evidence shows that storytelling can foster empathy (Hibbin 2016) and drama provides the possibility of deeper engagement and for promoting empowerment. Empathy is often referred to as the ability to share feelings with and relate to someone or something other than yourself. Research has shown that our innate human empathy towards other species is related with how closely they resemble us and in turn this affects how compassionate we feel towards them. This is similar to our empathy to other humans: we might empathise more naturally with an elderly neighbour than with all elderly people in the world (Bregman 2020), towards some of whom we may even feel xenophobic. This dilemma is addressed in the arts, and especially in drama education (Owens 2014), where moving between drama and real-world life creates the possibility to make the familiar seem strange and the strange seem familiar (Brecht 1964). One way to build empathy and therefore compassion towards a topic is to increase knowledge (Miralles et al. 2019). Empathy is also more likely to be elicited in response to cues that are *salient*. Kaninsky et al. (2018) used such principles, via data sets collected from local bat populations, to develop a multi-modal interface to evoke empathy and curiosity towards bats. A context for data exploration was provided in the form of an interactive story that relayed background information and also provided an entry point to visual, tactile, and auditory activities, such as allowing people to listen to different bat sounds, slowed down to make them audible to the human ear, or exploring live bat activity data via a visual map. These activities increased the salience of the data collected about the bats, thereby increasing the potential for empathy to develop.

Empathy is also considered to play an important role in addressing climate change. However, it may be hampered by what has been called an *empathy gap*, across **space** (direct climate effects are seen more in developing countries, and those in more developed countries perceive them as far away) and **time** (a problem for distant future generations, not directly relevant to here and now). Brönnimann and Wintzer (2019) have also coined the term *climate data empathy* to refer to contextual aspects such as political, economic, technological, and cultural histories that may affect climate data interpretation and use. For example, the coverage of climate data availability is unequal and developing countries may have fewer historical data from which to draw evidence of climate impacts and to advocate for change. Making such context more transparent and available alongside data sets may allow for more nuanced use of such data and in turn may do a better job at raising awareness of the issues and provide a more solid basis for decision making.

What these examples show is that empathy is important for understanding more-than-human concerns, but that empathy may not always be naturally present. Data sets may provide important information that can help empathy to develop, but without being interpreted towards an audience they may lack *salience* and they may lack other important context necessary for building empathy.

Arts-based approaches used in co-design

Co-design, and especially participatory elements of the process (Manzini & Rizzo 2011), holds a rich tradition of creative methods in engaging people and communities (traditionally seen as citizens) in urban planning (Wolff et al. 2021). However, engagement can be challenging for some people, such as those who do not find their place, power, or agency in the planning process (Krensky & Steffen 2008). In a situation like this, democratic citizenship is challenged and we need to learn together how to make change towards citizenship of the world (Nussbaum 2010). We remind ourselves here that the use of the concept 'Design' within the grand challenges of sustainability is in itself paradoxical. While being widely understood to be an integral part of the 'engine of economic growth within the consumerist system', there is an acute awareness of the fact that 'we cannot grow longer' (Ayvazova 2017). In other words, design as conventionally conceived is part of the problem when the fundamental ideology of design is as a consumer service where there are providers and producers and people are seen as users of, rather than actors in, a democratic system (Mouffe 2009).

One way to approach this paradox is to learn critical thinking together, following Freire's idea of the dialogical encounter conceptualised as a form of intervention in the world (Freire 1970/2000). In this alternative dialogical space participants' world views are incorporated into the learning process as a priority, and dialogue is rooted in the participants' real-life worlds brought into action through collective imagined experience. It is in this way that participants are encouraged to take up multi-perspective positions in order to move out of familiar circles of certainty and so support deeper thinking about a topic (Pässilä et al. 2013; Adams and Owens 2016). These are needed when the focus is on global environmental and social problems generated by the root causes of sustainability (Björgvinsson et al. 2012). In such perplexity, where differences of opinion around complicated ideas may lead to conflicting views, arts and arts-based approaches (Adams and Owens 2021) with their ability to create alternative dialogical spaces (Lehikoinen et al 2015; Biagioli et al. 2021; Eddy et al. 2021) offer one solution for civic agency in co-design (Berman and Allen 2012; Mchunu & Berman 2018).

In our study we conceptualise the form of our data-driven theatre practice—data drama—drawing on dialogical theatre practices that are applied to developmental learning processes. Our use of drama education conventions in a theatre setting

(Pässilä 2012; Owens 2014) focuses on the multi-voiced interpretation of existing situations; interpretation takes place between the theoretical frameworks of 'as *is*' and 'as *if*' and this resonates with Freire's fundamental pedagogical ideas. In this case participants are citizens of the world making sense of data affecting them, us, and the environmental, economic, political, social, and cultural ecosystem of which we are part. The drama-based approaches mentioned so far have taken a naturalistic, speculative approach to create imaginary worlds in which the distance between the drama and the phenomena being investigated is clear. However, the dramaturgical approach we take is pushing in a different direction such that it is concerned with metaphorical, affective staging of encounter where the intention is to make the familiar strange and the strange familiar.

A Framework for Data Drama

In previous sections we explored different aspects of data storytelling, empathy, and arts-based approaches, which led to the following hypotheses:

1. Data can foster empathy towards non-human concerns, *if curated to make the issues more salient.*
2. Data storytelling can make data easier to understand for a general audience. It can also foster empathy and build interest towards a topic, but to do so it should *go beyond trivial story structures towards stories that provide an element of surprise and foster curiosity to explore the topic further.*
3. Arts-based approaches also foster empathy towards problems but at the same time *support both imagination and criticality of thinking.* They can be effectively used to mobilise people to act around a common problem.

All of the above is important within more-than-human design scenarios for building consensus on the meaning of data in the local context and using local community knowledge. *Arts-based approaches therefore often require active involvement from participants that may not fit immediately to typical data storytelling media.* Thus, we have explored **data drama** as a method for framing environmental data and fostering empathy towards more-than-human concerns. We propose that data drama is an *interactive form* of data storytelling best suited to **collaborative explorations of data**.

We propose that a data drama should follow conventions of storytelling that include *suspense* in order to foster engagement and interaction of the participants to the story. For these reasons, we have envisaged data drama as something that is only half-formed—a series of frames that lead to questions and set up moments of tension, via a type of *benign manipulation.* As such, staging a data drama means organising a space for discussion—for example, about who owns data, what data means, and using an *evidence-driven* approach, but where the scenario is set in such a way that it is possible to explore these questions without any expectation that there is a single perspective to take in the search for an answer.

To understand data drama, note that merging data and theatre approaches is not a new concept. For over three decades different forms of drama and theatre have been used as methods of analysing data and translating findings for a wider audience than that comprised of the usual academics and professionals (Eisner 1993).

Here we use the distinction that theatre is performed towards an audience, whereas drama includes the audience into the performance in a way that it is partly driven by them. This may include elements of roleplay, although the audience may also participate as themselves but still perform activities that assist some critical part of the drama. In the last decade, the uses have extended further and now it is not unusual to see drama, theatre, and the other arts involved at all or any stages of the research process (Adams and Owens 2021) across the disciplines and a wide range of fields. This is because drama and theatre forms can engage people who are not experts in particular fields by presenting complex information, knowledge, and issues from those fields through use of the imagination with emotion in embodied ways. This can allow for shifts between inquiry-based information giving and exploration of feelings, attitudes, values; between the cognitive and the affective (Ball 1993); and between the worlds of logos and mythos. Rossiter et al. (2008) have explored theatre-based approaches to data exploration under the following categorisations, which they identified through analysing a number of health-related theatre projects: (1) **non-theatrical performances**, which employ a minimum of theatrical conventions to convey a story to a passive audience, though they might be to some extent scripted; (2) **ethnodramas**, which aim at realism (such as performing participant interviews) over theatricality and which can be either interactive (drawing from Boal's (1985) *Theatre of the Oppressed* methodology) or non-interactive (e.g., ethnotheatre); (3) **theatrical research-based performances**, which use data as a starting point for constructing the story, but which may move away from realism for aesthetic purposes; and (4) **fictional theatrical performances.**

According to these classifications, our own data drama framing bridges somewhere between an **ethnodrama**, which fosters audience interactivity and participation with real-life data and issues and a **theatrical research-based performance**, which draws in the audience with theatrical props and techniques and is therefore something slightly unique. We also find parallels with conventions of *science drama*, which is a participatory and facilitated approach to learning science through drama (Nicholas and Ng 2008) and which is contrasted with *science theatre*, which entails enacting science towards an audience (Wieringa et al. 2011). As such, we also create a distinction between a data drama and data theatre (Table 8.1). In a data drama, the participants are fully immersed within the storyworld and enact parts of the story, whether in a given role or as themselves.

Developing Our Data Drama

Our data drama took place in the city of Lahti, which is the ninth-largest city in Finland with a population of around 120,000 people. The city is on the edge of Lake Vesijärvi, a lake of over 100 square kilometres and that has been important to the city as a source of water, for summer and winter recreational activities, fishing, and business. In the 1960s and 1970s the lake became one of the most polluted in Finland due to the effects of sewage and industrial wastewater. Lahti then spent considerable money and effort to reverse the effects, which involved regular data collection to monitor indicators of lake pollution and introduction of measures based on the findings. The purpose of our data drama was to *engage participants in understanding the*

Table 8.1 Distinction between data storytelling, theatre, and drama.

	Description	Collaboration and Story Interaction
Data Storytelling	Often limited or no interactivity, lacking in theatrical elements or live performance.	Often engaged with individually. Little possibility to influence the story.
Data Theatre	Performed live and presented to an audience, using theatrical conventions.	Potential for collaboration between audience members, especially after a performance. Interactivity with the 'live' story is likely to be minimal and staged.
Data Drama	Designed for live audience interaction and enactment within a data story, supported by drama education conventions and dramaturgy.	Collaborative and designed for story interaction. Audience may actively roleplay and/or take a role in the drama to perform critical activities as themselves.

impact of pollution of the local lake, how it had been tackled in the past, and the potential dangers of allowing the lake to become further polluted in the future. To support this, we had access to lake data that had been collected since the 1970s, during which time different parts of the lake had been monitored—at different depths—to test for levels of phosphorous and chlorophyll, as well as testing for other minerals, water temperature, and so forth.

The data drama was a two-hour 'environmental learning' event that took place in SDO Theatrum Olga, Lahti, Finland, with the title *Veden Armoilla 'at the mercy of water'*. Theatrum Olga is an educational space following principles of phenomenon-based learning through convention of various arts-based methods. It is directed by a drama educator-artist (one of the authors) who has co-created in trans-professional setting a Theatrum Olga pedagogy. This means network-based collaboration with internal colleagues and collaborators beyond education for example museums, theatres, sinfonia orchestra, and third-sector cultural actors and artists. At the core of Theatrum Olga's pedagogy is a longitudinal relational co-design and co-creation with students. This is conducted by tailoring arts-based methods based on drama education and applied theatre. Thus, the data drama involved high school and vocational school students, teachers, art-educators, and scholars.

The space was set up as a *future water laboratory* where participants could experience the data drama. This was done using staging and props that were co-created by the vocational school's students and art-educators. It was supported by a drama pretext with one main character, called Näkkitär. Supporting video materials were created around the character and shown at the start of the event to set the scene.

The drama framing was intended as a *scaffold* to support exploration of the lake data, reducing barriers to understanding and also developing empathy to the concerns of the lake. As such, the lake data was carefully curated to fit the theme. The vocational school students, as well as co-creating the drama space and character, were trained in delivering the data activities to the high school students; further, their role during the event was as main facilitators while the scholars supported only as necessary. The event was documented by a professional video documentarist and two reflection sessions, and an inquiry took place after the event.

The event preparation and background work started in spring 2021 and there was one live-streamed testbed during March. In August 2021 the co-creation began with ten Theatrum Olga students, a make-up artist and hairdresser, a costume designer, and a drama teacher.

We organised ourselves into a **data team** and a **drama team** to both develop and work within the event. Activities of both teams are described below.

Data team

The data team were focused on making the lake data easily accessible in a short time period and linking this experience of data sensemaking to an overarching narrative. Since the goal was to use drama as a way to support the data sensemaking, the first step was to find a way to embed into the drama data that was collaborative and did not detract from the overall experience. It was felt that typical screen-based approaches to data exploration would not fit the context very well. Instead, the data team focused on creating tangible card games that participants could pick up and discuss. There were two games:

1. Speed data-ing, in which participants get to know key 'characters' relevant to understanding the data, in this case phosphorous and chlorophyll (Figure 8.1),

Figure 8.1 Speed data-ing example showing chlorophyll.

Reproduced courtesy of the authors.

the levels of which are linked to water pollution. This was presented in the form of a comic, drawing on the principle of data comic by Bach et al. (2017).

2. Hauki Bytes, which curated each decade of the water data onto a single card and also outlined key events in the decade that may have impacted on the quality of the lake. The participants had to answer a question from each card as to whether they thought the water quality would improve or not in the subsequent decade. At the end it was possible to compare the first decade and the last side by side since each card contained the full graph of the water readings for that decade. In this way it was possible to see very clearly that, despite fluctuations during each year, decade upon decade there was an incremental overall improvement to the extent that the water in the current decade is quite good. Figure 8.2 shows the two curated cards between 1970–1989 (reproduced courtesy of the authors).

In order to create the cards, a number of interviews took place with a water expert who helped to explain the data set.

Drama team

The core task for the drama team was to co-create a dramaturgical and pedagogical script to translate data into drama. We drew on the approaches of drama education in which performance, while important, is not the core. Rather, the focus is about asking important questions of us and of the world (Adams and Owens 2016; Heikkinen 2016). The learning process that ensues has the potential to develop students' cognitive and affective processes, can foster their capacity to explore diverse perspectives, problem-solving skills (Corbett 2019), and develop empathy. Empathy in this process is understood to involve affective and cognitive processes of the heart and mind (Wells et al. 2021) and the intent was to create rich contexts through imagined experience with others for encounters with the data.

A series of fictional scenes were sequenced in the drama script with the help of questions the students themselves found relevant in order 'to face change and to create capacity for building resilient futures'. Participants assumed roles, including as differently aged citizens, politicians, professionals (environmental researchers, fishers, and businesspeople), creatures—including fish, birds, and insects—as well as water plants and flora around the lake. The scenes were created through five different types of arts-based method drawn from drama education:

1. *Evocative encounterings*, in which theatre games framed in environmental focus were used to create as equal access as possible for everyone to explore the water analysis data.
2. *Drifting* within and around a theatre space, noticing and redefining space by finding unused areas and redefining them. For example, the theatre costume laundry room became a land of water secrets, created through theatrical staging using lights, tent materials, sound, and theatre props.
3. *Sketching initial ideas and thoughts* about lakes. There are thousands of lakes in Finland and most residents have their own lived experiences about these. This method allowed links to be made to the students' own local environment as we

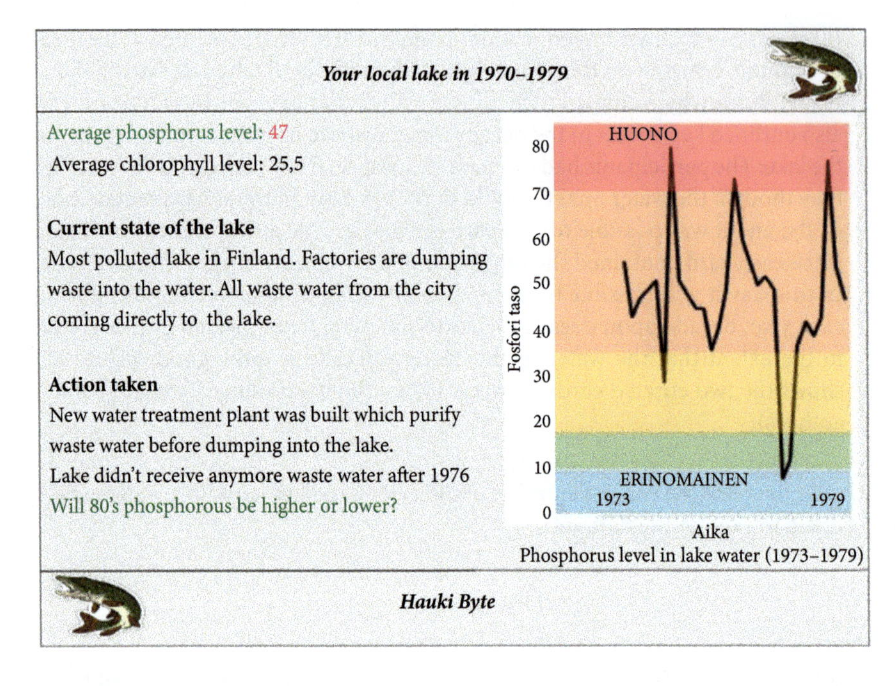

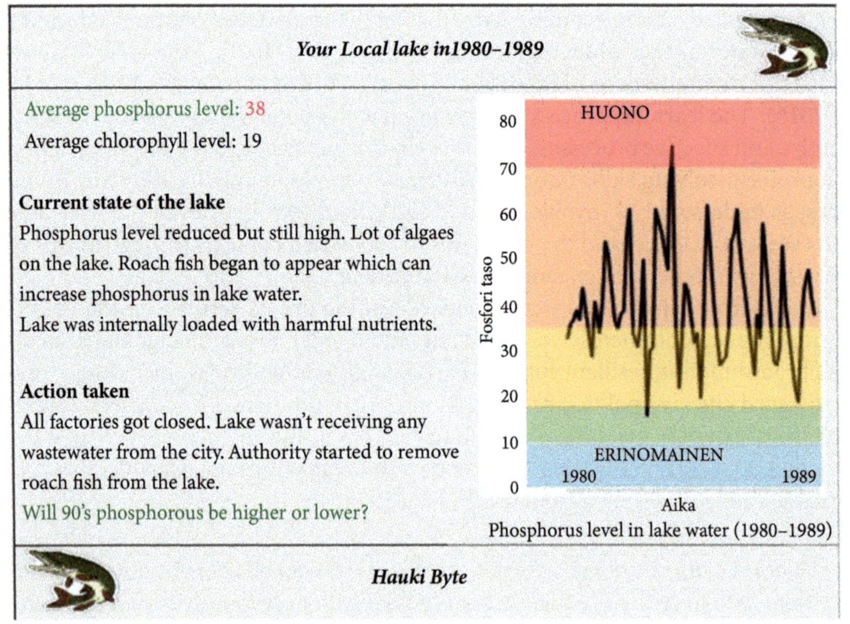

Figure 8.2 Hauki bytes game from 1970–1989.

simultaneously considered water issues on a global level through the making of a kind of explorative manifesto in the form of a short video.

4. *Sketching initial personal responses* to data to answer the question 'What does data actually mean to me in this context?' This was significant for the drama team, who were not so confident with what the water data meant to us personally and professionally. In this way, the learning process was collaborative; teacher, researcher, and visiting professor imagining, playing, and working alongside students, reading and seeking to understand what the data might mean. Findings were shared with each other in an organic way during the making and doing, rather than as a conclusion in the conventional seminar presentation form.
5. *Building scenes through drama education and theatre form.* Within the theatre space small groups were introduced to different drama and theatre forms in order to represent and play with their interpretations of the data. For example, one group worked in the form of object theatre in which they selected objects from a selection presented, which were then used to metaphorically represent their understandings. As they played with these objects, so their understanding continued to be modified and clarified. Another group worked with hand theatre form, in which they moved their hands individually and at times in sequence, creating patterns randomly through a large backdrop made of shredded black cloth. Appearing as disconnected hands on the cloth backdrop, the audience made their own interpretations about what this group were trying to convey about their understanding of the data.

The fictional scenes formed part of an overarching narrative which centred on the mythical figure of Näkkitär, drawn from Finnish Folklore, Arts and Cultural Studies. Acted by Pihla Karhu of Theatrum Olga, the participants slowly found out that Näkkitär had travelled back to their present from the future. She had been told by her old friend Raven Etiäinen that Lake Vesijärvi, and all that lived with/on/in it, might be lost. Raven Etiäinen (a disembodied bird figure on a laptop placed dramatically in the setting of the glowing water laboratory created in Theatrum Olga) had asked her to bring back with her from the future two samples of water and to meet with these young people who lived by the lake. They understood about the new, powerful, and mysterious thing called data. If Näkkitär could come to know what they understood about the Vesijärvi data, Raven Etiäinen believed she would no doubt have the power to stop everything being lost.

The staging of the mythical figure of Näkkitär was carefully undertaken around the scenes described and included the introduction of data by the data team. It allowed for a form of telling and inquiring in the learning environment of Theatrum Olga in which the rational and mythical were both valued and co-existed with mutual benefit. Attention was paid to the detail of the data and the detail of the imaginative setting. For example, props in the future water laboratory were placed carefully and symbolically in order to offer the possibilities of metaphor. In the same way that a specific small part of the huge data set was selected for investigation (i.e., the lake pollution rather than other aspects of the lake, such as changing depth) so only a small number of props were carefully selected and placed in the stage setting of Theatrum Olga for possible meaning. The use of masks, hair, make-up, lighting, and sound was similarly careful and selective. For example, the soundtrack playing throughout the encounter was 'Lake Sounds' recorded by sound artist David de la Haye, a field recordist, bassist, ecological artist, and sound engineer who records freshwater habitats using underwater techniques.

In summary, when scripting, the drama team were creating a series of playful tasks to engage the imagination of the participants in ways that sparked their curiosity and desire to know more about the data through the 'other worlds' of 'Data' and of 'Näkkitär' into which we were inviting them to enter (O'Neill 1995). Participants were 'making', 'doing', 'repeating', 'representing', 'interpreting', and using their own body, their own lived experiences, and their own local settings to collectively reflect—in this case on the data about the water of Lake Vesijärvi. In doing so, they were following the typical activities that occur within other drama education contexts.

Running the Event

At the start of the event, the students entered the drama space, while real underwater sounds were played. They walked through streamers and fish dangling from the ceiling. Part of the space was organised in a mini amphitheatre. Students then sat on steps around the edge of the amphitheatre and from there they could see Näkkitär sitting frozen on the stage, in front of a large blank canvas. In front of the stage there was a large roll of computer printout paper filled with zeros and ones, a prop to represent unstructured data that is difficult to interpret. There was a log with a light and smoke coming out of it, for extra atmosphere. Projected on the canvas was a video of Näkkitär emerging from lake Vesijärvi. The students were introduced to the drama team, who explained that Näkkitär had come from the future because something was happening in the local lake, and she had brought data with her that she knew could help to understand the problem, but that she couldn't understand it herself. She also brought two lake samples from two possible futures, one where the water was more polluted and one where it had stayed clean. The drama team then asked if participants would first help Näkkitär to understand this data in order to understand these futures. Next, the data team were introduced. After the introduction Näkkitär started to interact with the participants by inviting them—in role—to take paint brushes and paints from a large bag shaped like a lake fish (a hauki), which were to be used later to express ideas found from the data. Näkkitär did not speak but communicated through mime. The youth facilitators guided the students into two groups and led each group through the activities with the data cards, through which they started to understand the implications of the relationship between chlorophyll and phosphorus and activities that caused levels to rise or fall. They explained that, because Näkkitär did not understand human language, they would need to communicate their findings from the data without words. One group did this using hand theatre, where they enacted rising and falling phosphorous with hand movements. The other group selected objects from a display to which they assigned a meaning that they then used to communicate findings to Näkkitär, who started drawing her understanding onto the blank canvas, to show what she had learned from the student groups. The session concluded with the students gathering back in the amphitheatre space and participating in the final exercise, in which the students drew a huge painting about the possible future and presented it to Näkkitär, thereby revealing how the students envisaged the future and thought about what may have happened between now and then. Figures 8.3, 8.4, and 8.5 show different aspects of the event. As such, the drama aspects were communicated in three ways, through Näkkitär's mime, through the explanations (out of role) of the data and drama teams, and via the youth facilitators who bridged between these two. While the drama was pre-scripted it was conveyed in such a way that participants could construct their own story and meaning from the event.

Figure 8.3 Examples of prop making before the event (top left and bottom middle) as well as the participants expressing their imagined future through painting onto a large canvas (bottom left and right).
Photos by Lasse Kantola.

Figure 8.4 Students engaging with data cards.
Photos by Veijo Ruotanen (on the left) and Lasse Kantola (on the right).

Figure 8.5 Näkkitär at different moments throughout the event, drawing her learnings onto the canvas.
Photos by Lasse Kantola (bottom left) and Veijo Ruotanen (top and bottom right).

Finally, the participants were asked to make one reflection about the event, which was recorded. Quotations showed that they felt it was shared sense-making '... *we acted a little bit, a combination of painting and problem, what are the things related to this water pollution, we solved the problem together, we painted dreams, we thought about future'.*

Drama and a dramaturgical script were excuses, a pretext for collaboration and shared understanding: '*... to help Näkkitär to understand water pollution*'.

The collaborative learning process was simultaneously described as easy, accessible, and fun, as well as challenging: '*nothing was difficult*'; '*it was really exciting because I hadn't played games like this, everything went really well ...*'; '*there wasn't much new, I was little out of it, but I learned something new, this kind of interactive game was really fun*'; and finally, '*hopeful thoughts emerged, and I was excited*'.

Empathy towards data and lake by the Näkkitär actor: '*This has been amazing experience. I never thought I could do something like this in drama nor in science education. I feel I have now access to make sense of water analysis, I know more about Vesijärvi. Its history and present situation too*'.

In addition, participants (students and facilitators) were asked after the event to complete an open-ended survey about the event and these answers were analysed using inductive thematic analysis, yielding four themes related to the event and especially the data games:

1. **Sensemaking.** The data games helped people to learn more about the lake

    '*I learned a lot about Lake Vesijärvi and what things affect our water and how they relate to each other*'.

    '*I learned different ways to express information, which is for example but diagrams, how to make it clearer and can express it in different ways and practical terms. I also learned something about the health of the lake and the dangers to its health*'.

2. **Visualisation.** The visualisation made the data easier to use.

    '*The game was certainly a fun and different way for participants to learn and internalize things. I also learned a lot about this format and how it is utilized in teaching. Also, as a facilitator, I learned a lot about the topic and things stayed in my mind, I think the participants did too*'.

    '*I liked the simplicity of card games the most. For simplicity, the cards are easy to use in different ways*'.

    '*I liked the pictures of the cards the most*'.

    '*I liked the illustration, most informative*'.

3. **Interactivity.** The cards prompted conversation and collaboration.

    '*About teamwork and how everyone got involved and participated well*'.

    '*[the card games] work well to prompt a conversation*'.

4. **Design Issues.** Some participants identified areas for improvement in the design of the event.

    '*Evaluating what will happen in the future was difficult*'.

    '*We could have reviewed more in-depth information about what phosphorous and chlorophyll are, where else you can find them, etc. Now they remained only as chemical names. Lake history cards were all similar to each other, which makes sense, but made them boring in the long run*'.

Reflections

Our key learning is that data drama lowers barriers for data engagement, and we can use data for empathy building via immersive experience, using arts-based approaches combined with data curation techniques. Through the reflections and the survey, there is evidence that some aspects of the framing and the use of data cards helped participants to understand and engage with the history of the lake and also to do this collaboratively. Given the one-off nature of the event it is difficult to say exactly which parts of the overall event were most important for fostering engagement and critical thinking about the problems of the lake. For example, using the data cards without any of the drama framing would convey similar information. Overall, through the process we were trying to learn what is important and what is less important in order to engage people with environmental data sets and the issues to which they relate. We do not propose necessarily that planning processes should orchestrate complicated drama procedures in order to engage people in more-than-human thinking. We view our data drama approach as similar to designing for the catwalk—the clothes are not for everyday use but can be tailored to be practical. In this regard, we identify the following important steps we took towards helping people to feel more comfortable in engaging with the data:

1. Backgrounding. Finding data about the local environment.
2. Organising curation process. Understanding data (with expert help if needed) and curating data for the setting.
3. Conceptualising drama. Exploring metaphorical and symbolic elements which resonates to context, for example, based on cultural studies, drama education, folklore, and oral storytelling.
4. Scripting data via dramaturgical elements, creating learning stages, rehearsing.
5. Experimentally exploring data in a drama space by stepping into someone else's boots.
6. Providing a safe environment to try and to understand others, including non-humans, and their needs and dreams.

We respect the fact that data drama is still, for us, an aspiration—some parts were not realised as well as they could have been; specifically, we could have had a more seamless integration between the drama and the data sets. However, this is an iterative process. Still, both the data curation itself and the drama helped to bring possible futures closer to people, thus potentially helping to close the *empathy gap*, at least along the temporal dimension. An important concept of the narrative and the link to data was that the dramaturgical framing effectively created a **bridge to the future**. The data drama and data curation were conceived as a way to help participants to see trends in the data, to understand that the trends were related to many different and complex external activities, and to understand that even a positive trend might be reversed if bad practices started to occur again. The curated data on the cards represented what had been (in the past) and what is now (in the present) but in order to really understand the importance of the data we wanted the participants to be able to use their knowledge to predict what might happen (in the future). After learning about the history of the lake, through the rise and fall of pollution levels, would they feel hopeful for the future, or not? Thus, the data reveals trends that can be projected into the future, and it relates changes in lake quality to the local context, and in this way, the dramaturgical framing further reinforces these links to the future. In terms of the spatial gap, we do not address this through this work because we focus very much on the local nature of the data being interrogated, but it is something to consider for later.

Ultimately, we support the findings of researchers such as Elsden et al. (2017), Pschetz et al. (2019), and Pothong et al. (2021) that drama and roleplay are effective for empowerment, for supporting different viewpoints, and for creating experiential aspects to the processes of engaging with data. When it comes to more-than-human approaches and the need to advocate on behalf of others, we add in a new dimension and reflect on the importance of drama in building empathy and understanding about others, even when the others are the phosphorous, chlorophyll, and the fish (hauki) in the lake.

Acknowledgements

This project has received funding from: the European Union's Horizon 2020 research and innovation programme under grant agreement No 872500 within the project ParCos; Academy of Finland 'Building the Civic Datascape'; Yhteinen Mukkula: The Ministry of the Environment's Suburban Program/Lähiöohjelma, Resident-Oriented Development Experiments and Multilayer Data Collection in Mukkula project, LUT & LAB Universities, Finland; Reimagining Creative Democracy, Erasmus+ EU Project (2018–2021). We thank David de la Haye for providing underwater recordings, Theatrum Olga students and the Lahti teachers and students who came and took part, and the City of Lahti for continued support of our research activities.

References

Adams, J., & Owens, A. (2021) Beyond text: Introduction. In J. Adams & A. Owens (Eds.), *Beyond text: Learning through arts-based research practices* (pp. 1–11). Intellect LTD.

Adams, J., & Owens, A. (2016). *Creativity, education and democracy: The practices and politics of learning through the arts.* Routledge.

Alves, R., & Rosa, I. M. (2007). Biodiversity, traditional medicine and public health: Where do they meet? *Journal of Ethnobiology and Ethnomedicine, 3*(1), 1–9.

Ayvazova, D. (2017). Design paradox. The next chapter in the design process. *The Design Journal, 20*(suppl 1), S3059–S3067. doi: 10.1080/14606925.2017.1352813

Bach, B., Riche, N. H., Carpendale, S., & Pfister, H. (2017). The emerging genre of data comics. *IEEE Computer Graphics and Applications, 37*(3), 6–13.

Ball, S. J. (1993). What is policy? Texts, trajectories and toolboxes. *The Australian Journal of Education Studies, 13*(2), 10–17.

Berman, K., & Allen, L. (2012). Deepening students' understanding of democratic citizenship through arts-based approaches to experiential service learning. *South African Review of Sociology, 43*(2), 76–88.

Biagioli, M., Pässilä, A., & Owens, A. (2021). The Zine method as a form of qualitative analysis. In J. Adams & A. Owens (Eds.), *Beyond Text: Learning through arts-based research practices* (pp. 186–200). Intellect LTD.

Björgvinsson, E., Ehn, P., & Hillgren, P-A. (2012). Agonistic participatory design: Working with marginalised social movements, *CoDesign*, *8*(2–3), 127–144. doi: 10.1080/15710882.2012.672577

Boal, A. (1985). *Theatre of the oppressed* (C. A. McBride, Trans.). Theatre Communications Group.

Brecht, B. (1964). *Brecht on theatre*. Methuen.

Bregman, R. (2020). *Human kind: A hopeful history*. Bloomsbury.

Brönnimann, S., & Wintzer, J. (2019). Climate data empathy. *Wiley Interdisciplinary Reviews: Climate Change*, *10*(2), e559.

Corbett, S. (2019). *Influence of a drama-based education program on the development of empathy in year 10, Western Australian students* [Master's thesis, Edith Cowan University]. https://ro.ecu.edu.au/theses/2223

De Simone, F., Presta, R., & Protti, F. (2014). Evaluating data storytelling strategies: A case study on urban changes. In H. Lounis & D. Josyula (Eds.), *COGNITIVE 2014 : The Sixth International Conference on Advanced Cognitive Technologies and Applications* (pp. 250–255). IARIA.

Eddy, M., Blatt-Gross, C., Edgar, S. E., Gohr, A., Halverson, E., Humphreys, K., & Smolin, L. (2021). Local-level implementation of Social Emotional Learning in arts education: Moving the heart through the arts. *Arts Education Policy Review*, *122*(3), 193–204. doi: 10.1080/10632913.2020.1788681

Eisner, E. W. (1993). Forms of understanding and the future of educational research. *Educational Researcher*, *22*(7), 5–11.

Elsden, C., Chatting, D., Durrant, A. C., Garbett, A., Nissen, B., Vines, J., & Kirk, D. S., (2017). On speculative enactments. In G. Mark, S. Fussell, C. Lampe, m. c. schraefel, J. P. Hourcade, C. Appert, & D. Wigdor (Eds.), *CHI '17: Proceedings of the 2017 CHI Conference on Human Factors in Computing Systems* (pp. 5386–5399). ACM.

Freire, P. (2000). *Pedagogy of the oppressed* (M. Bergman Ramos, Trans.). Continuum. (Original work published 1970)

Heikkinen, H. M. (2016). Drama and citizenship: Devised drama for education. *Journal of Social Science Education*, *15*(4), 32–39. https://doi.org/10.4119/jsse-812

Hibbin, R. (2016). The psychosocial benefits of oral storytelling in school: Developing identity and empathy through narrative. *Pastoral Care in Education*, *34*(4), 218–231.

Hough, R. L. (2014). Biodiversity and human health: Evidence for causality? *Biodiversity and Conservation*, *23*(2), 267–288.

Kaninsky, M., Gallacher, S., & Rogers, Y. (2018). Confronting people's fears about bats: Combining multi-modal and environmentally sensed data to promote curiosity and discovery. In I. Koskinen, Y-K. Lim, T. Cerratto-Pargman, K. Chow, & W. Odom (Eds.), *DIS '18: Proceedings of the 2018 Designing Interactive Systems conference* (pp. 931–943). ACM.

Krensky, B., & Steffen, S. L. (2008) Arts-based service-learning: A state of the field. *Art Education*, *61*(4), 13–18 DOI: 10.1080/00043125.2008.11652063

Lehikoinen, K., Pässilä, A., & Owens, A. (2015, April 9–11). *Critical Reflection and the Arts as Third Spaces* [Conference presentation]. In Organizational Learning, Knowledge and Capabilities Conference, Milan, Italy.

Loukissas, Y. A. (2019). *All data are local: Thinking critically in a data-driven society*. MIT Press.

Manzini, E., & Rizzo, F. (2011). Small projects/large changes: Participatory design as an open participated process. *CoDesign*, *7*(3–4), 199–215. doi:10.1080/15710882.2011.630472

Matei, S. A., & Hunter, L. (2021). Data storytelling is not storytelling with data: A framework for storytelling in science communication and data journalism. *The Information Society*, *37*(5), 312–322. doi: 10.1080/01972243.2021.1951415

Mchunu, K., & Berman, K. (2018). Arts-based methods as tools for co-design in a South African community-based design co-operative. *Cubic Journal*, *1*(1), 34–51. https://doi.org/10.31182/cubic.2018.1.002

Miralles, A., Raymond, M., & Lecointre, G. (2019). Empathy and compassion toward other species decrease with evolutionary divergence time. *Scientific Reports*, *9*(1), 1–8.

Mouffe, C. (2009). *The democratic paradox*. Verso.

Nicholas, H., & Ng, W. (2008). Blending creativity, science and drama. *Gifted and Talented International*, *23*(1), 51–60.

Niemelä, J. (1999). Ecology and urban planning. *Biodiversity & Conservation*, *8*(1), 119–131.

Nussbaum, M. (2010). *Not for profit: Why democracy needs the humanities.* Princeton University Press.

O'Neill, C. (1995). *Drama worlds: A framework for process drama.* Heinemann.

Owens, A. (2014). Translating and understanding: Pre-text based drama. In P. Korhonen & R. Airaksinen,(Eds.), *Hyvä hankaus 2.0* (pp. 45–68). Draamatyö.

Pässilä, A. (2012). *Reflexive model of research-based theatre–processing innovation at the crossroads of theatre, reflection and practice-based innovation activities* [PhD Thesis, University of Tampere]. https://lutpub.lut.fi/bitstream/handle/10024/86216/isbn209789522653222.pdf?sequence=1

Pässilä, A., Oikarinen, T., & Harmaakorpi, V. (2013). Collective voicing as reflexive practice. *Management Learning, 44*(5), 1–20.

Pothong, K., Pschetz, L., Catlow, R., & Meiklejohn, S. (2021). Problematising transparency through LARP and deliberation. In W. Ju, L. Oehlberg, S. Follmer, S. Fox, & S. Kuznetsov (Eds.), *DIS '21: Proceedings of the 2021 ACM Designing Interactive Systems Conference* (pp. 1682–1694). ACM. http://doi.org/10.1145/3461778.3462120

Pschetz, L., Pothong, K., & Speed, C. (2019). Autonomous distributed energy systems: Problematising the invisible through design, drama and deliberation. In S. Brewster, G. Fitzpatrick, A. Cox, & V. Kostakos (Eds.), *CHI '19: Proceedings of the 2019 CHI Conference on Human Factors in Computing Systems* (pp. 1–14). ACM.

Puppim de Oliveira, J. A., Doll, C. N., Moreno-Peñaranda, R., & Balaban, O. (2014). Urban biodiversity and climate change. *Global Environmental Change, 1*, 461–468.

Rossiter, K., Kontos, P., Colantonio, A., Gilbert, J., Gray, J., & Keightley, M. (2008). Staging data: Theatre as a tool for analysis and knowledge transfer in health research. *Social Science & Medicine, 66*(1), 130–146.

Thakuriah, P. V., Tilahun, N. Y., & Zellner, M. (2017). Big data and urban informatics: Innovations and challenges to urban planning and knowledge discovery. In P. Thakuriah, N. Tilahun, & M. Zellner (Eds.), *Seeing cities through big data: Research, methods and applications in urban informatics* (pp. 11–45). Springer.

Wells, T., Sandretto, S., & Tilson, J. (2021). Learning 'what it's like to be someone else apart from yourself': Developing holistic empathy with process drama. *Pedagogy, Culture & Society, 31*(4), 809–825.

Wieringa, N. F., Swart, J. A., Maples, T., Witmondt, L., Tobi, H., & van der Windt, H. J. (2011). Science theatre at school: Providing a context to learn about socio-scientific issues. *International Journal of Science Education, Part B, 1*(1), 71–96.

Wolff, A., Pässilä, A., Knutas, A., Vainio, T., Lautala, J., & Kantola, L. (2021). The importance of creative practices in designing more-than-human cities. In: J. C. Augusto (Ed.), *Handbook of smart cities* (pp. 1643–1664). Springer. https://link.springer.com/referenceworkentry/10.1007/978-3-030-69698-6_74

SECTION 3
JUSTICE

9
Justice by Design
The Case for Equitable and Inclusive Smart Cities for Animal Dwellers

Clara Mancini, Daniel Metcalfe, and Orit Hirsch-Matsioulas

Introduction

Visionary urban architects such as Vincent Callebaut (vincent.callebaut.org) have produced ever-more imaginative designs of future smart sustainable cities, where elegant structures and lush vegetation blend together beautifully in spaces that seemingly provide perfect environments for human life to thrive. Aside from a few birds flying above the city, animals are either absent from these tame and sterile floral jungles or contained within sky-scraping urban farms, their perhaps less tameable and less sterile presence seemingly instrumentalised to or expunged from such anthropocentric utopias.

Urban planning theorists such as Houston et al. (2017) have challenged humanistic conceptions of cities as '*places of enlightened human value and technological mastery*' (p.193), because they perpetuate the dangerous idea of human separation from the rest of the biophysical world, giving rise to dichotomous categorisations between wanted and unwanted species, leading to the persecution of the latter; and because they assume the primacy of human interests over the interests of other beings, ultimately leading to the catastrophic changes the planet is currently undergoing. Instead, the authors urge city planners to acknowledge the complex '*multispecies and multi-thing*' (p.200) assemblages and relationships among humans, animals, fungi, bacteria, plants, rocks, water, and air, whose *becoming with* makes urban worlds; and to value all non-humans' participatory contribution to urban worlds (Forlano 2016), to enable the emergence of more inclusive and just cities.

However, while all organic and inorganic beings participate in the becoming of urban worlds, the diversity of agents involved needs to be acknowledged, precisely because humans' unwillingness to cohabit with other beings largely depends on our perception of these as potential competitors that may not be controlled. The space-temporal scale at which their agency manifests and the kinds of resources they seek mean that plants appear to be largely more controllable, less in competition with and often beneficial to humans. In contrast, many animals move more quickly, respond more autonomously, and produce more detectable signals, without yielding neither to the urban social and imaginative order of modern humans (Philo and Wilbert 2000; Wolch et al. 2000) nor to human social rules about animal mobility within urban physical and geographical borders (Braverman 2013). Moving according to

Clara Mancini, Daniel Metcalfe, and Orit Hirsch-Matsioulas, *Justice by Design*. In: *Designing More-than-Human Smart Cities*. Edited by: Sara Heitlinger, Marcus Foth, and Rachel Clarke, Oxford University Press. © Oxford University Press (2024). DOI: 10.1093/9780191980060.003.0011 their own needs and desires, animals challenge human socio-geographical orders (Michael 2004; Holmberg 2013) and often seek the same kinds of resources humans seek. In other words, the human–animal biological kinship is likely to set humans and other animals on a collision course that renders *making kin* (Haraway 2015) fraught with contradictions. If designing cities for cohabitation is to succeed in practice, moderating inter-agent competition and control in a way that decentres the human will be fundamental. Design models that can address this challenge in the context of human–animal relations are more likely to be extendable to a broader range of non-human agents.

In this regard, the development of *smart cities* provides an unprecedented opportunity. So-called *smart* technology is increasingly able to plan and manage complex systems by collecting and analysing vast amounts of multimodal data, and by making and implementing principled decisions (Bibri and Krogstie 2017) in relative autonomy. Thus, smart technology could play a fundamental role in decentring human interests within urban worlds. Throughout the history of our species, technological development has aimed at controlling, outcompeting, and ultimately exploiting the rest of the natural world, but this has evidently produced human-made imbalances that are destroying the planet. Although losing control and being outcompeted are considered two of the main threats that increasingly powerful artificial intelligence (AI) poses to humanity (Future of Life Institute 2022), have we now reached a point when technology could have a role in redistributing control, for example, by enabling animals' agency, in order to redress the imbalances we have created? Could technology that decentres the human promote and support a more relational approach to interspecies coexistence, akin to that which characterised some indigenous cultures (Graham 2014)? If so, the question is what ethical and design principles should inform such technology to give rise to more environmentally and ethically sustainable cities.

With this in mind, the rest of this chapter discusses the implications of extending the principles of *equity* and *inclusivity* that inform existing conceptions of *smart sustainable cities* to animal dwellers, leveraging Nussbaum's theory of multispecies justice, according to which a just smart city would offer animals opportunities to pursue biologically relevant goals and achieve basic species-specific capabilities. Two cases of human–animal cohabitation then exemplify requirements that a *just smart city* would need to meet to enable multispecies cohabitation: supporting animals' sensemaking of and interaction with urban affordances, enabling them to autonomously pursue their biological goals; managing affordances by balancing the interests of one species against the interests of other species, as well as the interests of individuals against the interests of groups; and accounting for different perspectives and narratives on interspecies relationships, when making and implementing decisions. Finally, the chapter proposes an iterative model of a *just smart city* in which technological interventions are informed both by principles of multispecies justice and by multispecies data to enable the emergence of cohabitation forms that are incrementally equitable and inclusive for a growing range of species and individuals.

Smart Sustainable Cities for Whom?

Smart technologies that combine big data analytics and context-aware computing—underpinned by digital sensing tools, cloud computing infrastructures, middleware architectures, and wireless communication networks—are becoming instrumental in the monitoring, analysis, operation, and planning of cities (Bibri and Krogstie 2017). As improving cities' *sustainability* becomes increasingly important, *smart sustainable cities* are expected to leverage these smart technologies to *meet the environmental, economic, social and cultural needs of its inhabitants* with *equity and inclusivity* (Angelidou et al. 2017; Bibri and Krogstie 2017), without compromising the ability of others or future generations to meet their needs (ITU 2014; Höjer and Wangel 2015). Thus, in a smart sustainable city, technology would ensure that citizens have equitable access to the resources, services, and opportunities they need to participate in society and enjoy a high quality of life within a healthy and pleasant environment that is not degraded by urbanisation or urban activity. This raises the question as to who counts as a citizen of such a city (Narayanan and Bindumadhav 2019).

Generally, aspirations of intra- and inter-generational equity and inclusivity regarding the benefits afforded by smart sustainable cities seem to be fundamentally limited to humans, as reflected by smart city applications, which aim to address environmental sustainability challenges but disregard sustainability challenges to biodiversity (Angelidou et al. 2017), signalling a widespread lack of concern for non-human city dwellers, particularly animals (Acari et al. 2021). As Beatley and Bekoff (2013) point out, although some animal species (e.g., macaques, racoons, foxes, rats) have adapted to living in urban settings, they are often perceived and treated as a nuisance or a threat, accused of carrying disease, damaging property and imperilling human safety. When conflicts of interest between humans and animals arise, they are often resolved by dispatching the animals. Except for a few protected species, animals' presence in cities is usually tolerated only if they are seen to add value to humans' urban experience without affecting humans' interests. For those whose presence is tolerated, cities are often inhospitable, whether by design (e.g., spikes fitted to the edges of buildings' windows and doorways to prevent pigeons from perching) or by indifference (e.g., glass-fronted buildings with which birds collide, misled by the surfaces' transparency). Instead, the authors advocate for the integration of animals' interests into city planning and practices, highlighting how this could benefit animals and humans alike; for example, because green spaces that provide habitats for animals also benefit human health, because encounters with wildlife enrich human experience, and because biodiversity is important for the preservation of the ecosystems that sustain human life.

Riffat et al. (2016) propose measures that smart cities could take to address environmental issues, including more efficient transportation systems, better waste management, increased carbon emission capture, reduced atmospheric pollution, greater use of renewable energy, lower-energy buildings, more compact urban design, and increased green spaces. While improving human life, these measures would likely also ameliorate living conditions for, and indeed attract, animals by improving the liveability of urban spaces and by reducing cities' environmental impacts. However, there is a fundamental difference between incidentally improving living conditions for animals and explicitly accounting for their interests, so that the urban environment can meet their needs with equity and inclusivity.

A Matter of Justice

The notions of *equity* and *inclusivity* in the organisation of smart sustainable cities are aligned with the idea of *fairness* underpinning influential theories of justice developed within the field of political philosophy, particularly the *social contract* tradition represented by Locke, Rousseau, and Kant, and reflected in Rawls's (2001) influential treaty. For Rawls, the functioning of a fair society should be informed by principles of justice that rational persons in an *original position* (where all are equal and have no vested interests) negotiate to reciprocal advantage. On this basis, while humans have a duty of compassion towards animals consistent with human dignity, the treatment of animals is not an issue of justice, since their lack of rationality and self-representation prevents them from negotiating and attaining societal membership.

Among the critics of contractarianism, Nussbaum (2006) rejects the assumption that those who negotiate the social contract must have equal capacity for rational reasoning and self-representation (a criterion that would also exclude humans with cognitive disabilities). She argues that, while animals might not be able to negotiate mutually advantageous principles of justice with humans, they are nevertheless subjects of justice for whom such principles must be negotiated. For Nussbaum, animals are *agents capable of a dignified existence, with corresponding needs for flourishing and related goals they actively pursue, to which they have a moral entitlement*. Therefore, how humans treat animals is not an issue of compassion, it is an issue of justice; their maltreatment is not contrary to human dignity, it is contrary to animal dignity.

Influenced by Aristotle's view that animals and humans are fundamentally akin because they are all made of organic matter (Deckha 2015) and by Marx's conception that one's true functioning depends more on the opportunity one has to engage in life activities than on quantifiable resources (Sen 2009), Nussbaum's multispecies theory of justice articulates fundamental entitlements for creatures of different types. Her *capability approach* differs significantly from utilitarian approaches, such as Bentham's hedonism (1823/1948) or Singer's preference-satisfaction (1980), because it regards the balance between pleasure and pain too crude a measure to evaluate animals' functioning. Within her approach, animals' functioning is evaluated based on the opportunity they have to pursue the capabilities they value (e.g., an animal may choose to engage in an activity that has value for them even if this causes them pain). Furthermore, unlike utilitarianism, the capability approach does not justify violating the rights of individuals to advance societal interests (i.e., reducing the pain of many does not justify inflicting pain on the few).

Nussbaum identifies *basic capabilities* for flourishing that animals are entitled to pursue: staying alive; maintaining one's bodily health and integrity; experiencing sensory and cognitive stimulation; enjoying nurturing emotions and attachments; setting goals and plans; forming intra- and interspecies affiliations and managing one's social life; having control over one's environment and safeguarding one's territorial integrity. Importantly, the relevance of capabilities is species-specific (e.g., being killed causes greater harm to animals capable of making plans frustrated by death than to animals with no such capacity). Additionally, relevant capabilities need to be fulfilled to an *adequate* threshold, below which justice is not done and above which inequalities are not unjust. While this does not eliminate conflicts of interest between competing needs, requiring some animals' (including humans') non-essential capabilities to be limited to enable the fulfilment of other animals' essential capabilities, it removes the need to admit species equality as a precondition for multispecies justice.

The capability approach to multispecies justice suggests that a *just smart city* would recognise animal dwellers' entitlement to a *dignified and flourishing existence* according to their species' needs and would afford them, with *equity* and *inclusivity* (Angelidou et al. 2017; Bibri and Krogstie 2017), the opportunity to pursue *biological goals relevant to their basic capabilities* at least to an *adequate* extent. Indeed, the capabilities identified by Nussbaum (2006) closely correspond to equivalent human needs identified for smart sustainable cities (ITU 2014): animals' goals might pertain to building, inhabiting, and traversing structures and spaces (*environmental goals*), to acquiring and managing resources (*economic goals*), to forming and maintaining social groups (*social goals*), to gaining and transmitting knowledge and skills (*cultural goals*). Thus, a just smart city would provide opportunities for animal dwellers to nest and travel safely; to hunt, forage, and store food; to communicate, meet, and mate; and to learn from others and their surroundings. While many urban environments disregard the needs of animal dwellers or deliberately seek to exclude them, others are far more welcoming, allowing animals to mingle with humans and to take advantage of the opportunities provided by the city. One example is the city of Istanbul's relation to its cat population.

Sensemaking, Interaction, and the Pursuit of Goals—Istanbul's Cats

Along with over fifteen million human inhabitants, Istanbul is populated by over a million cats (BBC News 2016). The documentary *Kedi* (Torun 2017) illuminates the world of felines living in the streets of this urban setting and the relationships they forge with humans.

In Islam, cats have a special status (Hart 2019) and the Muslim religion plays an essential role in shaping human–cat relations in the city, where countless water bowls and piles of dry cat food are scattered everywhere. Cats are largely allowed to take advantage of the city's urban architecture and practices: outdoor restaurant chairs provide comfortable resting places, awnings provide strategic lookout posts, and ledged buildings provide easy access to higher apartments; open markets are playgrounds where to frolic and hunt, jumping from place to place and snatching fish from stalls, while shopkeepers make unconvincing attempts to push back. Neither domesticated nor feral, the cats are free-living, and their caregivers devote much time and money to keep them safe and relatively healthy. When they show up ill or injured, usually someone takes care of them, and the local community sometimes share the financial burden of necessary veterinary treatment. Caregivers' and cats' life stories are thus intertwined, as humans and animals 'rescue' each other (Porter 2018): caregivers provide for the cats and, in turn, the cats give them purpose and joy.

However, the cats' existence and the human–feline bond in Istanbul are being threatened by accelerated urban development, the intensification of capitalism, and ongoing material and cultural changes (Hart 2019). Highways soon to be constructed will pose deadly dangers for the cats. New high-rise buildings will have no ledges or adjacent trees, so cats will not be able to enter higher apartments. The loss of old markets, narrow streets, and awnings will leave the cats unable to climb, hide, and interact with residents. In *Kedi* (Torun 2017), caregivers express their concern: '*We're more worried about what will happen to the cats than what will happen to us. If this area gets demolished, and it's very likely, they will be without anyone*'. Caregivers wish the design of modern buildings considered the cats' needs, because they belong to the city as much as its human inhabitants: '*The cat embodies the indescribable chaos, the culture and the uniqueness that is the essence of Istanbul. Without the cat, Istanbul will lose part of its soul*' (Torun 2017).

Thus, Istanbul's reality recognises cats' entitlement to co-own the city, which provides them with opportunities to shelter, travel, hunt, forage, communicate, socialise, and explore; and which humans willingly share with them, collectively caring for them, while respecting their autonomy as users of the urban space. But the cats' status as integrated urban dwellers, the cat–human bond, and Istanbul's very identity are threatened by urban developments that can take away their ability to make sense of and interact with their urban surroundings in pursuit of their *environmental*, *economic*, *social*, and *cultural* goals.

To pursue such goals, and achieve their essential capabilities, animals need to be able to interact with their surroundings effectively. To take advantage of their surroundings' potential for interaction, what Gibson (1977) called *affordances*, animals need to be able to make sense of their surroundings' elements within their *umwelt* (Uexküll 1909), that is within their world-model. This is informed by the animals' capacities of perception and interaction, and by their biological goals. Thus, sense-making requires that the elements of animals' surroundings be perceivable to them and responsive to their behaviour, consistent with semiotic mechanisms accessible to them and outcomes relevant to them, whether animals interact with their natural environment or with technological infrastructures and systems (Mancini 2023). For example, glass surfaces are difficult for birds to perceive, giving them the illusion that they can fly through, which often results in them crashing to their death (a typical example of *mis-perceived affordances*; see Gibson 1977); birds might perceive that buildings' windowsills afford perching on but may be prevented from interacting with those structures effectively by 'bird spikes'. In neither scenario does the city enable the animals to achieve goals biologically relevant to them: the former because it does not allow them to make sense of barriers that prevent them from safely traversing a space; the latter because it prevents them from taking advantage of an affordance that would provide them with a place to rest, socialise, and nest. Conversely, as Smith et al. (2017) note, structures such as wildlife crossings that feature local natural material and vegetation enable animals to make sense of a passage and to safely traverse an otherwise dangerous space to reach places where they can find food, build shelters, socialise with conspecifics, and develop their territorial knowledge. Communicating affordances unambiguously enables animals to make sense of what they can and cannot do, either encouraging them to pursue attainable goals or discouraging them from pursuing dangerously unattainable goals, such as attempting to cross a busy highway.

The case of Istanbul's cats exemplifies that, although the city is designed for humans, its urban architecture and practices afford the animals opportunities to fruitfully interact with their surroundings; and a culture that fosters humans' acceptance of the cats' presence allows them to take advantage of those affordances, which in turn allows humans and cats to form mutually beneficial relationships. But what about other relationships and competing interests? When a species is favoured over others, how are the other species impacted? What about the mice and rats, who also live in the city and who are hunted down by cats (Torun 2017)? When a species is allowed to expand in an urban environment providing limited resources, what happens to that species' many individuals who remain invisible, and succumb to starvation and disease (Arcari et al. 2021)? In brief, how is the flourishing of one species to be valued in relation to the flourishing of another species and how are the interests of individuals to be valued in relation to the persistence of their species? These dilemmas are highlighted by the relationships that, until early 2022, connected humans, dogs, and other animals at the Ukrainian site of Chornobyl.[1]

Individuals, Ecologies, and Decisions—Chornobyl's Dogs

The Chornobyl nuclear disaster in 1986 led to the evacuation of all residents within a thirty-kilometre radius of the plant. Over the years, this 'exclusion zone' became a liminal space: a cultural icon of pollution and death, and, in parallel, an apocalyptic urban paradise evolved into a nature reserve (Turnbull 2020).

When disaster struck, the authorities forced fleeing residents to permanently abandon their companion animals and soldiers were ordered to shoot all the dogs to prevent radioactive contamination from spreading. However, despite attempts to exterminate them, and despite Ukrainian winters' harshness, food scarcity, wolves, disease, and radioactivity, some dogs survived (McDowall 2018) and their great-great-grand-puppies still lived there in early 2022. The documentary *Dogs of Chernobyl: The Untold Story* (Camilleri and Chesnel 2020) depicts the silent streets of the exclusion zone, a monument to life that stood still, to families who left behind memories and dreams. For the dogs, this eerie habitat offered hiding places, empty roads, and drinking water, as well as multiple survival challenges, which made them bigger, stronger, and 'streetwise' through natural selection.

Until early 2022, every day, factory employees and checkpoint guards went to work in the exclusion zone, where hundreds of feral dogs roamed. Due to their hazardous conditions, which condemned them to hard and short lives, the dogs were the subject of concern for the workers. In this liminal space, bonds formed between humans and dogs (Turnbull 2020). Neither wild nor domesticated, the dogs had a special status, coming and going as they pleased through the zone's checkpoint, being both aloof and attached to checkpoint guards. The guards did not see themselves as dog owners, but some had formed partnerships with the canines, giving them names, and providing them with food, shelter, and medicines. In turn, the dogs defended the checkpoint and accompanied the guards on duty, providing a sense of home in a toxic and deserted place (Turnbull 2020).

The locals and the volunteers of US charity Clean Futures Fund, whose mission was to help humans and animals in the exclusion zone, disagreed on how to categorise and treat Chernobyl's dogs (Turnbull 2020). The locals believed that the dogs were accustomed to their living conditions and belonged in the exclusion zone's wilderness. Rather than radioactivity, they believed that freezing winters and wolves were the real danger for the animals. However, charity volunteers were keen to rescue the dogs from the radioactive zone and, if possible, send them abroad for adoption as pets. They examined every dog's condition to decide what was best for them: puppies, vulnerable, or poorly acclimated dogs were candidates for adoption; but, for dogs who had grown up in the exclusion zone and were used to its conditions, transplantation into a 'domestic situation' was deemed not in their best interest.

Thus, the liminal reality of Chernobyl's dogs existed in tension between different perceptions and narratives about who the dogs were, where they belonged, and what they needed. Were they citizens of the zone's wilderness, self-determining negotiators of their own mutualistic relations with humans? Were they disaster victims needing to be rescued from radioactive toxicity and other dangers to live within the safer bounds of domesticity? Were they not integral part of a new ecology that also sustained predators such as wolves? Did their preferential status in the humans' perception justify disregarding the wolves' survival needs? How would these kinds of evaluation, and any corresponding responses, be negotiated in a just city, and by whom?

A *just smart city* would need to address these kinds of tensions between individuals' identity, autonomy, and wellbeing on the one hand, and the interspecies dynamics that maintain ecological systems on the other hand. Thus, while enabling individual animals to make sense of and fruitfully interact with urban spaces and processes, the city would aim not to interfere with the multispecies ecologies existing within its bounds, in order not to advantage or disadvantage any one species and, thus, perturb the dynamics upon which said ecologies depend. Bekoff and Pierce (2009) demonstrate how different species have their own sense of fairness, which regulates their social interactions, and allows individuals to function within their social order. However, where, due to human activity, a particular species had a disproportionate advantage or disadvantage in relation to others, intervention might be required to neutralise the effect. This might involve limiting advantaged species' ability to pursue non-essential goals, while enhancing disadvantaged species' ability to pursue essential goals, by managing the opportunities for interaction that different species are afforded. For example, in North America, Eastern Bluebird populations have suffered greatly with the introduction of House Sparrows and Starlings, both invasive species that outcompete Bluebirds for nesting sites; the deployment of artificial nesting boxes with entrances too narrow for Starlings and too shallow for Sparrows discourages these larger birds while encouraging nesting for the smaller Eastern Bluebird (Rosenzweig 2003).

Nussbaum (2006) argues that justice is fundamentally concerned with the experience of individuals and that the continuity of species is only morally relevant to the extent that their decline involves individuals' suffering. For example, if the individuals of invasive prey species had to be culled, being killed by expert snipers would be less harmful than being torn apart by predators introduced as a control measure. However, while prey animals have evolved to sense and respond to predators in a way that enables them to take evasive measures (Lima 1998), they are less equipped to evade snipers' weapons, which impacts their ability to stay alive and calls into question the ethics of surreptitious killing. Additionally, the patterns of prey animals' avoidance behaviour stimulated by the presence of predators create ecological niches that allow other species, and their individuals, to flourish. For example, the reintroduction of wolves to Yellowstone National Park triggered a beneficial trophic cascade in the ecosystem (Fortin et al. 2005). Indeed, the ecological dynamics supported by biodiversity regulate key biotic and abiotic processes on the planet, providing the biosphere's long-term capacity to persist and adapt to abrupt and gradual changes (Steffen et al. 2015), so that generations of individuals can flourish.

As technological development has enabled humankind to progressively separate from and subjugate much of the natural world, the complex interconnections that make ecosystems have been increasingly disregarded to advance human interests with ever more disastrous consequences. So, how can humans make decisions on what interests should be prioritised by the just smart city, and what narratives should justify what interventions? If not humans, who should make and implement such decisions?

Imagining a Just Smart City

As we argue, a multispecies equitable and inclusive smart sustainable city would need to *meet the needs of **all** its inhabitants* (human and non-human) without compromising the ability of others or future generations to meet their needs; and that this would entail enabling its multispecies dwellers to *make sense of their urban surroundings and interact with them effectively to achieve biologically relevant goals*. With these fundamental principles in mind, we imagine what such a city might look like, the processes that could enable its functioning and the steps that would be needed to incrementally adapt existing cities to a more just model. Istanbul's example highlights the importance both of urban affordances, which enable animals to interact effectively with the urban environment, and of human sociocultural values that permit them to take advantage of said affordances, fostering a collective investment in mutually beneficial interspecies relationships. At the same time, Chornobyl's example highlights how different human sociocultural perspectives may impose particular values on ecological dynamics that, albeit unpalatable, may still need to be respected independently of human value systems. Thus, applying our proposed principles to the complex realities of existing urban multispecies dynamics raises key ethical and operational questions. For example, how to create lists of *species* to be considered? How to determine what *capabilities* different species value? How to define a minimum threshold for their *adequate* fulfilment? How to decide what each species *needs* to fulfil their basic capabilities? How to negotiate different species' conflicting needs? How to determine measures to compensate for the impacts of inherent urban and human activity? How to deal with human beliefs and norms that might influence the potential to adopt change? Who would get to decide the answers to these questions and how would the process be regulated?

The use of smart technology in ecological studies is on the rise as a way of addressing increasingly complex research questions and global challenges such as climate change and biodiversity loss (Allan et al. 2018). The *just smart city* would embody a gradual evolution of this trend, informed by multispecies justice principles, gradually shedding light on the kind of questions mentioned above. Starting from existing cities' physical and socio-cultural context, it would grow incrementally and iteratively, gradually evolving into an agent of *interspecies mediation and control re-distribution*. Figure 9.1 illustrates the different activities of a possible design cycle and, below, we discuss operational and ethical challenges that might arise at each stage, and how smart technology might help address them.

Data collection would be an essential activity of the *just smart city*. Ambient sensors could collect large amounts of data regarding the presence, frequency, and behaviour of different species within the urban environment, helping to shed light on species assemblages, behaviours, and preferences as to where and how they feed, nest, and socialise; what dangers they face; and what benefits the city already affords them. Notwithstanding the importance of protecting monitored animals' security and privacy (Paci et al. 2022), this data would help address some of the questions raised above within the context of specific cities. Monitoring applications could also support nature-based citizen science projects, enabling human citizens to take part in monitoring and collecting ecological data, with the added value of increasing emotional and cognitive connections to nature (Schuttler et al. 2018). In turn, this could encourage public acceptance of animal presence in cities and foster a culture of shared responsibility and collective caregiving (e.g., group monitoring of aspects of animals' behaviour to coordinate caregiving practices). As a starting point, the data collected would serve to highlight unjust situations for different species, which could be addressed incrementally through the existing governing mechanisms of the city. As more data was collected, it would be possible to identify different species' requirements for achieving basic capabilities (e.g., based on species-specific measures related to activities such as mating, feeding, and locomotion) and shift towards self-governing systems based on algorithmic decision making. These would serve as regulating mechanisms for ensuring that different species' needs were met to a minimum threshold defined based on collected data. Of course, how, where, when, and by whom data was collected might strongly influence decisions and outcomes (Kontokosta & Hong 2021). These concerns would be greater regarding species for whom there was no available data (e.g., if the animals were too small or too evasive) and, therefore, no representation in decision making. However, where species-specific data was missing, proxy measures, such as relevant parameters of ecosystem health, could be leveraged (Stephens et al. 2015).

While not immune to design bias, considered **data processing** approaches could help interpret the data in ways appropriate to the local urban context. For example, data regarding animals' behaviour could be combined with existing ecological and ethological knowledge to define basic species-specific capabilities based on what animals seem to value in specific situations. Because cities are novel ecosystems where animals' behaviour might vary from that of wild populations (Luniak 2004), it would be important to assess their behaviour in the local urban context to understand what the specific site does or should afford them. This could help assess to what extent

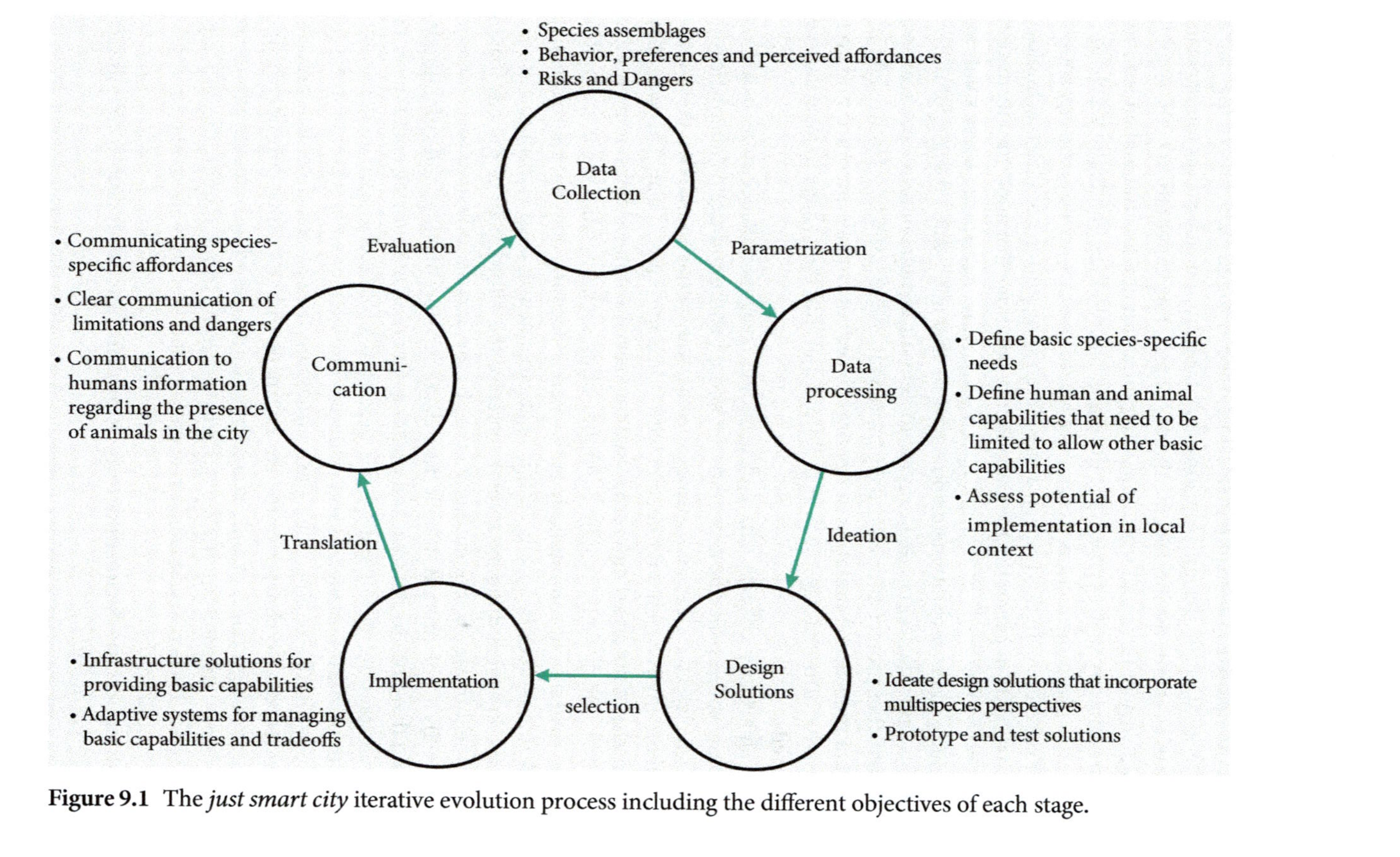

Figure 9.1 The *just smart city* iterative evolution process including the different objectives of each stage.

different animals were able to achieve their basic capabilities in their current urban settings and identify the best trade-offs towards achieving a minimum threshold for all. In cases where species groups were severely disadvantaged by human activity, compensatory measures could be proposed.

Insights generated and requirements identified through data processing could inform the ideation of **design solutions** that take into consideration multispecies perspectives as well as the local sociocultural context. **Implementation** of these solutions could vary in form and scale, including infrastructure features embedded into the design of the city such as green corridors, animal crossings, ponds and vegetation; and influence planning decisions, including where and in what ways the city should expand or regenerate. In this respect, a most interesting promise of smart technology might be its ability to generate agile and adaptive solutions that allow the city to shift and respond to the needs of multiple species over time and space. These solutions could include smart mobility regulation systems that allow safe crossing for different animals, sporadic feeders that respond to periodic changes in resources, seasonal reservations that protect animals during more vulnerable periods, adaptive lighting systems that reduce light pollution in response to certain animals' presence, and even transformative infrastructure, such as buildings that shift their shape to meet various species' needs.

As the smart city collects data and generates insights and decisions based on defined basic species-specific capabilities, it should **communicate** its affordances to different species in a clear and species-specific way, allowing individuals to make sense of their environment and interact with it in a meaningful way. This would be important also if the smart city recognised that certain animals' behaviours needed to be limited, which would require communicating such limitations. For example, a dangerous road should communicate both where it does and does not afford crossing (e.g., by featuring species-specific 'traffic lights' that deliver clear warnings).

The ways in which different animals perceive the affordances of the city, based on their world model, is influenced by many factors largely unknown to us humans (Uexküll 1909). The process of collecting data, decision making, and communication should therefore be iterative and ongoing. Ongoing monitoring could inform a better understanding of different species' perceived affordances based on their interaction with urban infrastructure and resources and help identify where affordances were misperceived. Adaptive solutions, harnessing AI and real-time data processing, could respond to changes in the environment and behaviour of residents, and provide increasingly relevant and perceivable affordances while reducing affordance misperceptions. In addition, involving human citizens in the monitoring and support of animal dwellers could familiarise the 'otherness' of animals, awaken biophilic sentiments, and improve environmental attitudes and behaviours, helping to overcome anthropocentric dichotomies (e.g., beneficial/harmful, desirable/undesirable; see Houston et al. 2017).

The ongoing iterative learning necessary to realise this vision could start by addressing only a handful of non-human species and gradually include more species, as better understanding is attained regarding the dynamics at play within the eco–socio–technical systems produced by the interactions among species, ecologies, and technologies. At the same time, although smart technologies could help redress the anthropocentric imbalances of current cities, they are likely to reflect human biases affecting every stage of the process, including data collection, processing, and interpretation, as well as design, implementation, and communication. Elsewhere, we propose an approach to support the design of animal-centred technology informed by multispecies justice principles, including design strategies to *disrupt* systems that go against animals' capabilities, to *reconfigure* anthropocentric notions that discriminate against animals, and to *pollinate* design thinking with animal-centred values; and a commitment to *expanded empathy* in pursuit of a deeper understanding of animals and their needs (Mancini et al. 2022). In the context of the *just smart city*'s evolution, such an approach could help challenge some of the human biases when considering possible choices related to the different stages of the process. However, there is no doubt that humans would need to be willing to learn from what the just smart city might have to teach us and gradually allow it to do its work, which would be more likely to happen if we gradually discovered that handing over some of our control had vital environmental and societal benefits.

From Just Smart Cities to Planetary Sustainability

Humans are but one among countless threads woven through an infinitely complex web of life that sustains all species. Yet, blinkered by anthropocentric interests and empowered by anthropocentric technology, we have disintegrated its delicate structures and undermined its systems' functioning. It is now incumbent upon us to use our technology to find sustainable forms of multispecies coexistence and prevent the ecological collapse that threatens all species, including humans.

Cities are ecological microcosms, both metaphor and metonym of the way in which we coexist with the multispecies individuals who inhabit the planet. As global urbanisation is expected to expand for decades to come (United Nations 2014), it is essential for future smart cities to recognise the citizenship of multispecies dwellers and afford them *equitable and inclusive opportunities to attain their essential capabilities*, as a matter of justice as well as of planetary ecological preservation. The examples of Istanbul's cats and Chornobyl's dogs highlight some of the fundamental complexities that designing this kind of *just smart cities* would have to consider. This is a daunting task, to say the least. But it is a task that can be tackled incrementally and iteratively, capitalising on the potential of big data analytics and context-aware computing, underpinned by digital sensing technologies, cloud computing infrastructures, middleware architectures, and wireless communication networks, which are expected to underpin the functioning of future sustainable smart cities (Vincent Callebaut Architectures 2014).

While futuristic visions of smart cities seem to still be largely anthropocentric, here we imagine an alternative ecologically and ethically sustainable vision, as a future destination towards which we attempt to provide a roadmap. In this vision, the city itself becomes an agent of *interspecies mediation and control re-distribution*, while the technology that powers it recedes quietly into the background and makes room for nature to take a more meaningful place in city life, helping human citizens to connect with nature experiences (Colding and Barthel 2017), to embrace more relational approaches to multispecies coexistence (Graham 2014), and to make kin with fellow urban critters (Houston et al. 2017). While many critical questions will need to be addressed, in order for *just smart cities* to become reality, the application of data collection and processing technology, informed by biologically and ecologically grounded principles of multispecies justice, could gradually enable some of the answers to emerge from the ground up. If successful, such technologically supported co-existence could redefine our relationships with other species not only within but also outside cities: beyond improving urban living and urban environments, designing *just smart cities* could provide a model for achieving ecological justice and sustainability for the planet as a whole.

Acknowledgements

While working on this chapter, we learned that the site of Chornobyl had been seized by Russian military forces, with dire consequences for animals and humans. Although Ukrainians have regained control of the site, we remain profoundly concerned for the safety of Chornobyl's animals and humans due to the threat of another invasion. This chapter is dedicated to them in solidarity.

Note

1. By choice, the Ukrainian spelling is used throughout this chapter, except in the bibliography, where the spelling used by referenced literature is maintained.

References

Allan, B. M., Nimmo, D. G., Ierodiaconou, D., VanDerWal, J., Koh, L. P., & Ritchie, E. G. (2018). Futurecasting ecological research: The rise of technoecology. *Ecosphere, 9*(5), e02163.

Angelidou, M., Psaltoglou, A., Komninos, N., Kakderi, C., Tsarchopolous, P., & Panori, A. (2017). Enhancing sustainable urban development through smart city applications. *Journal of Science and Technology Policy Management*, 9(2), 46–169.

Arcari, P., Probyn-Rapsey, F., & Singer, H. (2021). Where species don't meet: Invisibilized animals, urban nature and city limits. *Environment and Planning E: Nature and Space*, *4*(3), 940–965.

BBC News. (2016, November 7). Why are there so many stray cats in Istanbul? *BBC*. https://www.bbc.com/news/av/world-europe-37880274

Beatley, T., & Bekoff, M. (2013). City planning and animals: Expanding our urban compassion footprint. In C. Basta & S. Monori (Eds.), *Ethics, design and planning of the built environment* (pp. 185–196). Urban and Landscape Perspectives Springer Series, *12*. Springer.

Bekoff, M., & Pierce, J. (2009). *Wild justice: The moral lives of animals*. The University of Chicago Press.

Bentham, J. (1823/1948). *An introduction to the principles of morals and legislation*. Hafner.

Bibri, S.E., & Krogstie, J. (2017). Smart sustainable cities of the future: An extensive interdisciplinary literature review. *Sustainable Cities and Society*, *31*, 183–212.

Braverman, I. (2013) Animal mobilegalities: The regulation of animal movement in the American City. *Humanimalia*, *5*(1): 104–135.

Camilleri, L., & Chesnel, H. (Directors). (2020). *Dogs of Chernobyl: The Untold Story* [Film]. Independent. https://www.youtube.com/watch?v=y08oL0hbaFg

Clean Futures Fund. https://www.cleanfutures.org/programs/#dogsTop
Colding, J., & Barthel, S. (2017). An urban ecology critique on the 'smart city' model. *Journal of Cleaner Production, 164*, 95–101.
Deckha, M. (2015), Vulnerability, equality and animals. *Canadian Journal of Women and the Law, 27*(1), 47–71.
Forlano, L. (2016). Decentering the human in the design of collaborative cities. *Design Issues, 32*(3), 42–54
Fortin, D., Beyer, H. L., Boyce, M. S., Smith, D. W., Duchesne, T., & Mao, J. S. (2005). Wolves influence elk movements: Behavior shapes a trophic cascade in Yellowstone National Park. *Ecology, 86*(5), 1320–1330.
Future of Life Institute. (2022). Benefits & Risks of Artificial Intelligence. *Future of Life.* https://futureoflife.org/ai/benefits-risks-of-artificial-intelligence
Gibson, J. J. (1977). The theory of affordances. In R. Shaw & J. Bransford (Eds.), *Perceiving, acting, and knowing: Toward an ecological psychology* (pp. 67–82). Erlbaum.
Graham, M. (2014). Aboriginal notions of relationality and positionalism: A reply to Weber. *Global Discourse, 4*(1), 17–22.
Haraway, D. (2015). Anthropocene, Capitalocene, Plantationocene, Chthulucene: Making kin. *Environmental Humanities, 6*(1), 159–165.
Hart, K. (2019) Istanbul's intangible cultural heritage as embodied by street animals. *History and Anthropology, 30*(4), 448–459.
Höjer, M., & Wangel, S. (2015). Smart sustainable cities: Definition and challenges. In: L. Hilty, & B. Aebischer (Eds.), *ICT innovations for sustainability* (pp. 333–349). Springer.
Holmberg, T. (2013). Trans-species urban politics: Stories from a beach. *Space and Culture, 16*(1): 28–42.
Houston, D., Hillier, J., MacCallum, D., Steele, W., & Byrne, J. (2017). Make kin, not cities! Multispecies entanglements and 'becoming-world' in planning theory. *Planning Theory, 17*(2), 190–212.
International Telecommunications Union (ITU). (2014, March 5–6). Agreed Definition of a Smart Sustainable City. *Focus Group on Smart Sustainable Cities, SSC-0146.* International Telecommunications Union. https://www.itu.int/en/ITU-T/focusgroups/ssc/Pages/default.aspx
Kontokosta, C.E., & Hong, B. (2021). Bias in smart city governance: How socio-spatial disparities in 311 complaint behavior impact the fairness of data-driven decisions. *Sustainable Cities and Society, 64*, 102503.
Lima, S. L. (1998). Nonlethal effects in the ecology of predator–prey interactions: What are the ecological effects of anti-predator decision-making? *BioScience, 48*(1): 25–34
Luniak, M. (2004). Synurbanization: Adaptation of animal wildlife to urban development. In W. Shaw, L. Harris, & L. VanDruff (Eds.), *Urban Wildlife Conservation: Proceedings of the 4th International Symposium* (pp. 50–55). University of Arizona.
Mancini, C. (2023). A biosemiotics perspective on dogs' interaction with interfaces: An analytical and design framework. *Interaction Studies, 24*(2), 201–224.
Mancini, C., Hirsch-Matsioulas, O., & Metcalfe, D. (2022). Politicising animal–computer interaction: An approach to political engagement with animal-centred design. In D. van der Linden, I. Hirskyj-Douglas, & D. L. Roberts (Eds.), *ACI '22: Proceedings of the Ninth International Conference on Animal-Computer Interaction* (Article 1). ACM.
McDowall, J. (2018, February 5). Meet the dogs of Chernobyl—The abandoned pets that formed their own canine community. *The Guardian.* https://www.theguardian.com/lifeandstyle/2018/feb/05/dogs-chernobyl-abandoned-pets-stray-exclusion-zone
Michael, M. (2004). Roadkill: Between humans, nonhuman animals, and technologies. *Society and Animals 12*(4), 278–298.
Narayanan, Y., & Bindumadhav, S. (2019). 'Posthuman cosmopolitanism' for the Anthropocene in India: Urbanism and human–snake relations in the Kali Yuga. *Geoforum, 106*, 402–410.
Nussbaum, M.C. (2006). *Frontiers of justice: Disability, nationality, species membership.* Belknap Press.

Paci, P., Mancini, C., & Nuseibeh, B. (2022). The case for animal privacy in the design of technologically supported environments. *Frontiers in Veterinary Science: Animal Behaviour and Welfare, 8*, 784794.

Philo, C., & Wilbert, C. (2000). Animal spaces, beastly places: An introduction. In C. Philo & C. Wilbert (Eds.), *Animal spaces, beastly places: New geographies of human–animal relations* (pp. 1–36). Routledge.

Porter, P. (2018). For the love of cats (and dogs)! *Society & Animals, 26*(3), 339–343.

Rawls, J. (2001). *Justice as fairness: A restatement.* Harvard University Press.

Riffat, S., Powell, R., & Aydin, D. (2016). Future cities and environmental sustainability. *Future Cities and Environment, 2*(1), 1–23.

Rosenzweig, M. L. (2003). *Win–win ecology: How the earth's species can survive in the midst of human enterprise.* Oxford University Press.

Schuttler, S. G., Sorensen, A. E., Jordan, R. C., Cooper, C., & Shwartz, A. (2018). Bridging the nature gap: Can citizen science reverse the extinction of experience? *Frontiers in Ecology and the Environment, 16*(7), 405–411.

Sen, A. (2009). *The idea of justice.* Penguin Books.

Singer, P. (1980). Animals and the value of life. In T. Regan (Ed.), *Matters of life and death: New introductory essays on moral philosophy* (pp. 28–66). Random House.

Smith, N., Bardzell, S., & Bardzell, J. (2017). Designing for cohabitation: Naturecultures, hybrids, and decentering the human in design. In G. Mark, S. Fussell, C. Lampe, M. C. Schraefel, J. P. Hourcade, C. Appert, & D. Wigdor (Eds.), *CHI '17: Proceedings of the 2017 CHI Conference on Human Factors in Computing Systems*, (pp. 1714–1725). ACM.

Steffen, W., Richardson, K., Rockström, J., Cornell, S. E., Fetzer, I., Bennett, E. M., Biggs, R., Carpenter, S. R., de Vries, W., de Wit, C. A., Folke, C., Gerten, D., Heinke, J., Mace, G. M., Persson, L. M., Ramanathan, V., Reyers, B., & Sörlin, S. (2015). Planetary boundaries: Guiding human development on a changing planet. *Science, 347*(6223), 736–747.

Stephens, P. A., Pettorelli, N., Barlow, J., Whittingham, M. J., & Cadotte, M. W. (2015). Management by proxy? The use of indices in applied ecology. *Journal of Applied Ecology, 52*, 1–6.

Torun, C. (Director). (2017). *Kedi* [documentary film]. Oscilloscope, Turkey/USA.

Turnbull, J. (2020). Checkpoint dogs: Photovoicing canine companionship in the Chernobyl Exclusion Zone. *Anthropology Today, 36*, 21–24.

United Nations. (2014). World Urbanization Prospects: The 2014 Revision, Highlights (ST/ESA/SER.A/ 352). https://esa.un.org/unpd/wup

von Uexküll, J. (1909). *Umwelt und Innenwelt der Tiere.* Julius Springer.

Vincent Callebaut Architectures. https://vincent.callebaut.org

Vincent Callebaut Architectures. (2014). *Fertile cities: Ecoresponsible lifestyles inspired by biomimicry.* Liaoning Science and Technology Publishing House.

Wolch, J., Brownlow, A., & Lassiter, U. (2000). Constructing the animal worlds of inner-city Los Angeles. In C. Philo & C. Wilbert (Eds.), *Animal spaces, beastly places: New geographies of human-animal relations* (pp. 73–98). Routledge.

10

Decentring in More-than-Human Design

A Provocation on Spatial Justice and Urban Conflict in Palestine

Mennatullah Hendawy, Shaimaa Lazem, and Rachel Clarke

Introduction

We expand the discussion of socio-spatial justice to the more-than-human smart city discourse by questioning the practice of decentring (Forlano 2016). We highlight the added complexities when the imagined smart city is also the site of historical political conflict, taking Palestinian East Jerusalem (PEJ) as our case study. We take as a starting point recent scholarship that has moved from the technocentric view of smart cities towards a more dynamic understanding that builds on socio-technical (Nochta et al. 2021), hybrid (balancing top-down and bottom-up) (Hendawy & Kormann da Silva 2023), sustainability, and more-than-human concerns (Clarke et al. 2019; Celermajer, et al. 2021; Fieuw et al. 2022). Scholars in postcolonial urbanism and decolonial thinking, however, argue for greater awareness of northern European and Anglo-American perspectives that risk homogenising city planning and design in the Global South (Watson 2014; Datta 2019, p.408). Applications for, and knowledge produced on, the practicalities of smart cities can now be found in many different countries, demonstrating the significance of nuanced localised contexts (Datta 2019; Söderström et al. 2021).

More critical considerations of what concepts such as sustainability and more-than-human sensibilities mean in the context of smart city development for different religious and cultural orientations are also important (Rifat et al. 2020). With this, there is a need to support the creation of alternative stories and urban imaginaries of smart cities that diverge from the popularised mainstream (Estrada-Grajales et al. 2018). It also remains incumbent to more critically examine how more-than-human smart cities inhabit questions of spatial justice, governance, and power structures in different political contexts (Sheikh et al. 2023). The rise of digitalisation and visualisations of urban space can create socio-spatial injustices obscuring power asymmetries (Hendawy 2022). These require attention to spatial justice as the 'the fair and equitable distribution in space of socially valued resources and opportunities to use them' (Soja 2010, p.2).

In this chapter, we focus on PEJ and the position of 'the land'. Here the land is a more-than-human entity, a conjoined spiritual–naturalised space that encompasses a socio-political imaginary that forms the basis of urban conflict between Palestinian sovereignty and Israeli environmental protections (Braverman 2021). The division and fragmentation of spaces into borders and colonial states are made possible via

Mennatullah Hendawy, Shaimaa Lazem, and Rachel Clarke, *Decentring in More-than-Human Design.* In: *Designing More-than-Human Smart Cities.* Edited by: Sara Heitlinger, Marcus Foth, and Rachel Clarke, Oxford University Press.
 DOI: 10.1093/9780191980060.003.0012

the dispossession of land achieved through abstracting spatial technologies, including surveying, renaming, and mapping across visual and digital domains ascribing particular value (Pugliese 2020). In PEJ, non-human struggles are often positioned as 'protections' that sit at the nexus of the land, nature, race, and the state, thereby remaining a key battleground for ongoing dispossession of space from certain populations, including capital accumulation, political sovereignty, and decolonisation (Braverman 2021; Clarke et al. 2022).

In this chapter, we contribute a thought experiment using two fictional stories to problematise the practice of decentring in a context of struggle. Our discussion highlights the entangled spatial conflicts and the necessity of decolonial more-than-human–human relational configurations. We argue how decentring of marginalised humans to foreground more-than-human agencies for the design of smart cities may not result in visions that support longitudinal equity. We argue for multi-dimensional layers that recognise not only spatial centres and margins of power, but also hierarchical depths and temporalities that inform emergent forms of justice.

Theoretical Background: Decolonising Design with More-than-Humans

More-than-human conceptualisations of urban and environmental planning is an increasingly vital term to describe the future of smart and sustainable cities—that is, nature-positive (Birkeland 2022). It invites urban planners to question the conventional greenwashing approaches to smart cities (Yigitcanlar et al. 2019) and recognise the agencies of species other than humans in the city (Fieuw et al. 2022). Central to more-than-human scholarship is rejecting human exceptionalism, where humans are considered separate, autonomous, and superior to non-humans (Forlano 2016; de la Bellacasa 2017; Wakkary 2021). In an attempt to achieve a more just and democratic approach to urban planning, decentring human agency is postulated as one way of recognising the significance of multiple other-than-human worlds (Forlano 2016). Alternative modes such as collaboration and cohabitation between humans and other species are also proposed (Heitlinger et al. 2019).

Although more-than-human scholarship is critical of the Western dualist thinking in which human exceptionalism is rooted, traces of such dualism exist in the 'more-than-human' framing, whereby humans are separated from other entities. As described by Forlano (2016), acts of decentring human agency suggest shifting perceptions of what constitutes the centrality of human perception. Scholars such as de la Bellacasa (2017) highlight the contradictions and complexities of decentring when a presumed centre is already defined by and with particular humans. In response, we propose adopting a decolonial lens to further examine the nuance of more-than-human–human dualism in sites of political conflict.

The interest in decolonial thinking as a critical approach has been growing beyond its original role of describing the processes following the dismantling of colonial powers (Klose 2014) into other fields of investigation including design and Human–Computer Interaction (Ali 2016; Bidwell 2016; Abdulla et al. 2019; Akama et al. 2020; Lazem et al. 2021; Clarke et al. 2022). Central to decolonial thought is being critical of the dominance of Western knowledge systems and 'making Western systems of knowledge the object of critique and inquiry' (Denzin & Lincoln 2008, p.7). This is motivated by aspirations for self-determination by the formerly colonised (Hajibayova & Buente 2016; Ntuli 2002), and a desire for foregrounding and centralising local and indigenous voices (Zavala 2013; de Sousa Santos 2014; Datta 2017). This is underpinned by a lack of trust in Western models that, over time, have replaced local and indigenous knowledge systems (Battiste 2005; Tuck & Yang 2012). By focusing on the local previously marginalised non-Western voices, decolonial agendas seek to unsettle epistemological and ontological coloniality (Grosfoguel 2002; Mignolo 2012; Ali 2016). When centralising local voices is complemented with a critical reflection on the body-politics—or corpopolitics—of who is making design decisions and who is affected by them and the geopolitics of a site of inquiry, contextual power imbalances can be examined (Ali 2016; Torretta & Reitsma 2019).

Taking a decolonial thinking approach to more-than-human sensibilities, we provoke a discussion on human exceptionalism in an urban, occupied, non-Western city. Using a decolonial thinking lens to critically examine urban planning in PEJ, we show that human exceptionalism is a situated concept that should be understood within certain local socio-political, geographic, and economic realities. We bring to the fore the geopolitics of PEJ 'land' as a site of struggle. As decolonial scholars Tuck and Yang argue, 'Land is what is most valuable, contested, required.' and the disruption of particular relationships to land 'continues to represent a profound epistemic, ontological, cosmological violence' (Tuck & Yang 2012, p.5). We further scrutinise the corpopolitics of the 'humans' of this land. Indeed, the case of PEJ shows that Palestinian-humans-under-occupation, Israeli-human-settlers, and internationals can have very different embodied experiences of the city and its borders (Griffiths & Repo 2021; Clarke et al. 2022). Using terminology akin to decolonial thinking, one could say that humans in PEJ are distributed over multiple cores and geographical centres (Israeli government and settlers) and peripheries (Palestinian Authority and its people) in the city. Such views make palpable the power imbalances entrenched in PEJ and therefore foreground the implications of decentring Palestinian humans in favour of non-human actors.

Context: Designing Within Sites of Struggle (Palestinian East Jerusalem)

PEJ, although originally part of the West Bank, was annexed as part of Israel in 1967 and divided into smaller neighbourhoods under the occupation (See Figure 10.1). Many of the neighbourhoods in PEJ are disconnected from each other via a nine-metre-high concrete wall, separating PEJ from the West Bank and Israel. The barrier is only passable for Palestinians with appropriate permits via checkpoints (B'Tselem 2017).

Increased closures of routes, curfews, and checkpoints between Palestinian neighbourhoods have created significant fragmentation between families and communities (Richter-Devroe 2018). Within PEJ, the particular zoning of vacant areas as nature reserves and national parks, which have often been left vacant due to the inability of

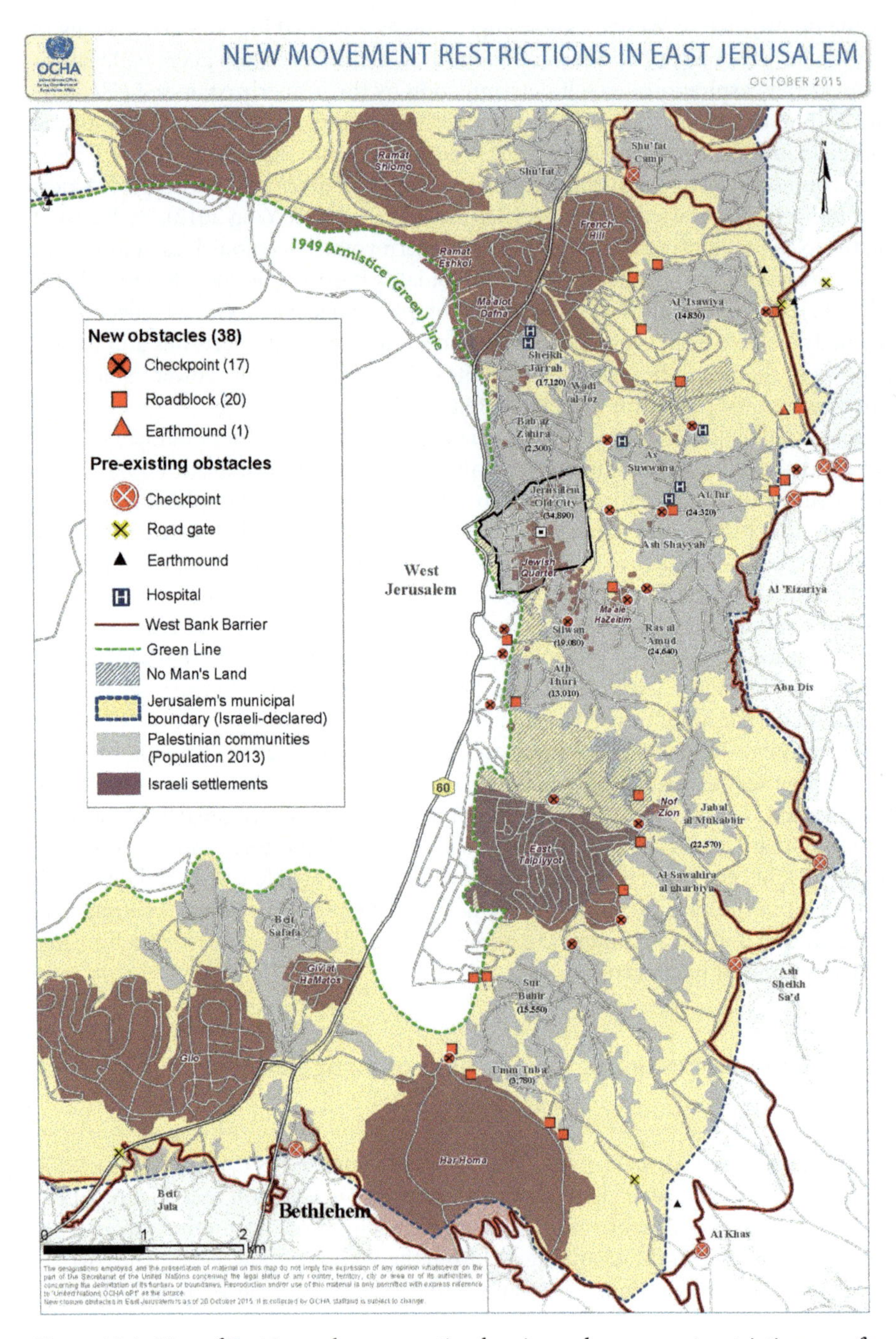

Figure 10.1 Map of East Jerusalem separation barrier and movement restrictions as of October 2015.

Map reproduced courtesy of the UN Office for the Coordination of Humanitarian Affairs in the Occupied Palestinian Territories, East Jerusalem, 2015.

families to gain access due to annexation, dispossession, and demolition, has continued to benefit green gentrification and tourism agendas at the cost of further spatial restrictions for everyday Palestinians (Bimkom 2018; Braverman 2021).

While neighbourhoods are coming together to challenge planning decisions, young Palestinian women in particular are often excluded from planning decisions, despite being heavily impacted by them. Planning decisions that limit the mobility or housing for Palestinians, through checkpoints, nature reserve designations, and segregation walls, can have a greater impact on young women's access to education, socialisation, employment, and new homes, thereby limiting transitions into independent adulthood (Sousa et al. 2014). Planning decisions can also inadvertently damage pro-environmental efforts by introducing new composite materials, dividing migration paths, reducing feeding habitats, and seed dispersal for plants and animals. Diverse habitats can be replaced with resource-intensive infrastructure unsympathetic to existing lower-impact traditional buildings (Braverman 2021).

International funders and non-governmental organisations (NGOs) supporting more sustainable urban design solutions expect women to be equally involved in future planning decisions and consultations to ensure decisions are more embedded in community concerns (UN Women 2019). This approach, however, is not without its complications and a focus on women's involvement can legitimise certain kinds of participation over others, serving as a tokenistic justification for key decision-making strategies (Jad 2018; Richter-Devroe 2018). Failure to consider the wider socio-cultural and intersectional sensitivities that encompasses ethnicity, religion, socio-economic background, and class hierarchies can further marginalise (Moser 2005). Most significantly, without international funding in combination with the lack of political backing and local knowledge, neighbourhoods within PEJ can find they have limited options that both respect their traditions and provide shared access to the land.

Palestinian Smart Cities

Investment in Palestine's technical infrastructure in the past decade has been heavily regulated by the Israeli government and international corporations (Fraiberg 2021). Concurrently there is no shortage of mapping and planning data available from local NGOs and academics engaged in mapping the injustices of service provision and problematic environmental degradation that affects water quality and pollution within Palestinian neighbourhoods (e.g., Shadeed et al. 2019). Yet, communities in PEJ can often struggle to gain access to such resources to help contribute meaningfully to the Israeli planning system without knowledgeable intermediaries (e.g., Teli et al. 2022), who understand both the logistics and complexities of planning legislation and the concerns of local communities.

Gaining access to and availability of planning skills is no small task. Legislation between Palestine and Israel is profoundly exclusionary, underpinned by decades of colonial division and occupation (e.g., JLAC 2021). Recourse to legal justice for Palestinians to remain on the land within PEJ is available, but the mechanisms to make this happen are often oblique and biased, drawn from laws created through a patchwork of international legislation distinguishing between different authorities and purposes of use. Limited availability of legal professionals experienced enough to master this level of complexity and overall a lack of trust in international mechanisms of justice mean few cases are successful (Jad 2018; Richter-Devroe 2018).

The smart city has emerged in this context as embodying the potential for an architectural high-tech modernity and form of resistance in the face of ongoing colonial restrictions and spatio-cidal injustices imposed by Israeli planning policy (Brocket 2021; Fraiberg 2021). In the cities of Ramallah and Rawabi, the integration of smart-city infrastructure has been described as creating efficiencies in service of the Palestinian people, alongside forming alternative governmentalities and state-building. This is in response to the limitations of governance provided by the Palestinian Authority and their quasi-state functionality (Brocket 2021; Fraiberg 2021).

Scholars have argued that such initiatives, however, have merely serviced the middle classes and elite Israeli and Palestinian populations, contributing to neoliberal global economic profits and politics that undermine justice and opportunities for everyday Palestinians (Grandinetti 2015). In the case of Rawabi, with a focus on building a new modern creative tech industry, this is predicated on material resources supplied by Israeli corporations. Entering Rawabi requires travelling through checkpoints, which many Palestinians are unable to do without permits (Fraiberg 2021).

Initiatives, such as renaming streets in Ramallah as part of a digitalisation process, further highlight ongoing tensions in Palestinian sovereignty. The desire for Palestinian relations with the land can counter the desire for a more depoliticised modernisation, breaking with the perceived problematic violent associations of terrorism and martyrdom (Brocket 2021), also considered by some to be a significant aspect of Palestinian resistance. These sites of struggle are also heavily mapped, surveyed, and prone to attacks by the Israeli military using a range of technologies (CCTV, observation towers, and drones; see Graham 2010; O'Malley & Smith 2020; Pugliese 2020), alongside the more everyday use of social media by Palestinians and activist groups.[1]

In this context, and given its historical-originated political conflicts, employing a duality between 'human vs non-human' in smart-city planning would fail to recognise the power differences and imbalance between Palestinian-humans-under-occupation and Israeli-human-settlers. In the following section we outline an approach to design in the form of thought experiments as fictional stories (Dunne & Raby 2013; Blythe & Encinas 2018) as a means of challenging alternatives that help demonstrate the frailty of the 'human' as a singular analytical category.

Methodology: Thought Experiments

Thought experiments are valuable in technology design to interrogate theories critically through fiction (Blythe & Encinas 2018) to bring to the fore debate on difficult topics and consequences of plans by 'fusing narrative and concept to produce functional fictions designed to get people thinking about something specific' (Dunne & Raby 2013; p.79). Beside 'being experiments and paradoxes, thought experiments are stories [and] many of the issues raised by thought experiments are prefigured in aesthetics and the logic of fiction' (Sorensen 1998, p.6).

Fictional experiments may sound like strange companions in responding to justice and conflict, particularly in a context of oppression and marginalisation. However, John Rawl's thought experiment, 'The veil of ignorance,' aims to ignite thinking about how justice can be achieved in decision making (Rawl 1971). As Rawls argues,

> The principles of justice are chosen behind a veil of ignorance. This ensures that no one is advantaged or disadvantaged in the choice of principles by the outcome of natural chance or the contingency of social circumstances. Since all are similarly situated and no one is able to design principles to favour his particular condition, the principles of justice are the result of a fair agreement or bargain (1971, p.11).

Rawls' experiment postulates that the decision maker is required to make decisions while being unaware of the role that they would be playing in the society, hence making an 'impersonal judgement' (Feiwel 1985, p.145) behind a 'veil of ignorance'. Rawls (1971) refers to this position as the 'original' position (Figure 10.2).

Key to Rawl's experiment is the assumption of 'symmetry of everyone's relations to each other, this initial situation is fair between individuals as moral persons.' Such presumed symmetry is indeed contested in decolonial thought (de Sousa Santos 2014), as previously outlined in the case of PEJ. The assumed symmetry in Rawl's experiment, we argue, echoes how 'humans' are envisioned in more-than-human sensibilities. Therefore, by using an adapted version of Rawl's experiment, our hope is to highlight the challenges of decentring humans when power asymmetrics and conflict persist.

We respond to issues of justice in more-than-human and marginalised worlds in conflict using a thought experiment with two differently positioned fictional stories. By writing fiction, we creatively work through and problematise how decentring humans without consideration of *who* is decentred may further marginalise. We aim to bring into dialogue a practice of decentring and recentring particular humans, Palestinian women, as marginalised actors in the PEJ planning process.

Troubling Stories

Despite the power of stories to generate visions of alternative preferable worlds, stories can also replicate stories of inequity. In wider traditions of science fiction, authors such as Octavia Butler have created preferable socially just worlds from the 'destruction and wounded flourishing' of the African diaspora, slavery, and migration (Haraway 2016, p.120). Haraway builds on a 'carrier bag' approach to stories that avoids reproducing monolinear grand narratives and heroes while embracing the entangled troubles of exploitation. Tabouda and Turner (2021) further suggest stories for speculating on an 'alternative to alternatives', drawing from the decolonial work of de Sousa Santos (2014). They argue for 'active imagination' that critically reveals,

Figure 10.2 An illustration of Rawls's veil of ignorance thought experiment. On the left are the decision makers tasked with creating more equitable futures for those most impacted by their decisions and on the right are representatives from a diverse society. The decision makers take on an 'original position', where they are not assigned with an identity but only asked to formulate ideas for a more inclusive society. The decision makers' identities remain uncertain behind a 'veil of ignorance' and hence they could be millionaires, unemployed youth, or any other part of the population. According to Rawls, this ensures decisions are more likely to be just and equitable as they cannot be influenced by self-interest.

explains, and avoids replicating linear narrative of progress that further support stories of colonial exploitation and domination.

We therefore acknowledge the burgeoning work of science fiction in Palestinian literatures that responds to an already dystopian, cyber-intense society where communities are disconnected through 'dischronotopia: multiple, hierarchised time-space configurations in one tiny geographical place' (Moore 2020). In the wider context of Palestinian literary traditions, Abu Hatoum (2021), suggests that stories about liberation feature heavily, containing cyclical temporalities between past and future; futures are haunted by the past, liberated futures are described in the past, and 'loss is enfolded into future traces ... when the everyday is subsumed by political (spatial, material, or symbolic) violence, the future oscillates in people's imagination between hope and suspicion.' (p.397). This aligns with the anticipatory concerns of

Palestinian authors and activists who argue for justice and sovereignty yet to come, despite segregation and violence (Jeronen et al. 2021).

Positionality

We recognise however, that in choosing a thought experiment, in the form of fictional stories to test notions of decentring, rather than a collaborative world building exercise (Tabouda & Turner 2021), we must acknowledge our own positionalities. We are not Palestinian and cannot speak on behalf of Palestinians. Rather, we draw from our respective experiences as Arabic and British women trained in urban planning, HCI, and design in a predominantly Western context in German, UK, and US institutions. We therefore embody multiple knowledges of these struggles, both through academic and Arabic literatures, research, and exposure to cultures that underpin our positionalities and lead to particular biases, some of which are sympathetic to Palestinian sovereignty. Indeed, there is a need, counter to the ideas proposed by Rawl (1971), in being open about our potential bias and limitations in constructing such fictions to avoid the 'god trick' of suggesting these stories come from nowhere and are not situated (Haraway 2016), and to commit to 'active imagination' that is also critically aware.

Prior Research

Despite efforts to engage with particular communities in PEJ, we have faced significant socio-political challenges, which we identify as a limitation of this work. The research insights and data that contribute to our fictional stories derive from real-world experiences; interviews, ethnographies, and design workshops, working with INGOs, designers, activists, and young people at risk of housing demolition in the West Bank between 2018–2020. In particular, we draw from research with an urban planning justice organisation in Jerusalem. In our prior research the focus was on designing a collaborative resource to engage young women (18–25 years) in alternative forms of collective data mapping that were meaningful for them and for their wider communities (see Clarke et al. 2022 and Figure 10.3.).

Given this context, the following fictions build on, invoke, and leverage the evocative metaphors of dischronotopia of multiple fragmented space-time configurations, oscillations of hope and suspicion, and carrier bags of wounded thriving and dispossession. Further, they build on lived experiences from our research (Clarke et al. 2022).

In the first story, we wear the veil of ignorance, which requires us to propose potentialities and consider the consequences of a just society. We do this here from the perspective of the land, as a spiritual and naturalised system of governance. We are asked to consider the benefits and burdens of our decisions in a newly formed society, and in this instance, a society that includes the agency of non-human entities. In this way, Palestinian identities are equalised alongside all other humans in order to

(a)

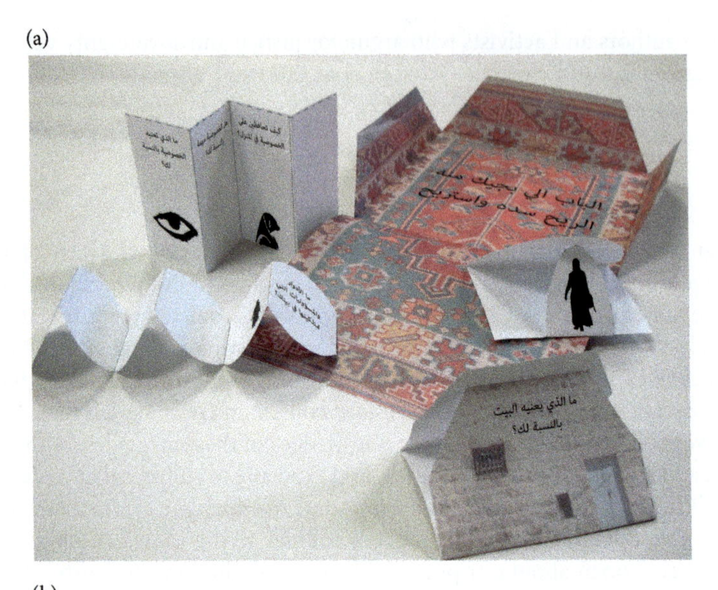

(b)

Figure 10.3a & 10.3b Example of co-design work to reconfigure data mapping in East Jerusalem. Working with a community neighbourhood planning facilitator in Jerusalem, we devised questions for young Palestinian women to discuss important areas of their neighbourhood combining different nature-cultures, local references, and spiritual connections to the land and its people.

foreground the significance of non-human entities, the land as an ecosystem for all its inhabitants.

In the second story, we remove the veil and centre the story on a Palestinian woman in an attempt to work towards a fiction that involves cohabitation that limits marginalisation and dispossession. We consciously focus on centring marginalised actors in PEJ planning. We recognise the agencies and voices of marginalised Palestinians-under-occupation (particularly young women), as well as the agencies of other marginalised non-human entities. This view implies that the needs of multiple actors should be accounted for in smart-city planning, and forces us, in line with decolonial thinking, to interrogate not only the geopolitics of where, but also the corpopolitics of who is affected and how, and how embodied intimacies in relation to the land are impacted by displacement and planning decisions. In each fiction we locate our story on a small vacant plot of land to illustrate different geographical scales and perspectives.

Fiction One: The Land

I am the land. I do my best to ignore the divisions, the walls, and the structures that sit on me, using rock and stone. I have taken millennia to form deep below the ground. I am continually supporting the plants and shrubs with nutrients and water that will eventually take down these walls and structures. Some are harder to break down than others when they are made from combined concrete and metal. It is more difficult for seeds to rest and for roots to grow.

There are sensors buried both deep in the earth and on the earth, encased in metals and plastics and on the buildings that record activity above and below; shifts in water flow, soil disruption and root activity, numbers of healthy plants and animals, insects and birds that have made this their home for feeding, sleeping, playing, mating. These sensors create a cacophony of data voices—numerical values of subtle dynamic changes over time converted to sound and speech. The data voices are used to make decisions about what should happen when planning new infrastructures as part of the city to sustain the land and its inhabitants for longevity.

There is a small plot of land on the outskirts of PEJ that people appear to have forgotten about, and the wilderness has taken over. The plot sits between two heavy houses with foundations that go for centuries deep into the soil and rock, with the voices of ancestors that further contribute to the cacophony. The people come and go but mostly ignore me, as to them perhaps I appear unruly and unkept, uneven, and uninviting. Maybe they just don't know what to do with me. But soon they will be gone. The data and voices have led to a decision to remove the houses so the land can support more wilderness. It is too overcrowded with people, and the structures are becoming too heavy to support other forms of life.

Fiction Two: Amal

I am Amal, a Palestinian woman. I have lived in this house with my family since I was born. Before this, my ancestors lived here for many decades, and after me, my future generations yet to come will be here. I am grateful for the strength of the rock and stone that make my home strong and secure, but also for the plants that grow between the cracks that help make a home for other creatures and sustain our family with medicine and herbs. They make our home stronger and cooler from the midday summer sun and heat and warmer in winter, protecting us from the rain and cold. They also protect us from hostile neighbours, providing privacy and shelter from attacks.

Once a week we check-in and spend time with a small plot of land next to our house, we feel how cool or dusty, muddy or damp it is; if there is new plant growth; and what creatures we are sharing our home with as this changes with the seasons and weather. We do this with our neighbours, with ancestors, elders, and the diaspora who are no longer living in our neighbourhood but are keen to maintain their connection with the land. Using pictures, food, and stories we exchange different ideas and share the different voices, sounds of the birds and crickets, old tales of how the land used to be before our houses were here, myths on how the landscape was moulded. We have access to the cacophony of data voices from sensors, too, which helps us understand some of the more scientific ways in which the land is constituted of different elements, water, minerals, certain grasses, insects, and birds.

These different perspectives help us ground our ideas and imagine new ways of being for how we continue to grow together with the land. With my family and neighbours, we make small changes each year to help work with the water flows that have carved the land and make use of resources already taken from the earth. We tread more carefully through pathways and entrances of the land appreciating how it has taken many lifetimes to forge these rocks and roots and how these offer stability in an uncertain turbulent way of life.

Discussion: Multiple Fictions, Multiple Realities

We presented a thought experiment (Rawl 1971; Dunne & Raby 2013; Blythe & Encinas 2018) through two fictional stories to explore the challenges of embracing more-than-human sensibilities in a Global South context of struggle, where land protections and conflicts prevail. Our goal was to contest the generalisable assumptions underpinning the term 'human' in taking a 'more-than-human' position when decentring human agency. These assumptions suggest humans should be considered equal with other planetary inhabitants, or to be considered of less import than other species. In our experiment we attempted to illustrate non-human concerns (the land) alongside marginalised humans (Palestinian women in PEJ). Examining these assumptions in the specific geopolitics of place in PEJ, where political conflict is omnipresent, has highlighted the risks of decentring humans when not identifying the power imbalances in more-than-human–human relations. Such examination further highlights the need for correspondence with and accounting for the complex realities of historical conflicts associated with land. In our final discussion, we reflect on the decentred and recentred perspectives taken in the two fictions and consider the value of thought experiments when positioned as decolonial spatial justice fictions. Such fictions open up opportunities for alternative framings of the more-than-human and multiple dimensions of justice to emerge.

Decolonial spatial justice fictions

In constructing two fictions concerning one small plot of land in PEJ, our first story attempted to wear Rawl's (1971) veil of ignorance and foreground the voice of the land, a non-human entity, that would not privilege either Palestinian or Israeli planning decisions. Through invoking this position, however, it was difficult to completely remove bias and not do this without highlighting how the land may prefer to return to a state without human presence. In doing so, this would inadvertently support the ongoing dispossession of homes, which positions the land as a naturalised space in need of environmental protections and clearance (Braverman 2021). In the second fiction we aimed to remove the veil and purposefully recentre the decolonial situated corpopolitics of occupation, the marginalised voice of a particular human, a young woman, as cohabitant with the land in dialogue with multiple perspectives across time and space. In constructing these two short fictions, what is clear is that, in wearing the veil of ignorance, justice cannot be achieved for those most impacted by occupation. While both fictions are prone to our particular biases in supporting Palestinian sovereignty, we became aware of the impossibility of creating fictions from nowhere if focused on a spatial justice orientation, without replicating the god-trick of exceptionalism (Haraway 2016) and recognising our own bias and privilege (de la Bellacasa 2017).

Adopting a decolonial lens that is sensitive to the politics of design encounters and of the construction of particular narrative tropes (Haraway 2016; Moore 2020; Abu Hatoum 2021) has demonstrated that decentring marginalised Palestinian humans (as presented in the first fiction) unintentionally might reinforce existing power imbalances pushing them further to the margins of the planning process. Interrogating not only the geopolitics but the corpopolitics of specific 'humans' is often absent in previous work promoting more-than-human integration (Forlano 2016; Fieuw et al. 2022). The thought experiment thereby works as a useful device, an illustration of how more-than-human–human relationships could be brought into focus with people and has provoked a refocus on 'marginalisation' as an analytical category as opposed to 'humanness' in the quest of spatial justice in smart-city planning. This focus, we argue, is in line with the ethos underpinning 'more-than-human' relations in the sense that it is attentive to power differences among inhabitants and attempts to rebalance excluded voices. Asking 'who is marginalised and by whom' reveals the significant historical and species relations connecting marginalised humans and non-human actors. Palestinian humans and non-human actors in PEJ are rendered inseparable, though not always equal, as it is their collective power that gives rise to Palestinian sovereignty in relation to the land (Braverman 2021).

Towards alternative framings of the more-than-human

A potential alternative framing is one where marginalisation and political histories of actors in PEJ are included. This can be achieved by seeing natural and cultural heritage as emerging from relationships between human and non-human actors (Roudavski & Rotten 2020). This view builds on critical heritage studies' notion of assemblage, where heritage could be perceived as a mixed social and material collective composed of humans and non-humans (including plants, animals, the environment, and institutions), between which agency is contingent and emergent (Harrison 2015). Under the assemblage framing, asymmetries of agency and domination-exclusion relations are recognisable and can be examined (Harrison 2013). This implies that if the concern is preserving and centring the land, then all actors involved in this assemblage have to be considered in smart-city planning and design encounters.

Drawing from Islamic perspectives on non-human actors offers another cohabitation frame. Humans act as trustees responsible for protecting the environment, including non-human actors (e.g., plants and animals). While on the surface, this view seems to resonate with human exceptionalism, a guardianship position comes with particular responsibilities for the sustainment of resources that, as a Muslim, you would be questioned in the afterlife if your actions have led to environmental destruction.[2] Therefore, in the case of PEJ, the dependencies of non-human actors on human actors in PEJ becomes unavoidable. Planning to centre non-human actors, therefore, would require us to centre the most relevant custodians of the land, alongside buildings and with neighbours.

Emergent dimensions of justice

Despite the challenges presented in reimagining spatial justice in the first fiction in particular, both fictions help surface alternatives to the smart city in relation to each other. In creating two fictions about the same plot of land, the fictions help to move away from a technocentric modernity, renaming and abstractly mapping resources for human consumption (Grandinetti 2015; Brocket 2021; Fraiberg 2021), in favour of a more diffuse, multi-faceted discursive vision of the smart city and spatial justice grounded in the complex day-to-day realities of people's lives. Most relevant is that while using the vocabulary of centres and margins as spatial metaphors helps clarify who is excluded, they also suggest further dualities if not situated within other dimensions of geopolitics, hierarchical depths and the importance of temporality and historicity. A two-dimensional 'mapping' of centres and margins may recreate the distanced borders of colonial surveillance and control (Pugliese 2020), rather than the messy entanglements that are woven through deep, slow time (Haraway 2016).

Linking back to the discussion on spatial justice and smart cities presented in the introduction of this chapter, alternative forms of justice need to be proposed to allow for the inclusion of more-than-human–human concerns. These may include techno-centric and socio-cultural, as well as political aspects to be incubated. In this alternative view, it is not about equalising humans and non-humans, but rather about the conscious decision to situate the network of actors in the socio-political and historical context it has emerged from. In this context, social, spatial, and material (technological) factors are all included.

Conclusion

The design of smart cities through a more-than-human conceptual lens continues to be significant in shifting focus from issues of sustainability and environmental protections to the importance of collaboration and cohabitation with non-human actors. Despite the relevance of designers responding to more-than-human concerns, issues of spatial injustices continue to govern how urban plans reproduce and enact inequalities. These plans often privilege particular visions, asserting power relations and inequitable disparities on who benefits, who loses out, and which agendas serve the decision-making process. While decentring human agency is one of many valuable strategies, such approaches may risk further marginalisation of people already excluded from the urban planning and the smart city discourse without further situated critical reflection. Therefore, reducing 'human' to one analytical category and assuming all humans are equally centred requires careful questioning on who constitutes the geographies of centres and margins. In the context of more-than-human smart-city design in the Global South, and in particular at sites of ongoing conflict, we have presented a case study on PEJ, offering a site of reflection and interrogation using fictional stories that are built on the veil of ignorance thought experiment (Rawls 1971). We suggest a reorientation to more purposeful decolonial more-than-human–human relations, recentring particularly quiet and slow human experiences already connected to the land through cohabitation. In utilising the thought experiment as an analytical device by creating multiple fictions from one situated place, we argue for a more multi-dimensional orientation—one that moves away from the dualities of centres and margins and instead considers the hierarchical depths and temporalities of pasts and futures that emerge from emergent forms of justice yet to come.

Notes

1. See Forensic Architecture's case on Sheikh Jarrah, for example: https://forensic-architecture.org/investigation/sheikh-jarrah
2. https://www.ecomena.org/sustainability-islam/

References

Abdulla, D., Ansari, A., Canlı, E., Keshavarz, M., Kiem, M., Oliveira, P., Prado, L., & Schultz, T. (2019). A manifesto for decolonising design [Essay]. *Journal of Futures Studies, 23*(3), 129–132. https://doi.org/10.6531/JFS.201903_23(3).0012

Abu Hatoum, N. (2021). Decolonizing [in the] future: scenes of Palestinian temporality. *Geografiska Annaler: Series B, Human Geography, 103*(4), 397–412. doi: 10.1080/04353684.2021.1963806

Ali, S. M. (2016). A brief introduction to decolonial computing. *XRDS: Crossroads, the ACM Magazine for Students—Cultures of Computing, 22*(4), 16–21

Akama, Y., Light, A., & Kamihira, T. (2020). Expanding participation to design with more-than-human concerns. In C. Del Gaudio, L. Parra-Agudelo, R. Clarke, J. Saad-Sulonen, A. Botero, F. César Londoño, & P. Escandón (Eds.), *PDC '20: Proceedings of the 16th Participatory Design*

Conference 2020: Participation(s) otherwise (pp. 1–11). ACM. https://doi.org/10.1145/3385010.3385016

Battiste, M. (2005). Indigenous knowledge: Foundations for First Nations. *WINHEC: International Journal of Indigenous Education Scholarship*, *1*, 1–17. https://journals.uvic.ca/index.php/winhec/article/view/19251

Bidwell, N. J. (2016). Decolonizing HCI and interaction design discourse: Some considerations in planning AfriCHI. *XRDS: Crossroads, the ACM Magazine for Students—Cultures of Computing*, *22*(4), 22–27.

Bimkom. (2018). Urban nature in Jerusalem. *Bimkom: Planners for Planning Rights*. https://bimkom.org/eng/urban-nature-in-jerusalem/

Birkeland, J. (2022). Nature positive: Interrogating sustainable design frameworks for their potential to deliver eco-positive outcomes. *Urban Science*, *6*(2), 35. https://doi.org/10.3390/urbansci6020035

Blythe, M., & Encinas, E. (2018). Research fiction and thought experiments in design. *Foundations and Trends® in Human–Computer Interaction*, *12*(1), 1–105. http://dx.doi.org/10.1561/1100000070

Braverman, I. (2021). Nof kdumim: Remaking the ancient landscape in East Jerusalem's national parks. *Environment and Planning E: Nature and Space*, *4*(1), 109–134. https://doi.org/10.1177/2514848619889594

Brocket, T. (2021). Governmentality, counter-memory and the politics of street naming in Ramallah, Palestine. *Geopolitics*, *26*(2), 541–563.

B'Tselem. (2017, November 11). The separation barrier. *B'Tselem*. https://www.btselem.org/separation_barrier

Clarke, R. E., Talhouk R., Beshtawi, A., Barham, K., Boyle, O., Griffiths, M., & Baillie-Smith, M. (2022). Decolonising in, by and through participatory design with political activists in Palestine. In V. Vlachokyriakos, J. Yee, E. Grönvall, R. Noronha, A. Botero, C. Del Gaudio, Y. Akama, R. Clarke, & J. Vines (Eds.), *PDC '22: Proceedings of the Participatory Design Conference 2022*, Vol. *1* (pp. 36–49). ACM. https://doi.org/10.1145/3536169.3537778

Clarke, R. E., Heitlinger, S., Light, A., Forlano, L., Foth, M., DiSalvo, C. (2019). More-than-human participation: Design for sustainable smart city futures. *Interactions*, *26*(3), 60–63. https://doi.org/10.1145/3319075

Celermajer, D., Schlosberg, D., Rickards, L., Stewart-Harawira, M., Thaler, M., Tschakert, P., Verlie, B., & Winter, C. (2021). Multispecies justice: Theories, challenges, and a research agenda for environmental politics, *Environmental Politics*, *30*(1–2), 119–140. doi: 10.1080/09644016.2020.1827608

Datta, A. (2019). Postcolonial urban futures: Imagining and governing India's smart urban age. *Environment and Planning. D, Society & Space*, *37*(3), 393–410. https://doi.org/10.1177/0263775818800721

Datta, R. (2017). Decolonizing both researcher and research and its effectiveness in indigenous research. *Research Ethics*, *14*(2), 1–40.

Denzin, N. K., & Lincoln, Y. S. (2008). Introduction: Critical methodologies and indigenous inquiry. In N. K. Denzin, Y. S. Lincoln, & L. T. Smith (Eds.), *Handbook of critical and indigenous methodologies* (pp. 1–20). SAGE.

de Sousa Santos, B. (2014). *Epistemologies of the south: Justice against epistemicide*. Paradigm.

de La Bellacasa, M. P. (2017). *Matters of care: Speculative ethics in more than human worlds*. University of Minnesota Press.

Dunne, A., & Raby, F. (2013). *Speculative everything: Design, fiction, and social dreaming*. MIT Press.

Estrada-Grajales, C., Foth, M., & Mitchell, P. (2018). Urban imaginaries of co-creating the city: Local activism meets citizen peer-production. *Journal of Peer Production*. http://peerproduction.net/wp-content/uploads/2018/02/issue11-urban-imaginaries-submitted-draft.pdf

Fieuw, W., Foth, M., & Caldwell, G. (2022). Towards a more-than-human approach to smart and sustainable urban development: Designing for multispecies justice. *Sustainability*, *14*(2), 948. https://doi.org/10.3390/su14020948

Feiwel, G. R. (Ed.). (1985). *Issues in contemporary macroeconomics and distribution.* SUNY Press.

Forlano, L. (2016). Decentering the human in the design of collaborative cities. *Design Issues, 32*(3), 42–54. doi: https://doi.org/10.1162/DESI_a_00398

Fraiberg, S. (2021). Unsettling start-up ecosystems: Geographies, mobilities, and transnational literacies in the Palestinian start-up ecosystem. *Journal of Business and Technical Communication, 35*(2), 219–253.

Graham, S. (2010). *Cities under siege: The new military urbanism.* Verso.

Grandinetti, T. (2015). The Palestinian middle class in Rawabi: Depoliticizing the occupation. *Alternatives, 40*(1), 63–78.

Griffiths M, & Repo, J. (2021). Women and checkpoints in Palestine. *Security Dialogue, 52*(3), 249–265.

Grosfoguel, R. (2002). Colonial difference, geopolitics of knowledge, and global coloniality in the modern/colonial capitalist world-system. *Review, 25*(3), 203–224.

Hajibayova, L., Buente W., Quiroga L., & Valeho-Novikoff, S. (2016). Representation of Kanaka Maoli (Hawaiian) culture: A case of Hula Dance. *Proceedings of the Association for Information and Science and Technology, 53*(1), 1–3.

Haraway, D. J. (2016). *Staying with the trouble: Making kin in the Chthulucene.* Duke University Press.

Harrison, R. (2013). *Heritage: Critical Approaches.* Routledge.

Harrison, R. (2015). Beyond 'natural' and 'cultural' heritage: Toward an ontological politics of heritage in the age of Anthropocene. *Heritage & Society 8* (1), 24–42. https://doi.org/10.1179/2159032X15Z.00000000036.

Heitlinger, S., Bryan-Kinns, N. and Comber, R. (2019). The right to the sustainable smart city. In S. Brewster, G. Fitzpatrick, A. Cox, & V. Kostakos (Eds.), *CHI '19: Proceedings of the 2019 CHI Conference on Human Factors in Computing Systems* (pp. 1–13). ACM.

Hendawy, M., & Kormann da Silva, I. F. K. (2023). Hybrid smartness: Seeking a balance between top-down and bottom-up smart city approaches. In R. Goodspeed, R. Sengupta, M. Kyttä, & C. Pettit (Eds.), *Intelligence for future cities: Planning through big data and urban analytics* (pp. 9–27). Springer Nature Switzerland.

Hendawy, M. (2022). *Spatio-visual co-constructions: Communication and digitalization of urban planning in a mediatized world—Cairo as a glocal case* [Doctorate thesis, Technische Universität Berlin].

Jad, I. (2018). *Palestinian women's activism: Nationalism, secularism, Islamism.* Syracuse Press.

Joronen, M., Tawil-Souri, H., Amir, M., & Griffiths, M. (2021). Palestinian futures: Anticipation, imagination, embodiments. *Geografiska Annaler: Series B, Human Geography, 103*(4), 277–282. doi: 10.1080/04353684.2021.2004196

JLAC. (2021). Al-Walajeh: A process of ongoing dispossession (Policy Paper). https://www.jlac.ps/public/files/file/legal%20papers/Walajah%20Eng%20Formated%20JCHR.pdf

Klose, F. (2014, July 25). Decolonization and revolution. *European History Online.* http://ieg-ego.eu/en/threads/europe-and-the-world/european-overseas-rule/fabian-klose-decolonization-and-revolution

Lazem, S., Giglitto, D., Nkwo, M. S., Mthoko, H., Upani, J., & Peters, A. (2021). Challenges and paradoxes in decolonising HCI: A critical discussion. *Computer Supported Cooperative Work, 31*, 159–196. https://doi.org/10.1007/s10606-021-09398-0

Mignolo, W. D. (2012). *Local histories/global designs: Coloniality, subaltern knowledges, and border thinking.* Princeton University Press.

Moore, L. (2020, June 25). Drones and clones: Mapping Palestinian sci-fi with Lindsey Moore. *Arab Lit Quarterly.* https://arablit.org/2020/06/25/drones-and-clones-lindsey-moore/

Moser, C. (2005). Has gender mainstreaming failed? A comment on international development agency experiences in the South. *International Feminist Journal of Politics, 7*(4), 576–590.

Nochta, T., Wan, L., Schooling, J. M., & Parlikad, A. K. (2021). A socio-technical perspective on urban analytics: The case of city-scale digital twins. *Journal of Urban Technology, 28*(1–2), 263–287. doi: 10.1080/10630732.2020.1798177

Ntuli, P. (2002). Indigenous knowledge systems and the African renaissance. In C. A. Odora Hoppers (Ed.), *Indigenous knowledge and the integration of knowledge systems: Towards a philosophy of articulation* (pp. 53–66). New Africa Books

O'Malley, P., & Smith, G. J. D. (2020). 'Smart' crime prevention? Digitization and racialized crime control in a smart city. *Theoretical Criminology, 26*(1), 40–56. https://doi.org/10.1177/1362480620972703

Pugliese, J. (2020). *Biopolitics of the more-than-human: Forensic ecologies of violence.* Duke University Press.

Rawls, J. (1971). *A theory of justice.* The Belknap.

Richter-Devroe, S. (2018) *Women's political activism in Palestine: Peacebuilding, resistance, and survival.* University of Illinois Press.

Rifat, M. R., Toriq, T., & Ahmed, S. I. (2020). Religion and sustainability: Lessons of sustainable computing from Islamic religious communities. *Proceedings of the ACM on Human-Computer Interaction, 4* (CSCW2), 1–32.

Roudavski, S., & Rutten, J. (2020) Towards more-than-human heritage: Arboreal habitats as a challenge for heritage preservation. *Built Heritage, 4,* Article 4. https://doi.org/10.1186/s43238-020-00003-9

Shadeed, S. M., Judeh, T. G., & Almasri, M. N. (2019). Developing GIS-based water poverty and rainwater harvesting suitability maps for domestic use in the Dead Sea region, West Bank, Palestine. *Hydrology and Earth System Sciences, 23*(3), 1581–1592. https://doi.org/10.5194/hess-23-1581-2019

Sheikh, H., Mitchell, P., & Foth, M. (2023). More-than-human smart urban governance: A research agenda. *Digital Geography and Society, 4,* 100045. https://doi.org/10.1016/j.diggeo.2022.100045

Söderström, O., Blake, E., & Odendaal, N. (2021). More-than-local, more-than-mobile: The smart city effect in South Africa. *Geoforum; Journal of Physical, Human, and Regional Geosciences, 122,* 103–117. https://doi.org/10.1016/j.geoforum.2021.03.017

Sorensen, R. A. (1998). *Thought experiments.* Oxford University Press.

Sousa, C. A., Kemp, S., & El-Zuhairi, M. (2014). Dwelling within political violence: Palestinian women's narratives of home, mental health, and resilience. *Health & Place, 30,* 205–214.

Soja, E. D. (2010). *Seeking spatial justice.* University of Minnesota Press.

Taboada, M. B., & Turner, J. (2021). Rolling stories: Re-imagining self and futures through fictional worlds. In R. M. Leitão, I. Men, L-A. Noel, J. Lima, & T. Meninato (Eds.), *Proceedings of Pivot 2021: Dismantling/Reassembling* (pp. 417–428). Design Research Society.

Teli, M., McQueenie, J., Cibin, R., & Foth, M. (2022). Intermediation in design as a practice of institutioning and commoning. *Design Studies, 82,* 101132. https://doi.org/10.1016/j.destud.2022.101132

Torretta, N. B., & Reitsma, L. (2019, June 18–21). *Design, power and colonisation: Decolonial and antioppressive explorations on three approaches for design for sustainability* [Conference presentation]. In Academy for Design Innovation Management 2019 (ADIM2019), London, England.

Tuck, E., & Yang. K. W. (2012). Decolonization is not a metaphor. *Decolonization: Indigeneity, Education & Society, 1*(1), 1–40.

UN Women. (2019) Innovation for Gender Equality. https://www.unwomen.org/en/digital-library/publications/2019/03/innovation-for-gender-equality

Wakkary, R. (2021). *Things we could design: For more than human-centered worlds.* MIT Press. https://doi.org/10.7551/mitpress/13649.001.0001

Watson, V. (2014). African urban fantasies: Dreams or nightmares? *Environment and Urbanization, 26*(1), 215–231. https://doi.org/10.1177/0956247813513705

Yigitcanlar, T., Foth, M., & Kamruzzaman, M. (2019). Towards post-anthropocentric cities: Reconceptualizing smart cities to evade urban ecocide. *Journal of Urban Technology, 26*(2), 147–152. https://doi.org/10.1080/10630732.2018.1524249

Zavala, M. (2013). What do we mean by decolonizing research strategies? Lessons from decolonizing, Indigenous research projects in New Zealand and Latin America. *Decolonization: Indigeneity, Education & Society, 2*(1), 55–71.

11

How Can Anyone be More than One Thing?

Dialogues on More-than-Humanity in the Smart City

Alison Powell and Alex Taylor

Introduction

This chapter experiments with the epistolary form, a model of intellectual dialogue that has histories in both the humanities and the sciences. As a literary device, the exchange of letters is used to unfold collaborations while permitting individual scholars to maintain their own voices (see Chang & Davis 2005; 2010). In this chapter, the letters specifically focus on the ideas of difference and perspective in relationships between humans and non-humans in urban settings. The authors write to each other in dialogue, together unfolding a shared perspective. The dialogue concludes with two speculative fiction narratives generated from the points of discussion and the scholars' shared interest in the idea of the 'more-than-human' city. In the speculative narratives, questions about data- and technology-driven practices of citizen participation are raised within a setting where many living beings, including animals, are accorded citizen rights. The fictions are intentionally opaque, queering the source or position of narration, and inviting questions of human, non-human, and more-than-human agency. The speculative 'smart city' that these fictions sketch works on policies of inclusion towards 'non-human citizens', including attempting to count and manage populations and to value the contributions they make to the public realm. Yet other blind spots begin to emerge in the narrative, drawing on points that both authors make in their dialogue.

The ideas and narrative development in this chapter also emerge from two closely connected projects: the *More-Than-Human Data Interactions in the Smart City* (or MoTH Cities—see https://mothcities.uk) and the *Algorithmic Food Justice* projects (Heitlinger et al. 2021; Heitlinger et al. 2022; Heitlinger et al. 2022; Houston et al. 2023). Both projects convened a diverse range of researchers and practitioners in varied habitats and stimulated ongoing and new threads of discussion for the authors. These were threads entangled with building and sustaining biodiverse and flourishing cities and the promise of technoscientific futures that might include non-human citizens.

Through the elaboration of separate and eventually interconnected threads of concern, including the speculative fictions, this chapter asks: how does understanding human and non-human Others hinge on technologies, including technologies of counting? What other relationships might be possible? How do these relationships also illuminate existing discussions of citizenship, identity, and belonging within and beyond cities?

Alison Powell and Alex Taylor, *How Can Anyone be More than One Thing?* In: *Designing More-than-Human Smart Cities.* Edited by: Sara Heitlinger, Marcus Foth, and Rachel Clarke, Oxford University Press.
DOI: 10.1093/9780191980060.003.0013

Dearest Alison,

We've talked about foxes before, I know. I have a little obsession with them—I think they're becoming part of London life in really knotty ways.

In a park just down the road from me, we have a fox that is, I think, curious about us—about me and the dogs (probably more the dogs than me). Most nights, it pops out from the bushes to watch us. The dogs strain against their leads compelled, I imagine, by the heavy scent, and I know, from past experience, desperate to give chase. Despite the energetic leaps and barks, though, our feral friend holds her ground. As a matter of fact, she sometimes approaches us, coming within 5 or 10 meters, all the time watching. She has also followed the three of us home, sometimes getting to within almost an arm's reach of our door. I wonder if she is teasing her distant tethered relatives? Perhaps she wants to play? Maybe she is lonely?

One evening, along with the two dogs, I managed to take a photo of a local fox (possibly our neighbourhood companion). Below, you'll see her on the road outside our house (Figure 11.1). She is quite clearly looking back at us, attentive to us looking at her.

It's urban-fox–canine–human encounters like this that have got me thinking about human–non-human relations in the city. As far as relations go, I'm curious about what's going on here? What should we make of our resident foxes? Why have they taken up living around and between us domesticated humans and non-humans? What are they in it for? What do they get back? What fox-non-fox-relations

Figure 11.1 Fox on a London street 'looking back' (Derrida 2002) at author and his dogs.
Reproduced with permission of author Alex Taylor.

are being made possible in the urban spaces we share? What other, new relations might (just) be possible?

For some, I'm sure the answers are easy. Foxes want our waste and our leftovers. Certainly, the strewn out remains left from our household black bags on rubbish-collection day would attest to this. Predictably, the headline grabbing tabloid stories want to point to 'the fox problem'. There are horror stories of babies being mauled after doors have been left open on hot summer days and because fox numbers are out of control.

I want to imagine there's something more than these so very limiting ideas. I've no doubt the foxes benefit from our waste and as a population are doing very well because of it. Could we begin, though, to think of our cities as spaces where more-than-human relations have some kind of investment, some kind of will, some kind of future to make?

Dear Alex,

For me what has always been wonderful about life in the city is the diversity of possibility, of encounter, and of difference. My research and practice have been focused on knowledge, participation and citizenship, as they are experienced through an urban lens. Your story of fox encounters reminds me that these differences of experience (which are profound) are not only interesting in themselves, as tales of multispecies encounter and possibility—they also provide some perspective on questions of how to live together in cities. If we take a close look at our lives, especially the tangled-together lives that the dense experience of urban existence makes possible, we see all kinds of competing experiences, proclivities and desires. We humans, too, want things to eat and drink that satisfy our physical needs. Like foxes we also might want companionship, connections across difference, or something fun to do on a summer evening. We might, in fact, want things that are contradictory. We might act in ways that don't seem consistent with how we are viewed from outside. It might be that humans are in some ways as inscrutable to each other as foxes.

Often, the ways that policy-makers think about 'living together' is in terms of how to perform governance. Compared to the richness of experience or even to the multiple desires of the fox, these are fairly narrow conceptions of what it's like to live together. Looking at these processes is important, because their purpose is to model ways of being together, of managing the urban world collectively, across difference.

In urban governance, participation and consultation are key pillars of 'participatory planning', which since the 1960s have been developed as a means of facilitating legitimacy and social justice (Davidoff 1965). Urban planners have thought about creating mechanisms for participatory planning to engage participation across a spectrum (IAPS 2007) or 'ladder' (Arnstein 1969), This would ideally extend beyond informing the public towards engaging in dialogue and drawing on different forms of knowledge. Yet what has transpired, especially as urban governance began to draw on 'smart' mechanisms, is that participation has become data-configured and data-driven. Humans are invited to fill out consultation surveys that structure and manage their opinions, so that these can become actionable or transactional, based around numbers and quantities rather than experiences. In this streamlined 'smart' participation, the kind of inchoate desires and encounters that you discussed in your letter cannot possibly be accounted for—indeed, the effort at accounting makes them even less capable of being part of the process of urban planning and governance. In the MoTH Cities project that we were involved with, this is one of the themes that started our conversation. I remember that's when we started to speculate on how to extend the modes and forms of participation out from humans to encompass non-human others, imagining which data layers on a neighbourhood map might be produced by birds, bats or bees.

I began to wonder what forms of participation were already in place, before we even speculated on techniques to better collect different perspectives. Noortje Marres' theory of 'material participation' (2016) identifies that political participation is sustained by material contexts and forms, which don't necessarily always align with the spaces and practices of formalised participation. Marres writes about the material infrastructure that pre-figures and sustains participation: things like the large tea-kettles whose presence are the backdrop for and the stage upon which political discussion can unfold around a cup of tea. She draws on Jane Bennett's (2010) idea of 'vibrant matter'—the elements of lively existence that Bennett thinks of as already political. These might include the relationships between entities and the energies that are produced as those relationships develop (much like our correspondence). Marres identifies the politics inherent in the division between the 'political' and the 'non-political'—the gendered and classed assumptions that make action taken at home or in private spaces not 'effective participation' and the disavowal of the material structures (including where we live and what objects we use to indicate relationships to each other). This concept always makes me remember the long trestle tables I sat under as a child while my mother participated in community meetings in dusty church halls. All of this in a human-driven world. Is there any way to pay attention to what other kinds of participation might be possible if we took non-humans seriously?

Alison,

I'm struck by the efforts we go to to keep all us animals separate–to find tidy ways of marking the differences. I find it very hard to imagine us acknowledging the complex human-non-human entanglements in our cities with so much work being put into keeping species separate.

Let me offer an example of what I mean. There are shall we say some more science-based approaches to studying 'The Fox Problem'. There is the radio-tracking of urban foxes done, for instance, to understand their range and mating/familial geographies. Illustrating this, Piran White has kindly allowed us to use visual representations of urban fox movements—using radio-tracking—from a paper he and his colleagues published in 1996 (White et al.1996) (Figure 11.2). There is also the PREDICTS database (Hudson et al. 2014), that while not specifically focused on foxes, is using global species datasets to model how local terrestrial biodiversity responds to human impacts. In other words, a database of the numbers of animals living and dying among us.

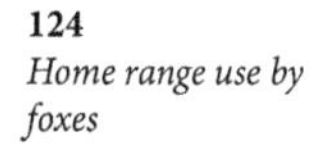

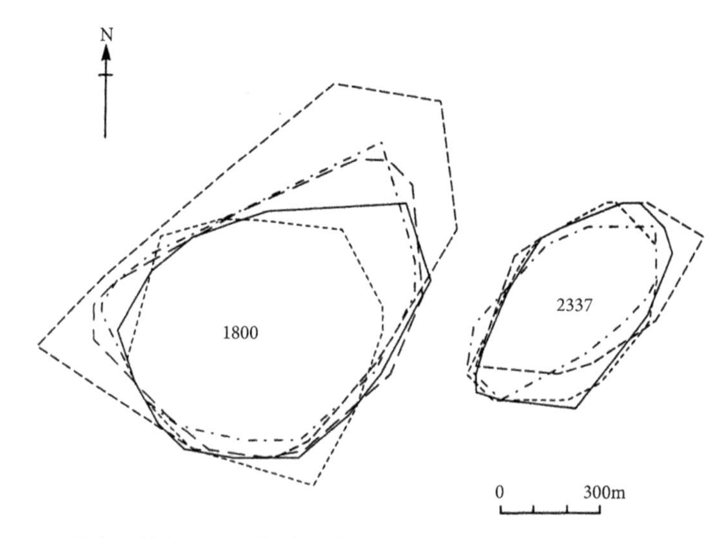

Fig.1. Seasonal stability of the home ranges of the male (1800) and female (2337) foxes radio-tracked for at least 1 year and showing extreme differences in the calculated range drift. Seasonal range boundaries are: summer 1990 (----), autumn 1990 (—), winter 1990/91 (--), spring 1991 (-·-·-·-·) and summer 1991 (——). The figures for range drift over the periods shown, calculated according to the method of Doncaster & Macdonald (1991), and expressed as percentages of the total range areas, are 5·6% for 1800 and 35·2% for 2337.

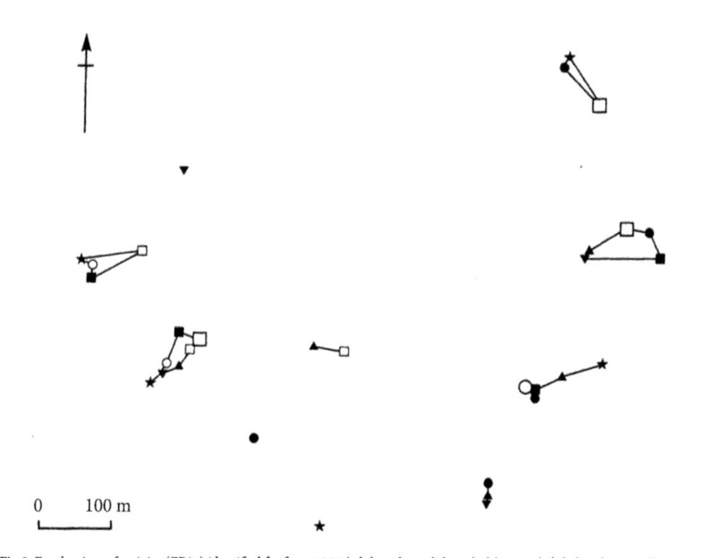

Fig.2. Focal points of activity (FPAs) identified for foxes 1800 (adult male - solid symbols), 2318 (adult female – small open symbols) and 2345 (sub-adult female – large open symbols) on the Group II range. Seasons are denoted by the following symbols: summer 1990 (▲), autumn 1990 (▼), winter 1990/91 (■), spring 1991 (●) and summer 1991 (★). The lines join FPAs that were identified as the same (see text). All FPAs identified for the adult female coincided spatially with ones used by the adult male, as did all three identified for the sub-adult female in winter. One of those used by the sub-adult female also coincided with one used by the adult female.

Figure 11.2 Example of visual mapping of seasonal home ranges and of focal points of activity, both for male and female foxes.

Reproduced with permission from White et al. (1996). Spatio-temporal patterns of home range use by foxes (*Vulpes vulpes*) in urban environments. *Journal of Animal Ecology*, *65*(1), 121–125. https://doi.org/10.2307/5705

I'm not sure what you think, but I feel like these sorts of spatial and numeric exercises are all about the urge to count, compute and model things. They enable us to see animals as a numerical aggregate of a species, of foxes thriving or of badgers being slowly but surely eradicated through their urban/peri-urban co-habitations with humans. Thus, our human eye is drawn to what species do, how they mate, what their geographies are, their sources of predation and food. As geographers such as McLean (2020) and Searle et al. (2023) write, the 'more-than-real' is assembled through such digital geographies—the question is not whether the spatial counts are real, but how they come to produce social, cultural, economic and environmental changes and feed affective and emotional forces. Much, then, is to be learnt from this work with numbers, I'm sure. The scale at which the data and computation operate provide firm insights into what is going on with species like foxes, and how their growing numbers are having an impact for us humans, in our cities.

But, you'll know well, there are things these approaches to mapping 'the fox' don't tell. I think that what we don't learn is why *the interrelations matter or indeed* how *they might come to matter. For a fox, how are we to understand what she is capable of, and what she is capable of with others, including ourselves? How should we account for what a human and two dogs give back to a fox? What conditions are created for the fox to be more than a data point in an aggregate and, in contrast, an actor becoming in and with the conditions it inhabits with others, much like the citizens whose perspectives on urban life are not able to be described or contained by the mechanisms of 'smart governance'. The problem here would seem to be less about the abundance of foxes in cities. To me, what seems a far more interesting problem to be starting with is what the relations could be between actors and in the spaces we share.*

Alex,

Your letter makes me consider this idea of capability and makes me think about how differences of opinion are represented. It also makes me consider what your Fox Problem illustrates about broader and deeper troubles with category, difference and Otherness. The 'otherness' of other species prompts reflections from humans about how to account for experiences that may not ever be able to be fully shared. In a New York Times *article, Ed Yong writes:*

In his classic 1974 essay, 'What Is It Like to Be a Bat?' the philosopher Thomas Nagel wrote that the conscious experiences of other animals are inherently subjective and hard to describe. You could envision yourself with webbing on your arms or insects in your mouth, but you'd still be creating a mental caricature of you as a bat. 'I want to know what it is like for a bat to be a bat', Dr. Nagel wrote. Most bat species perceive the world through sonar, sensing their surroundings by listening for the echoes of their own ultrasonic calls. 'Yet if I try to imagine this, I am restricted to the resources of my own mind, and those resources are inadequate to the task', Dr. Nagel wrote (Yong, 2022).

The tendency to anthropomorphise non-humans by attributing to them human qualities or intentions is of course an attempt to accommodate the distance created by this Otherness.

However, the effort at understanding and perceiving the world differently, from a perspective that is not one's own could also be seen as a foundation for seeking what is shared, universal and of value to all: what Myria Georgiou (2021) conceives of as a new kind of humanism that emerges from the recognition of difference amid shared struggle.

Some advocates argue that extending rights is a way to create belonging. Rights are often granted based on membership to a particular category. The citizenship rights I mentioned earlier are often allocated only to persons possessing formal citizenship in a nation-state. Across history, this kind of 'personhood' has been narrowly defined: property-owning men, but not women, people of colour, the enslaved or the incarcerated. Indeed, anyone incarcerated in the UK currently does not have the right to vote. Thinking about what rights non-human Others might want to claim should enhance, not detract from considering what systemic injustices might prevent claims on rights or action to exercise them, including existing rights. Engin Isin and Evelyn Ruppert (2020) argue that one of the key features of contemporary digital rights is that they include 'the right to claim rights'. Does the capacity of the PREDICTS database to count and describe the experience of foxes and other species get them any closer to having rights?

In some of my other work I've characterised this desire of humans to understand animal Others through technology as one of the paradoxes that results from technologically-driven models of smart governance. On the one hand the counting and measuring brings visibility and attention to large processes such as climate change: indeed, climate change as a phenomenon is indivisible from global processes of measurement and computation (Edwards 2010), and equally species loss and biodiversity protection are experienced through data even when they are highly personal (Powell 2021). Humans recognise our responsibility and exercise our grief in part through big-data mediated representations of the damage that we've done.

At the same time though, the human view alienates us from experience. This is what Donna Haraway calls the 'god-trick', the claim of objectivity that separates the observer from its object. In this way we are not really part of biodiversity. Instead, we are its descriptors, its protectors. As humans, we define what are objects and who are subjects. And as I've already described, becoming a subject is a contentious process.

Dear Alison,

Your thoughts on bats reminds me of Vinciane Despret's often evocative and always generous writings about animals. Anthropomorphism, as Despret (2013) writes, 'involves a dangerous flirtation':

is one putting himself [sic] in the animal's shoes or, on the contrary,
does one actually put the animal in human shoes?

So, what if we see anthropomorphism as one of a set of 'risky practices'—a tool from a wider panoply of practices that might allow us to be open to being affected by Others? This is one of Despret's many invitations to think-with-animals, and to become with them. Does this, I wonder, have anything in common with the new humanism you speculate on with its 'recognition of difference amid shared struggle'?

What I love about Despret's work is her persistence, her unceasing efforts to show—despite our best efforts—that human-animal worlds are always in intimate relation, always becoming together. Yes, we like to imagine our view from above, our God's eye view, and our radio-tracking plots and databases of species identification are nothing if not a pretension to this. But through our lab studies, field experiments, and other ways of actively seeing animals, are we not merely creating the conditions for new actors and new relations? As Despret writes:

Animals are invited to other modes of being, other relationships, and new ways to inhabit the human world and to force human beings to address them differently ... The identities upon which identification could ground itself do not pre-exist; the identity is created by the previous construction of affinities. Identity is the outcome, the achievement.

The god-trick, then, does not engrave an immutable picture, but would seem a stage setting for something more, for something new in the relations between critters of all kinds: animals in human worlds and humans in the worlds of animals, where so much more could happen.

So, then, can we begin to think here about new identities or even new actors? And can this give us some space to think about Noortje Marres' material participation *in some radically new ways (just as she invites)?*

Dear Alex,

Now we are really in the thick of it. There are experiences of difference that diverge across not only species lines but also across other lines of difference. How then shall we live together? This is no longer a question only of rights, but of justice. The right to claim rights can also be interpreted through the lens of justice: Iris Marion Young's (2011) conceptions of collective responsibility provide a counterpoint to the entrapments of neoliberal modes of governance. Young identifies that responsibility for justice includes addressing structural injustice and intergenerational justice: resisting efforts to limit or functionalize civic action.

Such a justice-oriented framing might also consider how different forms of Otherness complicate the capacity to claim or to exercise rights. The 'otherness' of other species prompts reflections from humans about how to account for experiences that may not ever be able to be fully shared. Thinking with Iris Marion Young's notion of responsibility for justice, what responsibilities do humans, who currently hold all of the official rights, hold for Others? On which timescales and in relation to which other potential fellow-citizens should these responsibilities be enacted? Across studies of governance as well as technology justice (see Franklin 1989), concepts of reciprocity are incredibly important in considering how long temporalities or uncertain outcomes should be considered. In ecological justice work, intergenerational justice and the rights of future (human) generations have begun to be considered in terms of adherence to the Sustainable Development Goals.

This is the setting into which discussions of 'more-than-human' citizenship are embedded. Projects like Furtherfield's Treaty of Finsbury Park 2025 engage with the long-term responsibility to create and sustain biodiversity by inviting existing (human) residents of the local neighbourhood to participate in a Live-Action Role Play taking on the perspectives and voices of their non-human neighbours: 'participants join Interspecies Assemblies to play as the species of Finsbury Park and plan a major collaborative event for the future: The Interspecies Festival of Finsbury Park. It is designed to explore new ways of building empathy pathways to non-human lifeforms through play. It is a critique of colonialism as expressed through the human domination of all living creatures and systems.' (https://creatures-eu.org/productions/treaty/).

The outcome of this consciously multispecies (and multi-stakeholder) process is the Treaty of Finsbury Park, which outlines the rights and responsibilities of all of the inhabitants of Finsbury Park. Explicitly drawing on the notion of rights (although treaty rights are distinct from citizen rights) the project itself performs a rights claim, while also drawing on the language and framing of participatory or democratic governance. What might the consequences be of establishing such a treaty? Furthermore, what kinds of responsibilities might be expected from non-human citizens? Within the organization of states, responsibilities of citizens include such actions as paying taxes, serving in the military or participating in collective acts of sacrifice. In her work, Wendy Brown identifies how significant the notion of 'sacrifice' has become in neoliberal governance. Sacrifice is not giving of oneself for mutual benefit: it is instead a destruction of one's capacity to work together. Once sacrificed, we are spent.

Brown's idea of 'sacrifice' as an expectation from the state to an autonomous individual also has a parallel with Judith Butler's (2020) defence of an expansive idea of rights, beyond an individualized rights-bearing subject. She believes that a social transformation is required in order to unseat the processes that justify racism and state violence. These efforts require making 'provisions for flourishing' for all, and beginning to question the necessity for distinctions between rights accorded to humans versus non-humans, and even the living versus the non-living.

What's interesting about the Finsbury Park project is how rights are described and extended, in line with some of these considerations. Our considerations of the connections between expectations of enhanced understanding of multispecies 'others' and the ability (or inability) to understand them highlight how technology, along with expanded conceptions of rights (and the rights to claim them) intertwine to reshape urban governance.

Governance, especially multi-stakeholder governance where participation and perspectives from a range of actors are ostensibly integrated into decision-making, is where collective decisions are legitimated and put into practice. Processes of governance do not always involve the exercise of rights. Winter and Davidson describe governance as values-based objectives created by different stakeholders (2019), which need to be achieved through different mechanisms. One such mechanism is the creation of legitimacy, either through democratic or quasi-democratic processes like voting, deliberation, or co-design. In both democratic or non-democratic settings this could include the exercise of state power, though increasingly governance is enacted through the use of market power. Governance is of course also enacted through design choices—participatory design processes are *intended to provide legitimacy to designs that anticipate, or even 'lock in' particular kinds of interactions and practices.*

Under what circumstances, in which ways and with which consequences might your fox neighbour be able to be considered a citizen? How might their interests be represented? What would be a more-than-human model for smart city governance?

Dearest Alison,

This is an exciting thread of thought. I hear you complicating the independence and autonomy of entities when it comes to participation. You make the connection between clumsy ideas of independence and autonomy, and neoliberal governance. This neoliberalism is of course all for independence but seems so unable to countenance the choice of collective *volition, and for that matter, where choice might be collectively defined or enacted.*

I see us thinking here with modes of governance and participation that resonate with the ideas of inter*dependence that have been so generative in disabilities scholarship from folks such as Solveig Magnus Reindal (2010), Christine Kelly (2013), Inga Bostad and Halvor Hanisch (2016), and Cynthia Bennett et al. (2018). For me, the attention we are giving to the more-than-human and multispecies relations intensifies the questions about the presumed units of independent participation and why we are so insistent on fixed lines separating our bodies from others.*

What seems especially important when we think of governance in our cityscapes, where we are amidst and becoming-with so many varieties of life is ... justice, as you suggest. I take this to be a recognition that values matter for all entities living in relation to one another. What we need to find is a way to live and govern with what matters on the table. This matter of justice is also a recognition of the need to bring many voices to the table to begin repairing human damage, even when the capacities for being-with and talking-with are partial and incomplete.

The radio-tracking of foxes and modelling of animal species (to name only two ways of technologically tooling-up our cities) is, then, just not enough in our smart city visions. What we need is a reciprocity, yes, but also I would argue reparation. Jenny Davis, Apryl Williams, and Michael Yang (2021) talk of an algorithmic reparation *and it's drawing from this that I'd like to pose my final thought to you.*

Algorithmic reparation, as Davis, Williams and Yang describe it, is a critical response to the fairness and equality research in machine learning and AI that has been spurred on by the recognised biases and discrimination amplified by algorithmic systems. Algorithmic reparation resists the idealism in this research that 'assumes a meritocratic society and seeks to neutralize demographic disparities'. (p.2). By contrast, a reparative frame acknowledges the embedded and pervasive structures of discrimination and, instilling action, it 'incorporates redress into the assemblage of technologies that interweave macro institutions and microinteractions, embedding an equitable agenda into the material systems that govern daily life' (p.4).

In talking about forms of justice and governance that are committed to city-scale, more-than-human flourishing, I want to ask if we might seek something akin to this algorithmic reparation. These would lead visions of the smart city that don't assume idealistic neutralities or where the propensities for injustice and discrimination can somehow be remedied through technology. These would be visions where a reparative mode seeks to redress human exceptionalism and its corresponding damage to our companion critters. Sought after would be technological interventions that project reparative change in whatever ways we can from local situated exchanges and subjectivities to wider institutional infrastructures and policies of governance. (This is just what we experimented in in the Algorithmic Food Justice Project (Heitlinger et al. 2021; Houston et al. 2023)). As Davis, Williams, and Yang (2021) phrase it, the goals would not be fairness and equality, but justice and equity.

Dearest Alex,

It strikes me that no matter what, our social institutions will need to change. As you mention, scholars in disability studies are rethinking the boundaries of the body and the necessities of care. In social theory, too, Judith Butler (2020) is rethinking these same boundaries and coming to some of the same conclusions: that 'a new imaginary is required - an egalitarian imaginary that apprehends the interdependency of lives' (p.203). Our conversation here illuminates two other ways to experience that interdependency. One of these is through the interdependency with other living beings different than ourselves. The other way is to think through the varieties of life that every individual experiences, that as Butler and Jane Bennett (2010) and Noortje Marres hint at as being aspects of experience that are differentially brought into formalized participation. Not only might reparative models shift away from a default human-centric position, but the movement from fairness and equality to justice and equity might allow for a more complex view of who, what, how many, and in which capacity we might become subjects.

Perhaps thinking from a multispecies perspective will allow us to move beyond the kinds of divisive categorizations that have been used to limit, rather than extend rights, and to consider how the capacity for participation and flourishing can be extended to more beings—as well as to different aspects of the same being. This aligns with other research from political theory and activism: Bart Cammaerts (2022) argues that the individualization of the self and the creation of distance to the other is part of the process through which 'conflictual polarization' occurs. Exclusion, othering and the creation of distance are, according to Cammaerts, part of the operation of hegemonic processes that undermine collective belonging, dismiss solidarity and intensify individualism. As I've tried to explain, individualism is damaging inside and out: when forms of participation are narrow and don't capture internal contradictions or the many different aspects of identity that make a self, something is lost. At the social level, both of us have identified different ways that collectivity, care, and reparation model more extensive and expansive ways to govern.

This exchange of letters, above, prompts questions about difference. That is, living together not just with different opinions and views but in urban worlds encountered, experienced and valued differently. Actors of all kinds—human, non-human animal, botanical, microbial, technological—relate and become through these differences, continually (re)producing worlds that despite hard technoscientific graft, resist reduction. But at the same time there remain words that cannot be exchanged, tables that can't be shared, representations that will never be proportionate. Worlds entangle and divide, sit atop and below other worlds.

So it is that we are left with the impossible, to tell a story of common experience and equity in agency, volition, participation, and governance. A story about participation and what it might make possible, as well as what it might demand. At best, our dialogue leaves ajar the possibility of something more. Ultimately, though, it remains provisional, incomplete, unsatisfactory. The absence of others—of more-than-human others—from the conversations resonates and rings, loudly.

The remains of this chapter extend and morph our thinking by using fiction to engage this impossibility. We imagine a setting where a local government is serious about extending citizenship to urban residents other than humans and is committed to using the kinds of technologies we discuss above to understand the needs and the potential contributions these 'non-human citizens' could make. In our speculative city, the government wants to take a census of humans and non-humans, but like all administrative technologies this census depends on setting categories from the beginning. Our imaginary local government then attempts to use technology to better understand the needs as well as the responsibilities of non-human citizens, which depends on the efforts of municipal workers working with technology that's limited, as it always is. Our story's anti-heroes are undefined: maybe-human, maybe-more-than-human, maybe-more-than-one-thing. Of course, as in all speculative fiction, aspirational technology and good intentions have unintended consequences.

City of Multitudes

1. The Census

The train is late.

I check my watch.

Still twenty minutes before I can no longer click on the registration link, but only eighteen minutes until moonrise.

We all know how important it is, in these unprecedented times, to share accurate and timely information with the government.

This is part of our responsibility, our deepest duty as citizens, as it is the duty of the state to recognize us in all our diversity, to support us to thrive, to retain that mystical safety net below, as frayed as it might be.

So it's for that reason that I'm leaping up the stairs from the train platform three at a time—to act responsibly, to do my duty, to be recognized.

I get to the top with three minutes to spare and stand under the awning just outside the station. It's so damp that the rain no longer seems separate, more like a watery curtain reaching all the way to the ground.

There's no way to see the sky. I open the app, and the first screen reminds me that my answers given AT THIS MOMENT are taken to be true, correct, and indicative of how I will be recognized by the state. I begin, the app crashes, and I begin again, while the rain descends, my hands shaking as I look at my watch while the app's new page loads and I see the question, the one that I waited for, expected and dreaded, and while it rains and the tiny wheel on my phone spins and the timer on my watch ticks down I wait and finally read:

At this moment, are you:

A. *Human*

B. *Animal*

Please note that your response will be used to deliver specific social services which you may require now or in the future.

And before I can select anything the timer clicks around, the moon icon opens on my phone, and I transform.

2. Policy Options

In the small room behind the committee room, one of the ceiling tiles had come partially unstuck. A brownish stain, a little like a feather, spread across the tile from the corner. Ursula looked up at it as she listened to Paul go over it all again. Around the edges of the room, behind the desks and pushed up against the air conditioners that ground, leakily, in a hum almost obscuring the noise of the excavation next door, were boxes of sensors, coils of cables. They smelled of fresh rubber and insecticide, and the curving script on the side suggested they had just been imported from Xantian.

'I just don't understand what's behind this', muttered Paul, hooking his fingers into his belt loops just below his belly. 'Why would anyone want to disrupt the census? We've consulted. We've done our due diligence. When I've taken this on the road I've got so much feedback that our approach is on the cutting edge, that we're really doing something new here. The journey we've made, as a local authority, towards understanding our citizens, really being responsive, being smart and also clever, no one else is doing this. And Nigel's insight—so brilliant—that our non-human citizens . . .'.

Ursula bristled, while Paul bounced back and forth on his shiny brown shoes.

'. . . more-than-human citizens, of course. The census is the mechanism for creating policy options. Policy options . . . obviously people are going to need all kinds of things we haven't thought of yet, that's why we've got these participatory planning processes in place, the pheromone mapping and the budget allocations for dark corridors and hides and rat-runs and what have you, and now the census is the main mechanism to diversify the tax base. Without knowing who we're dealing with how can we determine the relative level for contribution?'

Ursula sighed heavily. 'We can look at the first issue, that's the stability of the app itself. Could be an easy win.' She shifted around the office bulkily, picking up a box of sensors—these ones were ultrasound, intended to 'gather ambient information from Chiroptera citizens'.

But Paul was in his flow, bobbing back and forth between his feet beneath the leaky tiles.

'Well, a rights claim? To the tribunal? That will take ages to resolve, and if it gets into the papers it'll undermine the whole project. We were just starting to get traction on it, the Revenue Office got all those young graduates involved, the first time in two centuries that taxation is interesting, not to say that I didn't meet smart people in my accountancy training, that's not what I'm saying at all but you know, this is the biggest breakthrough in urban management in decades and now this? Besides, it seems a tiny bit overblown to me. How can anyone be more than one thing?'

Ursula looked again at the ceiling, at the windows, at the piles of boxes of equipment donated by the Universe Group as part of this new initiative to fully understand 'the diversity and contributions of all our citizens, in service of expanded participation, fairer contributions and a chance for progress for all'. For the last six months they'd been sending out these boxes to their local partners, and she'd been monitoring the feeds as they went online. The bats were complaining—there were really only a few families left in the area and they were isolated—starting to compete over what had been traditional territories. Most of what the sensors picked up was bitter gossip: Ysilda had lost a nursling and her cousin Rory spent all night speculating that it was because she'd been out under hazel trees and everyone knew there was an old curse on them. So far nothing of what they'd collected gave any indication of what Chiroptera Citizens might plausibly contribute to the tax base. Besides bat guano.

'How can anyone be more than one thing?', thought Ursula. This morning, she'd got up at 5, used a meditation app, programmed the details for her run into her phone, headed out by 6, back by 7, laid out the kit for the little ones, unpacked the dishwasher, put on the coffee, pulled up the data from the sensors, shouted up the stairs 'Out of bed, now!', put on the radio to hear more about this week's flood warnings and the 'planned remediation of the Thames Barrier', yelled up the stairs again, put on the toast, saw a message from her sister saying she couldn't stop in on the parents today, could Ursula do it before work?, drank the coffee, ate a protein bar just as 'Mama! Mama! I forgot, today we need to bring an artifact from our family's history, can you find something for me?', bundled the littles into the bike, grateful for the high wheelbase today in the puddles, got to school just as the gates opened, then to the parents' flat, no time to deal with the smell in the kitchen sink but enough time for a small hug to her mother. Ursula didn't remember her mom's head hitting her chest during those hugs before—how did her mother get so small?

Ursula can't remember anything about that last part of the ride, the second coffee she poured in the lounge, the report she ran from the Chiroptera and Cornu overnight data, the message from her parent's cleaner about the sink. She can't remember, and Paul is bouncing so quickly on his feet now and crowing 'It's the data that will make all the difference', so she pushes back the chair, sits heavily and puts her head on the desk.

How can anyone be more than one thing?

Speaking for another can only ever be a failed endeavour. Our letters, our stories, the projects that we undertake in order to establish more expansive ways of thinking about living together in cities—about what 'the other' might want, or even who 'the other' might be—these are doomed always to be at best partial successes, and at worst mere fantasy. However, perhaps both fantasy and failure are in fact desirable. One significant challenge for contemporary intellectual and activist projects is to address the experience of difference in relation to collective life—to contend with the fact that we can never fully know another, and yet that if we are to live well together there must be a way to reckon with that unknowable difference in the context of shared rights, responsibilities, and encounters. Acknowledging that this reckoning might never be completely optimised, perfected, or aligned ensures that citizens of more-than-human cities retain the humility and grace that allows us to continue to investigate the conditions of collective flourishing. It may never be possible for a human to imagine what a fox wants. In this chapter we have wandered through the complexities of using such imagination to think about more-than-human connections, ethics, practices, and potentials. We hope these lead to more conversations.

References

Arnstein, S. R. (1969). A ladder of citizen participation. *Journal of the American Planning Association 35*(4), 216–224.

Bennett, C. L., Brady, E., & Branham, S. M.(2018). Interdependence as a frame for assistive technology research and design. In F. Hwang, J. McGrenere, & D. Flatla (Eds.), *ASSETS '18: Proceedings of the 20th International ACM SIGACCESS Conference on Computers and Accessibility* (pp. 161–173). ACM.

Bennett, J. (2010). *Vibrant matter: A political ecology of things.* Duke University Press.

Bostad, I., & Hanisch, H. (2016). Freedom and disability rights: Dependence, independence, and interdependence. *Metaphilosophy, 47*(3), 371–384.

Butler, J. (2020). *The force of nonviolence.* Verso.

Cammaerts, B. (2022). The abnormalisation of social justice: The 'anti-woke culture war' discourse in the UK. *Discourse & Society, 33*(6), 730–743. https://doi.org/10.1177/09579265221095407

Chang, R. S., & Davis, A. D. (2005). The adventure(s) of blackness in western culture: An epistolary exchange on old and new identity wars. *UC Davis Law Review, 39*, 1189–1235.

Chang, R. S., & Davis, A. D. (2010). Making up is hard to do: Race/gender/sexual orientation in the law school classroom. *Harvard Journal of Law & Gender, 33*, 1–59.

Davidoff, P. (1965). Advocacy and pluralism in planning. *Journal of the American Institute of Planners, 31*(4), 331–338.

Davis, J. L., Williams, A., & Yang, M. W. (2021). Algorithmic reparation. *Big Data & Society 8*(2). https://doi.org/10.1177/20539517211044808

Derrida, J. (2002). The animal that therefore I am (more to follow). *Critical Inquiry, 28*(2), 369–341.

Despret, V. (2013). Responding bodies and partial affinities in human–animal worlds. *Theory, Culture & Society 30*(7–8), 51–76.

Edwards, P. N. (2010). *A vast machine: Computer models, climate data, and the politics of global warming.* MIT Press.

Franklin, U. 1989. *The real world of technology.* House of Anansi.

Furtherfield. (2022). The Treaty of Finsbury Park 2025. https://www.furtherfield.org/the-treaty-of-finsbury-park-2025/

Georgiou, M. (2021). Making an urban human? The digital order and its curious human-centrism. *Communication and Critical/Cultural Studies, 18*(4), 395–403.

Heitlinger, S., Houston, L., Taylor, A., & Catlow, R. (2021). Algorithmic food justice: Co-designing more-than-human blockchain futures for the food commons. In Y. Kitamura, A. Quigley, K. Isbister, T. Igarashi, P. Bjørn, & S. Drucker (Eds.), *CHI '21: Proceedings of the 2021 CHI Conference on Human Factors in Computing Systems* (pp. 1–17). ACM.

Heitlinger, S., Houston, L., Choi, J., Taylor, A., & Catlow, R. (2022). More-than-human computer interaction for urban food governance. In A. Moragues-Faus, J. Clark, J. Battersby & A. Davies (Eds.), *Routledge handbook of urban food governance* (pp. 1–16). Routledge.

Heitlinger, S., Houston, L., & Taylor, A. (2022). Nature 3.0 blockchain for extraction or care? In R. Catlow, & P. Raffety (Eds.), *Radical friends: Decentralised autonomous organisations & the arts* (pp. 1–8). Torque Editions.

Houston, L., Heitlinger, S., & Taylor, A. (2023). Algorithmic food justice. In D. Papadopoulos, M. Puig de la Bellacasa, & M. Tacchetti (Eds.), *Ecological reparation: Repair, remediation and resurgence in social and environmental conflict* (pp. 379–396). Bristol University Press.

Hudson, L. N., Newbold, T., Contu, S., Hill, S. L. L., Lysenko, I., De Palma, A., Phillips, H. R. P., Senior, R. A., Bennett, D. J., Booth, H., Choimes, A., Correia, D. L. P., Day, J., Echeverría-Londoño, S., Garon, M., Harrison, M. L. K., Ingram, D. J., Jung, M., Kemp V., . . . Purvis, A. (2014). The PREDICTS database: A global database of how local terrestrial biodiversity responds to human impacts. *Ecology and Evolution* 4(24), 4701–4735

International Association for Public Participation (IAP2). (2007). IAP2 Spectrum of Public Participation. International Association for Public Participation. https://cdn.ymaws.com/www.iap2.org/resource/resmgr/pillars/Spectrum_8.5x11_Print.pdf

Isin, E., & Ruppert, E. (2020). *Being digital citizens*. Rowman & Littlefield.

Marres, N. 2016. *Material participation: Technology, the environment and everyday publics*. Palgrave Macmillan

Kelly, C. (2013). Building bridges with accessible care: Disability studies, feminist care scholarship, and beyond. *Hypatia*, *28*(4), 784–800.

McLean, J. (2020). *Changing digital geographies: Technologies, environments, and people*. Palgrave Macmillan.

MoTH Cities. (2021). More than human data interactions in the smart city. https://mothcities.uk/

Powell, A. B. (2021). *Undoing optimization*. Yale University Press.

Reindal, S. M. (2010). What is the purpose? Reflections on inclusion and special education from a capability perspective. *European Journal of Special Needs Education*, *25*(1), 1–12.

Yong, E. (2022, June 20). How animals see themselves. *New York Times*. https://www.nytimes.com/2022/06/20/opinion/how-animals-see-themselves.html

Young, I. M. (2011). *Responsibility for justice*. Oxford University Press.

Searle, A., Turnbull, J., & Adams, W. M. (2023). The digital peregrine: A technonatural history of a cosmopolitan raptor. *Transactions of the Institute of British Geographers*, *48*(1), 195–212. https://doi.org/10.1111/tran.12566

White, P. C. L., Saunders, G., & Harris, S. (1996). Spatio-temporal patterns of home range use by foxes (*Vulpes vulpes*) in urban environments. *Journal of Animal Ecology*, *65*(1), 121–125. https://doi.org/10.2307/5705

Winter, J. S., & Davidson, E. (2019). Big data governance of personal health information and challenges to contextual integrity. *The Information Society* *35*(1), 36–51.

SECTION 4
FUTURES

12

A City of Good Ancestors

Urban Governance and Design from a Relationist Ethos

Mary Graham, Michelle Maloney, and Marcus Foth

Introduction

When considering the future of cities, there are many urgent and immediate issues to consider: the impacts of climate change and sea level rise; effective and socially just planning; access to affordable housing; the role of technology, digital inclusion and citizen surveillance; the sustainability of food and other materials coming into the city; the management of waste and pollution coming out of the city; and so much more.

But what if we also take a long view? As an organising structure for human societies, cities have experienced their first 10,000 years of development. What if we contemplate the future of cities and other human settlements for the coming 10,000 years? Given the current threats of climate change, as well as the ecological and social justice challenges humans face, this is an exercise in deep optimism and what Krznaric (2020) calls 'cathedral thinking—the art of planning into the distant future'. If human beings and their societies are to survive for another 10,000 years, what governance principles should guide us, and how can we ensure cities turn from an agglomeration of human settlements and infrastructure into habitats that are regenerative, socially just and capable of supporting a thriving more-than-human ecosystem (Panelli 2010; Metzger 2019)? How do we design not just smart cities but 'seven generation cities' (Engle et al. 2022) or—borrowing from both Krznaric (2020) and the late Aboriginal elder Maureen Watson[1]—*a city of good ancestors* that will serve the generations of humans and more-than-humans who follow us well into the future?

To begin exploring these questions, in this chapter we employ a philosophical approach and turn to one of the oldest human societies on earth—the Aboriginal societies of the continent that is now called Australia. We say 'now' to duly acknowledge the settler-colonial history of this country, which saw foreigners invade and establish permanent settlements on unceded Indigenous lands. Settlers sought to acculturate First Nation peoples by imposing their own societies and institutions, which displaced and marginalised Indigenous peoples. This process involved cultural erasure, land theft, and the imposition of settler norms and governance (Moreton-Robinson 2015). It perpetuated unequal power dynamics and curtailed Indigenous peoples' rights, autonomy, and access to resources. While Aboriginal Peoples have endured colonisation and continue their culture and ancient practices, Australia's history of settler-colonialism has had profound and enduring consequences on Aboriginal

Mary Graham, Michelle Maloney, and Marcus Foth, *A City of Good Ancestors*. In: *Designing More-than-Human Smart Cities*. Edited by: Sara Heitlinger, Marcus Foth, and Rachel Clarke, Oxford University Press. © Oxford University Press (2024). DOI: 10.1093/9780191980060.003.0014 and Torres Strait Islander communities, shaping their socio-political, economic, and cultural realities.

We ask 'what if'—what if cities were built on the foundational principles and governance systems of Australian Aboriginal societies, which developed some of the most stable, spiritually rich, and long-standing governance systems in the history (and prehistory) of humanity (Gammage 2012)? How might these foundations forge future cities over the coming millennia? What difference might they make to how human societies operate?

In Part 1, we introduce key foundational principles within what Dr Mary Graham calls a 'pan-Aboriginal' governance system, including the Relationist Ethos, the Custodial Ethic, and law of obligation as the principles of a 'Civilisational Culture' needed for peace and security. Part 1 is thus primarily concerned with introducing some of the foundational principles that can be applied to a relationist city. We refrain from referring to smart cities discourse until we reach Part 2, where we present an applied example of how smart cities professionals can employ a Relationist Ethos in their praxis. Here, we embark on a normative adventure, and explore what it would look like if smart cities were built on the foundations of the Relationist Ethos and Custodial Ethic. As part of this, we also provide an outline of one of the frameworks developed by Dr Michelle Maloney, called *Greenprints*, which is being used to help people in existing cities and settlements in Australia to connect with and live within the capacity of nature, and transform our systems to adopt the Relationist Ethos.

Foundational Principles of a Relationist City

Indigenous peoples and cities

In looking at an ancient culture like Aboriginal societies, it would be easy to assume a high level of incommensurability between their complex understanding of principles of organisation and the Western ideas of complicated, highly technological systems such as smart city infrastructure.

Cities arose approximately 10,000 years ago, predating the rise of large-scale agriculture (Graeber & Wengrow 2022). Various forms of the city-state later emerged in other parts of the world, including Europe, China, and South America. By 'cities' we broadly refer to large congregations of human communities, living within a defined area, with structured systems of governance. While various concepts, criteria, and definitions exist, we note the two approaches—often used in tandem—endorsed by UN Habitat (2018) to develop a functional definition of the city for the purposes of UN Sustainable Development Goal 11: Sustainable Cities and Communities. They are: 1) a city as defined by its urban extent, that is, built-up and urbanised open space; and 2) a city as defined by its degree of urbanisation ('DEGURBA').

Aboriginal Peoples—past and present—had highly organised societies, often in what would be described as large villages. But Aboriginal people did not develop large cities as we know them today, because the spiritual, material, and practical elements of the principles outlined in the following sections of this chapter guided the nature and size of Aboriginal societies. Aboriginal societies embedded themselves within the patterns of the more-than-human world (what we call nature and the intimacy of place), curated resources across an ancient continent efficiently, and managed their population sizes carefully. Populations in specific Places[2] did not naturally increase greatly over time, and due to the relative isolation of the continent, there were few people migrating from other Places up until the arrival of settler-colonialists (Russell 2001). However, despite the differences between traditional Aboriginal societies and city-based societies around the world today, like most human groups, and for other life forms throughout history, everything starts with the relationship to Place. For Aboriginal people security was to be found in the development of a system of co-existence with Place, that is, the more-than-human world, or the life force, in all its forms. This Relationist Ethos formed the deep foundations of Aboriginal societies and created a remarkable governance system and culture.

What is the purpose of human culture? This is a question that could be (and probably was) asked by all societies and individuals, as exemplified by Western thinkers such as Socrates (Williams & Moore 2006). It could be suggested that the purpose of human culture is to achieve (and maintain) coherence about human relationship to, and understanding of, the environment, human attributes, relations with other humans and collectives, and Place.

Relationalism and the Relationist Ethos

Relationality[3] literally means 'concerning the way in which two or more people or things are connected' (Houseman 2006). In Australian Aboriginal societies, the primary relationship is between people and Country.[4] Other relations, including those with more-than-human relatives, are always contingent/built upon the relationship between people and Country.

Aboriginal relationalism—traditionally the foundation of Aboriginal law—is an elaborate, complex, and refined system of social, moral, spiritual, and community obligations that provides an ordered universe for people. Within the context of this system, relationalism: embraces uncertainty and imprecision; accords primacy to feelings, intuitions, intimations, etc. over mere thoughts; accepts and makes room for conflict (yet is at odds with notions of invasion or conquest); resolves the contradiction between (Western hierarchical) power and (Aboriginal distributed) authority; provides coherence about the meaning of life; and assumes that not only groups, but all people and more-than-human relatives, are autonomous beings (Graham 2014).

So, any notion of Aboriginal social and political order has to begin with the Aboriginal relationship to Land, which is primary: 'the land is the source of the law' (Black 2010). Expanding one's sphere of influence by conquest of other lands does not confer security: just the opposite. Rather, it ensures insecurity in a number of ways, not least of which is the long-standing grievance of the 'conquered', which may or may not express itself in myriad ways. Coercion in relations sooner or later rebounds—the act(s) of coercion is not forgotten. They are solidly embedded in the narratives of all those involved in conquest projects.

The establishment and maintenance of relationalism rests with its attributes, which are—autonomy, balance, place/kinship, and the Custodial Ethic.

Autonomy

Autonomy, in the Aboriginal sense, is a state of being for human and non-human life. All beings are autonomous. Their self-hood is owned by ones-self alone, that is, the individual is a self-governing agent, but is not and cannot be a law unto themselves. Nor can they be enslaved or owned by another, be a conscious isolate, or a discrete, detached individual.

The Law of Obligation (Boulous Walker 2022; Graham 2023) prevented autonomous beings distancing themselves from each other, by way of the Autonomous Regard method of conduct. Autonomous Regard is not respect in the ordinary sense; rather, it is self-awareness, plus awareness of the other's autonomy, thoughtfulness, subtlety, discretion, and other qualities closer to diplomacy. Holding all beings—human and more-than-human—in Autonomous Regard, this deep form of interconnectedness and respect is a profoundly important practice within Aboriginal societies, and can empower non-Indigenous people to transform their relationships with each other, and the more-than-human world of which they are part (Brigg & Graham 2021).

Balance

Autonomous Regard is used in achieving balance. Balance is necessary for a positive, stable society.[5] Balance is not about bending people to one's will, but sponsoring and accounting for the interests of others, sharing, and being reckoned with. This is what and how one's place in the world is determined—not through domination of one's environment.

Autonomous Regard is the fulcrum or central balancing tool, infused with the Custodial Ethic, enabling and inviting two or more different perspectives from/within thought, action, and intent, practice in physicality or spirituality to observe the essence or truth in the other.

Relationist, not conflated with competitiveness or rivalry, can be individual or plural (with others). It acts like a foil (in fencing, it is the blunt end sword for training) in that it prevents the extreme from manifesting. It could be called the essential conservatism. As a concept, balance via Autonomous Regard interrupts tribalism, identity politics, ideology, religious beliefs, and politics.

Place/kinship

If Aboriginal societies had an equivalent of the Descartes's (1998) statement: 'I think, therefore I am', it would be: 'I am located, therefore I am' (Graham 2023). While a person has autonomy as a spiritual being inextricably tied to Place as a spiritual landscape, the Aboriginal individuality is not centred on the idea of a rational, autonomous self alone in the world as a discrete entity or conscious isolate searching for meaning. Kinship and meaning come from Country, from Place, and from community.

Custodial Ethic

A common Western view is that people have to have some kind of belief system in order to have a spiritual justification for agency. Western humanism is not a unified system; it is a rationalist outlook or system of thought attaching prime importance to human rather than divine or supernatural matters. The rational self is individualistic, self-centred, egoistic.[6] In contrast, the Aboriginal system of governance—the Custodial Ethic—is not a faith-based religion or belief system. Instead, it employs a sense of propriety and shame related to one's conduct. The system of relationalism was effective, efficient, rational, stable, and sustainable with a meritocratic system of governance and inclusive, with an absence of domination by any one group over another or others. This coexistence was underpinned by laws, that is, guidelines for engagement; non-hierarchical social and political structures both within and between clan groups; very different notions of power and authority (the two are not conflated in Aboriginal thinking); and a system for territorial integrity rather than the expansion of spheres of control/influence by invading another's Country—the preferred Aboriginal word for one's own land/territory—or, the impulse to forced clan unification.

Conjointly, these laws embedded in a system of relationalism comprise a monumental, all-encompassing governance system called the Custodial Ethic (Graham 2023).

Survivalism

Relationalism and survivalism go hand in hand (Table 12.1). Survival(ism) can be either an everyday small event or a large event. Examples of general survival include almost getting hit by a bus in traffic, swimming in shark-infested waters, or losing one's job after a long career or in an economic downturn. It could also encompass being affected by large-scale events like being a refugee fleeing war/revolution or

Table 12.1 Relationalism and Survivalism sit beside each other.

Relationalism	**Relationist Reasoning**	**Relationist Ethos**
Lateral organisational structures; land/environment partnership	Aboriginal Logic and the intuitive mind; Reflective Motive; Resource management	Place, Autonomy, Balance and Ethics (the Law) Land becomes Country not territory
Survivalism	**Survivalist Reasoning**	**Survivalist Ethos**
Hierarchies; territory/ land and resources capture	Logic; Unreflective Motive; Economic and Technological dominance and endless growth.	Security guarantee, strategic autonomy and the zero-sum game; land becomes property/territory

trying to survive in a war-torn, impoverished country. Indigenous people everywhere are trying to survive colonialism—in the immediate sense and over centuries. Additionally, the human and non-human world is trying to survive any large-scale global crisis like climate change or pandemics.

However, having an idea of the world and life as a place of constant struggle and/or danger, requires a permanent striving through life. One could say that people who see themselves as 'battlers' are like 'survivalists'. Survivalists follow survivalism as a frame of reference even after achieving reasonable or moderate security. Economists and anthropologists have always evinced struggle (the survivalist life) as a natural state of being for the indigent and the Indigenous (cf. Payne 2020).

However, the true Survivalist Ethos arises when individuals, groups, or Peoples and states conclude that the hard, relentless experience of fighting for survival in any of the above-named experiences, for any length of time, in any range of different circumstances, is indeed what life is all about. That is, the crucial importance is when the survivalist starts to see the environment, natural, social, or political situation as inherently hostile and therefore tends to see others (and their actions) as the competitive Other and so becomes alert and wary, that is, to see only one's self as autonomous and the Other as potential threat and rival. The whole canon of international relations writing is based on the survivalist ethos.

A survivalist ethos can lead a state to see the global space as a hostile environment and therefore pursue a policy of strategic autonomy, with a moderate but growing nationalist self-regard. Furthermore, like the survivalist person who runs the risk of becoming an extreme discrete entity or conscious isolate trapped in a hostile world, the state with this ethos imperils itself when their own nationalist self-regard becomes extreme. With the gradual increase in survivalist ethos thinking, the capacity for self-correction—via policy analysis, economic and community development of communities and states—decreases. The ultimate survivalist ethos entity/example that is most clear is the state that pursues global hegemonic control.

Not just nation-states but cities, too, show qualities and tendencies towards a survivalist ethos. Examples include firewalls and protective design elements in the old days, as well as competition expressed through national performance dashboards (Kitchin et al. 2015), rankings (Giffinger et al. 2010), and new forms of protectionism such as military urbanism (Graham 2010; Iveson 2010).

A city of good ancestors: coherence, proportionality, predictability

If we consider that cities came into being about 10,000 years ago (give or take a few thousand years) and that great social, political, economic, and technological change within cities have forged hierarchical and often unjust social systems, and have transformed—and in many places—utterly depleted the more-than-human world—then how do we deal with the outcomes of this period of time? Do we want our cities to continue to grow as they have done? Or can we see that human settlements have grown out of proportion with the capacity of the living world to support them? Perhaps, in order to design a city of good ancestors that is fit for the next 10,000 years, we need to reconnect with the Relationist Ethos and with the non-human world.

Aboriginal people were engaged in creating and maintaining a long-term, regenerative system of governance. Their human, spiritual, and social (political, economic, technological) endeavours took place for generations based on principles of coherence, proportionality, and predictability, and they thus sustained vibrant human and more-than-human communities until coming face-to-face with imperialism and its colonial projects. The 'wild card' in this view is the pathway possibilities that any/all crisis/challenge situations present. Will the long-term or short-term view be taken? Will the strategic or tactical response be more advantageous? Will the relationist or survivalist ethos be the preferred choice, in making these decisions, the more rewarding socially, culturally or otherwise?

This crisis and challenge situation is present for cities also—cities globally even. Perhaps cities need to work out a new design approach of their own for the next 10,000 years to achieve harmony with the more-than-human world.

Coherence—the beginning of the reflective self

Coherence emerges from the experience of relating to the Land, which, again, is best expressed as: 'the land is the source of the law' (Black 2010). Land invented human and non-human beings, it has thrown us up into the world and into the imaginative ability to create society, ecology, and culture, it helps us (continually) to form society and keeps us alive and creative through its resources, its changes, and its enabling capacities. We (humans) are ultimately, inextricably, and will forever be obliged to Land for our existence. The obligation is expressed in broad reciprocal social and cultural arrangements where human collectives—clan and language groups—'look after' Land within particular local regions recognised by other collectives. Arrangements, or to be more exact, a complex systematisation takes place. That is, the Law, in all its manifestations, enters the world, becomes embedded within and between groups, and the world becomes ordered as the following:

- **Cultural** (narratives, languages, representations, the Custodial Ethic)
- **Ceremonial** (spiritual integrity, Land as a moral, living, conscious, communicative entity, duties to ancestral spirits)
- **Practical** (attending the consensus, consensus decision making, primacy of the extended (not nuclear) family, especially children, young people and kin)
- **Organisational** (non-hierarchical structure with gender balance, Elders are an authority, but they do not rule)
- **Personal** (non-competitiveness, maintenance of harmonious relations, careful management of the ego, positive conflict management and group dynamics).

Combined, these five arrangements can also be understood as the Custodial Ethic. Such an ethic serves the valuable purpose of suspending social and political judgement, especially between groups, and promotes autonomy.

Proportionality—the environment of the reflective self

How do we measure up in our own Country, that is, how do we measure ourselves (not in a competitive sense) to/with the Country/landscape/ground itself, to others

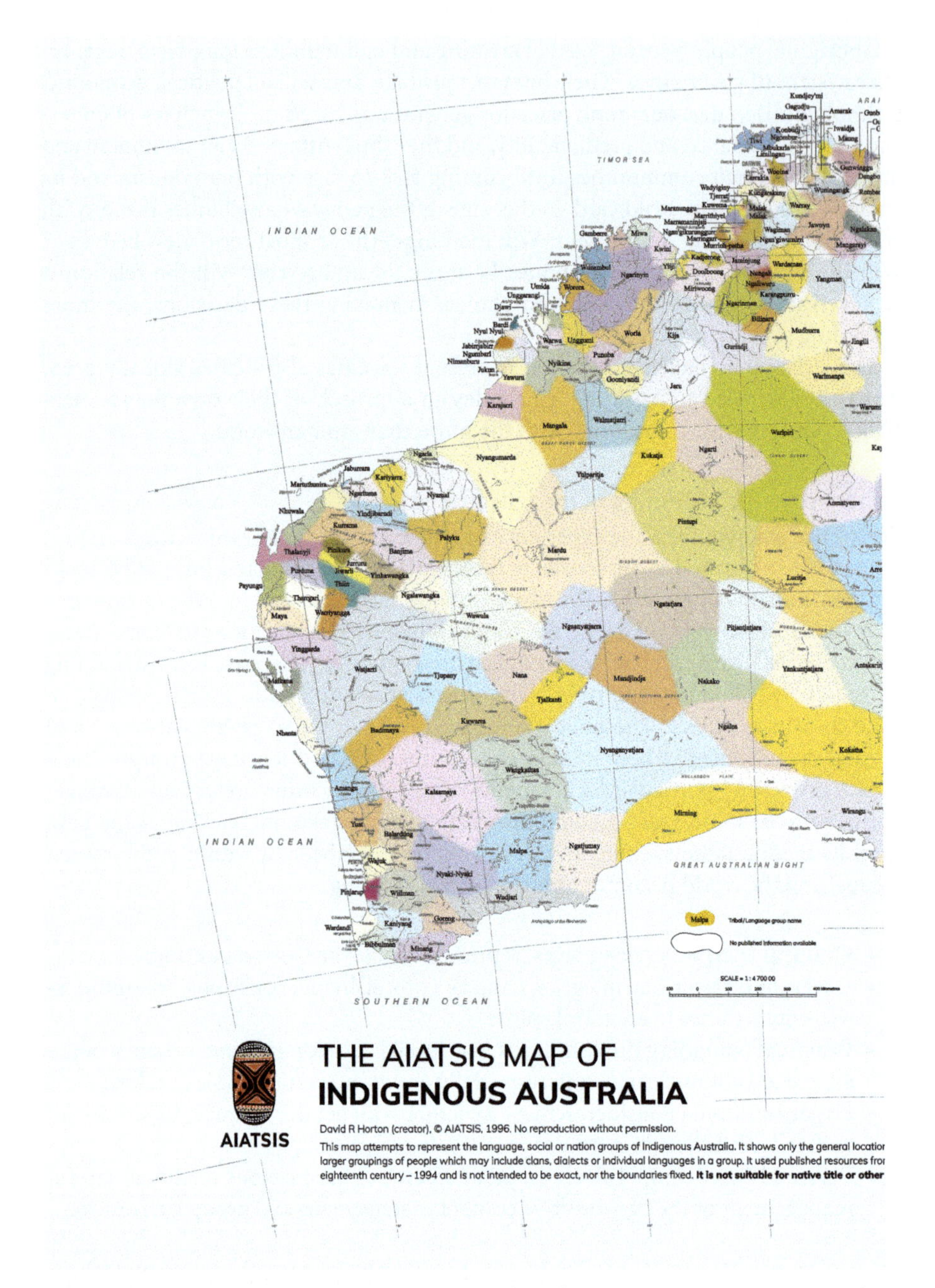

Figure 12.1 AIATSIS map of Indigenous Australia. This map attempts to represent the language, social, or nation groups of Aboriginal Australia. It shows only the general locations of larger groupings of people, which may include clans, dialects, or individual languages in a group. It used published resources from the eighteenth century–1994 and is not intended to be exact, nor the boundaries fixed. It is not suitable for native title or other land claims.

David R Horton (creator), © AIATSIS, 1996. No reproduction without permission. To purchase a print version visit: https://shop.aiatsis.gov.au/.

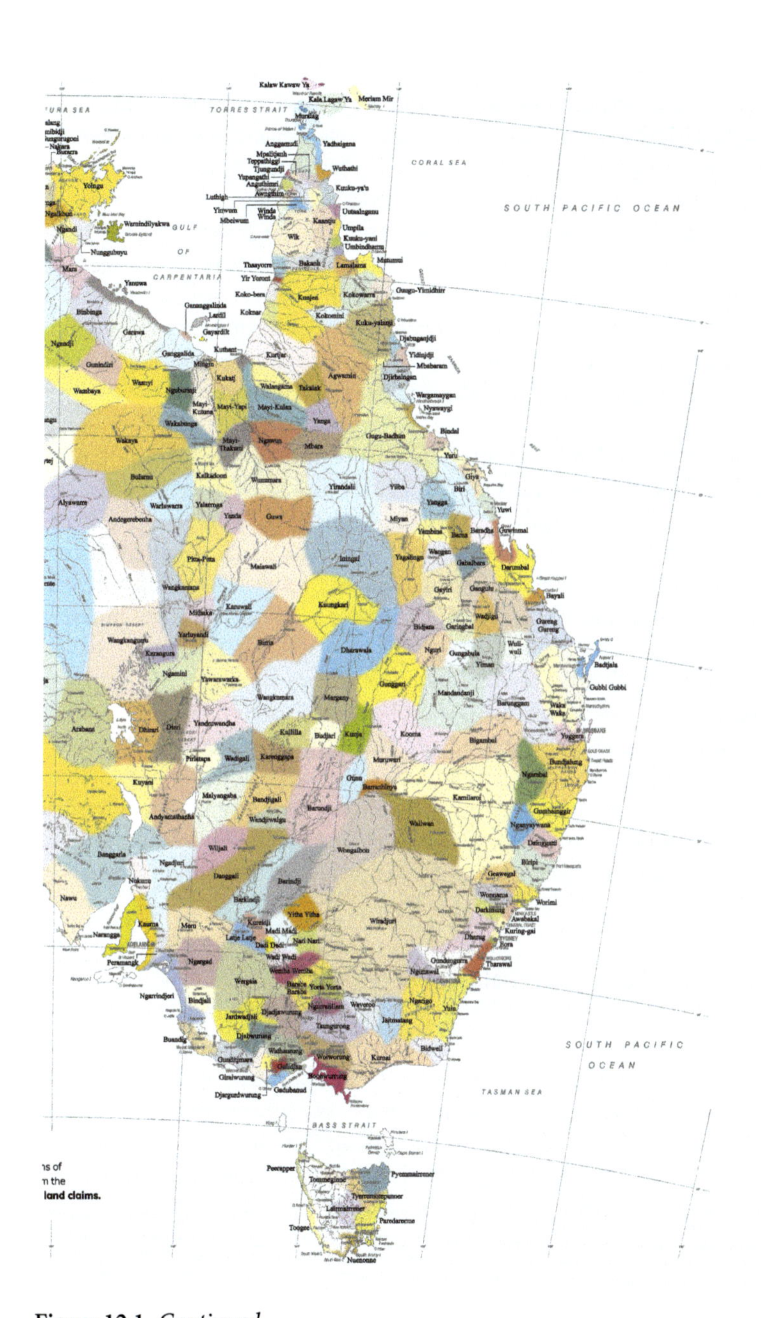

Figure 12.1 *Continued*

in and outside the group, to the ancestors, to Spirit Beings? How do we fit in the Place and Country we are in? More to the point: how do we find this good fit? The best way to start seems to be the measure utilised by ancestors—how did those who went before us do it? If the exact, correct, measured relationship with our surroundings can be understood properly, it can be only in the state of the environment as it was left to us to be Custodians. As good ancestors our obligation is to learn and reflect on the intent of previous generations (Brand 1997; Yunkaporta 2019). This adds proportionality to our own significance. The intention was clear—the Land does not actually need any human—or, for that matter, any more-than-human—life form to care for it, and yet here we are—it created us with the most complex and yet the most contradictory qualities and states of being, like human will, logic, reflective and unreflective motives, vulnerabilities, and fears, including some proclivity for violence.

Within a moral/spiritual landscape the Custodial Ethic—in the form of the Law of Obligation (Boulous Walker 2022; Graham 2023)—has to be maintained by people being lawful. Yet, simultaneously the ego, the wild card of human nature, is not deemed to be sinful or bad. Rather, it is viewed as a potentially volatile substance to be treated with something like a combination of caring stewardship, referee-like supervision, watchful guardianship, and prompts towards attentive, measured persuasion.

The primacy of Place, identity, and autonomy is shown clearly in the Aboriginal language map (Figure 12.1)—a map that is also about the representation of a locality-based, social, and political organising principle, rather than an ideological one.

Having a Law of Obligation gives communities and populations a deep sense of confidence, and therefore security, which is what makes the ancient system sophisticated. The Law of Obligation is worldly, in the sense of being within the world and with the world across time, whereas an individual is just in the world. This is what also makes it elegant.

Predictability—the reflective self challenged

Aboriginal logic or, if this is too challenging for some, logic with Aboriginal characteristics, follows specific organising principles (Figure 12.2).

The equation may also be proposed as: Place = Dreaming[7] Multiple Places = Multiple Dreamings = Multiple Laws = Multiple Truths = Multiple Perspectives = All perspectives (truths) are valid and reasonable (Graham 2009).

The two systems—*the Custodial Ethic* and *the logic that all perspectives are valid and reasonable*—are in the Aboriginal context like first principles, that is, a priori in that they are simply assumed and exist prior to our ability to reason. The two

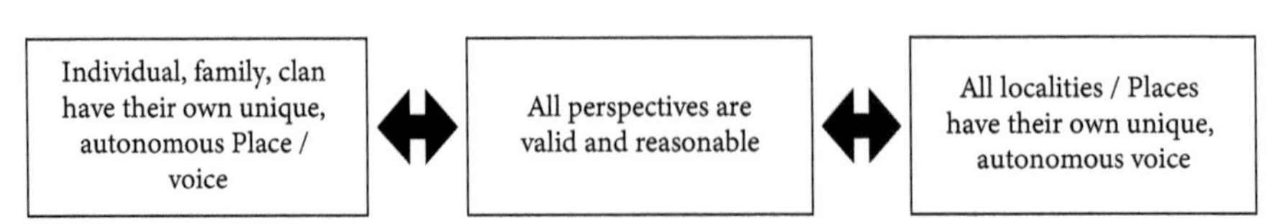

Figure 12.2 Organising principles of Aboriginal logic.

principles together are very effective—ideally one cannot stand without the other. The *logic that all perspectives are valid and reasonable* on its own is quite cold-blooded as it can lead to a kind of extreme relativism where there is no meaning at all, especially with regards to moral dilemmas or ethical judgements. The logic is an instrument to suspend or soften judgement, and to aid and sharpen a correct sense of proportionality where good judgement, prudence, or discernment are required.

The Custodial Ethic is an ethic of obligation to family, clan, community, and Country—the Law of Obligation—involving the vast array of expressions of Aboriginal Lawfulness, which is part of the overall solemn and sublime Aboriginal Law covering the whole of existence, time, and space. The purpose of this is also to give ourselves purpose—spiritually, psychologically, socially, and culturally. This then gives people the general feeling of confidence that one's environment—including seasonal variability—is predictable. For Aboriginal people this predictability came through the Relationist Ethos, that is, the primary relationship between people and Land/environment and the relationship between people or society; the latter is always contingent on the first.

If culture is the expression of human attempts to acquire coherence about existence, then understanding proportionality and predictability (long-term), among other factors, are the main prerequisites for attaining the relationist aspect of effective security for both the individual and the collective while living culturally. The pathway towards achieving personal and social/communal security, that is, the security that is coherent, proportional, and predictable, is through a measured equilibrium between notions of relationalism and survivalism.

This interpretation of predictability stands in stark contrast with smart cities created using an urban science approach embedded in a positivist paradigm. The latter vows to collect and analyse urban data to find the single truth to satisfy Western notions of predictability (Kitchin 2020; Rittenbruch et al. 2022). Yet, in this ongoing quest of discovery even 'big data' is never *enough* data, which renders the city in a perpetual state of incompleteness (Fredericks et al. 2019), based on a limited epistemological basis (Foth et al. 2007; Mattern 2021), and risking to paralyse any action that is urgently needed (Hulme 2014; Glavovic et al. 2021).

Cities Governed by Relationist Ethos and Custodial Ethic?

Since 1788, Australian cities and towns have been established on Aboriginal lands, as part of the British Colonial Project. Many Aboriginal people were either removed from their Country and displaced to reserves, driven off, or killed, but some were able to remain in a life-saving compromise to find employment enabling them to stay on Country—a security tactic undertaken by many Aboriginal communities across the continent.

Today, Australia's population of twenty-six million people live predominantly along our coastlines and within cities and large urban settlements. The Australian Institute of Health and Welfare (2022) reports that 'Indigenous Australians live in all parts of the nation, from cities to remote tropical and desert areas. Indigenous Australians are more likely to live in urban and regional areas than remote areas, though the proportion of the total population who are Indigenous is generally higher in more remote areas'. The ABS (2019) projects for 2022 that among Indigenous Australians: 38% (344,800) live in major cities; 44% (395,900) live in inner and outer regional areas; and 17% (155,600) live in remote and very remote areas combined. The proportion of the total population who were Indigenous increased with remoteness, from 1.09% in major cities, to 32% in remote and very remote areas. So how can future cities be transformed by the Relationist Ethos and Custodial Ethic?

In a chapter of this length, we cannot hope to discuss all the complex elements of a future city that might be shaped by a new focus on the Relationist Ethos and a Custodial Ethic. However, we have chosen to briefly explore three elements:

(i) **Bringing cities into relationship with the more-than-human world.** What would it look like if people living in cities were in relationship with the living world?
(ii) **Bringing people into a deeper relationship with each other**. What would it look like if people in cities used their relationship with the land as the template for their relationships with each other—and they governed and designed their communities for the collective good, respecting the autonomy and wellbeing of all its human and non-human communities?
(iii) **Bringing it all together to transform our cities.** What are the steps or processes that can be used to create the type of change discussed in this chapter?

Linking cities and the more-than-human world

If human communities within a modern city's boundaries truly understood that the land—Place—is the source of the law, it would trigger a cascade of governance and urban design reform (Graham & Maloney 2019; Sheikh et al. 2023). People would work to develop their understanding of the biophysical realities of their Place and the intricate web of life that supports them and their more-than-human kin and neighbours. Further, they would ensure they live in proportion to the capacity of the surrounding bioregion to support life within the city and that they act as good global citizens, living within planetary boundaries (Persson et al. 2022). Further, the peoples of a city would embrace what is now called 'nature positive' design (Birkeland 2022; Fieuw et al. 2022; Jones et al. 2022): the idea that not only does a human community have to minimise harm to the environment through sustainability practices, but that it also has an obligation to nurture regenerative life and 'give back' to nature. In effect, a city could be transformed to be a haven of abundance for all life in the bioregion (McGinnis 1999; Liaros 2019).

A city that exists in deep relationship with the living more-than-human world, requires a set of different 1) governance and 2) design principles that fundamentally decentre the human (Forlano 2016; Clarke et al. 2019) in order to achieve what Graham (2023) terms *sacralised ecological stewardship*, which dovetails with the notion of 'sacred civics' by Engle et al. (2022). First, with regards to governance, we posit that the local culture would celebrate, reflect, and support the more-than-human world of which it is part—people would see themselves in relationship with the plants, animals, and ecosystems in and around the city. Nature would not just be 'property' or a natural resource (Rühs & Jones 2016; Graham & Maloney 2019), or the 'background' to human activities. Rather, nature would be foregrounded in all aspects of human society and caring for Country and our planetary health and wellbeing would be an obligation (Poelina et al. 2022). This cultural approach to identifying with local natural features and other members of the earth community can be connected to the modern concept of 'bioregionalism' (McGinnis 1999), and is deeply embedded in many Indigenous cultures and thus also prompts reflection on bioregionalism's capacity for decoloniality (Mignolo & Walsh 2018; Paradies 2020; Wiebe 2021). This type of cultural engagement with ecocentrism and seeing 'the land as the law' is critically important to building a Civilisational Culture. Collective and individual responsibility would be demonstrated towards natural systems within the local, regional and global context. This would translate into ecocentric governance in so many ways, including customs, ceremonies, festivals, seasonal calendars, education curricula, and societal funding priorities; it would infiltrate all aspects of life for the people of a city.

Local laws would reflect the importance of the living world and would enshrine the primacy of the regenerative capacity of the unique ecosystems that humans and non-humans live within. Local laws would prevent harm to nature, and support earth-centred economics and human activities. Local laws protecting and sacralising local places would not be able to be overridden by other legal processes (e.g., from other scales—such as Federal or State laws) and would be managed by effective processes involving local people. Local laws would also embed a range of processes to promote local custodianship of natural places. Governance structures would include mechanisms such as 'eco-representation' (Eckersley & Gagnon 2014; Gray & Curry 2020; Kopnina et al. 2021), so that the interests of the more-than-human world would be prioritised in all decision making processes. In today's cities, processes such as Councils of All Beings, Rights of Nature Tribunals, and Citizen's Assemblies that include eco-representation might flourish.

Second, with regards to city design, we argue that a city in deep relationship with the more-than-human world would be designed so that the health and wellbeing of natural ecosystems are considered an obligation, and are always understood, respected, and cared for. Ecocentric approaches to designing cities might include ensuring that extensive natural habitat flourishes throughout the city, and interconnected corridors of life are protected in perpetuity, so that biodiversity can flourish (Steele 2019; Steele et al. 2019; Yigitcanlar et al. 2019; Wiesel et al. 2020; Fieuw et al. 2022). It also means ensuring waterways are held in deep respect, and developments are managed to prevent harm and pollution that would detrimentally affect waterways. Strategies such as 'daylighting' (Lee et al. 2020), that is, bringing covered waterways back to life, would be critical. As noted, the cultural aspects of an ecocentric society would require ceremonies and community practices to reinforce the sacralised respect for natural systems, including waterways. Urban design and planning would engage in re-wilding efforts (Steele 2019) to enable urban wildlife to thrive in their city habitats by ensuring that suitable habitat and food plants exist, and by preserving pathways for animal movement and migration, as natural overpasses, bridges, tunnels, and the like can support their free movement around the city. Looking at the planning and design of human habitat, the concept of 'green buildings' has started to be critically assessed with regards to their limited focus on energy efficiencies and architectural aesthetics (Loh et al. 2020). Instead, human settlements must be designed to be genuinely sustainable, that is, net positive, circular, and relational (Birkeland 2020, 2022; Liaros 2021; Sheikh et al. 2022), and replacing chemicals, plastics, and other novel entities that are harmful to life with biodegradable and sustainable materials (Persson et al. 2022).

Deeper relationships between people: social justice and the Relationist Ethos

In addition to recognising the primacy of the more-than-human world and local/bioregional ecosystems, building cities on the principles of the Relationist Ethos would mean actively promoting and protecting peoples' collective responsibilities and obligations to each other.

With regards to governance features, such a city might include features such as a relationist governance structure using consensus-based decision making, and support processes such as Citizens Assemblies, so that all people can have a voice in the governance and allocation of resources within a city. Relational and social justice values and frameworks would ensure affordable housing, food and transport for all people. Cities would develop new governance structures to respect the wisdom and knowledge of Elders and ensure gender balance within the city's decision-making processes. Relationships between communities and suburbs would be actively nurtured and supported, through proactive grassroots governance structures and financial, cultural and psychological support systems. Relationships within and between families would be highly valued and supported by collective responses and resources wherever possible—including innovative and free child-care and educational options. A relationist city would also ensure people were educated in a wide variety of ways necessary to support harmonious relations, including learning how to create and nurture cooperative work relationships (rather than competitive structures) and learning how to undertake effective conflict management.

With regards to design, cities built on the Relationist Ethos would have extensive public spaces designed to support harmonious relationships between human and more-than-human life, including places for ceremonial practices, and places to celebrate Land as a moral living agential entity; places for public learning—libraries and schools—would be prioritised and well resourced; human settlements including urban renewal and new residential developments would be designed to maximise wildlife habitat and safe green spaces, and maximise community spaces and support for families and all people; and industrial zones and economic activities would be designed and built to maximise a circular economy with zero-waste and zero-emissions—and ensure space and habitat corridors for biodiversity.

Combined, the above arrangements would build a Custodial Ethic, so that people would care for Country and care for each other.

Bringing it all together: the Greenprints approach

There are many different ways that proposals like those listed above can be initiated—and are being initiated—in cities around the world. Policy, regulation, and economic incentives can all be used to progress such ideas. In this final part of our chapter, we provide an outline of a framework being used in Australia—'the Greenprints approach'.[8] The Greenprints framework has been created specifically to support earth-centred systems change and encourage the adoption of the Relationist Ethos and Custodial Ethic, systemically by non-Indigenous communities, in solidarity with Indigenous communities. The Greenprints approach offers an example of just one of many ways to create the type of long-term cultural and governance change discussed in Part 1 of this chapter.

Designed by Dr Michelle Maloney of the Australian Earth Laws Alliance (AELA; earthlaws.org.au), the Greenprints approach has been created in collaboration with Indigenous colleagues from Future Dreaming Australia (futuredreaming.org.au) and other organisations. It engages deeply with ecocentrism and Relationism, and AELA is currently working in several communities around Australia to build a movement of people who are empowered with knowledge and approaches to build relational, ecocentric, regenerative settlements and societies. The name 'Greenprints' came from the observation that, although there are 'blueprints' to guide careful construction of engineering and building projects, we do not yet have 'greenprints' that help guide industrialised societies to build regenerative communities and economies within healthy ecological limits. The Greenprints framework addresses this gap by providing a practical methodology—a step-by-step process—to help people rethink and transform their societies to connect with and live within the capacities of nature. Greenprints has eight basic steps that are used as scaffolding to support a wide range of projects, including community 'think-tank' methods. The whole process has been designed to create cultural change and generate scenarios for ensuring local places are governed and cared for within the spirit of the Custodial Ethic.

Greenprints begins by inviting people to 'think differently' about Australia's colonial history and Western notions of nature merely as property, and engage with Indigenous knowledge systems and ecocentrism. It enables people to understand the unique ecology and healthy limits of their local bioregion and community ecosystems; analyse past, present, and possible future human economic activity within their bioregion (including land use, consumption, production, carbon and other emissions); and develop bioregion-specific strategies for transitioning to new, regenerative economic systems that are supported by relationism, ecological law, and ecological governance.

Step 1: Think differently

The first step in the Greenprints approach is to *change the way we think* about our place in the world. Greenprints start by enabling people to connect with paradigm shifting concepts inspired by Indigenous knowledge and the Relationist Ethos, and also by earth jurisprudence (Berry 2011; Cullinan 2011; Burdon 2012; Rühs & Jones 2016; Graham & Maloney 2019). If we accept that humans are simply one part of the wider, interconnected community of life on this planet, and we accept that all of life and life-supporting systems have the intrinsic right to exist, thrive, and evolve, then our expectations of how we should live change dramatically.

In this first stage of the Greenprints process, participants explore ecocentric theories—including bioregionalism—and Indigenous Place-based governance through a range of interactive exercises, peer-to-peer learning, and workshops and activities featuring experts and special guests. It includes engaging with the traditional custodians of the Place, and wherever possible, working together in a culturally appropriate way that ensures Indigenous peoples' perspectives and knowledge are respected and they themselves are leaders, advisors, and participants in the longer-term project, should they wish. The first stage of the process also introduces the concepts of planetary boundaries, ecological limits, and a range of economic theories and approaches that can inform the transition to an economic system that can 'fit' within ecological limits, including Steady State (Daly 1991) and Doughnut Economics (Raworth 2017).

Step 2: Define ecological boundaries

The second Greenprints step is to identify and choose the most appropriate ecological boundaries, for the relevant project or endeavour. In her Nobel Prize-winning work on the commons, Elinor Ostrom (1990) highlighted the importance of setting clear boundaries when designing commons management projects (Gibson-Graham et al. 2016; Teli et al. 2020, 2022)—and if we are to transition industrial societies away from their current abuse and overconsumption of the natural world, we need to start by focussing on the ecological integrity and resilience of the natural world. But what 'scale' or 'unit of analysis' is the best way to start? What are these ecological limits within which we need to work? As a starting point for non-indigenous communities, ecological boundaries recognised by western science—such as local ecosystems, catchments (watersheds), and/or bioregions and sub-bioregions—can be extremely useful. In the case of cities, this typically means locating the political boundaries of the city in the catchment and bioregion within which the city is located.

It is important to distinguish between bioregion and 'bioregional*ism*'. Bioregionalism is a body of thought that evolved to 'reconnect socially just human cultures in a sustainable manner to the region-scale ecosystems in which they are irrevocably embedded' (Aberley 2005). It has a rich, vast literature and despite its critics, has created an enduring legacy. Greenprints draws on some of the powerful ideas from the bioregionalism movement, but unlike the movement itself, does not place a priority on redrawing our current political boundaries to comply with bioregional boundaries. In contrast, bioregions are a scientifically defined boundary that describe the unique geology, vegetation, and natural features of a place.

Step 3: Understand ecological foundations

The third step of the Greenprints process focuses on developing a deep understanding of Place—the geology, soils, topography, biodiversity, climate, water cycles, and local seasons of the local bioregion, sub-regions, and catchments. It connects with the knowledge and practices of Indigenous peoples, together with western science, including local citizen science projects and published scientific information. It also draws on the knowledge of local organisations actively involved in ecological restoration, land care, and biodiversity protection. The purpose is to enable people to get to know their local ecosystems—and address the disconnection many modern people have from the natural environment upon which they depend. This stage sees local participants working with local and visiting experts, and hosting collaborative events such as workshops and webinars, to bring an ever-increasing number of people into the process.

Step 4: Understand human activities—past and present

The fourth step of the Greenprints process is, in many ways, the largest task—this stage requires understanding past and present *human activities in the Place* (bioregion/catchment). Information is drawn from existing assessments of the current ecological condition and current patterns of human activities in the bioregion, which are regularly carried out by catchment management and natural resource management groups in Australia. It includes more deeply engaging with Indigenous peoples' relationship and interaction with the Place, understanding the colonial history of the Place, and mapping out past and current economic activities undertaken in the bioregion. The impacts of past and current activities are analysed, including land use changes since colonisation, and the various impacts on the bioregion's ecological health. The Greenprints mapping tool is particularly useful in this stage, as it includes the layering of a number of datasets that show, in some detail, how the bioregion has been and is being used and impacted by human activities. This stage includes a full analysis of economic frameworks and activities relevant to the human communities of the bioregion, including analysis of economic and social justice issues. It can also facilitate an investigation into the interconnections between participants' local bioregion and neighbouring bioregions that may be impacted by their activities.

This step involves a detailed analysis of the current and future ecological limits within which human activities must operate. This includes using the IPAT framework (**I**mpact = **P**opulation, **A**ffluence, and **T**echnology) where decisions made within an ethical framework (Brown et al. 2009). A range of tools and methods are explored at various scales for determining a range of impacts, including: 1) how local actions affect the local bioregion; 2) how local actions affect neighbouring bioregions; and 3) how local actions affect places further away, through direct relationships such as trade, and through indirect relationships such as contributing to the use and pollution of the global commons, including climate emissions.

Step 5: Health check—are we in overshoot?

Step 5 is to assess if, and to what extent, a community, town, or city is in 'overshoot'. A primary tool for this stage is the Ecological Footprint Method, which can assist in the calculation of local consumption and includes the impacts of importing goods and services from other regions (Wackernagel & Rees 1998; Wackernagel & Beyers 2019). Connected concepts include downscaling the concept of planetary boundaries, upscaling local activities to connect to planetary boundaries (Häyhä et al. 2016,

2018) and approaches used in operationalising the concept of Doughnut Economics (Raworth 2017).

Step 6: Develop scenarios for change

The Greenprints approach then encourages the development of a number of possible 'scenarios' for the future of a particular Place. 'Business as usual' examines what the impacts would be of continuing to carry out existing growth-oriented economic activities, with details specific to the bioregion in question. Such activities might include destructive industrial-scale agricultural practices, mining, water consumption, logging, rapidly growing populations, and residential and urban developments and other activities. Other scenarios are then developed, including scenarios that include degrowth, building an ecocentric Relationist society and establishing regenerative economics and land use. The goal is to examine what could realistically be done in a region, across various time frames, that would ensure living systems thrive, regenerate and continue to support human societies. This goes beyond just 'visioning' a different future—the extensive research, analysis, and peer-to-peer sharing that will have taken place in the previous 'steps' enables the development of rigorous scenarios that can show how significant, place-specific transitions of human activities can be undertaken, and how they can build a regenerative, relationist future.

The scenarios, along with land use maps generated with the Greenprints mapping tool, can be powerful techniques for 'showing' what earth-centred and Relationist governance options exist. The ultimate decisions about which 'scenario' to aim for will be made by the communities involved.

Step 7: Choose collective decision-making processes

Step 7 focuses on the democratic and participatory processes that need to be used—such as Citizens Assemblies—for large groups of people within a participating community, to decide which long-term scenarios and short-term goals should be pursued, and how action will be taken. Note that, in reality, this step begins when the Greenprints framework begins, as power structures, local governance, local decision-making approaches, and new collective processes are discussed throughout the high levels of community participation developed during the previous Greenprints steps.

Step 8: Develop transition action plans and begin implementation

Once optimal scenarios are identified in Step 7, Step 8 looks at developing long-term, medium-and short-term actions to build the desired futures. These Greenprints for action will include land use transition plans, economic activity transition plans, funding proposals, collaborative public-private partnerships, and other strategies for creating new pathways for human societies—including cities.

An important (and radical) part of the planning process is the rethinking of governance structures, to support the optimal scenarios communities want to grow in their Place. The Greenprints process can provide local people with important insights into how to work towards radically reframing local governance for their unique Place. This is a particularly important 're-connecting point' for Greenprints and the Relationist Ethos and Custodial Ethic.

After the work of the previous stages has been comprehensively carried out, the Greenprints approach involves a legal team reviewing and reimagining the legal and governance rules that would effectively govern the bioregion and local places. Other publications about Greenprints (Maloney 2020) and other literature about environmental law note that Australia's environmental governance system is 'top down', and most resource management takes place at the State or Federal level. By working through the Greenprints approach and developing place-specific transition scenarios for a regenerative future, Greenprints can be used to also develop place-specific law and governance recommendations. While there will still be a range of legal and economic issues that will need to be governed nationally and regionally, the Greenprints approach will equip people with a deeper understanding of how to advocate for laws that would effectively support their unique places, and advocate for greater local control over local land use, local biodiversity protection, local planning laws and local community economics. Instead of a predominantly top-down system, Greenprints will enable people to advocate for the implementation of principles of subsidiarity and community-based ecological governance, in order to more effectively protect and manage ecosystems and bioregions, than distant, nationally and state 'standardised' laws (Moulis et al. 2020).

Finally, an important part of Greenprints is building the Custodial Ethic through the '8 Steps' but also by embedding in community processes, the need for regular citizen reviews of scenario plans, Greenprint actions and the ongoing requirements of citizens within an ecological society.

Conclusions

We propose that the advantages of a relationist approach to urban governance and design towards a city of good ancestors is longevity and (genuine) sustainability. It is efficient, rational, and builds and maintains people's confidence in their city's governance system. Security and stability maintained in the *organisational* steady state system is maintained, leading to a steady state *economic* system. For the individual being, this governance model arises from a polity (organisational principle) that recognises people as persons with autonomy, more exactly, persons who practise Autonomous Regard. The beginning of justice starts with treating all people as persons with Autonomous Regard. It is imperative to cultivate the system of Autonomous Regard not the culture of impunity.

Politically, the city of good ancestors recognises that exploiting the world's resources for profit is anathema to generational thinking and the Relationist Ethos. A foundational principle like the Law of Obligation underpins state and city responsibilities, policies, rules, and services. The city of good ancestors could, in its own self-interest, start to seriously explore, consider and take on board some aspects of a civilisational culture. Cities, any city, could begin the next 10,000 years by determining what a civilisational culture could be, as opposed to being a civilisational state which was (and still is) one of the essential originators of large-scale competitiveness, extractivism, oppression, and social, economic and political violence (Harvey

2012; Monbiot 2016; Gilmore 2023). Prior to the rise of states, there was (and still is) conflict between groups. This conflict will continue.

The preparation for this long-term view of human civilisation and its most important obligation is for future generations and descendants to be in receipt of an authentically stable and secure (in all senses of the terms) world. This will happen because the principle of a sacralised, ecological, collaborative, stewardship system (based on the system of values and governance we have outlined in this chapter) will have become learned, socialised, internalised, and practised as civilisational culture.

How do we get there? One of the key premises of conventional smart cities is their claim to bring about sustainability goals through data analysis for resource optimisation (Yigitcanlar et al. 2019). However, more and more commentators across design, architecture, technology, and building construction are pointing out the limitations of an approach to sustainability that is just focused on energy efficiencies at best and greenwashing at worst (Loh et al. 2020; Bedford et al. 2021; Foth et al. 2021). In a quest to find more genuine and authentic approaches to sustainability, designers have recently started to engage with post-humanist theories and concepts from the environmental humanities with a much longer history. This has brought about the more-than-human turn in design research (Forlano 2016; Giaccardi & Redström 2020). This development identifies the issues and flaws with an approach to design grounded in human exceptionalism that is inherent to human-centred design. In response, scholars argue that we need to decentre the human and adopt new methods to engage and 'design with' the more-than-human world (Forlano 2016; Clarke et al. 2019; Tomitsch et al. 2021) including multispecies investigations (Liu 2019; Fieuw et al. 2022; Sheikh et al. 2022) and hybrid nature cultures (Puig de la Bellacasa 2010; Smith et al. 2017).

In this chapter, we sought to offer a new perspective based on ancient Australian Indigenous philosophy that serves as a reminder that the more recent more-than-human turn in design is perhaps taking us back to where we started. This more-than-human turn that seeks to undo the pitfalls of linear thinking and bestow a circular paradigm is in fact grounded in a Relationist Ethos, which recognises the connectedness and entanglements between humans, more-than-humans, and the planet. Our chapter outlined the foundational principles of how the Aboriginal peoples of Australia practised the Relationist Ethos through their laws, customs, and cultural values, and how we are currently engaged in the Greenprints initiative to translate some of these values into urban design and planning practice. Applying this Relationist Ethos to the design of future cities prompts us to ponder that perhaps—as Yunkaporta (2019) put it—it is ancient Indigenous thinking that can help end the current destructive world system as we know it, so it can be reborn anew.

Notes

1. We acknowledge and pay our respects to the late Maureen Watson—poet, actress, storyteller who was known for using the term 'honourable ancestors'. In his eulogy in 2009, her son Tiga Bayles remembered her by saying, 'she taught us [. . .] how all of us, individually, collectively and globally—can empower ourselves to become honourable ancestors to our future generations by bequeathing them a healthy Mother Earth' (cited by Gwyther 2009, p.7).

2. The word 'Place' has been capitalised to juxtapose Western notions of land (the raw physical material) from the sacralised meaning similar to 'Country'.
3. We distinguish the way we use the term relationality here from the notion of the 'relational city' and 'relational urbanism' (Sullivan 2018). Rafferty defines relational cities as 'cities whose geographical-historical profiles position them as urban nodes connecting regional-global-national systems of flows under globalised capitalism' (2022, p.183). However, we acknowledge that some scholars have started to bring this concept to bear on issues of human relationality and environmental sustainability (Robertson 2018; Lejano 2019).
4. In Aboriginal English the word 'Country' denotes this conjunction yet entails further cultural meaning (Gay'wu Group of Women 2019).
5. We acknowledge that Aboriginal societies have certainly not been immune to patriarchy and predatory behaviour of individuals, yet it is the Relationist Ethos that aspires to regain balance.
6. The ego is seen as a potentially volatile substance to be treated with something like a combination of caring stewardship, referee-like supervision, watchful guardianship, and prompts towards attentive, measured persuasion. These terms/qualities underpin the Aboriginal social praxis and ontological and epistemological basis of existence.
7. 'The Dreaming', also known as 'Dreamtime', is a central concept in Aboriginal culture. It refers to the belief that ancestral beings, through their actions during creation, shaped the land, animals, and people. It encompasses spiritual and cultural knowledge passed down through generations, encompassing stories, laws, rituals, and relationships with the environment. The Dreaming is not confined to the past but exists in the present and future. It connects Aboriginal people to their ancestors, their land, and their identity, guiding their worldview and providing a profound sense of interconnectedness with the natural world and the cosmos (Faulstich 1998; Page & Memmott 2021; Graham 2023).
8. For practical tools, cases, and examples, see https://www.greenprints.org.au

References

Aberley, D. C. (2005). Interpreting bioregionalism. In M. V. McGinnis (Ed.), *Bioregionalism* (pp. 27–56). Routledge. https://doi.org/10.4324/9780203984765-12

ABS. (2019, November 7). Estimates and Projections, Aboriginal and Torres Strait Islander Australians. Australian Bureau of Statistics. https://www.abs.gov.au/statistics/people/aboriginal-and-torres-strait-islander-peoples/estimates-and-projections-aboriginal-and-torres-strait-islander-australians/latest-release

Australian Institute of Health and Welfare. (2022, July 7). Profile of Indigenous Australians. Australian Institute of Health and Welfare. https://www.aihw.gov.au/reports/australias-health/profile-of-indigenous-australians

Bedford, L., Mann, M., Foth, M., & Walters, R. (2021). A post-capitalocentric critique of digital technology and environmental harm: New directions at the intersection of digital and green criminology. *International Journal for Crime, Justice and Social Democracy, 11*(1). https://doi.org/10.5204/ijcjsd.2191

Berry, T. (2011). *The great work: Our way into the future.* Crown.

Birkeland, J. (2020). *Net-positive design and sustainable urban development.* Routledge. https://doi.org/10.4324/9780429290213

Birkeland, J. (2022). Nature positive: Interrogating sustainable design frameworks for their potential to deliver eco-positive outcomes. *Urban Science, 6*(2), 35. https://doi.org/10.3390/urbansci6020035

Black, C. F. (2010). *The land is the source of the law.* Routledge-Cavendish. https://doi.org/10.4324/9780203844380

Boulous Walker, M. (2022). Nature, obligation, and transcendence: Reading Luce Irigaray with Mary Graham. *Sophia, 61*(1), 187–201. https://doi.org/10.1007/s11841-022-00907-2

Brand, S. (1997). *How buildings learn: What happens after they're built* (rev. ed.). Phoenix Illustrated.

Brigg, M., & Graham, M. (2021, July 27). The relevance of Aboriginal political concepts (7): Autonomous regard. *ABC News.* https://www.abc.net.au/religion/aboriginal-political-concepts-autonomous-regard/13472098

Brown, P., Brown, P. G., & Garver, G. (2009). *Right relationship: Building a whole earth economy.* Berrett-Koehler.
Burdon, P. D. (2012). A theory of earth jurisprudence. *Australian Journal of Legal Philosophy, 37,* 28. https://heinonline.org/hol-cgi-bin/get_pdf.cgi?handle=hein.journals/ajlph37§ion=4
Clarke, R., Heitlinger, S., Light, A., Forlano, L., Foth, M., & DiSalvo, C. (2019). More-than-human participation: Design for sustainable smart city futures. *Interactions, 26*(3), 60–63. https://doi.org/10.1145/3319075
Cullinan, C. (2011). *Wild law: A manifesto for earth justice* (2nd ed.). Chelsea Green Publishing Company. https://philpapers.org/rec/CULWLA
Daly, H. E. (1991). *Steady-state economics: Second edition with new essays.* Island Press.
Descartes, R. (1998). *Discourse on method and meditations on first philosophy* (D. A. Cress, Trans.; 4th ed.). Hackett.
Eckersley, R., & Gagnon, J.-P. (2014). Representing nature and contemporary democracy. *Democratic Theory, 1*(1). https://doi.org/10.3167/dt.2014.010105
Engle, J., Agyeman, J., & Chung-Tiam-Fook, T. (2022). *Sacred civics: Building seven-generation cities.* Routledge. https://doi.org/10.4324/9781003199816
Faulstich, P. (1998). Mapping the mythological landscape: An aboriginal way of being-in-the- world. *Philosophy & Geography, 1*(2), 197–221. https://doi.org/10.1080/13668799808573645
Fieuw, W., Foth, M., & Caldwell, G. A. (2022). Towards a more-than-human approach to smart and sustainable urban development: Designing for multispecies justice. *Sustainability: Science Practice and Policy, 14*(2), 948. https://doi.org/10.3390/su14020948
Forlano, L. (2016). Decentering the human in the design of collaborative cities. *Design Issues, 32*(3), 42–54. https://doi.org/10.1162/DESI_a_00398
Foth, M., Mann, M., Bedford, L., Fieuw, W., & Walters, R. (2021). A capitalocentric review of technology for sustainable development: The case for more-than-human design. In A. Finlay (Ed.), *Global information society watch 2020: Technology, the environment and a sustainable world—responses from the global South* (pp. 78–82). Association for Progressive Communications. https://giswatch.org/node/6216
Foth, M., Odendaal, N., & Hearn, G. (2007). The view from everywhere: Towards an epistemology for urbanites. In D. Remenyi (Ed.), *Proceedings ICICKM 2007: 4th International Conference on Intellectual Capital, Knowledge Management and Organisational Learning* (pp. 127–134). Academic Conferences Limited. https://eprints.qut.edu.au/9149/
Fredericks, J., Caldwell, G., Foth, M., & Tomitsch, M. (2019). The city as perpetual beta: Fostering systemic urban acupuncture. In M. de Waal & M. de Lange (Eds.), *The hackable city: Digital media and collaborative city-making in the network society* (pp. 67–92). Springer. https://doi.org/10.1007/978-981-13-2694-3_4
Gammage, B. (2012). *The biggest estate on earth: How Aborigines made Australia.* Allen & Unwin.
Gay'wu Group of Women. (2019). *Songspirals: Sharing women's wisdom of country through songlines.* Allen & Unwin.
Giaccardi, E., & Redström, J. (2020). Technology and more-than-human design. *Design Issues, 36*(4), 33–44. https://doi.org/10.1162/desi_a_00612
Gibson-Graham, J. K., Cameron, J., & Healy, S. (2016). Commoning as a postcapitalist politics. In A. Amin & P. Howell (Eds.), *Releasing the commons* (pp. 192–212). Routledge. https://doi.org/10.4324/9781315673172-12
Giffinger, R., Haindlmaier, G., & Kramar, H. (2010). The role of rankings in growing city competition. *Urban Research & Practice, 3*(3), 299–312. https://doi.org/10.1080/17535069.2010.524420
Gilmore, R. W. (2023). *Change everything: Racial capitalism and the case for abolition.* Haymarket Books.
Glavovic, B. C., Smith, T. F., & White, I. (2021). The tragedy of climate change science. *Climate and Development,* 14(9), 829–833. https://doi.org/10.1080/17565529.2021.2008855
Graeber, D., & Wengrow, D. (2022). *The dawn of everything: A new history of humanity.* Penguin Books.
Graham, M. (2009). Understanding human agency in terms of place: A proposed Aboriginal research methodology. *Philosophy Activism Nature, 6,* 71–78. https://doi.org/10.3316/informit.590560058861546

Graham, M. (2014). Aboriginal notions of relationality and positionalism: A reply to Weber. *Global Discourse, 4*(1), 17–22. https://doi.org/10.1080/23269995.2014.895931

Graham, M. (2023). The law of obligation, Aboriginal ethics: Australia becoming, Australia dreaming. *Parrhesia, 37*, 1–21. https://www.parrhesiajournal.org/index.php/parr/article/view/410/305

Graham, M., & Maloney, M. (2019). Caring for country and rights of nature in Australia: A conversation between earth jurisprudence and aboriginal law and ethics. In C. La Follette & C. Maser (Eds.), *Sustainability and the rights of nature in practice* (pp. 385–399). CRC Press. https://doi.org/10.1201/9780429505959-19

Graham, S. (2010). *Cities under siege: The new military urbanism*. Verso. https://www.versobooks.com/books/365-cities-under-siege

Gray, J., & Curry, P. (2020). Ecodemocracy and political representation for non-human nature. In H. Kopnina & H. Washington (Eds.), *Conservation: Integrating social and ecological justice* (pp. 155–166). Springer International Publishing. https://doi.org/10.1007/978-3-030-13905-6_11

Gwyther, S. (2009). In memoriam: Maureen Frances Watson 1931–2009. *Queensland Journal of Labour History, 8*, 6–7. https://www.labourhistory.org.au/wp-content/uploads/2012/10/QJLH-No-08-March-2009-final.pdf

Harvey, D. (2012). *Rebel cities: From the right to the city to the urban revolution*. Verso Books.

Häyhä, T., Cornell, S. E., Hoff, H., Lucas, P., & van Vuuren, D. (2018). *Operationalizing the concept of a safe operating space at the EU level—first steps and explorations*. Stockholm Resilience Centre. https://www.stockholmresilience.org/publications/publications/2018-07-03-operationalizing-the-concept-of-a-safe-operating-space-at-the-eu-level—first-steps-and-explorations.html

Häyhä, T., Lucas, P. L., van Vuuren, D. P., Cornell, S. E., & Hoff, H. (2016). From planetary boundaries to national fair shares of the global safe operating space: How can the scales be bridged? *Global Environmental Change: Human and Policy Dimensions, 40*, 60–72. https://doi.org/10.1016/j.gloenvcha.2016.06.008

Houseman, M. (2006). Relationality. In S. Mayhew (Ed.), *A dictionary of geography* (5th ed.). Oxford University Press. https://www.oxfordreference.com/display/10.1093/acref/9780199680856.001.0001/acref-9780199680856-e-3606

Hulme, M. (2014). *Can science fix climate change? A case against climate engineering*. John Wiley & Sons.

Iveson, K. (2010). The wars on graffiti and the new military urbanism. *Cityscape, 14*(1–2), 115–134. https://doi.org/10.1080/13604810903545783

Jones, D., Vlieg, M., Ashar, S., Friend, L., & Gomez, C. C. (2022). Learning to quantify positive futures. *International Journal of Environmental Impacts Management Mitigation and Recovery, 5*(2), 128–145. https://doi.org/10.2495/ei-v5-n2-128-145

Kitchin, R. (2020). Urban science: Prospect and critique. In K. S. Willis & A. Aurigi (Eds.), *The Routledge companion to smart cities* (pp. 42–50). Routledge. https://doi.org/10.4324/9781315178387-4

Kitchin, R., Lauriault, T. P., & McArdle, G. (2015). Knowing and governing cities through urban indicators, city benchmarking and real-time dashboards. *Regional Studies, Regional Science, 2*(1), 6–28. https://doi.org/10.1080/21681376.2014.983149

Kopnina, H., Spannring, R., Hawke, S., Robertson, C. D., Thomasberger, A., Maloney, M., Morini, M., Lynn, W., Muhammad, N. Z., Santiago-Ávila, F. J., Begovic, H., & Baranowski, M. (2021). Ecodemocracy in practice: Exploration of debates on limits and possibilities of addressing environmental challenges within democratic systems. *Visions for Sustainability, 15*, 9–23. https://doi.org/10.13135/2384-8677/5832

Krznaric, R. (2020). Cathedral thinking: The art of planning into the distant future. In *The good ancestor: How to think long term in a short-term world* (ch. 6). Random House. https://www.romankrznaric.com/good-ancestor

Lee, C. S., Lee, H., Kim, A. R., Pi, J. H., Bae, Y. J., Choi, J. K., Lee, W. S., & Moon, J. S. (2020). Ecological effects of daylighting and plant reintroduction to the Cheonggye Stream in Seoul, Korea. *Ecological Engineering, 152*, 105879. https://doi.org/10.1016/j.ecoleng.2020.105879

Lejano, R. P. (2019). Climate change and the relational city. *Cities, 85*, 25–29. https://doi.org/10.1016/j.cities.2018.12.001

Liaros, S. (2019). Implementing a new human settlement theory: Strategic planning for a network of regenerative villages. *Smart and Sustainable Built Environment*, *9*(3), 258–271. https://doi.org/10.1108/SASBE-01-2019-0004

Liaros, S. (2021). A network of circular economy villages: Design guidelines for 21st century garden cities. *Built Environment Project and Asset Management*, 12(3), 349–364. https://doi.org/10.1108/BEPAM-01-2021-0004

Liu, S.-Y. (2019). Designing for multispecies collaboration and cohabitation. In E. Gilbert & K. Karahalios (Eds.), *CSCW '19 Companion: Companion Publication of the 2019 Conference on Computer Supported Cooperative Work and Social Computing* (pp. 72–75). ACM. https://doi.org/10.1145/3311957.3361861

Loh, S., Foth, M., Caldwell, G. A., Garcia-Hansen, V., & Thomson, M. (2020). A more-than-human perspective on understanding the performance of the built environment. *Architectural Science Review*, *63*(3–4), 372–383. https://doi.org/10.1080/00038628.2019.1708258

Maloney, M. (2020). Practical pathways to ecological law: Greenprints and a bioregional, regenerative governance approach for Australia. In K. Anker, P. D. Burdon, G. Garver, M. Maloney, & C. Sbert (Eds.), *From environmental to ecological law* (pp. 237–251). Routledge. https://doi.org/10.4324/9781003001256-21

Mattern, S. (2021). *A city is not a computer: Other urban intelligences*. Princeton University Press.

McGinnis, M. V. (Ed.). (1999). *Bioregionalism*. Routledge. https://doi.org/10.4324/9780203984765

Metzger, J. (2019). A more-than-human approach to environmental planning. In S. Davoudi, R. Cowell, I. White, & H. Blanco (Eds.), *The Routledge companion to environmental planning* (pp. 190–199). Routledge. https://doi.org/10.4324/9781315179780-20

Mignolo, W. D., & Walsh, C. E. (2018). *On decoloniality: Concepts, analytics, praxis*. Duke University Press.

Monbiot, G. (2016). *How did we get into this mess? Politics, equality, nature*. Verso Books. http://www.monbiot.com/2007/08/28/how-did-we-get-into-this-mess/

Moreton-Robinson, A. (2015). *The white possessive: Property, power, and Indigenous sovereignty*. University of Minnesota Press.

Moulis, A., Pilon-Summons, C., Maloney, M., & Lee, J. K. (Eds.). (2020). *Earthwords and artlings anthology, Volume 1: Voices of nature*. Australian Earth Laws Alliance. https://www.earthlaws.org.au/resources/aela-publications/earthwords-vol1-2020/

Ostrom, E. (1990). *Governing the commons: The evolution of institutions for collective action*. Cambridge University Press.

Page, A., & Memmott, P. (2021). *Design: Building on country*. Thames & Hudson.

Panelli, R. (2010). More-than-human social geographies: Posthuman and other possibilities. *Progress in Human Geography*, *34*(1), 79–87. https://doi.org/10.1177/0309132509105007

Paradies, Y. (2020). Unsettling truths: Modernity, (de-)coloniality and Indigenous futures. *Postcolonial Studies*, *23*(4), 438–456. https://doi.org/10.1080/13688790.2020.1809069

Payne, M. (2020). Survivalist anthropology. In *Flowers of time* (pp. 128–162). Princeton University Press. https://doi.org/10.1515/9780691206400-005

Persson, L., Carney Almroth, B. M., Collins, C. D., Cornell, S., de Wit, C. A., Diamond, M. L., Fantke, P., Hassellöv, M., MacLeod, M., Ryberg, M. W., Søgaard Jørgensen, P., Villarrubia-Gómez, P., Wang, Z., & Hauschild, M. Z. (2022). Outside the safe operating space of the planetary boundary for novel entities. *Environmental Science & Technology*, *56*(3), 1510–1521. https://doi.org/10.1021/acs.est.1c04158

Poelina, A., Wooltorton, S., Blaise, M., Aniere, C. L., Horwitz, P., White, P. J., & Muecke, S. (2022). Regeneration time: Ancient wisdom for planetary wellbeing. *Australian Journal of Environmental Education*, *38*(3–4), 397–414. https://doi.org/10.1017/aee.2021.34

Puig de la Bellacasa, M. (2010). Ethical doings in naturecultures. *Ethics, Place & Environment*, *13*(2), 151–169. https://doi.org/10.1080/13668791003778834

Rafferty, M. (2022). Relational urbanisation, resilience, revolution: Beirut as a relational city? *Urban Planning*, *7*(1), 183–192. https://doi.org/10.17645/up.v7i1.4798

Raworth, K. (2017). *Doughnut economics: Seven ways to think like a 21st-century economist*. Chelsea Green Publishing.

Rittenbruch, M., Foth, M., Mitchell, P., Chitrakar, R., Christensen, B., & Pettit, C. (2022). Co-designing planning support systems in urban science: The questions they answer and the questions they raise. *Journal of Urban Technology, 29*(2), 7–32. https://doi.org/10.1080/10630732.2021.1980319

Robertson, S. A. (2018). Rethinking relational ideas of place in more-than-human cities. *Geography Compass, 12*(4), e12367. https://doi.org/10.1111/gec3.12367

Rühs, N., & Jones, A. (2016). The implementation of earth jurisprudence through substantive constitutional rights of nature. *Sustainability: Science Practice and Policy, 8*(2), 174. https://doi.org/10.3390/su8020174

Russell, L. (2001). *Colonial frontiers: Indigenous-European encounters in settler societies.* Manchester University Press.

Sheikh, H., Foth, M., & Mitchell, P. (2022). More-than-human city-region foresight: Multispecies entanglements in regional governance and planning. *Regional Studies, 57*(4), 642–655. https://doi.org/10.1080/00343404.2022.2045266

Sheikh, H., Mitchell, P., & Foth, M. (2023). More-than-human smart urban governance: A research agenda. *Digital Geography and Society, 4*, 100045. https://doi.org/10.1016/j.diggeo.2022.100045

Smith, N., Bardzell, S., & Bardzell, J. (2017). Designing for cohabitation: Naturecultures, hybrids, and decentering the human in design. In G. Mark, S. Fussell, C. Lampe, m. c. schraefel, J. P. Hourcade, C. Appert, & D. Wigdor (Eds.), *CHI '17: Proceedings of the 2017 CHI Conference on Human Factors in Computing Systems* (pp. 1714–1725). ACM. https://doi.org/10.1145/3025453.3025948

Steele, W. (2019). *Planning wild cities: Human–nature relationships in the urban age.* Routledge. https://doi.org/10.4324/9781315688756

Steele, W., Wiesel, I., & Maller, C. (2019). More-than-human cities: Where the wild things are. *Geoforum; Journal of Physical, Human, and Regional Geosciences, 106*, 411–415. https://doi.org/10.1016/j.geoforum.2019.04.007

Sullivan, R. (2018). The relational city. In *Twenty-first-century urbanism: A new analysis of the city* (pp. 48–62). Routledge. https://doi.org/10.4324/9781315549484-4

Teli, M., Foth, M., Sciannamblo, M., Anastasiu, I., & Lyle, P. (2020). Tales of institutioning and commoning: Participatory design processes with a strategic and tactical perspective. In C. Del Gaudio, L. Parra-Agudelo, R. Clarke, J. Saad-Sulonen, A. Botero, F. César Londoño, & P. Escandón (Eds.), *PDC '20: Proceedings of the 16th Participatory Design Conference 2020: Participation(s) otherwise* (pp. 159–171). https://doi.org/10.1145/3385010.3385020

Teli, M., McQueenie, J., Cibin, R., & Foth, M. (2022). Intermediation in design as a practice of institutioning and commoning. *Design Studies, 82*, 101132. https://doi.org/10.1016/j.destud.2022.101132

Tomitsch, M., Fredericks, J., Vo, D., Frawley, J., & Foth, M. (2021). Non-human personas: Including nature in the participatory design of smart cities. *Interaction Design and Architecture(s), 50*, 102–130. https://doi.org/10.55612/s-5002-050-006

UN Habitat. (2018). *What is a city?* UN Habitat. https://unhabitat.org/sites/default/files/2020/06/city_definition_what_is_a_city.pdf

Wackernagel, M., & Beyers, B. (2019). *Ecological footprint: Managing our biocapacity budget.* New Society Publishers.

Wackernagel, M., & Rees, W. (1998). *Our ecological footprint: Reducing human impact on the earth.* New Society Publishers.

Wiebe, J. (2021). Cultural appropriation in bioregionalism and the need for a decolonial ethics of place. *The Journal of Religious Ethics, 49*(1), 138–158. https://doi.org/10.1111/jore.12342

Wiesel, I., Steele, W., & Houston, D. (2020). Cities of care: Introduction to a special issue. *Cities, 105*, 102844. https://doi.org/10.1016/j.cities.2020.102844

Williams, B., & Moore, A. W. (2006). Socrates' question. In *Ethics and the limits of philosophy* (pp. 1–21). Routledge. https://doi.org/10.4324/9780203969847-3

Yigitcanlar, T., Foth, M., & Kamruzzaman, M. (2019). Towards post-anthropocentric cities: Reconceptualizing smart cities to evade urban ecocide. *Journal of Urban Technology, 26*(2), 147–152. https://doi.org/10.1080/10630732.2018.1524249

Yunkaporta, T. (2019). *Sand talk: How Indigenous thinking can save the world.* Text Publishing.

13
Informed by Microbes
Biofilms as a Platform for the Bio-Digital City

Rachel Armstrong

Introduction

When we think of a city, we think of an architectural system imagined and constructed by *homo sapiens* between 4000 and 3000 BCE, when early peoples began to develop networks of urban settlements. Bolstered by the rise of *homo faber* (Arendt 1958, pp.153–158), where human beings controlled their fate and their environment by using tools to initiate agriculture and trade, these settlers could enjoy surplus food and economic stability. Communication technologies—spoken languages, alphabets, numeric systems, signs, ideas, and symbols—enabled societal cohesion leading to technological development, cultural exchange, economies, modes of government, and the kinds of human civilisation that we recognise today. The lethal pairing of bending nature to our will to consume its resources at increasing speed using our increasingly powerful technologies has resulted in the well-documented Anthropocene, with notorious environmental consequences expressed in various ways through the climate emergency.

This essay examines an alternative framework for human settlement, which draws on the incredible environmental knowledge of microbes, which can be (at least in part) accessed using advanced biotechnologies. The aim is to establish which aspects of microbial cities, or biofilms, can help us turn around the Anthropocene by establishing new kinds of (more than) human infrastructures and modes of co-inhabitation to establish a *culture of life*. By working meaningfully with the oldest terrestrial residents, and engaging different kinds of intelligences, at different scales and kinds of embodiment, we may learn from how microbes sustain themselves while enriching their environments so that we can become ecological collaborators, and vastly better neighbours.

Introducing Microbes

While humans have invented elaborately built cooperative settlements known as *cities*, we are not the first to do so. Collectively, two to three billion species of microbes make up more than 60% of the earth's living matter. These most numerous, oldest, and robust of all creatures constitute nearly all earth's biodiversity and for most of its history, were the only forms of life. Today, there are likely a trillion microbial species, but most environmental microorganisms are *nature's dark matter*, remaining

Rachel Armstrong, *Informed by Microbes*. In: *Designing More-than-Human Smart Cities*. Edited by: Sara Heitlinger, Marcus Foth, and Rachel Clarke, Oxford University Press. © Oxford University Press (2024). DOI: 10.1093/9780191980060.003.0015 unidentified and uncultured (Locey and Lennon 2016; Wiegand et al. 2021). While tiny, microbes are not always invisible. Around 3.25 billion years ago, discrete microbial ecosystems (microbiomes) swarmed together to form the first types of urban structures on this planet called *biofilms* (Hall-Stoodley et al. 2004). Forged from a soft, sticky matrix termed extracellular polymeric substances (EPS), these microbes (bacterial, fungi, archaea, viruses, protists) collectively built a physical, social platform, which increased their tolerance against multiple environmental stresses. This same material also established a discrete site for the exchange of *microbial goods*, like metabolites and genetic information such as plasmids,[1] enabling these communities to quickly adapt to changing circumstances. The outputs of this system have endured since the origin of life and collectively form the *living* base of the biosphere establishing a *primordial culture of life* (Margulis 1981). For example, not only are microbes integral to our experience of the world, but also their 'webs of histories and bodies' catalyse biodiversity (Tsing et al. 2017, M3). While the microbial cells within biofilms are too small to be seen by the human naked eye, the overall structure is often clearly visible at the human scale. Although biofilms are nothing like human cities, being soft and formless with the outward appearance of slime, algal blooms, dental plaque, or pond scum, at the microscopic level, they are organisationally complex, dynamic, and multifaceted. As different kinds of microbes thrive in different environments, so biofilms express a rich variety of different metabolisms, and can produce different kinds of goods. A basic distinction between biofilm types is aerobic (requires oxygen) and anaerobic metabolism (does not require oxygen). Both kinds of metabolisms are important but generally, aerobic biofilms exist at the interface with air, while anaerobes tend to live deeper in their matrix with some, or no, oxygen availability. Remarkably, biofilms even share some of the characteristics of multicellular organisms, acting *as if* they are multicellular to accomplish tasks that are impossible as *mere individuals* (Miller and Bassler 2001). Given the versatility of such an arrangement, perhaps unsurprisingly, biofilms are the preferred mode of habitation for more than 80% of all microbes today (Römling 2022).

Conventionally, human narratives are centred on the primacy of our species, but twenty-first-century visualisation methods such as *metagenomics* and *high-powered microscopes with stains that highlight specific characteristics*, reveal that our world is fundamentally microbial. The 'natural history' of microbes forms an epic narrative, where advanced biotechnologies can 'read' the organic information within the biofilm, tracing its evolution back to biogenesis. During the Archean era, ancient cyanobacteria transformed the planet's atmosphere from a reducing system into to an oxidising one through the massive-scale use of photosynthesis to draw energy from the sun, generating massive amounts of biomass and oxygen as a by-product in the process, which created the conditions for the subsequent emergence of multicellular life. These insights are decentring human experience as the originator of all knowledge and enabling new proposals that reposition our role with respect to the planet's histories before humans, which Bruno Latour (2013) calls 'geostory'. For the first time, we can glimpse a tiny tip of the iceberg that comprises the invisible realm of world-making microbes all around us.

It is hard to positively relate to a microbe. As they are individually invisible to the naked eye, it is difficult for us to form independent opinions about them, and an incredible amount of mediation already shapes our relationship with and expectations of microbes—from visualisation tools to the values we associate with their presence (dirt, infection, contamination). Our encounters with microbes are framed in such a way that, even before we encounter them, we have already judged them negatively. This adverse view of microbes arises from a specific realm of study in the nineteenth century that focused on infectious diseases, where Robert Koch first demonstrated the relationship between specific types of microbes and diseases such as anthrax (1876), tuberculosis (1882), and cholera (1883). Louis Pasteur advanced this new version of germ theory, firmly equating microbes with contagion in the public imagination. Enabled by modernity's Reign of Hygiene (Lahiji and Friedman 1997), the microbial realm was positioned as an invisible enemy upon which to wage a war of sterility. Consequently, modern buildings were designed to uphold specific health and safety standards where the presence of any microbes was considered 'contamination', and where good house husbandry necessitated the liberal use of ecocidal chemicals that kill 'all known germs dead'. The prevailing negative microbial worldview reinforces behaviours that cause environmental disequilibrium, where Rachel Carson's (1962) *Silent Spring* drew attention to wide-scale ecological disruption caused by our modern industrialised paradigms, inviting us to consider a new relationship with the living world.

Most microbes, however, are not pathogens and more than 99% of them coexist quietly alongside us, assimilating and responding to—or constructing and transforming—their surroundings, as well as each other. The impacts of natural biofilms are overwhelmingly in dynamic equilibrium with their environment and toxic biofilms are indicative of environmental disequilibrium often caused by anthropogenic factors such as nitrogen run-off from farms or illegally discharged untreated sewage. Their powerful ability to transform matter even modulates key processes that turn the substrates of the world into life-bearing activities such as plant growth, soil nutrient cycling, and marine biogeochemical cycling. They are constantly (re)worlding the world by fixing gases and breaking down dead plant and animal matter into simpler substances that (re)enter the food chain. Without the activities of this collective 'microbial commons' (Dedeurwaerdere 2010), which redistributes nutrients and energy in a way that promotes biodiversity, life as we know it would simply not exist.

Today, microorganisms and their biofilms are ubiquitous, existing in every terrestrial location from infiltrating marine sediments in the continental subsurface to forming close association with higher organisms such as plants, invertebrates and humans. In fact, the ecosystems of microbes inhabiting our bodies (*human microbiome*) (Sender et al. 2016) and living spaces (*microbiome of the built environment*) (Kembel et al. 2012) are so intrinsic to our health that we can even think of them as extended organs, which contribute to our wellbeing—digesting our food, elevating our mood, and acting as a first line immune system. Humans are edifices, or living terrains, where microbial cities flourish. In turn, our microbial residents and neighbours entangle our vital needs and actions with a much broader community of life through the realm of metabolism,[2] which extends into the human city (*urban microbiome*) (King 2014) where they perform ecosystem services at little, or no resource cost to their human co-inhabitants (Bell et al. 2005; Balvanera et al. 2006; Fenchel et al. 2012).

Although morphologically speaking biofilms appear to have nothing in common with cities, organisationally they share many analogous features with human settlements, specifically via the fundamental sociability required for communities to live together (Hird 2009; Clark and Hird 2018).

Biofilms are organised according to specific principles that enable certain microbial communities to persist within the slimy EPS matrix. These organisational rules form the physical basis of their *commons*, demonstrating open and horizontal forms of biological information-sharing. As in human cities, the social lives of microbial inhabitants are organised around the provision of 'public goods', which include metabolites, active biomolecules (Griffin et al. 2004), toxins, and their antidotes (Raymond et al. 2012), that are distributed freely within the EPS. Some microbes even specialise in the production of essential resources that are obtained through trade with other microbes, which promotes increased intercellular exchange, analogous to modern economic markets (Tasoff et al. 2015). While the production of these metabolites is costly for individual microbes, they are a worthwhile investment in maintaining the integrity of the biofilm community (Stewart and Franklin 2008).

Additionally, microbes use sophisticated chemical signals to communicate in groups by counting their own siblings, and when there are enough of them together, their group behaviour is shaped by specific chemical 'words'. Known as *quorum sensing* (QS), this complex lexicon enables bacteria to hold private conversations, as well as public ones that even extend beyond their own species (Raut et al. 2013). QS molecules therefore regulate a range of microbial behaviours that confer collective advantages on the community, such as biofilm formation, migration towards food sources, and pathogenicity (Diggle et al. 2007; Stewart and Franklin 2008). The material nature of microbes and their languages used to establish new territories may be considered as ways of *walking the boundary*[3] that provides a spatial basis for negotiated transactions and principles of co-existence (Fischel 2017). While biochemical signals rely on diffusion to produce their effects, microbes can communicate more rapidly, and even at a distance, using electron transfer to generate electrical signals that ripple from cell to cell across the biofilm. On reaching their intended destination (often the outer edges), the electrons instruct growing cells to change their behaviour. For example, microbes may pause their growth, enabling nutrients to diffuse inward into the centre of the biofilm (Humphries et al. 2017). The coordination of these near and far communications strategies enable biofilms to carry out incredibly complex functions, rather like the communications systems in human cities.

Microbes also have a basic justice system whereby the biofilm community can stop opportunistic individual organisms, or 'cheaters', from working against the dynamics of a biofilm community by, for example, stealing energy and nutrients from their neighbours, rather than making their own resources from scratch. The justice system comprises resistant cells (cooperators) that outcompete susceptible cells (cheats) and are effective even when the frequency of cooperators is low (Doebeli and Hauert 2005; Brown and Taddei 2007).

Although biofilms share many analogous organisational features with human cities, they differ significantly in terms of their environmental impact. Overall, the rich variety of microbial goods produced by biofilms has resulted in the general enlivening of the planet by fuelling biodiversity and enabling regeneration through recycling dead matter in our silts and composts. If we genuinely seek sustainable human cities that go beyond zero environmental impact, then we have much to learn from biofilms, which bioremediate the environment as well as making new, and useful, environmental 'goods' as an exemplar of *effective resource circularity*.

The Challenge of Human–Microbial Diplomacy

To achieve the regenerative impacts that microbes have already demonstrated throughout the ages requires us *to actively live better alongside microbes*, while, at the same time, retain valued aspects of our human selves. Such a goal is immensely problematic, as our relationship with microbes is contradictory: the advent of the human microbiome means that microbes are formally part of 'us', while their slimy materiality and stealthy omnipresence is, instinctively speaking, completely alien. Not only do we face incommensurate challenges of scale and medium, but on a bad day, our bodies are also their food. Coupled with our general poor microbial literacy and cultural conditioning to destroy them, our rapport with microbes is woefully inadequate for negotiating on mutually recognisable terms (Timmis et al. 2019). A transactional system is needed that provides a communications interface to enable interspecies conversations. Such a conversational Babel[4] requires intelligible languages and ways of interacting that meaningfully translate between radically different systems, creating interfaces for exchange that do not privilege one over the other, but approach a concordant understanding.

Typically, microbial activity is deciphered using the tools of biochemistry but in human terms the interpretation process is quite slow. Tapping into the much faster electron flows within biofilms, however, provides a real-time way of understanding the behaviour of a microbial population at any given moment and, depending on the sensitivity of electrodes, creates the possibility of developing a communications platform between human and microbe. Anaerobic microbes convert organic matter into a range of metabolites and excrete electrons that are detectable at the human scale. This electron flow can be both empirically measured and tested in real time using conventional electronics systems to provide electrical power and data for digital systems. A specific platform dedicated to this purpose was developed in 1911 by Michael Cressé Potter (1911), who brought the worlds of electricity and biology together using a bioreactor that harvested electrons from naturally formed anaerobic biofilms. The resultant 'living' battery, or microbial fuel cell (MFC), produced several hundred millivolts of energy from *Saccharomyces* bacteria that converted the chemical energy of organic matter into electrons that flowed into an external circuit to provide electrical power for as long as they continued to be fed (Figure 13.1). This highly mediated relationship established a power-sharing relationship across mechanical and natural bodies that is neither entirely biological, nor exclusively mechanical. The resultant *cyborg being* thrives on different types of organic fuel to perform a range of metabolic tasks at room temperature, such as cleaning wastewater, generating bioelectricity, and detoxifying pollutants. While bioelectrical systems (BES) like the MFC cannot compete with the sheer power of other electricity generating systems (renewables, fossil fuels), their (material) circularity is unsurpassed providing

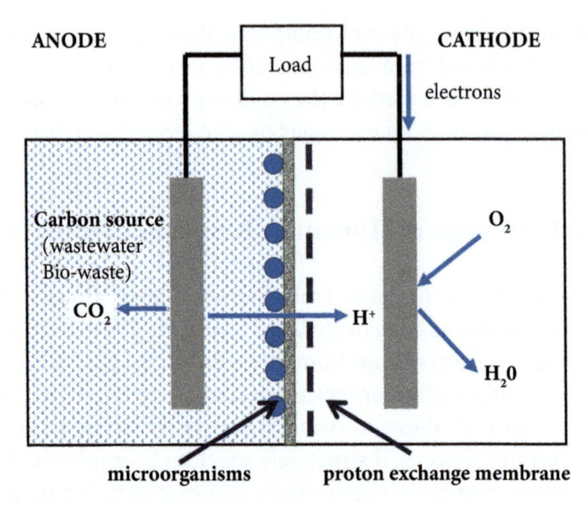

Figure 13.1 Diagram of a microbial fuel cell showing the anode, cathode, semipermeable membrane, electrodes, and biofilm.
Drawing by Rachel Armstrong, 2018. Reproduced courtesy of the author.

essential natural limits to our consumption. Situating design at the interface between the biochemical metabolic realm and low-powered electrical technologies, like LEDs and low-power digital platform design, the electron-excreting metabolism of anaerobic biofilms enables the formation of a legible, real-time communications platform between human and microbe.

Even with an identified platform, finding the sweet spots for interspecies exchange and discovering appropriate ethical relations in response to received signals requires a suitable interface and modes of interpretation where humans and microbes can meet on a discursive footing. While an accessible space is unlikely to reach any notion of real equality owing to incommensurate difficulties of scale, time, embodiment, language, etc., taking our first faltering steps towards interspecies diplomacy through design and communication, is vital for discovering what it *could be.*

Prototyping Elements of the Bio-Digital City

To learn from biofilms how we may better organise, power, and develop our human cities, I have explored various aspects of a human–microbial interface that is based on choreographed bioelectrical exchanges between microbes and humans in the following case studies. Having conceived the concept by considering how biofilms and human cities could be interlaced, I initiated my studies within the framework of EU grant proposals, where the excretion of waste electrons by anaerobic biofilms comprises a low-powered electrical system. Given the alien materiality of microbes and their natural prevalence in our waste streams, the interweaving of biofilm and human seemed possible within the design and distribution of our utilities and building infrastructures. Translating this concept into a scientific proposal led to immediate compromises. Conceiving designable and implementable systems required a degree of utility and ingenuity using established platforms, whereby the bio-digital interfaces imagined as the primary platform for human–microbial communication were still fundamentally modern—using metal wires, silicon circuits, a range of plastics, and computer hardware. Additionally, there was very little room for unconventional approaches to convince the funders to support these projects. The risk of this opportunistic method is that my initial explorations can never go beyond the entirely service-based arrangement that characterises the fundamentally anthropocentric, neoliberal *innovation drivers* underpinning science and technology grants. However, within the logic of these frameworks, I sought opportunities to subvert the industrial logic, while being mindful of anticipating (and trying to prevent) the *integral accident* (Virilio 2007)[5] and have resisted to narrativise microbes as a building block, rather than a plastic material where biofilms retain a 'dark element of withdrawal that fundamentally escapes humanity's grasp, the grasp of *homo faber*' (Neyrat 2018). Given these significant limitations, the aim of these cases is not to resolve every issue of human/microbial cohabitation but to take important first steps away from the mores that frame the Reign of Hygiene and propose alternative, designable approaches—which may always already lie outside the grasp of *homo faber*. Rather than seeking solutions, my explorations comprise a pedagogical role, confronting the human designer at each turn with the many aspects of nature that simply cannot be fully controlled or influenced, but with which we must remain engaged in conversation. Each of these four selected case studies engages with human–microbial interactions the level of biofilm organisation, which, enabled by electron flow, provide the scaffolding for interspecies communications based on metabolic transactions that are typical of soil and silt metabolism. The resultant successes, imperfections, and inevitable misunderstandings are therefore an attempt to alter human hygiene rituals and establish preliminary considerations of just how achievable the *culture of life* is. Although these case studies are far from the necessary paradigm shift needed to change our thinking and practice, it is possible that with increasing microbial understanding, our city infrastructures will, at some stage, be informed by a true microbial materiality[6] organised according to biofilm logic and will herald the advent of (more-than) human development to establish a *culture of life* (Armstrong 2021).

Living Architecture

The *Living Architecture* project (2016–2019) takes the form of 'living' bioreactor wall. It was developed within the framework of a European Union (EU) Horizon 2020 Future Emerging Technologies Open funding programme, which focused on the biotechnical challenge of creating discrete microbial communities that do not normally co-inhabit spaces—some communities are photosynthetic (feeding on light and are not poisoned by oxygen), while others are anaerobic (live in lightlessness and are poisoned by oxygen). The project was contextualised as a building infrastructure that could draw on world-making microbial actions as an alternative way of providing household resources for human inhabitation. At the same time, the trade-off was that humans had to find a way of welcoming living alongside those kinds of microbes with which the Reign of Hygiene waged war (Armstrong et al. 2017). Taking the form of a freestanding, next-generation, selectively programmable bioreactor, the *Living Architecture* apparatus is effectively a city of microbes composed of integrated building blocks (MFC, algae bioreactor, and genetically modified processor), which also function as standardised building segments—or bricks.

Each 'brick' is both a structural unit and an enabling environment for populations of microbes, which are assigned a particular task, where communities are housed in technologically enabled hollows. Such a *cyborgian* arrangement of built and natural structures is in keeping with biofilms' capacity to act beyond their natural forms using their environments, and proximate relationships to accomplish tasks that are impossible as *mere individuals.* From a human perspective, 'programming' is achieved by altering the microbial populations and spatially sequencing them, so the system can be thought of as a *metabolic app,* which can materially compute, and process, one set of substances being transformed into another, depending on its inputs. The hardware configuration for wild type modules is based on the MFC, which consists of an anode, selective membrane, and cathode, where natural microbes in the incoming waste streams decide to live together and form a biofilm on the membrane. Capturing electrons from the bioelectrical activity of the biofilm, using an electrode generates small amounts of usable electricity. As the electron flow varies proportionally to the over biofilm, packets of electrons can be thought of as 'data' that reflect the embodied intelligence of the biofilm. The processes information is fundamentally environmental, being concerned with the biochemical processing of nutrient streams that pass into its stomach, or anode, and pass through its 'gut wall'—fashioned as a carbon fibre, or ceramic semipermeable membrane. During this process, the fuel cell cleans water, produces a range of metabolites, and excretes electrons that self-power the system and are captured by conductive wires—evidenced through the activity of electronic devices.

The microalgae photobioreactor is connected to the cathode where it provides oxygen as a by-product from photosynthesis to boost the bioelectrical power from the MFC, by acting as an end-terminal receptor. The proof-of-principle system is a synthetic bioreactor, which explores just how far the actual metabolic reactions in the bricks can be designed using synthetic biology techniques being uniquely able to reclaim 100% of the phosphate introduced in the system from discarded washing powders and detergents, as well as remove nitrous gases from the feedstock. 'Fed' by liquid domestic waste (urine and grey water), by air and sunlight, when combined, the microbial populations turn these substrates into a set of metabolites—where each bioreactor moves its waste products on to the next chamber in the sequence of 'apps', where further transformations take place, and so on. The whole process is coordinated by an artificial intelligence (AI) that detects the amount of electricity being produced by the MFC and—as the metabolisms are interlinked—modifies the systems inputs accordingly to produce various forms of *housework* that mitigate the negative environmental impacts of human occupancy by removing pollutants, providing electricity, making biomolecules, and recovering water.

Rejecting the Reign of Hygiene logic, microbes are welcomed into this domestic apparatus by providing food, welcoming surfaces for biofilm settlements, removing electron waste, and providing more versatile tools to enable them to respond to their environment via synthetic biology techniques. Within a domestic setting, our own microbiomes are added to this community becoming part of hygiene rituals, microbial caring, and understanding our own contributions to resource recycling within domestic, and ultimately, urban spaces. In this way, apparatus is a new kind of sanitation ritual emerges, of feeding and emptying microbial products, creating an alternative arrangement with biofilms, besides their eradication. Importantly, resident microbes do not have to comply with the terms specified by the apparatus, and the cooperation of the biofilm community must be invested in through the provision of organic matter, cared for in terms of the integrity of the different 'brick' compartments and fine-tuned to ensure the optimum conditions for biofilm flourishing are maintained. While these routines are conducted at the human, or architectural, scale, the living biofilms continue to act according to their own social logic and modes of justice. An initial marker of microbial contentedness is the production of electrons, which is used as data that provides a snapshot of the whole biofilm. We do not have technology that works at a level of metabolic sensitivity that can understand the welfare of individual live microbes, so we must assume that a healthy biofilm reflects the welfare of its constituents.

This arrangement between apparatus and biofilm is no strange brain-in-a-box, but a communicable *fundamentally environmental* intelligence—one that pays attention to microbial wellbeing and can be modulated (or crudely interacted with) by human interactions that take place across electrical, physical, and chemical interfaces. Establishing a kind of metabolic trading system, *Living Architecture* generates an interdependence between human and microbes in this mode of inhabitation. Implicit in these entangled relationships, the microbiota of human inhabitants is inevitably incorporated into the nutrient waste streams, so they become part of the holistically operating, 'living' system (Figure 13.1). Rendering obsolete instrumental practices, microbes housed in the apparatus establish themselves within various bioreactor types to make kin and community in microbial consortia and biofilms. Inhabited through rituals of daily life and care for things, *Living Architecture* not only 'computes' the material flows within a household (via QS that then summate to generate microbial behaviours reflected in changes in electron flow) but also provides an apparatus that exemplifies alternative paradigms for domestic economies—where through a designed relation with microbes, human activities of daily living are transformed into world-making actions (Armstrong and Hughes 2021). When, through habituation, the overall performance and wellbeing of the constituents cannot be meaningfully separated out from each other, then *Living Architecture* acquires the status of *holobiont* (Gordon et al. 2013).

Throughout the project, the human social acceptability of the technology was considered through various 'brick' prototypes that were exhibited in biennales and international exhibitions, enabling the narrative framing of the apparatus to be explored in more inclusive terms pertaining to human–microbial relations. The first prototype was a simple hack of a brick, turning it into an MFC, which brought together structure and process and was displayed at the Building Centre in London (2018), as well as during the Venice Architecture Biennale (Figure 13.2). Such an arrangement enabled discourses concerning co-housing humans and microbes, modes of cohabitation through the kinds of affordances such building elements

Figure 13.2 Two vernacular Venetian bricks 'hacked' to become a bioelectricity-generating unit, or microbial fuel cell, exhibited during the Venice Architecture Biennale.
Photograph reproduced courtesy of the Living Architecture project, 2016.

provide, and co-constitutive actions that arise from (inter)actions between human and microbial inhabitants. The biofilm too appeared content with the arrangement, continuing to generate a maximum power of 1.2 mW (You et al. 2019).

Even more complex 'brick' structures, or city spaces for microbes, were developed that increased the surface area between different metabolic microbial worlds and were displayed at the 4th Tallinn Architecture Biennale (Figures 13.3, 13.4). Each element could simultaneously host photosynthetic and anaerobic organisms, enabling them to exchange metabolites with each other across incommensurate environmental conditions, which is something they cannot do in nature. In soils and other natural environments, anaerobic and photosynthetic organisms are separated by redox gradients and spaces that enable a broader range of intermediary metabolisms to process the biochemistry in this transitional zone. On approximating these microbial populations, the abrupt interface sets the boundaries for biofilm settlement and speeding up metabolism in the anaerobic biofilm as the proximity of oxygen captures the excreted electrons, increasing the electrical power within the electronic system (Figure 13.5). As electron flow is only a broad indication of biofilm activity, it is not known whether this arrangement compromises individual microbes within the biofilm, or whether they are frustrated by not walking the boundary with the degrees of freedom they are accustomed to and, in this sense, they retain a *dark element of withdrawal.*

999 years 13sqm (The Future Belongs to Ghosts)

The original version of *Living Architecture* could not be exposed directly to the public owing to the presence of genetically modified organisms. *999 years 13sqm (the future belongs to ghosts)* provided an alternative wild-type MFC bioreactor

Figure 13.3 Living 'brick' chassis for housing photosynthetic and anaerobic organisms designed by Simone Ferracina and exhibited at the Tallinn Architecture Biennale.
Photograph reproduced courtesy of the Living Architecture project, 2017.

wall system as an installation that was developed for the *Is this tomorrow?* exhibition at the Whitechapel Gallery (Figure 13.6), in collaboration with artist Cecile B Evans (Bevan 2019; Whitechapel Gallery 2019). This group show was themed on the Whitechapel Gallery's former landmark exhibition *This Is Tomorrow* (1956). The original exhibition featured thirty-seven British architects, painters, and sculptors, including Richard Hamilton, Eduardo Paolozzi, and Alison and Peter Smithson, working collaboratively in small groups. *Is this tomorrow?* featured experimental propositions from contemporary leading architects and artists responding to twenty-first-century issues at a time when humanity is facing new challenges posed by big data, bioengineering, and climate change.

We were one group of ten artist/architect collaborations that were invited to offer our visions of the future in the technological world of tomorrow. Our experimental project took the form of a future apartment space, where the installation housed a screen-based system powered by natural anaerobic biofilms within an array of 'living bricks' (Figure 13.6). Comprising a post-human household powered by microbes, we imagined the space being inhabited by digital ghosts of the past, present, and future, as the only traces of human life fundamentally mediated by microbial presences interlaced with the human scale at an infrastructural level. While the bioenergy levels produced by the BES would ultimately generate around 12V using parallel arrays of MFC units, the overall electrical outputs are much lower than compared with fossil fuels that are delivered to our homes as 230V power supplies. From an ecological

Figure 13.4 Fully inoculated *Living Architecture* 'wall' and apparatus installed at the University of the West of England, Bristol.
Photograph reproduced courtesy of the Living Architecture project, 2019.

perspective, these limits are creative. The unlimited energy offered by fossil fuels encourages wasteful patterns of behaviour, which accelerates consumption. Moreover, the performative agency of microbes to collectively act to generate electrical power, electronic data and chemical transformation highlights their life promoting functions.

Active Living Infrastructure: Controlled Environment (ALICE)

The *Active Living Infrastructure: Controlled Environment* (ALICE) prototype (2019–2021), was the first digital interface powered and informed by microbes. This pioneering bio–digital platform was funded within the EU's funding framework via an Innovation Award. The instrumental purpose of this project was to visualise and interpret electrogenic biofilm activity in ways that could reveal its extraordinary environmental intelligence. From a human–microbial perspective, a real-time interface was sought enabling microbes to be perceived and imagined beyond our usual unpleasant encounters with 'slime' (the natural 'face' of microbial colonies). The digital platform was chosen as a medium for this interaction, as it is sufficiently well positioned to help challenge human/microbial interactions, where 54% of people in the EU aged 16–74 have at least basic digital skills (Eurostat 2021).

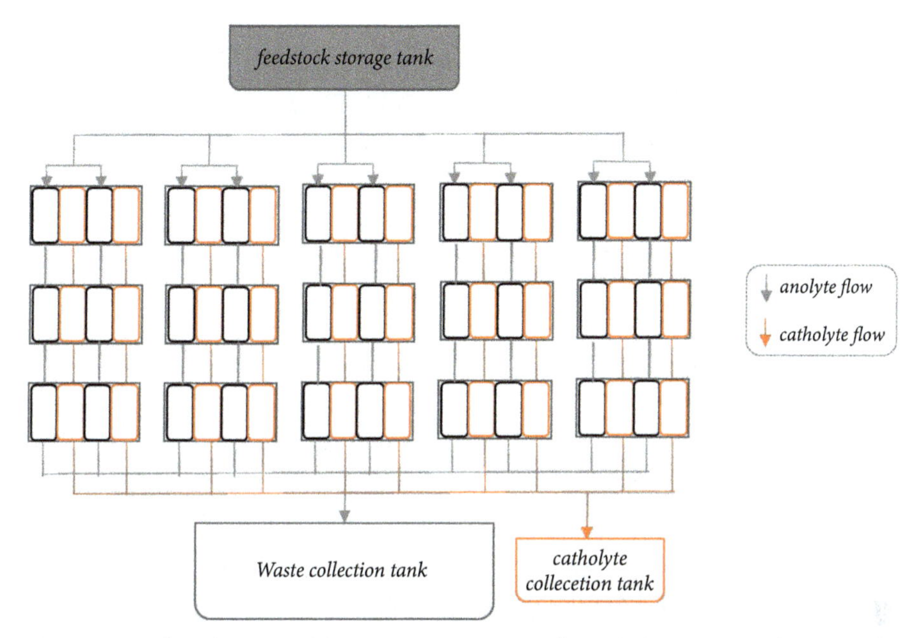

Figure 13.5 Flow diagram of the wastewater passing through the Living Architecture bioreactor array.
Diagram reproduced courtesy of the Living Architecture project, 2019.

MFCs were used as the interface between humans and anaerobic biofilms, by directly linking microbial metabolism with electronic systems. Harvested electrical activity from the biofilm was a source for both power and data, which was translated by data artist Julie Freeman into animations that conveyed the overall status of the biofilm. Participants could interact with the data in an exploratory exchange—as if they were caring for a pot plant, or even a pet. This world of 'Mobes'—a characterful term coined for the data-based representations of microbes—took the form of ALICE gallery installations[7] and is also a permanent online exhibit.[8] It can be accessed under the section Bio-Digital Interface by clicking the *Launch Artwork* button, where visitors meet an animated community of Mobes whose behaviour is informed by electrical data arising from a real MFC biofilm installed in a scientific laboratory at the University of Southampton. Visitors interact with the Mobes by selecting different options from drop-down menus such as different microbial stains, or observing their environmental behaviour (temperature, pH) and overall electrical performance (power output). Depending on how the visitor interprets the Mobes' behaviour, they can choose to feed them using a remotely operated valve system, or gently warm them by turning on an LED in the laboratory (Figure 13.7). With habituation, both human and microbe use the ALICE interface to continually negotiate their position and relevance to the living world through myriad investments of work, the formation of affective bonds, and a transactional alterbiopolitics, expressed through different aspects of 'care' (Tronto 1993).

Figure 13.6 The installation *999 years 13 sqm (the future belongs to ghosts)* is a collaboration between Cecile B. Evans and Rachel Armstrong for the *Is This Tomorrow?* exhibition at the Whitechapel Gallery, London.
Photograph by Rolf Hughes. Reproduced courtesy of the author, 2019.

Mobes are a crude but appealing way of reading biofilm activity and there is plenty of opportunity for misinterpretation. While electronic signals are literal for microbes being produced by their bodies, animated characters are symbolic for us, so we remain at a distance from events where we will not feel the physical effects of electricity. ALICE can help microbial and human actors actively share a life world by providing a communications platform that enables a condition of mutual liveability, inviting innovators to *step inside the skin of the entities they are designing with* as living beings and adopt a more-than-human perspective, decentring their human contribution in the process. While necessary for constructive negotiation, deanthropocentrisation does not imply devaluing a person, but rather giving equal attention and status to the non-human agents in the innovation process. Altering the status of the 'substrate' requires an ethics, and alterbiopolitics, so that we can better comprehend, and equitably re-deploy, the myriad linkages that connect our everyday lives with the environment in biodiversity-promoting ways.

Immunological City (IM-CITY)

IM-CITY searches for a *commons* where meaningful exchange can take place between humans and microbes by drawing on the innate characteristics of biofilms. This ambitious (and unfunded) proposal was conceived as a Starting Grant for the

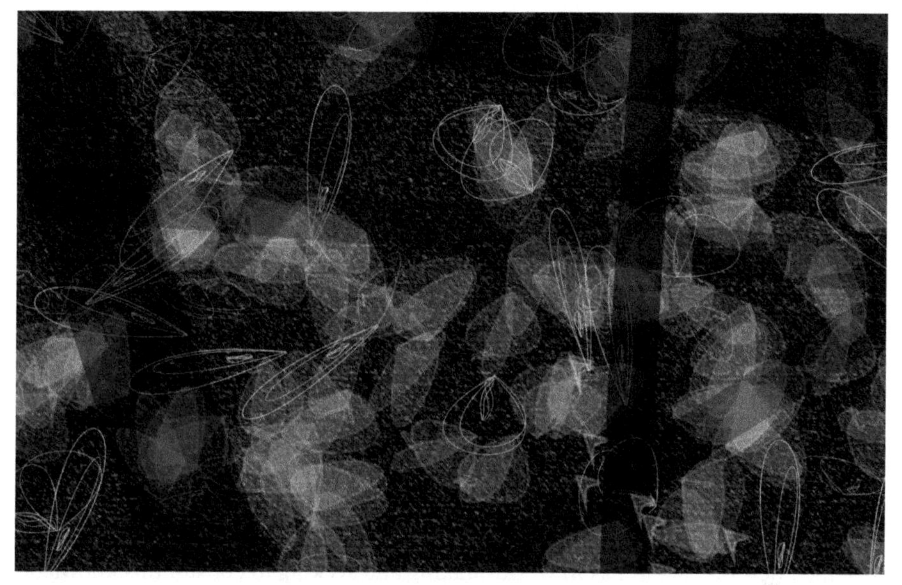

Figure 13.7 'Mobes', from the ALICE website (http://alice-interface.eu) showing dynamic, interactive, graphical representations of microbes.
Photograph reproduced courtesy of the ALICE project, 2021.

European Research Council. It considers how the environmental embeddedness and dynamic, self-regulating processes within biofilms—justice systems, economies, languages, etc.—can be effectively deployed as a network in the urban environment to provide a readable, relatable, eco-friendly immune system.

IM-CITY's immune system is composed from a network of self-powering MFCs embedded in waste streams, which provide protected spaces and stable environments where microbes can thrive undisturbed. Constantly 'reading' the biochemical character of their surroundings in real time, biofilms detect environmental 'harm' exacerbated by urbanisation itself in the form of pollutants, physical changes, noxious agents, and pathogenic microbes. The biofilm metabolisms within the MFCs provide packets of electrical data, which are combined with physical data from electronic sensors,[9] to train low-power computer systems via machine learning[10] and deploy a range of actuators—resulting in bioremediation, and removing pathogens from wastewater streams (Ieropoulos et al. 2017). Powered and informed by MFC bioelectricity, these biofilms are integrated into smart-city infrastructure to become an urban-scale cyborgian entity. This heterogeneous identity is analogous with immune system principles, which are complex networks (Jerne 1974) that learn to recognise different entities (antigens), memorise, and learn from them (Jerne 1960).

Working at the cell-population level, individual immune cell interactions, like biofilms, respond to their surroundings to make sense of highly situated information, being able to distinguish between harmless and harmful agents, and act accordingly via a range of actors. Also, in keeping with biofilm organisation, immune systems are highly situated, embodied, and tuneable being informed by robust, interconnected molecular circuits that learn from real time experiences (Grossman 1992, 1989; Grossman & Paul 1991, 1992, 2000). Importantly, IM-CITY's operations are informed by an immunological model called Danger Theory (DT) (Matzinger 2002) that rejects notions of immunity as self and other, working instead on a no-harm principle. Recognised as a feminist model of the immune system, DT has important epistemological value in changing narratives about the health of urban environments from *being at war* with 'foreign invaders' like microbes (Weasel 2001) to establishing an alternative value system based on the contributions of citizens (of all species). These founding principles based on mutual care and an exchange (economy).

There is no quick fix for urban pollution and even productive transactions with microbes will take time to scrub from our cities centuries of poor environmental hygiene. In practice, establishing a networked communications protocol with microbes is likely to be anthropocentric, and therefore frustrating, as we discover that we do not know as much about microbes as we had assumed. However, the attempt to make a shared platform for the exchange of environmental data with microbes is, in itself, an important ethical position—as a move towards acknowledging the expertise the microbial realm has in world-making and seeking to consult this knowledge for bioremediation and improved practices for human development. The outcomes of these less-than-perfect exchanges will likely shape our urban imaginaries, inform decisions about how we live better alongside nature, challenge our assumptions about what environmental health may be, and help us establish new rituals and habits that build towards a *culture of life.*

Conclusion

> *I sit on a man's back, choking him and making him carry me, and yet assure myself and others that I am very sorry for him and wish to ease his lot by all possible means—except by getting off his back* (Tolstoy 1925, p.99).

Microbial cities are already here and have existed since life's origins. Biofilms are not something humans invented, but rather advanced technologies provide new insights about their fundamental importance in world-making. This new knowledge is the starting point for realisable synergies that can underpin new modes of co-inhabitation that enable more-than-human cities. However, all the adjustments are the burden of human responsibility, as biofilms already thrive, and will continue to do so long after our civilisations have gone.

While this chapter aims to identify tangible synergies with the microbial realm that provide a starting point for changing our ways of designing and working, it remains doggedly anthropocentric. Perhaps necessarily so. Each case study is described from the perspective of the human innovator based on scientific research where the overall benefits are aimed at human recipients, while microbes self-organise around the proposed interventions and are narrativised in terms of microbial benefits. The different case studies may well be differently viewed by microbes but, to date, it is impossible to communicate with them on an equal footing to establish their view.

To go beyond rhetorical flourishes requires concrete alternatives and, in this sense, the cyborgian nature of the MFC is intriguing, as it provides a site where the macroscale of the human world and microscale of the microbes converge in a sustained manner. This is the building block of the bio-digital city. Resident biofilms can persist for over a decade in this context—and likely much longer under the right conditions. Biofilms are notoriously resilient despite deliberate human attempts to remove them, but even when they are actively engaged, they set their own limits on the proposed transactions. For example, MFCs must be fed and watered appropriately, or they will shut down. Moreover, they will only produce the number of electrons that can be metabolised from the feedstock. The generation of low-power bioelectricity is eye-opening as it reminds us that the natural world works within the limits of metabolism. When arranged in arrays and stacked together, MFCs will ultimately generate around 12V, which is much lower than compared with fossil fuels that are delivered to our homes as 230V power supplies. From an ecological perspective, these limits are creative.

The unlimited energy offered by fossil fuels encourages wasteful patterns of behaviour, which accelerates consumption (Garrett et al. 2020). Moreover, the performative agency of microbes to collectively act to generate electrical power, electronic data and chemical transformation spotlights their overall potency as an agentised, collective body to generate life-promoting downstream environmental impacts. The case study proposals based on MFCs—*Living Architecture*, ALICE, and *999 years 13sqm (the future belongs to ghosts)*—are prototype expressions of this platform that provide human–microbial interfaces that enable their interrogation from many different perspectives. In this way, these prototypes are pedagogical systems that inform imaginaries through which future iterations for more-than-human city proposals like IM-CITY can be conceived. Such first steps are always hard and inevitably imperfect, but through collective engagement and persistence, the narratives that discuss them will change, then the apparatuses, then the interactions, then our expectations. At that point, the kinds of systems that can be implemented to establish our more-than-human cities will emerge and develop into a working reality.

The smart microbial city of the near future will draw fully on the world-making characteristics of biofilms. These settlements will be biodiverse with native, fertile soils, and renewable energy will be deployed for heavy-duty work (>12V). It is a place of organic generosity where notions of commodity are replaced with those of metabolism, where metabolic cycles are the fundamental currency, and the concept of 'waste' disappears into the starting point for new metabolic processes. The emerging *cultures of life* are celebrated—not by excessive wealth—but what we put back into the landscapes that sustain us. How we develop our smart-city infrastructure to consciously coexist with microbes is of great importance, as we cannot take their cooperation for granted. By upholding a *parliament of things*, where microbes, creatures, rivers, places, and peoples can meet and negotiate the laws, power structures and modes of living for mutual enlivening on-their-own-terms (Latour 1993), we can establish a model for living that can be thought of as an ecological Babel, where hotly negotiated differences form the foundations of our living together and do not drive us apart. We will remain vigilant to the needs and moods of our microbial kin by the data-images provided by AI systems, and actuated by machine learning, that show us on a meta level just how our invisible landscapes are 'feeling'. Gradually microbes will become an everyday part of our conversations and daily lifestyles, establishing the principles for succession towards bio-digital cities. Recognising the intelligence and foundational material transformations invested by microbial life into healthy urban spaces these systems will make more liveable space for all earth's species through the increased fertility of urban soils and landscape. With time, our cities and nature will converse and converge, so we can no longer tell where one stops and the other begins.

Acknowledgements

Living Architecture is Funded by the EU Horizon 2020 Future Emerging Technologies Open programme (2016–2019) Grant Agreement 686585 a consortium of six collaborating institutions—Newcastle University, University of Trento, University of the West of England, Spanish National Research Council, Explora Biotech, and Liquifer Systems Group. ***The Active Living Infrastructure: Controlled Environment (ALICE)*** project is funded by an EU Innovation Award for the development of a bio-digital 'brick' prototype, a collaboration between Newcastle University, Translating Nature, and the University of the West of England (2019–2021) under EU Grant Agreement no. 851246. **999 years 13sqm (the future belongs to ghosts)** installation by Cecile B. Evans and Rachel Armstrong at the Whitechapel Gallery at the group exhibition 'Is this Tomorrow?', London (2019) was possible with contributions by: Bioengineering Team: Ioannis Ieropoulos (lead; University of the West of England), Simone Ferracina (University of Edinburgh), Rolf Hughes (Newcastle University), Pierangelo Scravaglieri (Newcastle University), Jiseon You (University of the West of England), Arjuna Mendis (University of the West of England), Tom Hall (University of the West of England), Patrick Brinson (University of the West of England); Microbial Fuel Cell Bioreactor Brick Installation Design: Pierangelo Scravaglieri and Jiseon You, under the guidance of Ioannis Ieropoulos; Structure Designer: Dominik Arni; Structure Fabricator: Weber Industries; Contributing Writer: Amal Khalaf; Animator: Tom Kemp; Composer: Mati Gavriel; Research and Production Assistance: Anna Clifford; Installation Team: Richard Hards, Hady Kamar; Sponsorship from Personal Improvement Ltd. and Living Architecture (EU Grant Agreement no. 686585). In-kind support provided by Andrew Hesketh; Audioviz (UK FogScreen); the Bristol BioEnergy Centre at the Bristol Robotics Laboratory and their research into alternative, sustainable sources of power for the home and infrastructure.

Notes

1. Plasmids are circular strands of genetic information that are independent from the organism's chromosomal identity and can be transmitted from one microbe to another. Plasmids are mainly found in bacteria, but also exist naturally in archaea and in eukaryotes such as yeast and plants.
2. Metabolism is a biochemical mode of empowerment, based on a fundamental currency and flow of electrons that, in many ways, comprises the living world and keeps all living bodies from reaching their energetic ground state.

3. Walking the boundary, beating the bounds, or perambulating the bounds, is an ancient custom still observed in parts of England, Wales, and the New England region of the United States, where inhabitants walk the geographic boundaries of their locality for the purpose of maintaining the memory of their precise location.
4. The decoding of such impossible conversations invokes the 'Babelfish', a term invented by Douglas Adams in *The Hitchhiker's Guide to the Galaxy*. It referred to a creature that could translate brain waves, and in effect, translate all languages for anyone who had a Babelfish placed in their ear.
5. The integral accident is a term devised by French philosopher Paul Virilio, who observed that technology cannot exist without the potential for accidents.
6. Microbial materiality is characteristic of biodesign practices, where living microbes (e.g., fungi and bacteria) organise waste matter (e.g., agricultural waste and sand) into a material composite form. Our increasing understanding of these processes are leading to a range of different materials with characteristic properties and can even be hybridised with construction and demolition waste.
7. ALICE was exhibited at the Digital Design Weekend, V&A, London, UK, as part of the London Design Festival from 24–26 September 2021, and was installed at the Electromagnetic field Festival, from 2–5 June 2022.
8. Online access to the interactive ALICE website is available under the section Bio-Digital Interface at: http://alice-interface.eu
9. Some of the most common environmental sensors measure temperature, air quality, moisture, VOCs (volatile organic compounds), and seismic vibrations.
10. Machine learning is the term used when computer systems use algorithms and statistical models to analyse and draw inferences from patterns in data, thereby learning and adapting their outputs without following explicit instructions.

References

Arendt, H. (1958). *The human condition*. University of Chicago Press.

Armstrong, R. (2021). *Safe as houses: More-than-human design for a post-pandemic world*. Lund Humphries.

Armstrong, R., & Hughes, R. (2021). Metabolic architecture: Dialogues with microbes. In L. Succini, L. Arboritanza, A. Chiara Benedetti, K. Rochink Costa, S. Gheduzzi, R. Grasso, I. Gorzanelli, S. Rinaldi, I. Ruggeri, & I. Zedda (Eds.), *The ecological turn: Design, architecture and aesthetics beyond 'Anthropocene'* (pp. 10–20). BK Books.

Armstrong, R., Ferracina S., Caldwell, G., Ieropoulos I., Rimbu, G., Adamatzky, A., Phillips, N., De Lucrezia, D., Imhof, B., Hanczyc, M. M., Nogales, J., & Garcia, J. (2017). Living Architecture (LIAR): Metabolically engineered building units. In F. Heisel & D. Hebel (Eds.), *Cultivated building materials: Industrialized natural resources for architecture and construction* (pp. 170–177). Birkhauser.

Balvanera, P., Pfisterer, A. B., Buchmann, N., He, J. S., Nakashizuka, T., Raffaelli, D., & Schmid, B. (2006). Quantifying the evidence for biodiversity effects on ecosystem functioning and services. *Ecology Letters*, *9*, 1146–1156.

Bevan, R. (2019, February 14). Is this tomorrow? Review: Installations show a troubled mood of the future. *The Standard*. https://www.standard.co.uk/culture/is-this-tomorrow-review-installations-show-a-troubled-mood-of-the-future-a4066551.html

Bell, T., Newman, J. A., Silverman, B. W., Turner, S. L., & Lilley, A. K. (2005). The contribution of species richness and composition to bacterial services. *Nature*, *436*, 1157–1160.

Brown, S. P., & Taddei, F. (2007). The durability of public goods changes the dynamics and nature of social dilemmas. *PLoS One*, *2*, e593.

Carson, R. (1962). *Silent spring*. Houghton Mifflin Harcourt.

Clark, N. & Hird, M. (2018). Microontologies and the politics of emergent life. In M. Coleman & J. Agnew (Eds.), *Handbook on the geographies of power* (pp. 245–258). Edward Elgar.

Dedeurwaerdere, T. (2010). Self-governance and international regulation of the global microbial commons: Introduction to the special issue on the microbial commons. *International Journal of the Commons*, *4*(1), 390–403.

Diggle, S. P., Griffin, A. S., Campbell, G. S. & West, S. A. (2007). Cooperation and conflict in quorum-sensing bacterial populations. *Nature*, *450*, 411–414.

Doebeli, M., & Hauert, C. (2005). Models of cooperation based on the Prisoner's Dilemma and the Snowdrift game. *Ecology Letters, 8*, 748–766.

Eurostat (2021). How many citizens had basic digital skills in 2021? https://ec.europa.eu/eurostat/web/products-eurostat-news/-/ddn-20220330-1

Fenchel, T., King, G., & Blackburn, T. H. (2012). Biogeochemical cycling in soils. In T. Fenchel, G. M. King, & T. H. Blackburn (Eds.), *Bacterial biogeochemistry: The ecophysiology of mineral cycling* (pp. 89–120). Academic Press.

Fischel, S. (2017). *The microbial state: Global thriving and the body politic.* University of Minnesota Press.

Garrett, T. J., Grasselli, M., & Keen, S. (2020). Past world economic production constrains current energy demands: Persistent scaling with implications for economic growth and climate change mitigation. *PLoS One, 15*(8), e0237672.

Gordon, J., Knowlton, N., Relman, D.A., Rohwer, F. and Youle, M. (2013). Superorganisms and holobionts. *Microbe, 8*(4), 152–153.

Griffin, A. S., West, S. A., & Buckling, A. (2004). Cooperation and competition in pathogenic bacteria. *Nature, 430*, 1024–1027.

Grossman, Z. (1992). Contextual discrimination of antigens by the immune system: Towards a unifying hypothesis. In A. S. Perelson & G. Weisbuch (Eds.), *Theoretical and experimental insights into immunology* (pp. 71–88). Springer-Verlag.

Grossman, Z. (1989). The concept of idiotypic network: Deficient, or premature? In: H. Atlan & I. R. Cohen (Eds.), *Theories of Immune Networks* (pp. 38–52). Springer-Verlag.

Grossman, Z., & Paul, W. E. (2000). Self-tolerance: Context dependent tuning of T cell antigen recognition. *Seminars in Immunology, 12*, 197–203.

Grossman, Z., & Paul, W. E. (1992). Adaptive cellular interactions in the immune system: The tuneable activation threshold and the significance of subthreshold responses. *Proceedings of the National Academy of Sciences of the United States of America, 89*, 10365–10369.

Grossman, Z., & Paul W. E. (1991). Hypothesis on cell learning outside the brain. *Journal of Neuroimmunology, 35*, 28.

Hall-Stoodley, L., Costerton, W., & Stoodley, P. (2004). Bacterial biofilms from the natural environment to infectious diseases. *Nature Reviews Microbiology, 2*(2), 95–108.

Hird, M. (2009). *The origins of sociable life: Evolution after science studies.* Palgrave Macmillan.

Humphries, J., Xiong, L., Jintao Liu, J., Prindle, A., Yuan, F., Arjes, H. A., Tsimring, L., & Süel, G. M. (2017). Species-independent attraction to biofilms through electrical signaling. *Cell, 168*, 200–209.

Ieropoulos, I., Pasternak, G., & Greenman, J. (2017). Urine disinfection and in situ pathogen killing using a microbial fuel cell cascade system. *PLoS One, 12*(5), e0176475.

Jerne, N. K. (1960). Immunological speculations. *Annual Review of Microbiology, 14*, 341–358.

Jerne, N. K. (1974). Towards a network theory of the immune system. *Annals of Immunology, 125C*, 373–389.

Kembel, S. W., Jones, E., Kline, J., Northcutt, D., Stenson, J., Womack, A. M., Bohannan, B. J. M., Brown, G. Z., & Green, J. (2012). Architectural design influences the diversity and structure of the MBE. *International Society of Microbial Ecology Journal, 6*, 1469–1479.

King, G. (2014). Urban microbiomes and urban ecology: How do microbes in the built environment affect human sustainability in cities? *The Journal of Microbiology, 52*(9), 721–728.

Lahiji, N., & Friedman, D. S. (1997). *Plumbing: Sounding modern architecture.* Princeton Academic Press.

Latour, B. (2013). Once out of nature: Natural religion as a pleonasm. *Gifford Lecture Series*, University of Edinburgh. http://www.youtube.com/watch?v=MC3E6vdQEzk

Latour, B. (1993). *We have never been modern.* Harvard University Press.

Locey, K. J., & Lennon, J. T. (2016). Scaling laws predict global microbial diversity. *Proceedings of the National Academy of Sciences of the United States of America, 113*(21), 5970–5975.

Margulis L. (1981). *Symbiosis in cell evolution: Life and its environment on the early earth.* WH Freeman.

Matzinger, P. (2002). The danger model: A renewed sense of self. *Science, 296*, 301–305.

Miller, M. B., & Bassler, B. L. (2001). Quorum sensing in bacteria. *Annual Review of Microbiology, 55*, 165–199. doi.org/10.1146/aaurev.micro.55.1.165
Neyrat, F. (2018). *The unconstructable earth: An ecology of separation*. Fordham University Press.
Potter, M. C. (1911). Electrical effects accompanying the decomposition of organic compounds, *Proceedings of the Royal Society B, 571*(84), 260–276.
Raymond, B., West, S. A., Griffin, A. S., & Bonsall, M. B. (2012). The dynamics of cooperative bacterial virulence in the field. *Science, 337*, 85–88.
Raut, N., Pasini, P., & Daunert, S. (2013). Deciphering bacterial universal language by detecting the quorum sensing signal, autoinducer-2, with a whole-cell sensing system. *Annals of Chemistry, 85*(20), 9604–9609.
Römling, U. (2022). Is biofilm formation intrinsic to the origin of life? *Environmental Microbiology, 25*(1), 26–39. https://doi.org/10.1111/1462-2920.16179
Sender, R., Fuchs, S., & Milo, R. (2016) Are we really vastly outnumbered? Revisiting the ratio of bacterial to host cells in humans. *Cell, 164*, 337–340.
Stewart, P. S., & Franklin, M. J. (2008). Physiological heterogeneity in biofilms. *Nature Reviews Microbiology, 6*, 199–210.
Tasoff, J., Mee, M. T., & Wang H. H. (2015). An economic framework of microbial trade. *PLoS One, 10*(7), e0132907.
Timmis, K., Cavicchioli, R., Garcia, J-L., Nogales, B., Chavarría, M., Stein, L., McGenity, T. J., Webster, N., Singh, B. K., Handelsman, J., de Lorenzo, V., Pruzzo, C., Timmis, J., Martín, J. L. R., Verstraete, W., Jetten, M., Danchin, A., Huang, W., Gilbert, J., Harper, L. (2019) The urgent need for microbiology literacy in society. *Environmental Microbiology, 21*(5), 1513–1528.
Tolstoy, L. (1925). *What then must we do?* Oxford University Press.
Tronto, J. (1993). *Moral boundaries: A political argument for an ethic of care*. Routledge.
Tsing, A. L., Swanson, H. A., Gan, E., & Bubandt, N. (2017). *Arts of living on a damaged planet: Ghosts and monsters of the Anthropocene*. University of Minnesota Press.
Virilio, P. (2007). *The original accident*. Polity Press.
Weasel, F. (2001). Dismantling the self/other dichotomy in science: Towards a feminist model of the immune system. *Hypatia, 16*(1), 27–44.
Whitechapel Gallery. (2019). Is this tomorrow? https://www.whitechapelgallery.org/exhibitions/is-this-tomorrow/
Wiegand, S., Dam, H. T., Riba, J., Volmers, J., & Kaster, A-K. (2021). Printing microbial dark matter: Using single cell dispensing and genomics to investigate the *patescibacteria*/candidate phyla radiation. *Frontiers in Microbiology, 12*. https://doi.org/10.3389/fmicb.2021.635506
You, J., Rimbu, G. A., Wallis, L., Greenman, J., & Ieropoulos, I. (2019). Living architecture: Toward energy-generating buildings powered by microbial fuel cells. *Frontiers in Energy Research, 12*. https://doi.org/10.3389/fenrg.2019.00094

14
Intimate Translations
Transforming the Urban Imagination

Ann Light, Lara Houston, and Ruth Catlow

Introduction

This chapter looks at governance for an urban green space through a game of futures-making called *The Treaty of Finsbury Park* (hereafter, *Treaty*). *Treaty* invites people to listen to the grass and trees, and to the creatures that inhabit them. We use this intimate approach to rethinking relations—the outcome of *Treaty*'s gameplay—to challenge smart city narratives.

Treaty has been sponsored by CreaTures (Creative Practice for Transformative Futures), an EU-funded action research project that worked with creative practitioners and sought to inspire care, collaboration, and reflection so that different relations, values, and priorities can emerge in society. The authors have a stake in *Treaty* as members of the research team (two being academic researchers—Lara and Ann—and one, a researching artist and co-creator of *Treaty*—Ruth) and as people with connections to London and an interest in social change.

Treaty is a project concerned with representation and access in a park between the life forms that inhabit it. It belongs to an emerging genre of creative practices that make conditions for people to change their relations in/with our worlds towards greater eco-social wellbeing. CreaTures has been aggregating examples of this genre, drawing attention to its potential and helping to identify its characteristics. By showing the significance of this style of creative practice—intervening at diverse points in a system, staying approachable while keeping ambitious changes in sight, and working to change people's relations with other beings—the intention is to affect how to conceive of and legislate for futures.

Treaty links the big dimensions of society, governance, and social justice and even bigger geological and ecological concerns of climate futures, with the experience of everyday life and the goings-on in a specific park. The tactics used are *intimate*: focusing on peoples' everyday practices, working person-by-person and group-by-group, and linking personal meaning to the values that underpin civilisations. In practicing intimacy in this way, it becomes possible to create convivial and reassuring spaces that nurture close-knit relations and allow groups to take risks together. This is to look past historically derived binary boundaries, such as global–local, culture–nature, and urban–rural, on a collective journey to see what new thresholds are relevant. In doing so, *Treaty* focuses on the affective context and the experiencing of body and relations in formation: aspects that are often overlooked in planning future cities.

Ann Light, Lara Houston, and Ruth Catlow, *Intimate Translations*. In: *Designing More-than-Human Smart Cities*.
Edited by: Sara Heitlinger, Marcus Foth, and Rachel Clarke, Oxford University Press. © Oxford University Press (2024).
DOI: 10.1093/9780191980060.003.0016

The game of *Treaty*

Treaty occupies the heart of this chapter, described as a challenge to the planning of future (smart) cities. We note that there are both stable and evolving parts to this artwork and the materials we draw from in this chapter come from 2021–22.

> *'It's the dawning of interspecies democracy—a new era of equal rights for all living beings. Where all species come together to organise and shape the environments and cultures they inhabit, in Finsbury Park, urban green spaces across the UK, the world, and beyond.'* (Introductory notes to Treaty, Furtherfield, October 2021).

Treaty is a game of Live Action Role Play (or LARP) designed by the art organisation Furtherfield, which invites humans to act as part of an interspecies forum for navigating a notional new future for an actual park. It deals in issues of custodianship, representation, asset management, and power relations. Stepping behind masks—cardboard (in the park) or digital (online)—people engage in multispecies co-operation, then debrief to consider the experience. It is a vehicle for sensitising humans to the impacts of current global systems on all life forms. In representing key park species (dog, squirrel, Canada goose, stag beetle, bee, grass, and London plane tree), the agenda is to go beyond *social* inequality to look at the fall-out from destructive patterns of dominion on all life. As Furtherfield (2021) explains, in the game materials:

> We are catapulted several years into the future where all the species of the park have risen up to demand equal rights with humans. After much unrest, it has been agreed that a treaty will be drawn up, designating these rights, but first, humans must learn to better relate to and understand non-humans so they can cooperate better together. Thankfully there has been a new invention—The Sentience Dial—which allows humans to tune into all the flora and fauna of Finsbury Park.

Furtherfield's offer is unusual: 'Think like a dog, bee or even grass and help change the way we all see and participate in our local urban green spaces forever' (2021). Through this intimate co-creative experience, players are prompted to imagine themselves as non-human agents of future change.

Furtherfield, the producer

Furtherfield's stated aim is to diversify the people involved in shaping emerging technologies through an arts-led approach. In 1996, artists Ruth Catlow and Marc Garrett initiated an online platform for collaboration and experimentation, informed by community arts, pirate radio, activism, and street art. A grassroots network and programme emerged, which continues to thrive with a commitment to free and open-source methodologies. Furtherfield's Gallery and Commons came later, in the middle of London's Finsbury Park. And, while 'Adventurous digital arts experiences radiate from these venues, transforming the urban park into a platform where people can explore how they want live in our globally connected world' (https://www.furtherfield.org/about-us/), there are also local concerns that bring the park itself, rather than the network or gallery space, into relief. In *Treaty*, the park's future is a principal concern.

Treaty's development was hit hard by controls to manage the Covid-19 pandemic, with knock-on effects of delay, digitisation, and uncertainty. It was launched online[1] and only moved into the park early in 2022, after controls were lifted (See Figures 14.1).

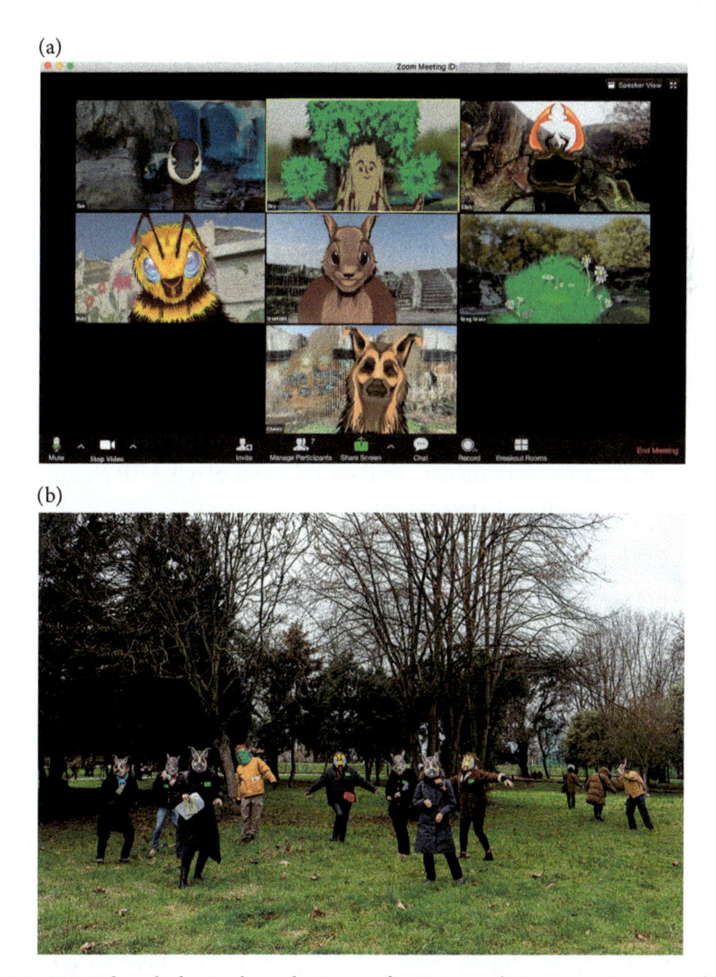

Figure 14.1 Digital and physical masks in use for Treaty. a) Interspecies Assemblies 2022, part of The Treaty of Finsbury Park. Screenshot of online play. b) The first in-park assembly of local dignitaries 2022, part of The Treaty of Finsbury Park.
Photograph by Hydar Dewachi. Images reproduced courtesy of Furtherfield, 2022.

The setting

Treaty is set in Finsbury Park, a large inner-city urban green space in London, of forty-six hectares, fraught with governance struggles, questions of financial sustainability, and environmental issues from noxious gasses to traffic noises. Created in 1869, it became a municipal liability during the late twentieth century when facilities fell into disrepair. More recently, it has seen renovation and renewal as a venue for cultural activity, sport, and leisure, but it is still a site of conflict. *Treaty* takes its flora and fauna from the park and in playing out some of the tensions, raises issues affecting many community and public urban resources, as well as the global context of colonial systems.

CreaTures, the project researching *Treaty*

Treaty was formed under the auspices of CreaTures, a project investigating the role of participatory-oriented creative practices in helping people imagine liveable futures and bring them into being. A central tenet of CreaTures is that creative practices (broadly understood) are already actively linking designers, artists, cultural workers, and citizen-led collectives around the complex issues of climate change and social inequalities and using a wide range of aesthetic, affect-driven, and participatory approaches to achieve change. However, these practices are fragmented, often poorly resourced, and badly understood (Light et al. 2019). The project has supported twenty subprojects to redouble their efforts, making them more visible and legible to policymakers. This means *Treaty* is a test site for transformation produced with accompanying researchers to discuss its development, play LARP characters, reflect on learning, and contribute to evaluation.

Experiencing Treaty

Human players join *Treaty's* 'Interspecies Assemblies' either online (via a videoconferencing platform) or in person at the Furtherfield gallery in Finsbury Park. In either case, they consult the Sentience Dial to be matched with the 'Mentor Species' that they will perform throughout the role-play. In the online version, participants work through a series of email prompts to receive a virtual filter of a dog, squirrel, Canada goose, stag beetle, bee, blade of grass, or London plane tree. These characters are representative of key groups of park dwellers (e.g., the bee speaks on behalf of all the pollinators of Finsbury Park). In the in-person role-play, participants consult a hooded figure to be awarded their printed Mentor Species mask. Before the Assembly begins in earnest, participants put on their masks and begin to act as their Mentor Species. They continue this make-believe improvisation throughout the Assembly.

When the Assembly starts, participants are given a poetic welcome by the convenor, and led through a mindfulness exercise to fully attune to their own character and to the more-than-human richness of the Assembly. Then the convenor moves on to the main agenda—planning the world's first Interspecies Festival in Finsbury

Park in 2025. Participants are sorted into small groups to brainstorm ideas for activities, using all the Park's biodiverse habitats. Participants introduce themselves to each other and chat about their needs and desires. Staying in character throughout, they brainstorm activities that all species might enjoy, for example, an Interspecies Spa and Daycare, where the participants groom each other, forming new symbiotic relationships, or the Poop Festival, celebrating the diversity of something that all participants can do, with benefit to the soil. Before the Assembly ends, each breakout group reports back to the main Assembly and receives feedback on their ideas.

At the end of the Assembly, participants again go through a mindfulness exercise to 'de-role' and come back into their human selves. The group then holds a de-briefing session, reflecting and learning on the experiences of performing as their Mentor Species and the issues that came up in the game.

The sites and briefing materials were developed with the park ranger and a bi-annual review meeting keeps these up to date. Participants include members of Furtherfield's extensive art network and people living by the park, including children. There are no specific requirements for involvement and the existence of both in-person and online versions makes it open to a wide range of players. Although there are significant differences in the experience of these two versions, we focus, in this account, on the more general features of asking people to inhabit a different life form.

Treaty Antecedents

In the design of *Treaty*, we see influences from art, design, ecology, computer science, philosophy, geography, critical animal studies, and performance studies. Across these, we are interested in how to evaluate playing the game. Many questions fall from this. How much play is needed to affect people's sensibilities? How, if at all, are people changed? Does the role affect the impact? What post-play reflection best enables people to make meaning from the experience? How might Furtherfield know that *Treaty* activities are transformative and in which ways? We wonder if playing a tree or stag beetle creates identification with the represented group, whether the camaraderie of humans as other beings is memorable, and how to learn of the communal aspects—not just experience of other species but imagining the interplay of seven non-human species. To explain its development and our conclusions, we look here at elements that have fed our analysis and the questions they raise.

Live Action Role Playing (LARPing)

Treaty reflects interest in design and computer science fields in using performative methods (Márquez Segura et al. 2019) to sensitise humans to other species. Researchers argue that 'role-playing experiences can produce moments of temporary identity transformation by placing a player into the role of a character in a story', potentially sparking empathic connections (p.390).

Live Action Role Playing (LARPing) is performative: it involves adopting the part of a character and acting out their presence physically, alongside a group of other players. Unlike a scripted and staged theatre play, the players at a LARP event create many aspects of the world collaboratively, using improvisational techniques and 'make-believe'. When the game begins, players improvise their character for the entirety of the game. While some games are elaborate multi-day events with sophisticated storylines and staging, shortened 'chamber' LARPs take place in a single room over hours. *Treaty*'s LARP is a short-form game, lasting a couple of hours and currently involving about fifteen to twenty people in any session, including Ruth as leader to oversee the interactions.

Over the past five years, Ruth has developed this kind of LARP for use within live art events that bring LARPs to wider public audiences. This approach is playfully known in Furtherfield as LAARRPing (Live Art Action Research Role Play), developed through a range of other research collaborations (see Pothong et al. 2021). *Treaty* holds an intention to change people's (inter)subjectivities through play. When used for educational purposes like this, LARPing bears a resemblance to pedagogical movements in teaching, such as educational drama (Heathcote 1984) and psychodrama/sociodrama (Moreno 1946), where, likewise, there are no audients, just players and improvised roles.

The current LARP has antecedents in a LARP called *Now London is a City Farm*, organised by Ruth and Lara, with Ann as participant. Set in the year 2025, at a point when London is trying to become self-sufficient in growing food, players held human roles, but were also charged with representing a 'companion species' so would shift to speak as (or on behalf of) soil, plants, sensors, air, farm animals, trees, or weather (see Heitlinger et al. 2021; Houston et al. 2023). Players spent time addressing the complaints of their companion species (e.g., a bees' strike) yet spoke mostly as humans. The framing of food crisis and self-sufficient Londoners led to a focus on provision for people, despite the city farm being a 'multispecies commons'.

Land use and human-centricity

At the same time, Ann was working with colleagues on agricultural relations, analysing more-than-human farming as a challenge to what they called 'anthropocentric functionalism' (Bardzell et al. 2021). This team looked at alternative agriculture by exploring the practices of Taiwanese farmers resisting a mainstream, cash-crop, approach. Here, prioritisation of (more-than-human) respect, intimacy, and interdependence found expression in principles of preserving life, letting things take their course, and restorative agriculture, led by people departing from industrial jobs, caught in the farming collective's ethos: 'the important thing is not so much about how to make a living here; it is whether one has the desire to live here that matters the most' (Bardzell et al. 2021). The *desire to live 'here'* is an intuitive measure of wellness for community, resourcing, and land. We concluded that generating economic wealth often happens at the expense of that feeling—and the conditions that create it.

Running through this account, like *City Farm*, is a tension between human needs and desires and those of other co-located life forms. There is no resolution. The practices are human-shaped and remind us that sharing of space requires compromises in which some lives give way to others. *Treaty* picks up these concerns. Ecologies involve balances that shift over time and can never be fixed once and for all. Feral creatures may run over a place (and a crop) and thrive on/in disturbed soils. Others flourish only when effort is invested to protect them. *Treaty* takes this understanding and invites participants to play out the tensions.

More-than-Human?

Treaty combines two fields of inquiry key to CreaTures' investigations, making *playful encounters* of the *more-than-human* kind. Thus, the game and its reflective processes are, we might say, *creaturely*. So how does thinking through this creaturely avant-garde art piece help us understand the more-than-human smart city?

The relevance is that *Treaty* seeks to address what the more traditional smart-city agenda needs and lacks (Rose & Willis 2019). We are struck by the sterility of the images that accompany smart city promotional materials, being 'semi-schematic, many with data symbols marked over them . . . most resembl[ing] the Manhattan skyline. Trees and green spaces are almost absent and there are few people, fewer animals, and only a couple with bike lanes' (Light 2021a, p.189). Plants are featured in these smart city visualisations only as optimised performers vertiginously rising up and away from the land. Green-trimmed tower blocks or precision-engineered vertical farms are the new visual totems of 'algorithmic food' (Houston et al. 2023).

While there is always a gap between vision and actuality, this sterility is frightening to contemplate for it seems to sever ties for inhabitants to all that is playful, visceral, and spiritual, leaving only the bureaucratic, informational, and functional—pointing to 'ecocidal' smart cities (Heitlinger et al. 2018). In contemplating these images, we wonder how it is possible to know that we are alive. There are no allusions to the rest of the ecology in which we are formed and survive. And we speculate that it is harder to achieve justice if we cannot see other beings' worlds. Last, we feel sad that glorious life forms that are already struggling to survive in hostile human-made spaces seem to have no place in these cities. The fate of pollinators may be linked to our own species' survival, but beyond that is our care for intricate living beings of all kinds made vulnerable by inhospitable habitats.

Design scholars point to the need to more actively decentre 'human-centred design' in urban space to be inclusive to plants and animals in our rapidly expanding cityscapes (Forlano 2016). These go beyond people- and sustainability-centred critiques (Borjesson Rivera et al. 2015; McLaren & Agyeman 2015) to new ways of designing for and with more-than-humans, from speculations on multispecies worldings (Westerlaken 2021) to methods that include more-than-humans in the design process (Tomitsch et al. 2021). Radically new embodied and performative methods, such as Clarke's masked walks in the fictional 'Ministry of Multispecies

Communications' (2020), bring fresh perspective to familiar urban spaces. This speaks to both understanding the gap between smart city visions and realities (Shelton et al. 2015) and telling stories of more-than-human smart city entanglements that account fully for the agency of other beings, not treating life as an object of technological surveillance and control (Gabrys 2016). Resistance comes in accounts of citizen-led, DIY infrastructures that write against dominant logics of optimisation (Powell 2021) to collaborate with or accommodate more-than-human lives (Jungnickel 2014).

In CreaTures, we see every stretch of ground as an ever-changing cluster of specific instances of (more-than-human) life. To value the more-than-human is to adopt some generic acknowledgment of the need for better relations. By contrast, to dwell with other species is to remember that, by virtue of being alive and irreplaceable, every blade of grass has some right to existence (as well as the genus and subspecies it hails from), and also that a goose might peck that blade at any time. With these perspectives, the concept of 'nature' has little value: this is neither an essentialist account of different species' characteristics, nor an attempt to place humans in something 'external' to them. Humans, like other species, exist and become formed in their relatings and in their interdependence with all other life.

Thus, the more-than-human smart city in which our *Treaty* and our park might be based is not one that merely caters to other animals beyond humans and remembers nature. It is a city that acknowledges interdependencies between life forms: that air breathed in by fauna is emitted by flora. It is a world in which slime moulds can flourish, herbs are not merely a garnish for high-end eating establishments, and a mosquito is not automatically denied a place. The authors celebrate London as a National Park City (https://www.nationalparkcity.london/) and note that London leads the world in urban blue and green spaces. We prefer this view to the rhetoric appearing in smart cities literatures on managing relations.

Intimacy and Play

The strengths of the more-than-human view are *relational*, occurring between lives, not centred in individuals and their management. Bardzell et al. (2021) suggest the farm collective's labour 'is infused with intimacy'. This is, they say, more than the regular acquaintance that arises out of daily work with plants, soil, and fauna, and more than an intellectual understanding of the effects of nonhumans living, intimacy is a 'shared way of being and a feeling of recognition, of mutuality' (Bardzell et al. 2021).

What is intimacy?

Cultural theorist Lauren Berlant (1998) writes eloquently to produce an understanding of intimacy that detaches it from sexuality and other forms of tight coupling. She asks: 'What if we saw it emerge from much more mobile processes of attachment?' She goes on:

> While the fantasies associated with intimacy usually end up occupying the space of convention, in practice the drive toward it is a kind of wild thing that is not necessarily organised that way, or any way. It can be portable, unattached to a concrete space: a drive that creates spaces around it through practices. [. . .] Intimacy seen in this spreading way does generate an aesthetic, an aesthetic of attachment, but no inevitable forms or feelings are attached to it (Berlant 1998, pp.284–285).

In the chapter, we are using intimacy to refer to a coming-together to experience moments of such power that they stay as connections between people, forged as shared encounters in a temporary space drawing on mobile processes of attachment, such as the one of which Berlant speaks. What we take from intimacy, which makes it particular to the work we describe, is the frisson in these encounters, so that people are brought into relations that form brief new structures, with no institutional bearings and pre-conceptions of the work to be done in making sense of the encounter yet offering a quality that is precious and inter-subjective. It is a quality that is impossible to produce at scale, for it loses the significant connection brought by the charge of mutual recognition and subsequent affective change. It is hard to speak about in general, but particularly as a researcher. Sehlikoglu and Zengin (2015, p.23) ask 'How might one provide evidence of intimacy, especially when it is one of the least describable experiences in human life? The most intimate moment is the most difficult to describe, one that poets dwell on and novelists are haunted by—and which seems to enchant ethnographers too'. We face this challenge, yet it is a dimension of *playful encounter* that seems especially salient when we need to reflect on what matters and how it comes to matter (Grossberg 2002). Jane Bennett (2001) says, 'one must be enamored with existence . . . to be capable of donating some of one's scarce mortal resources to the service of others' (p.4). Affective charge relates to memorability and choosing where to place one's efforts.

Further, sociologist Anthony Giddens (1999) proposes a link between intimacy and democracy, such that 'self-disclosure is the basic condition of intimacy' and this involves 'a relationship of equals, where each party has equal rights and obligations' and 'each person has respect, and wants the best, for the other' to build trust and resist 'arbitrary power, coercion or violence'. This too has bearing, for in agreeing to LARP, participants are thrown into a negotiation of structures and stories without hierarchy, accepting that others operate in good faith and will co-construct a generous experience for all. The link is even stronger in an encounter like *Treaty*, for its bones are about democracy and governance. (We note that the word democracy—the rule of the people—has to be stretched if it is to include all life, just as it was stretched to include women and working-class men, who were not franchised in Ancient Greece).

Within more traditional framings of urban planning, concern for relations often centres round security and privacy, protecting individuals from each other and from the institutions they interact with. The addition of the digital structures of 'smartness' makes issues of privacy and data control yet more salient, as digital personal information is aggregated for service provision. To prioritise intimacy might seem to fly in the face of these concerns. Intimacy speaks to the values of conviviality that we want in our cities: feelings of *between-ness*, rather than protections that respond to individual anxieties. It exists alongside these other types of care, to be managed within protective care systems for individuals, but challenging even what we understand these to be.

Invitations of intimacy in *Treaty*

We suggest that LARPing—and an invitation to devise a new treaty (i.e., a new way of relating)—creates the conditions for intimacy. LARPing is usually associated with the building of empathy (for the character one steps into). In *Treaty,* Ruth used a fiction called the 'Sentience Dial' to set the basic expectation that all species in the LAARRP could speak to each other. The Dial is described as 'allowing humans to tune into all flora and fauna' and 'supporting communication between humans and all other living entities' (Catlow's notes on designing Treaty, 2021). Tuning in and communicating both offer something more and less than empathy. Sentience speaks to something discernible in our cognitions and is speculative, while empathy may be absent yet to be desired, even between humans amongst themselves. Intimacy speaks to a bringing-close that may be mute and subject to an emotional intensity that we inevitably fail to express. Intimacy happens in the game, human on human, and inspires thoughts of empathy—and empathetic thoughts—more broadly, asking participants to question the nature of empathy. Players seem variously cautious and curious about the degree to which they can empathise with another species. This feels, in itself, like a pathway to increased respect.

Play, then, makes spaces for informal intimacies to grow and happen on many levels, recognised in the catching of the eye or shared gasp of recognition. This co-production of intimacies is particularly salient when masked players begin to adopt the behaviours of other species. Canine players may well want to sniff each other's rears in shared greeting but have to navigate the physical taboos of human mutual existence, using the cover of the species' masks (and taking the freedoms allowed in play) to explore the edges of permission, sniffing shoulders and nuzzling strangers. Here, rather than talk of emotional intimacy (though this may be invoked), we talk of *participative intimacy* (Light 2021b), as the quality of brief coming-together to share an encounter that holds the seeds of transformation in it (rather than making the base of enduring partnerships, though it may).

Discussion

Of course, it is not possible to measure a move to greater 'inter-species justice' by evaluating the outcomes of a LAARRP, even one as dedicated to species equality as *Treaty*. It is not possible to use a Sentience Dial to tune into other life forms' wavelengths either, even though that is the metaphor informing the dial. We know that even if we could speak the local dialect of squirrel language, we would not know what it means. *Treaty*, as we stated at outset, is a sensitising tool aimed at changing humans' perceptions and appetite for care of other species, not an unmediated bid for new park relations, though what is supposed to fall out of it is a sense that, in the minds of the species (humans) that legislates about park use and can lobby for more ecologically sensitive management, new park relations could come about.

And, beyond that, *Treaty*, in existing and in being played, suggests that a different way of thinking about other species could animate discussions of social justice. After all, in designing the perfect city, there seems no reason why either human workers or livestock should be denied the freedom to move, to love, and to be with their family in an environment they find appealing. And yet we do not talk about this as part of our aspirational future cities, because these abuses happen outside their borders or in hidden quarters. In the promoted urban lifestyle, the consumerism of cheap garments, mobile phones, and meat can prevail. In reality, the fastest growing form of city is the quasi-temporary and chaotic one: the refugee camp and the shantytown.

There are further politics to navigate. People talked about sharing the space more equitably, but this raised the political status of different species. Playing a tree might give insight into one's lack of tree knowledge and a sudden desire to learn more. But, as one early participant noted, even most of the representative species that Furtherfield chose (Canada goose, lawn grass, grey squirrel, bee, London plane tree, dog, stag beetle) are called to the space by humans or human-made habitats; only stag beetles represent enduring denizens of the land, rather than of the park placed on it. This was deliberate; Ruth's choices were based on who/what is present in the park and their familiarity to park users, not their historic claim. In other words, the team heard 'invasive species' set against 'indigenous species' in ways that would be awkward and inappropriate were we talking about human patterns of migration. Such a distinction reinforces our sense that there can be no real justice, only a recognition that, despite the fact that we can never achieve a just and permanent balance of power between life forms (any more than we can achieve such a thing between people), this is not a reason to stop asking about justice or to keep trying to move to more equitability. This is a goal for our designing (Costanza-Chock 2020). The journey is where the learning comes.

So, when we use the game to consider more-than-human aspects of smart cities, we can take multiple paths. We can wonder at the questions that the creation of a Sentience Dial raises and take a philosophical path and/or we can consider the changes that came about in people's thinking as a result of performing as a different animal for a few hours and look at the practical influence of the LAARRP on publics and playfellows. Both can tell us about cities and what our priorities should be.

Learning about the design of cities

Creative practice intervenes at multiple, diverse points of relevance for cities, how they are structured, and how we live in them. If we follow the approach of *participative intimacy*, we stay approachable in our transformations while keeping ambitious changes in sight. This links global climate futures with the experience of everyday life. But existential re-evaluation cannot be launched at the scale of the city, which is an emotional abstraction, even if city-scale activity is important for a sense of belonging to a place and for the organisational structures of effective management.

What we can do with these practices is proliferate them and work on increasing reach by multiplying the playful encounters possible.

Every neighbourhood might have its encounters as a means of staying fresh and agile. They could, perhaps, use it for their own ends to advocate for better environmental agendas. Furtherfield is already thinking of building a network of people interested in further imagining multispecies activities. And technologies might be configured to engage local councils, residents, and political activists to intervene in planning policy, consultation, or protest as animals and plants. Yet most platforms for engagement are designed to be sober, even if they are bottom-up and participatory in their aims. What would it be like if space were made among the decision making for playing, with non-human representation? In the emerging zo-op structure (an ecologically motivated legal mechanism for organisations to consider broader life forms: https://zoop.hetnieuweinstituut.nl/zoop-model), there are 'non-human' board members. But this is to change the purpose of the encounter and exchanges remain more formal and relate directly to the future of the organisation, not experiments in imagining living together as such.

The change of sensibility aspired to in LARPing depends on intimacy and play and it cannot be infinitely scaled, though experiments in working remotely were successful in inspiring playful encounters. But the groups remained small—if anything smaller online. Intimacy is not something that can be mandated as part of urban policy or beamed into every household. Only the opportunity for intimacy (and transformation) can be made available and then a whole system of creative practitioners could be employed (at far less cost than new technology) to inspire small groups to imagine how things could be different and enact it.

In terms of city building, the game play of *Treaty* is focused on who occupies a real place and how they are welcomed, encouraged or allowed to do so. We have already raised many of the political issues (which species and how they relate, the vulnerability of smaller beings vs the prevalence of their species, the invasive species and what to do with them, competition for food, etc.) and the philosophical issues (whose right to life, how we consider sentience, what interrelations can exist between instances of different species). The game takes these issues out of their abstractions, creating new encounters and new salience and bringing up some of these matters to consider together. While it cannot dictate what thoughts participants leave with, the mere acts of making the game and making it known that such a game exists will change (in some small way) the ideas that are broached in considering futures and cities, the importance of parks, of what is playful, visceral and spiritual and of finding accommodations for our part in sustainable world systems (Veselova & Gaziulusoy 2021).

This approach is timely, given that cities across the world are experiencing rapid warming and weather upheavals, exacerbated by design decisions (Kendon et al. 2021). While smart-city systems may help us manage increased protection, there remains the need for communities to negotiate how we live convivially together, as we strive to take properly into account the needs of more-than-humans that live alongside us and avoid 'ecocidal' smart cities (Heitlinger et al. 2018) and the needs of fellow humans who are living with prejudice, exploitation, and oppression. The ability of creative practitioners to take playful approaches to near-future challenges and opportunities provides resources for communities to think through rapid eco-social change.

How we ask matters

We have presented playful encounters as a method, because among other learning, CreaTures has been able to show that creative practitioners bring novel tools of engagement, ones that summon intimacy in fleeting yet profound ways, and that these touch people as information alone cannot. We will not be certain how people react or what the parameters are for who will engage, so we do not offer a predictable tool of transformation; indeed, it would be ridiculous to do so, given the diverse cognitive architectures and cultural dynamics in play. But we can point with some confidence to the components to a lively engagement with making-a-difference:

- a generous invitation
- a protected time and space for experimenting
- curious others with whom to connect
- stimuli that are challenging to norms, but not to the individuals' own sense of emotional security
- reflection on the experience that embeds it as significant.

So, another point that could inform the more-than-human smart city is how creative work can create the milieu and mood of the places we inhabit by activities of place-making. All this is quietly incorporated in play (a permission to experiment with new forms and relations) without dictating outcomes. Where the smart city may aim for control of mechanisms and a means of managing incipient challenges, the contribution of playfulness, viscerality, and the spiritual—all to be cultivated in activities like *Treaty*—is, on the one functionalist hand, to protect from unknown unknowns through flex and flux, while on the other (and less functionally), to remind us why our lives are worth living.

Conclusion

We have reported on the first phase of the *Treaty* project. The project culminates with a multispecies *Treaty of Finsbury Park*, which includes an attempt to create a consensus on the 'rights' of multispecies park users and dwellers at a time when rapid climate change will be affecting the habitats of the park, just as it is—more imperceptibly—now. It works kindly with its strange more-than-human relations. It promises us cities where life is more important than data—be that the life of a bee, dog, squirrel, or blade of grass—and where quality (and wanting to live 'here') takes precedence over control. If we are to overcome the challenges facing our neighbourhoods and our planet, it will be with these charms, which bring us together and make us care, not the efficiency model that underpins smartness and the engineering paradigms of the cities that are beholden to it.

As with other work focused on multispecies communication and justice (e.g., Pitt 2015; Houston et al. 2023), *Treaty* acknowledges the limits of experiencing more-than-human perspectives inside human bodies, inside the very human practice of LARPing. Yet perhaps this ultimate inaccessibility is the overall point of the project. We can never create multispecies justice since justice remains a very human concept. In our design of smart urban green spaces, we can be 'justice-seeking'. This may be uncomfortable for smart-city stakeholders to embrace (in commercial rather than playful contexts), but it must be central to the design of transformative futures.

Acknowledgments

The CreaTures project received funding from the European Union's Horizon 2020 research and innovation programme under grant agreement no. 870759. The content presented in this document represents the views of the authors, and the European Commission has no liability in respect of the content.

Note

1. Furtherfield originally collaborated with Cade Diehm of New Design Congress on the concept and online version of *Treaty.*

References

Bardzell, J., Bardzell, S., & Light, A. (2021). Wanting to live here: Design after anthropocentric functionalism. In Y. Kitamura, A. Quigley, K. Isbister, T. Igarashi, P. Bjørn, & S. Drucker (Eds.), *CHI '21: Proceedings of the 2021 CHI Conference on Human Factors in Computing Systems* (Article 293). https://doi.org/10.1145/3411764.3445167

Bennett, J. (2001). *The enchantment of modern life: Attachments, crossings, aesthetics.* Princeton University Press.

Berlant, L. (1998). Intimacy: A special issue. *Critical Inquiry, 24*(2), 281–288

Borjesson Rivera, M., Eriksson, E., & Wangel, J. (2015). ICT practices in smart sustainable cities: In the intersection of technological solutions and practices of everyday life. In V. Kvist Johannsen, S. Jensen, V. Wohlgemuth, C. Priest, & E. Eriksson (Eds.), *Proceedings of EnviroInfo and ICT for Sustainability 2015* (pp. 317–324). Atlantis Press. https://doi.org/10.2991/ict4s-env-15.2015.36

Clarke, R. E. (2020). Ministry of multispecies communications. In R. Wakkary, K. Andersen, W. Odom, A. Desjardins, & M. Graves Petersen (Eds.), *DIS '20 Companion: Companion Publication of the 2020 ACM Designing Interactive Systems Conference* (pp. 441–444). ACM. https://doi.org/10.1145/3393914.3395845

Costanza-Chock, S. (2020). *Design justice: Community-led practices to build the worlds we need.* MIT Press.

Forlano, L. (2016). Decentering the human in the design of collaborative cities. *DesignIssues, 32*(3), 42–54.

Gabrys, J. (2016). *Program earth: Environmental sensing technology and the making of a computational planet.* University of Minnesota Press.

Giddens, A. (1999, April 28). Family. Reith Lectures 1999: Runaway World. *BBC*. http://downloads.bbc.co.uk/rmhttp/radio4/transcripts/1999_reith4.pdf
Grossberg, L. (2002). Is there a fan in the house? The affective sensibility of fandom. In L. A. Lewis (Ed.), *The adoring audience: Fan culture and popular media* (pp. 50–65). Routledge.
Heathcote, D. (1984). *Collected writings on drama and education*. Heinemann Educational.
Heitlinger, S., Foth, M., Clarke, R., Di Salvo, C., Light, A., and Forlano, L. (2018). Avoiding ecocidal smart cities: Participatory design for more-than-human futures. In L. Huybrechts, M. Teli, A. Light, Y. Lee, C. Di Salvo, E. Grönvall, A. M. Kanstrup, K. Bødker (Eds.), *PDC '18: Proceedings of the 15th Participatory Design Conference: Short Papers, Situated Actions, Workshops and Tutorial*, Vol. 2 (Article 51). ACM. https://doi.org/10.1145/3210604.3210619
Heitlinger, S., Houston, L., Taylor, A., & Catlow, R. (2021). Algorithmic food justice: Co-designing more-than-human blockchain futures for the food commons. In Y. Kitamura, A. Quigley, K. Isbister, T. Igarashi, P. Bjørn, & S. Drucker (Eds.), *CHI '21: Proceedings of the 2021 CHI Conference on Human Factors in Computing Systems* (Article 305). ACM. https://dl.acm.org/doi/10.1145/3411764.3445655
Houston, L., Heitlinger, S., Catlow, R., & Taylor, A. (2023). Algorithmic food justice. In D. Papadopoulos, M. Puig de la Bellacasa, & M. Tacchetti (Eds.), *Ecological reparation* (pp. 379–396). Bristol University Press.
Jungnickel, K. (2014). *DIY WiFi: Re-imagining connectivity*. Palgrave Macmillan.
Kendon, M., McCarthy, M., Jevrejeva, S., Matthews, A., Sparks, T., & Garforth, J. (2021). State of the UK climate 2020. *International Journal of Climatology 41*(S2), 1–76. https://doi.org/10.1002/joc.7285
Light, A. (2021a). Not a research agenda for smart objects. In M. C. Rozendaal, B. Marenko, & W. Odom (Eds.), *Designing smart objects in everyday life: Intelligences, agencies, ecologies* (pp. 185–194). Bloomsbury.
Light, A. (2021b). Participative intimacy. *Light Stuff*. http://lightstuff.co.uk/participative-intimacy/
Light, A., Wolstenholme, R., & Twist, B. (2019). *Creative practice and transformations to sustainability: Insights from research*. Sussex Sustainability Research Programme.
Márquez Segura, E., Spiel, K., Johansson, K., Back, J., Toups, Z. O., Hammer, J., Waern, A., Tanenbaum, J., & Isbister, K. (2019). Larping (live action role playing) as an embodied design research method. In S. Harrison, S. Bardzell, C. Neustaedter, & D. Tatar (Eds.), *DIS '19 Companion: Companion Publication of the 2019 on Designing Interactive Systems Conference* (pp. 389–392). ACM. https://doi.org/10.1145/3301019.3320002
Mason, D., Wakeford, T., Wolstenholme, R., & Hielscher, S. (2018). *Creative practice and transformations to sustainability: Making and managing culture change*. UK Arts and Humanities Research Council. https://doi.org/10.13140/RG.2.2.10760.88321
McLaren, D., & Agyeman, J. (2015). *Sharing cities: A case for truly smart and sustainable cities*. The MIT Press.
Moreno, J. L. (1946). *Psychodrama, Vol. 1*. Beacon House.
Pitt, H. (2015). On showing and being shown plants—a guide to methods for more-than-human geography. *Area 47*(1), 48–55. https://doi.org/10.1111/area.12145
Pothong, K., Pschetz, L., Catlow, R., & Meiklejohn, S. (2021). Problematising transparency through LARP and deliberation. In W. Ju, L. Oehlberg, S. Follmer, S. Fox, & S. Kuznetsov (Eds.), *DIS '21: Proceedings of the 2021 ACM Designing Interactive Systems Conference* (pp. 1682–1694). ACM. http://doi.org/10.1145/3461778.3462120
Powell, Alison B. 2021 *Undoing optimization: Civic action in smart cities*. Yale University Press.
Rose, G., & Willis, A. (2019). Seeing the smart city on Twitter: Colour and the affective territories of becoming smart. *Environment and Planning D: Society and Space, 37*(3), 411–427. https://doi.org/10.1177/0263775818771080
Sertaç S., & Zengin, A. (2015). Why revisit intimacy? *Cambridge Journal of Anthropology, 33*(2), 20–25.
Shelton, T., Zook, M., & Wiig, A. (2015). The 'actually existing smart city'. *Cambridge Journal of Regions, Economy and Society 8*(1), 13–25.

Tomitsch, M., Fredericks, J., Vo, D., Frawley, J., & Foth, M. (2021). Non-human personas: Including nature in the participatory design of smart cities. *Interaction Design and Architecture(s)—IxD&A, 50*, 102–130.

Veselova, E., & Gaziulusoy, I. (2021). When a tree is also a multispecies collective, a photosynthesis process and a carbon cycle: A systemic typology of natural nonhuman stakeholders when designing for sustainability. In J. C. Diehl, N. Tromp. & M. van der Bijl-Brouwer (Eds.), *RSD10: Proceedings of Relating Systems Thinking and Design* (pp. 25–35). SDA.

Westerlaken, M. (2021). It matters what designs design designs: Speculations on multispecies worlding, *Global Discourse, 11*(1–2), 137–155.

15
More-than-Human Biographies
Designing for their Endings

Ron Wakkary

This chapter is an exercise in *designing-with* (Wakkary 2021). Designing-with is a reworking of design that foregrounds relationality and shared agencies in more-than-human worlds. The approach articulates a practice of designing in which humans are neither central nor exceptional but are ecologically interdependent with the non-human world. Designing-with creates *things*. Things are non-humans, made by both humans and non-humans. And so, in writing about things, it is unsurprising that a bird feeder, a water-lily pond, a concrete sink, traffic lights, cars, bicycles, gutter spouts, a peanut butter shrub, zoning by-laws, policies, and mobile phones populate this chapter. Despite the convenience of naming things as if they are self-contained and fixed, things are fluid, and without distinct boundaries given they are fundamentally relational. Things are co-constituted, meaning they only make sense in relation to other things and the multiple species worlds they cohabit. And so also present in this chapter are Northwestern crows, New Caledonian crows, Hawaiian crows, African elephants, *Mansonia* mosquitoes, humans, comet goldfish, racoons, blue mussels, hazelnuts, climbing hydrangea, and Wanvisa water lilies. Some of the naming of these living beings preceded settler occupations, so the Northwestern crow is first known as *spó*:l in the Coast Salish dialect of Halq̓eméylem, on whose unceded lands I am on as I write, or the Hawaiian crow is first known as *alalā* and the elephant is *oldome* in Maa, the language of the Maasai. In this more-than-human world there are no universalities underlying concepts like humans or crows despite what the language suggests. Rather, in its place are differences grounded in the intersectionalities of race, colonisation, and gender in human life, such as my presence as a settler immigrant from a family of Javanese, Sundanese, and Menadonese. And situatedness such as the very Northwestern crows who nest during breeding season in our neighbourhood set at the city limits of a century ago, in our backyard, perched in the gutter spouts of our neighbours or in our peanut butter shrub.

The discussion in this chapter is about designing-with and cities. In designing-with, a designer is not exclusively human but is an assembly of humans and non-humans in which each have qualities of agency or agentic capacities, and so together, or collectively, they design (Wakkary 2021). A designer is also co-constituted, meaning that it only makes sense in relation to the things it creates and how, together, designer and thing cohabit more-than-human worlds. In designing-with, the concept of *biography* accounts for this co-constitution of designer and thing. A biography is an identifiable human and non-human life force (creative entity) that constructs and inscribes itself into the world. Further, the notion of a biography is prescriptive: it

Ron Wakkary, *More-than-Human Biographies*. In: *Designing More-than-Human Smart Cities*. Edited by: Sara Heitlinger, Marcus Foth, and Rachel Clarke, Oxford University Press. © Oxford University Press (2024).
DOI: 10.1093/9780191980060.003.0017

aims to make clear that the good in designing things is the cohabiting of the designer and thing in a shared world that is accountable for what it inscribes and leaves behind (Wakkary 2021). For example, the *Bag with handle of weldable plastic material* or more commonly, the plastic bag, patented in 1965 by the industrial designer Sten Gustaf Thulin and the company Celloplast, became a global product of convenience but also one of ongoing colossal waste and toxicity, environmental injustices, and belated legislations to curb its use. All of this together, form the shared biography of the plastic bag, Thulin, and Celloplast (Thulin 1965). We may be closing in on the end of the plastic bag biography—yet its last chapter has the resiliency to last for up to a thousand years, only to result in microplastics that will never decompose (Stevens 2001). Other biographies, extant ones like a traffic intersection, are very much in the process of being written and rewritten.

The concept of biography conceptualises a practice of accountability by identifying the relations that gather to create a thing and keeping these relations, and new ones that form, visible throughout the life of the biography through to its end. This concept readily applies to things that can come to constitute cities. An important feature of biographies is that it makes explicit that things have endings long after their human use and value. This contrasts with the blinding attention given by designers to the beginning of a thing, its newness or perpetual promise of human value—an imaginary of progress that hides and forestalls the eventual ending of things. This understanding of biography is best acted upon while making or remaking things, well before their endings, so in essence things can be designed for their ending rather than their beginnings as a strategy to better cohabit. While arguably clear as a concept, there is much work to be done to reveal, articulate, and understand biographies better, especially their endings. This chapter sets out to do that by seeing things as fragile, breaking down, and without human value to make visible their endings or signalling of their end.

The aims of this chapter are twofold. First, I want to extend the idea of biographies, with particular attention given to their endings, to understand things and cities in more-than-human terms. Second, the chapter aims to get a glimpse of futures with respect to cities; not through the imaginary of human innovation and progress, but rather to trace possible futures as endings that highlight the non-human temporalities and non-human futures that are a part of the biographies of things.

This attention to the end of biographies comes with the commitment to more-than-human worlds that require care, attention, and attunement to non-human agencies, multi-species, and non-human temporalities that constitute and inform things and their gatherings. Gathering is what others have called geo-graphs (Sundberg 2014), assemblages (Deleuze & Guattari 1987), and networks (Latour 2007) and in designing-with refer to the coming together of humans and non-humans to design a particular thing or to consider designing (Wakkary 2021).

More-than-human worlds epistemologies have long been central to and are ongoing within Indigenous thinking and ways of knowing (Lewis et al. 2018; Tuhiwai Smith 2021) and much more recently in Western European thinking (e.g., Latour 1999; Haraway 2003; Braidotti 2013; Puig de la Bellacasa 2017). Further, it is important to hold more-than-human thinking to its commitments and goals of expansiveness and pluriversality through decolonial approaches and critical Indigenous scholarship such as the work of Vanessa Watts (2013), Juanita Sundberg (2014), Joanne Todd (2015), and others. More-than-human approaches have been applied to understanding or conceptualising cities, including cities as multispecies configurations that raise deeper questions of sustainability (Fieuw et al. 2022), strongly question the planning of cities around the ontological exceptionalism of humans and the need for human and non-human co-production (Houston et al. 2018), all of which calls for decentring the human in the making of cities (Forlano 2016). Within more-than-human and human-centred thinking, grasping a metaphor for the complex entanglements that make cities is an ongoing effort.

The philosopher Graham Harman (2016) argues a city is an enduring ontological object that cannot be reduced to its components of people, culture, and infrastructure that are always changing. The architect and design theorist Christopher Alexander (2015) argued a city is a 'complex fabric' or a semi-lattice, a complicated mathematical abstraction that sees a well-designed city as sets of overlapping structures rather than a centralised pattern like a tree. The design and media theorist Shannon Mattern (2021) updates and extends Alexander in arguing that a 'city is not a computer'. She counters and critiques the appropriation of Alexander's semilattice city into a networked and algorithmic city, a metaphor that lurks behind every variation of the idea of the 'smart city' (see Eremia et al. 2017). Mattern reclaims Alexander by ironically reinvoking the tree metaphor as a corrective to the city as a metaphorical computer. She offers 'grafting' as a way to see how independent and local structures attach themselves onto other structures in ways that decentralise and hybridise. Grafting is a technique in which tissues of plants are joined to grow together, like grafting a branch from one tree onto another. This chapter also explores the idea of a decentralised city but as a collection of biographies. The idea fits in part with Mattern's observation of city administrators and corporate partners '*grafting* twenty-first-century "smartness" onto existing urban scaffolds and substrates' like attaching sensors and cameras to legacy infrastructures such as utility poles and traffic signals (Mattern 2021, p.5). I see this 'grafting' and want to investigate it as different biographies, like what comes together to form a water-lily pond or a traffic intersection, and in turn parts of a city. More apt descriptively is the metaphor of a braid offered by Robin Wall Kimmerer (Kimmerer 2015). For Kimmerer, her braid of stories is the coming together of Indigenous ways of knowing, scientific knowledge, and her story as an Anishinabekwe scientist to address what matters most. In this chapter, I humbly borrow the braid as a heterogeneous gathering as an ongoing life of a place, a coming together to form a biography, and the braiding of different biographies to make and unmake a city in ways that matter.

The Biography of a Water-Lily Pond

Last summer, I created a water-lily pond in my backyard; unfortunately, it lasted no more than a week. I say I created it, but in fact there were many humans and non-humans who gathered to make (and unmake) the water-lily pond with me. I say 'pond' when it was a concrete sink of less than a meter squared and half a meter deep that contained the water, soil, pottery shards, gravel, rocks, and two Wanvisa water lilies. The sink came with our house that dates to 1909. So, both the house and the sink are quite old by Pacific Northwest standards. Sometime ago, my partner, Resja and I hauled the sink from the dirt floor basement of our house into the garden. It is a double basin concrete sink once used for laundry that now sits at the foot of the small deck that extends from the main floor of the house. In one basin is soil, a fern, and a climbing hydrangea. In the other, for a time, were water and water lilies.

Wanvisa water lilies are small but hearty water plants that survive year-round in the Pacific Northwest. I plugged the sink basin for the 'pond' and purchased the lilies from our local nursery. The lilies sat on shards of pottery, rocks, and gravel, so they just broke the water surface. In a matter of days, I could see *Mansonia* mosquito larvae wriggling just below the surface of the water. The mosquito eggs could have come with the lilies or were already in the sink. It would be a matter of days before they would become adults. The difference between a water-lily pond and a mosquito hatchery is no doubt a very blurry line. Not wanting to breed *Mansonia* mosquitoes or any mosquitoes, the options were to install a water bubbler that disturbed the eggs but not the lilies, use a water dunk, which is a chemical pesticide to kill the larvae, or add fish like comet goldfish to my pond that would feed on the larvae. I did not want to use pesticides for all the obvious reasons.[1]

My partner Resja likes to feed the crows, who are often around our house. Normally, all the Northwestern crows in the city roost together a few kilometres from where we live. This is a daily migration, so come evening time our sky is filled with murders of crows from all over the city flying to their roost. During the day, the crows tend to return to the same place and during the breeding season, they forego their city-wide migration to roost nearby with their young. Whether they reside only in the day or evenings, too, our backyard is home to resident Northwestern crows. Resja calls the male crow, Cy, after the painter Cy Twombly. At first, Resja would place dry cat food on the railing of our deck for Cy, his mate, and younger crows (see Figure 15.1). On occasion, other crows would also come by. While feeding, they often knocked food off the railing that would at nighttime attract raccoons looking for leftovers. To remedy the situation, my son Andre made a crow-feeder with more surface area than the deck railing. The crow feeder was attached to a post of the deck, about three metres directly above the concrete sink. And as it turns out, the crows would still knock food off the feeder and into the water-lily pond.

To 'solve' the *Mansonia* mosquito larvae problem, I purchased three comet goldfish that are typically sold as food for larger fish. I thought it was the perfect solution. Not only would the goldfish eat the larvae when they hatched, but during dormant periods, they would be fed by the leftover dried cat food that fell from the feeder each time the crows were fed. The water-lily pond was a gathering of two Wanvisa water lilies, three comet goldfish, a concrete sink, water, pottery shards, rocks, gravel, short-lived mosquito larvae, and spilled cat-food-cum-crow-food (see Figure 15.2).

However, this was not the final equilibrium of this gathering. More would gather in the biography of the water-lily pond. And it was by no means the 'perfect solution', at least not from my human perspective. It was the perfect solution for the family of racoons that visited nightly. The five toes of a racoon's front paws are quite dexterous, so they can easily grasp objects like doorknobs, latches, lids, pottery shards, rocks, potted water plants, and fish. A racoon's keenest sense is its touch, as its front paws

Figure 15.1 Northwestern Crow we call Cy, on our deck railing

Photo by the author.

are very sensitive. And, as I learned later, the sensitivity of its paws increased when underwater such that, when possible, racoons will examine objects in water.

One further bit of information about racoons necessary to understanding this biography is that they are omnivores.

No doubt, you the reader are far ahead of what I am about to write. During the week of the water-lily pond biography, after the goldfish became part of the pond, I awoke each morning to one devastating scene after another within the basin of the concrete sink. In the sink were remnants of whatever existential drama played out the night before. The first morning, the Wanvisa water lilies were uprooted or clearly moved, the pottery shards were moved aside, and I could only see two of the comet goldfish in the muddied water. At the time, I did not fully suspect the racoons. I spent the next day adding large flagstones of Pennsylvania Sandstone to better anchor the potted roots of the lilies and create hiding spaces for the fish. And each morning the devastation was even worse, as there seemed to be no rock too heavy or large to be turned over. The Wanvisa water lilies appeared as if they were plucked out of the water, roots and all, closely scrutinised, then dropped back in the sink. The goldfish were eventually eaten, yet even still each morning the lilies were uprooted, scrutinised, and left barely alive. Even without the fish, the racoons would hunt and peck for morsels of cat food lying at the bottom of the pond and in the roots of the lilies. The lives of the water lilies and the comet goldfish were over. The water-lily pond was dead, and its biography had come to an end.

A designer biography in its most common parlance is easy to understand as biographical relations between designer and designed, like the architect Marina

Figure 15.2 The peak of the water lily pond biography.
Photo by the author.

Tabassum, who designed the Bait ur Rouf Mosque in Dhaka, Bangladesh (Griffiths 2017). There is also a biographical relation between me and the water-lily pond. And unlike the Bait ur Rouf Mosque, the water-lily pond is only known by my family and as a backyard catastrophe, brought up over dinner for a good laugh. However, in designing-with, a biography is much more. In this meaning of a biography, the water-lily pond is a thing. Unlike Harman (2018) and his philosophy known as *object oriented ontology*, I don't look upon the water-lily pond as an ontological object distinct from the material effects it has on the world. Though like Harman, I see the water-lily pond as more than its components, what in a biography would be seen as a gathering or assembly. As I have shown, the biography gathered many humans and non-humans in its making or coming into being in the world. But what is important, with respect to the designing-with of the pond, are the relations between what gathered to make it and what effects or agentic forces were at work in this collective of humans and non-humans. That is designing-with water, Wanvisa water lilies, *Mansonia* larvae, Northwestern crows, crow feeder, concrete sink, and so on to produce the water-lily pond. Each of these influenced the outcome, pushing the design in different directions and creating new outcomes, like the addition of comet goldfish and hiding places for the fish. These are forms of non-human agentic forces that I'll elaborate on further in the chapter. For now, the biography reveals the relationalities at work in designing and an expansive understanding of what or who is designing. While the designer is the collective gathering, in designing-with terms, I hold a special place as a speaking subject, the key human actor in the assembly of the water-lily pond. I have language that is shaped by my particular situation and history, and can rationalise the gathering to others and be at the origins of the biography: 'Wouldn't it be great if we had a water-lily pond in that old concrete sink in the garden?' As the *speaking subject*, I am accountable for mobilising the gathering, getting others—especially non-humans—to participate in the making of the thing, and for dissuading others from joining the gathering, like the *Mansonia* larvae. This requires intense listening and striving for other intimate connections. As the speaking subject, I have the dubious role of speaking on behalf of the assembly, though I could never be sure if I was speaking for them or for me.

The short life of the biography of the water-lily pond allows the retelling of its story and to see the dynamics and complex gathering before it became too rich and entangled to ever tell properly. I can account for how it inscribed itself in the world, becoming part of the urban ecology of our backyard and a family project of kinship across species. In this sense, its effects were minimal or largely compatible with whatever else it cohabited with during the week. The story also includes the end of the biography and what is left behind. Its end, in part, was a result of belonging to an urban ecology that includes racoons. It is not that the racoons ended the thing, but rather that the overall agentic forces at work created the outcome and brought the racoons to the gathering. What did it leave behind? Given that I did not use pesticides, the ongoing effect of the water-lily pond is negligible. The ravaged lilies dried up and were thrown on the compost. The water drained into the soil. The Pennsylvania Sandstone and pottery shards were redistributed in the garden and the concrete sink remains, partly filled with gravel and crow food (that the raccoons still eat). Interestingly, the concrete sink is its own biography, over a hundred years old, that was grafted onto the temporary water-lily pond in line with Mattern's (2021) tree thinking. It remains, perhaps, to be a legacy addition in another biography, not unlike old utility poles or other legacy infrastructures of a city. Throughout this episode, the resident crows, incidental but key actors in the biography, observed the life of the water-lily pond from above, involved but unconcerned.

The Biography of a Traffic Intersection

Northwestern crows feed on blue mussels. In Vancouver, near the water, I often see broken mussel shells that have been dropped by crows onto rocks, sidewalks, or roads, so they can get at the protein inside. Similarly, across the Pacific Ocean in Sendai, Japan, Carrion crows have been observed dropping or placing walnuts in traffic intersections to be run over by cars to be cracked open and eaten (Nihei & Higuchi 2001). Crows are well known for their resourcefulness to adapt to urban environments and incorporate things, such as the toolmaking proficiency of New Caledonian crows (Jelbert et al. 2018). These are examples of natureculture and the idea that human and non-human animals are 'prosthetic creatures' (Wolfe 2010). Nihei and Higuchi claim that the walnut-cracking routines of Carrion crows began in the 1970s in Sendai at an intersection near a driving school and spread from there (Nihei & Higuchi 2001). I now turn my attention toward another intersection that is in The Netherlands that also gathers car traffic lights, pedestrian traffic lights, bicycle traffic lights, bicycles, cars, mobile phones, drivers, pedestrians, and cyclists. In all likelihood, at times, the odd crow may well have perched on the traffic lights in this intersection. The biography of the water-lily pond was clearly vital, especially since it gathered non-humans that were very much alive in the biological sense. However, in this biography of a traffic intersection, I can show how a biography can be equally animated by non-human forces that do not require biological life.

In 2017, in the town of Bodegraven in The Netherlands, a prototype called +Lichtlijn (Ricker 2017) was installed at the intersection of Goudseweg and Vrije Nesse (see Figure 15.3). The system embeds LED strips in the sidewalk that are synchronised with the existing traffic light system. +Lichtlijn is at the right angle for mobile phone users who, while looking down at their phones, can see the traffic signal within their line of sight. The concept came under criticism from the Veilig Verkeer Nederland (Safe Traffic Netherlands) for 'rewarding bad behaviours' that can be assumed to be the dangers of technology overuse (Scully 2017). However, the intersection, like other traffic intersections, in designing-with is seen as a co-constitution

Figure 15.3 +Lichtlijn by HIG Traffic Systems in Bodegraven, Netherlands

Source: Photo by Joost Hoving Fotographie.

through technological use that does not separate us from technology; it is what Donna Haraway (1985) sees as cyborg relations in which the boundaries between humans and technologies break down. In the context of a biography, +Lichtlijn helps to reveal how a traffic intersection redesigns itself and inscribes itself into the world through the agency of inert materials, technologies, and things themselves.

So far in this chapter, I have used phrases like 'non-human agency' or 'agentic forces'. In designing-with, the specific term is *agentic capacities* (Wakkary 2021). This concept draws heavily on Jane Bennett's description of non-human agency as a matter of affects rather than consciousness. Bennett in turn draws on the work of Diana Coole (2005), who investigated the idea of distributed agencies that resulted in political actions. Agentic capacity can be described as having different qualities such as *efficacy* and *trajectory* (Bennett 2010, p.31).

Efficacy is the creative force of agency, the ability to create new things; trajectory is the direction of the force, a movement or progression without suggesting 'purposiveness'. In the biography of the water-lily pond, I described how the relations between those that gathered fostered a trajectory that moved the concerns in the making of the water-lily pond in one direction or another.

From creating a water habitat for the lilies to working with the birth and feeding cycles of mosquitoes and goldfish. And how the efficacy of the agentic capacities created new participants and new configurations like the comet goldfish and stone hiding places for them.

Thinking about this in relation to the traffic intersection in Bodegraven, the addition of the mobile phone user to the gathering brought its own agentic capacities to the biography that in many respects added to a trajectory, a direction that in a sense precipitated the +Lichtlijn and it became a matter of efficacy, the creation of something new. However, in the ongoing biography of the intersection and its past, how different is this from creating traffic lights for pedestrians and cyclists in addition to lights for cars? Designing-with speaks to another agentic capacity drawn from Bennett's (2010) descriptions of *causality*. Here Bennett refers to Hannah Arendt's (1951) distinction between 'origins' and 'causes'. With agentic capacities, there is no linear cause and effect; rather, agency plays a role at the origins of an effect, which can be quite indeterminate (Bennett 2010, pp.33–34). As I described earlier with the water-lily pond, I was at the origin as the speaking subject of that biography. The same can be said about HIG Systems, who are at the origins of the +Lichtlijn as the speaking subject. But unlike the simplicity of the water-lily pond, the +Lichtlijn is taken up into the larger assembly or biography of the traffic intersection of Goudseweg and Vrije Nesse. As Mattern would say, +Lichtlijn has been grafted on to the existing configurations or another biography to hybridise and become a part of it. HIG Systems is one speaking subject in a past of multiple speaking subjects that were at the origins and spoke on behalf of things like the pedestrian or cyclist traffic lights.

The French philosopher of technology, Gilbert Simondon (1958/2017), would describe this coming into being of the traffic intersection biography as the *concretisation* of a technical object. For Simondon, a technical object originates as an immature invention that iterates to become more refined and concretises or comes into being in ways not foreseen by the human designer at the origin. The refinements are driven by the technical relations between non-human components, more so than human creativity or decision-making. A given part or change in a part simply requires another specific part to keep the whole functioning. Simondon calls this form of iteration the 'condensing' of the technical object in a way that intensifies or creates new functionalities (+Lichtlijn or audio signals for the blind and visually impaired who are part of the gathering at the intersection) while simultaneously simplifying and reducing the object to essential components or relations. In this way, the technical object or thing evolves almost on its own.

Biographies are not equal gatherings of humans and non-humans. Shifting powers were evident between the Wanvisa water lilies, racoons, and comet goldfish in the water-lily pond biography. It is clear that at the intersection of Goudseweg and Vrije Nesse, the driver and car are dominant, and the gathering organises around this dominance. Seeing +Lichtlijn as a matter of encouraging technology overuse overlooks the larger gathering or biography it has become a part of. In these wider relations, the moving car poses an immediate existential threat to a mobile phone user of being in a fatal accident—far greater than an addiction to Instagram. The traffic light system of car signals, bicycle signals, pedestrian signals, and mobile phone user signals are militating against the dominance and dangers of the driver and car. The car dominates in other ways as well, as a matter of consumption, it consumes vast amounts of non-humans as extracted resources and further generates vast amounts of carbon dioxide (CO_2) and nitrogen dioxide.

The privileging of certain relations over others in a biography offers insights into the political nature of things designed or what Latour refers to a thingpolitics (Latour 2005), in which things gather matters of concern. Matters of concern are differences that are to be negotiated and possibly addressed. In the water-lily pond, the choice to avoid pesticides did not need to be negotiated, but if it did, the municipal by-laws regulating pesticide use in Vancouver would become part of the gathering. Some may have reflected on or even objected to the marginalised set of relations concerning the non-human animals that gathered in the biography. The politics of these relations also offer a way to consider the ending of a biography like a traffic intersection. This negotiation of the matters of concern of a biography can come by design, political action, governance, or some combination, any of which can intervene to dramatically shift the dynamics and privileged relations. In The Netherlands, the Stop de Kindermoord [Stop the murder of children] movement in the 1970s led to the first city-wide infrastructure of cycling paths that are now largely taken for granted across the whole country (van der Zee 2015), and so shifting the political relations between cyclists and drivers. Some twenty years ago, the socialist mayor of Pontevedra asked the question: 'How can it be that private property—the car—occupies the public space?' and so banned cars from the city centre and imposed severe traffic restrictions elsewhere (Burgen 2018). It is now commonplace for European cities to create low-emission zones that shift the balance away from cars such that biographies, like those at the intersection of Goudseweg and Vrije Nesse, can become obsolete or unwanted (Jones 2018). The COVID-19 pandemic—a massive human–non-human commingling—has usurped countless human and technical configurations; the surrendering of car infrastructure to pedestrians to allow for two-metre physical distancing between people is creating a collapse in carbon output that while it may be temporary, it has created a new trajectory in the biographies of a city (Batty 2020).

A City as a Collection of Biographies and Constituencies

The city council of Vancouver passed a motion to create a by-law to prohibit intentional feeding of wildlife, including crows. The motion was passed just prior to the making of the water-lily pond. I only learned this recently, well after the end of the water-lily pond. Such by-laws exist elsewhere, including in Victoria, a neighbouring city. The motion 'B.6 Don't Feed the Wildlife' makes clear that the speaking subject (me) is never aware of all the non-humans including municipal regulations that gather in a biography. Nonetheless, this matter of concern, so clearly expressed, cast doubts on the kinship practice of my family feeding Cy and his family. The concerns of the motion and most discussions on such human interventions include the health and wellbeing of the animals as well as the risk of cross-species disease or zoonotic diseases, like avian flus or coronaviruses. Conservationists have long argued that human interventions can be detrimental to animals' nutritional physiology (see Birnie-Gauvin et al. 2017) and can come at a wider ecological cost (see Dunkley & Cattet 2003). While the general reality portrayed here is not disputed and has much practical merit, questions remain, such as what is the difference between human intervention and human relations with non-human animals?

Charis Thompson makes this point in her study of elephant conservationists in Kenya's Amboseli National Park (Thompson 2002) in which biologists are caught in competing notions of nature that ultimately question what or who are the elephants that are being conserved. The competing worldviews come down to the degree to which conservation is seen as a relational concern or not. Thompson depicts one group of conservationists who see the African elephant in its biological essence, with limited ecological relationships, and requiring separation from humans and containment within the boundaries of the park (excluded from the boundaries of a city) to be conserved and recover their naturalness. While another group sees the elephant as part of a broad set of ecological relations that includes humans, arguing that the elephants need to be allowed to travel their migration paths beyond the park that includes cohabiting and interchange with the Maasai peoples whose territories include that of the park and the elephant migration paths. Thompson sides with the 'relationalists', seeing the need for conservation 'to be responsive to and expressed within the existing political potentialities' (Thompson 2002, p.167).

Thom van Dooren, in his studies of the conservation of the Hawaiian crow or *alalā*, encounters similar issues that he sees as authenticity, or what is an authentic crow (van Dooren 2016)? The alalā are extinct, save for the hundred or so that are in captivity, as part of an effort to eventually restore them to their original habitats. Like Thompson, van Dooren sees the successful return of the alalā happening in a context in which emergence is accounted for across human and non-human divides. He cites the example of one conservationist, who would like to see a 'soft release' of the alalā in which the aviary remains open for a period as a reliable locale for food. As part of monitoring the released crows, food might be dispensed in bowls at the trunks of the trees where they are nesting when offspring are born, and even antibiotic treatments may be necessary at times. Van Dooren makes clear that this is a minority position among the biologists, as many would oppose this degree of intervention and human–non-human relationship. However, there is a clear survival argument for this type of soft release as the environment has changed since the alalā became extinct, in which commingling with humans is unavoidable, new diseases have developed, and a range of new predators have emerged.

On a philosophical level, van Dooren argues for what he sees as the 'performative identity' of the alalā rather than an imagined 'authentic crow' of the past:

> The simple fact of inter-generational difference cannot be so easily read as the 'loss' of anything, certainly not an ideal authentic state. Instead, our attention is drawn towards the agency of non-humans in the shaping of their own individual species identities: as crows conduct experiments in emergent forms of crow-ness. Far from any singular telos, individuals and species are engaged in multiple forms of becoming, all of them reiterative and ongoing, all of them co-constitutive and collaborative (even if unequal) (van Dooren 2016, p.38)

Seeing the identity of crows as performative, he draws on Karen Barad's (2003) idea of 'posthumanist performativity' in which materiality and material bodies are iteratively and reiteratively produced. For Barad, this process of materialisation is one in which the separate categories of humans and non-humans are questioned. Not unlike Haraway's (1994) 'materialised refiguration' that is emblematic in the game of cat's cradle—a game in which string figures, patterns of looped and knotted string, are created by passing a loop of string back and forth between the hands and fingers of multiple players. The game creates the string figure by maintaining the pattern while simultaneously experimenting with new possibilities and doing so collectively. For Haraway, it is a metaphor for non-human kinship. It is a heterogeneous collective that works across species and non-humans, knotted, and entangled in ongoing configurations and *refigurations*. It is a collective self-formation or collectively producing entity that she refers to as *sympoiesis*, a boundaryless form of autopoeisis (Haraway 2016). Not unlike Kimmerer's description of braiding sweetgrass that is best done with another. Braiding also suggests time and performativity as a journey of reciprocity as the braid gets finer and thinner as it continues until it is down to individual blades of grass that are tied off together (Kimmerer 2015). Van Dooren assigns this performativity to the biological identity of the crow that is co-constituted in its environments and through its relations with others and through time. This is the same performativity of biographies. As previously discussed, a biography is an ongoing process of inscribing and reinscribing itself, as with the traffic intersection in Bodegraven or the concrete sink in my backyard. The performativity of biographies means that it also includes the historical not unlike the crows and their past, and hence political processes that iteratively form and reform the speaking subjects and the ongoing thing. Further, biographies like the water-lily pond or the Bodegraven traffic intersection do not simply appear; rather, they emerge from the heterogeneous participants that hold up the strings in Haraway's cat's cradle or Kimmerer's blades of sweetgrass. In designing-with, this is referred to as a *constituency*.

A constituency is the assembly of humans and non-humans from which designers of things are gathered to go on to design things and form biographies (Wakkary 2021). To imagine a constituency when thinking about cities is to start with thinking of the sociomaterial interdependencies that make up cities. These include human actors (e.g., speaking subjects, residents, families, politicians, immigrant settlers, Indigenous peoples, business people, activists, unhoused, city workers, and so on, that are racialised and intersectional) as well as non-human actors (e.g., neighbourhoods, electricity, sewage, materials, technologies, houses, buildings, parks, homeless shelters, walk-in medical clinics, non-human animals, plant life, organisations, institutions, activist groups, by-laws, cars, bicycles, sidewalks, speed bumps, crosswalks, rain, wind). These interdependencies form the geographies or locations that have their own histories and geopolitics, from which constituencies actively gather. Juanita Sundberg (2014), informed by the Zapatista principle of walking with, carefully describes such *geo-graphs* (what I call gatherings) as situated and fostering of 'multi-epistemic literacy' and political engagement. Further, in designing-with, a gathering is constituted through an ongoing intention to design something. That is, a gathering to negotiate and consider the making of things and assembling the designer before things are made or biographies form. My backyard garden is the constituency from which the water-lily pond biography was formed.

The biography can be said to be a product or an outcome of the constituency. Within this gathering of the garden, which has spawned other biographies such as our vegetable garden, there are the humans and non-humans assembled, some of which were needed to participate in the making of the water-lily pond, others who did not participate (or who I did not want to participate), and others that had to be brought into the constituency, such as the water lilies and comet goldfish. Constituencies are where the politics and intentionalities are negotiated such as cities as settler occupations, plots of land divided as settler properties, pesticide-free growing, planting of only local plants, and organic fertilisers. The constituency is not a physically bound place, and as is evident in the political agreements that gather on their own in our backyard constituency such as unceded territories, pesticide by-laws, and a wildlife feeding motion for a by-law.

If a city is a braiding of biographies, to accept the gift of the metaphor from Kimmerer (2015), it is also a braiding of constituencies that precede biographies. Further, constituencies are not only the collectives in which biographies form, but also the collectives in which they end. The water-lily pond ended within the constituency it began, in my backyard, whereas the Bodegraven traffic intersection will be inherited by other constituencies when it comes to an end, and the plastic bag biography is inherited or 'exported' to constituencies unwillingly, unknowingly, and exploitatively as waste when it ends.

The Endings of Biographies

The end of the water-lily pond biography is a story of fragility. My backyard constituency is relatively stable for the Northwestern crows, the concrete sink, the climbing hydrangea, and the racoons but less so for Wanvisa water lilies. This contrast between fragility and stability is evident in how short the biography lasted and how easily its gathering dispersed and found places in other gatherings in the backyard such as compost; and how easily the biological lives of the lilies, mosquito larvae, and fish came to an end. Of course, this contrast can only be drawn within the short time span of the water-lily pond, over time in relation to other gatherings my backyard could also be seen as fragile—perhaps at its end. Nevertheless, I told the story of the water-lily biography through what is called a *repertoire* in designing-with (Wakkary 2021).

Repertoires are the methods and positionalities by which speaking subjects seek ways to understand non-humans through listening and touching as well as speaking, to aid in their representation and participation in biographies and constituencies. Specifically, I utilised a repertoire called *noticing through fragility*, developed by Doenja Oogjes (Oogjes & Wakkary 2022). This repertoire of noticing draws on Anna Tsing's (2015) art of noticing. It focuses on precarity and disturbances to increase attention, to notice the relations between non-humans in non-anthropocentric ways to the extent that's possible. The method of noticing follows a particular non-human, like the Wanvisa water lilies, through its fragile relations with others in the gathering to draw out the relations and agentic capacities at work. The repertoire lends itself to events of fragility, in which relations are often tentative and uncertain.

As a braiding of biographies, cities are inscribed and reinscribed by such fragile biographies, such as temporary and ad hoc shelters for or by the unhoused. This example makes clear that the performativity of fragility is not enacted solely in the active undoing of the relations as with the failure of the water-lily pond, but also in the potential undoing or fragility as with ad hoc shelters. This constant potential to be fragile extends to traffic intersections like at Goudseweg and Vrije Nesse in Bodegraven. As described earlier, even ongoing biographies like traffic intersections or other forms of urban transportation can be undone by political and ideological change, whether by a grassroots movement like Stop de Kindermoord or through reclaiming of public property as in the city of Pontevedra (van der Zee 2015; Burgen 2018) or municipal by-laws to prevent the feeding of crows. Climate change and global pandemics also deftly strip away the certainties of biographies to reveal the possibility of underlying fragilities.

Biographies that endure despite the constant possibility of coming undone, are seen as stable, like the Bodegraven traffic intersection. The stability successfully masks the underlying fragility to the extent it makes things and biographies unnoticeable. Biographies become like infrastructure, submerged as a substrate upon which the daily life of humans and non-humans go about their business. Whether it is commuters getting to work or Carrion crows settling in to feast on walnuts. Stability fosters reliance, making many biographies unremarkable and invisible. However, as infrastructure studies show, stability is an effect that results from ongoing maintenance and repair that not only staves off potential fragility but attends to the related idea of breakdown. Ultimately, infrastructures fall prey to decay, ruin, and destruction (Steinhardt 2016). This holds clear lessons for the performativity of biographies and their end. Like infrastructures, a constant in the life of a biography is breakdown and repair, these are central and ongoing performances. The other lesson is that breakdown is a constant reminder, an abject reminder, of the inevitable decay or feeble resilience in the face of political or catastrophic forces that may cause a biography's abrupt end.

Breakdowns that necessitate repair are what makes stable biographies like infrastructures visible again. It is commonly understood among those who study infrastructures that it 'becomes visible upon breakdown' (Star & Ruhleder 1996, p.113). Steve Jackson (2014) goes so far as to say that repair offers an epistemic position from which technologies, infrastructures, and in our case things can be seen more clearly. Seeing breakdowns as part of the performativity of biographies opens it to the epistemological lens of repair. And in this chapter, we can extend this knowing to what makes a city. Traditionally, in what can be described as the 'dominant productivist imaginings of technology' (Jackson 2014, p.227), technologies like the +Lichtlijn are seen as innovative and progressive, intrinsically valuable by bringing the traffic intersection into a new and interconnected world—the very idea of a smart city. Conversely, seeing the world through repair, +Lichtlijn is the repair of a breaking down biography. The relations that make up the biography of the traffic intersection need being fixed, namely, the need to repair the relations with pedestrians that use mobile phones, which if left unrepaired means the traffic intersection is outmoded, failing to achieve its goal of minimising accidents, fatal and otherwise. Jackson would describe this as a 'constant process of fixing and reinvention, reconfiguring and reassembling into new combinations and new possibilities ... ' (Jackson 2014, p.222). This epistemological view moves past the occlusion of technological progression to better see the performative nature of biographies, in which repair keeps it alive and effective in the world. There is of course labour in repair (Llorente-González & Vence 2020), in the case of things this is aptly described by Hamid Ekbia and Bonnie Nardi (2017) as *heteromation*—labour divided between humans and machines done at the lowest costs to keep things running. If breakdowns make biographies visible again through repair, this reappearance is disruptive, unlike its first appearance as something new and innovative. Breakdown, as when a traffic signal fails, is disruptive. And if repair makes biographies visible again, it does so abjectly. Repair signifies ruin and so is best hidden from view, done during off-hours. Surely, breakdown withholds functionality and makes a thing unreliable, which is reason enough to be upset. Yet arguably, repair makes a thing visible in a way that disrupts the imaginaries of innovation and progress, as Jackson (2014) argues. More to the point, the abjection of repair and breakdown arises from the clarity that the biography will eventually end. The real emotions of despair caused by disrepair are the opposite of the gleeful fantasies of innovation and newness of a thing in perpetuity.

To best understand biographies is to shield them from the imaginaries of innovation and progress. In addition to keeping the end of things in sight, this shielding offers the additional gain of moving past narrowly anthropocentric perspectives. Things can certainly be described as the performances of humans and machines entangled together in a biography but can also be seen as competing or cooperating agencies across multiple species, that also shape or co-constitute what a thing is. Again, we can learn from infrastructures. Maan Barua (2021) offers a wider, more-than-human ontology, for understanding infrastructures. He describes three types of more-than-human infrastructures that also navigate fragility and breakdown: 1) *Repurposing infrastructures* such as termites that inhabit and enflesh infrastructures to construct habitats that require working with or against when it comes to maintenance and repair; 2) *Recombinant infrastructures* in which novel compositions form within estranged gatherings such as peppered moths, lichen, and sulphur dioxide from pollutants to thrive together in industrial towns; and 3) *Reconciliation infrastructures* that entails infrastructures that support and modulate non-human life engagements like green roofs and wildlife bridges (Barua 2021). These descriptions of more-than-human configurations can readily be applied to biographies.

They help articulate the role in the gatherings of the biographies I've described in this chapter, like the Northwestern crows repurposing of my backyard deck; Carrion Crows recombinant traffic intersection into a feeding locale; and the attempted reconciliation of comet goldfish in a water-lily pond.

I've described how the fragilities and breakdowns that occur throughout the life of biographies, and especially at their end, are often hidden or masked. A recurring theme is that, despite these attempts, these qualities that mark the end of biographies cannot be kept from view. This is also true of the remaining quality that signals the end of a biography: waste. Waste is very much an anthropocentric concept with the sole purpose of categorising things to be removed and excluded from human culture—to be removed from the city. Waste is defined by its exhaustion of value for humans such that it requires removal. In its desired form, it is a non-human ontology, in that its world relations are exclusively non-human once transformed into waste. In this anthropocentric sense, the end of the biography of the plastic bag is to strip it of its relations that make up the biography by transforming it from a thing into waste. As waste, it is no longer a bag; it is solely seen as waste material, specifically polyethylene. Ideally as waste, removed to a landfill it is expected to fragment into microplastics through photo and thermal oxidation, broken down by sunlight or heat in addition to mechanical movements of soil and various chemical reactions that contribute to its fragmentation (Canopoli et al. 2020).

In reality, landfills are not exclusively non-human, but rather very entangled with being human. Waste is never relieved of its human relations. This is most visible when considering the significant amounts of polyethylene waste that escapes landfills to participate in human and non-human ecologies, such as circulatory pathways of wind, rivers, and oceanic currents. Waste material settles alongside roads, shorelines, and gathers offshore and into the oceanic gyres across global transport routes like the Pacific Garbage Patch (Lebreton et al. 2018).

Polyethylene and other plastics reach the most remote places like mountaintops (Van Cauwenberghe et al. 2013; Free et al. 2014), though also the most biologically intimate human locales (we can assume non-human animals as well) by entering food chains (Barboza et al. 2018), to then enter the human body, including placentas (Ragusa et al. 2021), bloodstream (Leslie et al. 2022), and lungs (Amato-Lourenço et al. 2021). Waste and e-waste follow paths of inequity and oppression of being consumed in the Global North to be disposed of in the Global South, what Frey et al. (2018) describe as exploitative and unequal ecologies of exchange. Some argue that trade patterns show a lessening of exporting of waste from the Global North to the Global South (Lepawsky 2015) when in reality it may signal the rise in illegal trade of waste that goes unrecorded, particularly e-waste that is characterised by illicit, deceptive, and criminal practices of exploitation (Bedford et al. 2022). A practice that includes ontological sleights of hand in which waste is relabelled as 'second-hand' goods with some human value, so it can be exported widely only to become waste again with no human value on arrival in Asian and African countries (Bedford et al. 2022).

Biographies, seen through a relational understanding of waste in which waste remains entangled as both human and non-human, uncover inequities and exploitation as discussed above and can also reveal racial entanglements that are very much a part of biographies through to their end. Michelle Huang (2017) sees this relationality through her framework of *ecologies of entanglement* that are networks of circulation that make porous the boundaries between humans and their environment. The framework shifts attention toward the discursive and material relations that culturally produce forms, including racialised forms like Asian American. She critically examines this transpacific meaning by seriously including the role of the non-human Pacific Ocean and its waste that binds the transnationality of Asian Americans: 'Viewing the Great Pacific Garbage Patch as an ecology of entanglement means seeing *humans in the gyre* and the *gyre in the humans*' (Huang 2017, p.104). In other words, reclaiming the non-human ontology of waste into its relational ontology with humans. Huang sees in the ocean's plastic waste the opportunity to investigate how the racial form of Asian American materialises and circulates in the absence of racially identified human bodies. Things transmuted into the ontologies of plastic waste are removed from their origins, deracinated, to be seen to proliferate western shores and litter city streets, to migrate from the east in inevitable though unwanted ways. Plastics, like Asian Americans, are feared for their potential ubiquity though desired for their perceived mutability. For Huang, plastic is the model minority like Asians, 'foreign menace and diligent' (Huang 2017, p.108).

The Future of Biographies

That cities and things in cities take on racialised entanglements is not new, Langdon Winner (1980) long ago pointed out the racist politics of artefacts in city infrastructure. Rather, the contribution of this article is to show that a more-than-human view discloses ecologies of radically generous entanglements, diverse in their agencies, temporalities, and politics. Like the crows in this article, whether Northwestern crows perched on deck railings or Carrion crows on traffic signals, we are involved, certainly more concerned, but we are not the exclusive actors in determining the 'future' of cities.

The contribution of extending the idea of biographies, to pay particular attention to their endings, moves designing past the imaginary of progress and innovation. I aimed to make clear the capacities of non-human agencies and temporalities in designing. I wanted to detail how biographies inscribe themselves in a multispecies world and what is left behind in an abrupt fashion or slowly unfolding over countless generations of human life. Biographies also reveal the fragility, breakdown, and shifting ontologies of waste that are central to the making and remaking of things. The hope is that these disclosures shift attention toward the endings of what is made. That is to encourage us to start designing at the end, so to speak. To gather, to speak on behalf of a more-than-human assembly that designs endings as much as beginnings. To design an end is not to predict an ending, but rather to account for endings at the beginning.

A further contribution is to glimpse the futures of cities by tracing the myriad endings of its biographies of things. Throughout this article, I chose to see the city as a braiding of biographies. I aimed to find futures by tracing endings. And by doing so, shifting the understanding of cities from the algorithmic to the ecological. A city that gathers, grafts, grows, decays, breaks down, repairs, and ends. A city that is a political ecology revealed by tracing the endings. What this offers is the possibility to see the making of cities as both development and devolvement, making and unmaking, growth and degrowth, beginnings and endings.

Conclusion

In summary, the chapter offers a view of cities by paying close attention to how the biographies of things end. The hope is that to see the end of things more clearly, that is to privilege the ending of biographies, is a path to move beyond the privileging of human experience and use, as the lens by which things and cities are understood. Whether that means seeing things through the haptically sensitive wet paws of racoons or pandemic-induced traffic calming. This decentring of humans is not to erase human relations, but rather to emphasise the more expansive relationality of humans with the more-than-human world.

Another goal of the chapter was to get a glimpse of futures with respect to cities. Here again, following the ending of biographies is a way to trace possible futures or, more specifically, to trace the non-human temporalities of things. This means seeing futures as endings, to acknowledge and foreground that all things end but to also open up futures of cities to include non-human futures like the thousand years to fragment plastic or residing as waste in deterritorialised gyres of the Pacific Ocean. Additionally, biographies occur alongside each other along different temporalities whether as new, ongoing, or ending. Seeing a city as braided biographies is to see it as different temporalities braided together. In this respect, futures exist in trajectories of non-human agencies originating in the past, as well as in the present as futures deferred through successful repair or futures as endings that suddenly arrive as irreparable only to live on as waste.

The boundaries of cities are diffused temporally as well as geographically. They are hard to see and even harder to encapsulate as an abstract entity, which is why I approached cities through the particulars of my water-lily pond and a traffic intersection in Bodegraven. This also allowed me to trace the endings of biographies along the dimensions of fragility, breakdown, and waste that I saw as performativity, or the ongoing life of the ending and its continuance of matters of concerns, entanglements, and cohabitation.

Note

1. For a detailed discussion of the relationship between humans, cities, and mosquitoes, see the chapter by Jonathan Metzger and Jean Hillier in this same collection.

References

Alexander, C. (2015). *A city is not a tree* (50th anniversary ed). Sustasis Press.

Amato-Lourenço, L. F., Carvalho-Oliveira, R., Ribeiro Júnior, G., dos Santos Galvão, L., Augusto Ando, R., & Mauad, T. (2021). Presence of airborne microplastics in human lung tissue. *Journal of Hazardous Materials, 416*(August), 126124. https://doi.org/10.1016/j.jhazmat.2021.126124

Arendt, H. (1951). *The origins of totalitarianism*. Schocken.

Barad, K. (2003). Posthumanist performativity: Toward an understanding of how matter comes to matter. *Signs, 28*(3), 801–831. https://doi.org/10.1086/345321

Barboza, L. G. A., Vethaak, A. D., Lavorante, B. R. B. O., Lundebye, A-K., & Guilhermino, L. (2018). Marine microplastic Debris: An emerging issue for food security, food safety and human health. *Marine Pollution Bulletin, 133*(August), 336–348. https://doi.org/10.1016/j.marpolbul.2018.05.047

Barua, M. (2021). Infrastructure and non-human life: A wider ontology. *Progress in Human Geography, 45*(6), 1467–1489.

Batty, M. (2020). The Coronavirus crisis: What will the post-pandemic city look like? *Environment and Planning B: Urban Analytics and City Science, 47*(4), 547–552. https://doi.org/10.1177/2399808320926912

Bedford, L., Mann, M., Foth, M., & Walters, R. (2022). A post-capitalocentric critique of digital technology and environmental harm: New directions at the intersection of digital and green criminology. *International Journal for Crime, Justice and Social Democracy, 11*(1), 167–181. https://doi.org/10.5204/ijcjsd.2191.

Bennett, J. (2010). *Vibrant matter: A political ecology of things*. Duke University Press.

Birnie-Gauvin, K., Peiman, K. S., Raubenheimer, D., & Cooke, S. J. (2017). Nutritional physiology and ecology of wildlife in a changing world. *Conservation Physiology 5*(1): cox030. https://doi.org/10.1093/conphys/cox030.

Braidotti, R. (2013). *The posthuman*. Polity.

Burgen, S. (2018, September 18). 'For me, this is paradise': Life in the Spanish city that banned cars. *The Guardian*. https://www.theguardian.com/cities/2018/sep/18/paradise-life-spanish-city-banned-cars-pontevedra

Canopoli, L., Coulon, F., & Wagland, S. T. (2020). Degradation of excavated polyethylene and polypropylene waste from landfill. *Science of the Total Environment, 698*(January), 134125. https://doi.org/10.1016/j.scitotenv.2019.134125

Coole, D. (2005). Rethinking agency: A phenomenological approach to embodiment and agentic capacities. *Political Studies, 53*(1), 124–142. https://doi.org/10.1111/j.1467-9248.2005.00520.x

Deleuze, G., & Guattari, F. (1987). *Thousand plateaus: Capitalism and schizophrenia* (2nd ed). University of Minnesota Press.

van Dooren, T. (2016). Authentic crows: Identity, captivity and emergent forms of life. *Theory, Culture & Society, 33*(2), 29–52. https://doi.org/10.1177/0263276415571941

Dunkley, L., & Cattet, M. R. L. (2003). A comprehensive review of the ecological and human social effects of artificial feeding and baiting of wildlife. *Canadian Cooperative Wildlife Health Centre: Newsletters & Publications*. University of Nebraska. https://digitalcommons.unl.edu/icwdmccwhcnews/21

Ekbia, H. R., & Nardi, B. A. (2017). *Heteromation, and other stories of computing and capitalism*. MIT Press.

Eremia, M., Toma, L., & Sanduleac, M. (2017). The smart city concept in the 21st century. *Procedia Engineering, 181*(January), 12–19. https://doi.org/10.1016/j.proeng.2017.02.357

Fieuw, W., Foth, M., & Amayo Caldwell, G. (2022). Towards a more-than-human approach to smart and sustainable urban development: Designing for multispecies justice. *Sustainability, 14*(2), 948. http://dx.doi.org/10.3390/su14020948

Forlano, L. (2016). Decentering the human in the design of collaborative cities. *Design Issues, 32*(3), 42–54. https://doi.org/10.1162/DESI_a_00398

Free, C. M., Jensen, O. P., Mason, S. A., Eriksen, M., Williamson, N. J., & Boldgiv, B. (2014). High-levels of microplastic pollution in a large, remote, mountain lake. *Marine Pollution Bulletin, 85*(1), 156–163. https://doi.org/10.1016/j.marpolbul.2014.06.001

Frey, R. S., Gellert, P. K., & Dahms, H. F. (Eds.). (2018). *Ecologically unequal exchange: Environmental injustice in comparative and historical perspective.* Springer International Publishing.

Griffiths, A. (2017, March 5). Daylight filters in through the roof and walls of Bangladeshi mosque by Marina Tabassum. *Dezeen.* https://www.dezeen.com/2017/03/05/bait-ur-rouf-mosque-dhaka-bangladesh-marina-tabassum-brick-aga-khan-award/

Haraway, D. (1985). A manifesto for cyborgs: Science, technology, and social feminism in the 1980s. *Socialist Review, 5*(2), 65–107.

Haraway, D. (1994). A game of cat's cradle: Science studies, feminist theory, cultural studies. *Configurations, 2*(1), 59–71. https://doi.org/10.1353/con.1994.0009

Haraway, D. (2003). *The companion species manifesto: Dogs, people, and significant otherness.* Prickly Paradigm Press.

Haraway, D. (2016). *Staying with the trouble: Making kin in the Chthulucene.* Duke University Press Books.

Harman, G. (2016). *Immaterialism: Objects and social theory.* Polity.

Harman, G. (2018). *Object-oriented ontology: A new theory of everything.* Pelican.

Houston, D., Hillier, J., MacCallum, D., Steele, W., & Byrne, J. (2018). Make kin, not cities! Multispecies entanglements and 'becoming-world' in planning theory. *Planning Theory, 17*(2), 190–212. https://doi.org/10.1177/1473095216688042

Huang, M. N. (2017). Ecologies of entanglement in the Great Pacific Garbage Patch. *Journal of Asian American Studies, 20*(1), 95–117. https://doi.org/10.1353/jaas.2017.0006.

Jackson, S. J. (2014). Rethinking repair. In T. Gillespie, P. J. Boczkowski, & K. A. Foot (Eds.), *Media technologies: Essays on communication, materiality, and society* (pp. 221–240). MIT Press. https://doi.org/10.7551/mitpress/9780262525374.003.0011

Jelbert, S. A., Hosking, R. J., Taylor, A. H., & Gray, R. D. (2018). Mental template matching is a potential cultural transmission mechanism for New Caledonian crow tool manufacturing traditions. *Scientific Reports, 8*(1), 8956. https://doi.org/10.1038/s41598-018-27405-1.

Jones, S. (2018, November 30). 'It's the only way forward': Madrid bans polluting vehicles from city centre. *The Guardian.* https://www.theguardian.com/cities/2018/nov/30/its-the-only-way-forward-madrid-bans-polluting-vehicles-from-city-centre

Kimmerer, R. W. (2015). *Braiding sweetgrass: Indigenous wisdom, scientific knowledge and the teachings of plants.* Milkweed Editions.

Latour, B. (1999). *Pandora's hope: Essays on the reality of science studies.* Harvard University Press.

Latour, B. (2005). From realpolitik to dingpolitik. In B. Latour & P. Weibel (Eds.), *Making things public* (pp. 14–44). MIT Press.

Latour, B. (2007). *Reassembling the social: An introduction to actor-network-theory.* Oxford University Press.

Lebreton, L., Slat, B., Ferrari, F., Sainte-Rose, B., Aitken, J., Marthouse, R., Hajbane, S., Cunsolo, S., Schwarz, A., Levivier, A., Noble, K., Debeljak, P., Maral, H., Schoeneich-Argent, R., Brambini, R., & Reisser, J. (2018). Evidence that the great Pacific garbage patch is rapidly accumulating plastic. *Scientific Reports, 8*(1), 4666–15. https://doi.org/10.1038/s41598-018-22939-w

Lepawsky, J. (2015). The changing geography of global trade in electronic discards: Time to rethink the e-waste problem. *The Geographical Journal, 181*(2), 147–159. https://doi.org/10.1111/geoj.12077

Leslie, H. A., van Velzen, M. J. M., Brandsma, S. H., Vethaak, A. D., Garcia-Vallejo, J. J., & Lamoree, M. H. (2022). Discovery and quantification of plastic particle pollution in human blood. *Environment International, 163*, 107199. https://doi.org/10.1016/j.envint.2022.107199

Lewis, J. E., Arista, N., Pechawis, A., & Kite, S. (2016). Making kin with the machines. *Journal of Design and Science, 3.5.* https://doi.org/10.21428/bfafd97b

Llorente-González, L. J., & Vence, X. (2020). How labour-intensive is the circular economy? A policy-orientated structural analysis of the repair, reuse and recycling activities in the European Union. *Resources, Conservation and Recycling, 162*, 105033. https://doi.org/10.1016/j.resconrec.2020.105033

Mattern, S. (2021). *A city is not a computer: Other urban intelligences*. Princeton University Press.
Nihei, Y., & Higuchi, H. (2001). When and where did crows learn to use automobiles as nutcrackers? *Tohoku Psychologica Folia, 60*, 93–97.
Oogjes, D., & Wakkary, R. (2022). Weaving stories: Toward repertoires for designing things. In S. Barbosa, C. Lampe, C. Appert, D. A. Shamma, S. Drucker, J. Williamson, & K. Yatani (Eds.), *(CHI '22): Proceedings of the 2022 CHI Conference on Human Factors in Computing Systems* (Article 98). ACM. https://doi.org/10.1145/3491102.3501901
Puig de la Bellacasa, M. (2017). *Matters of care: Speculative ethics in more than human worlds* (3rd ed). University of Minnesota Press.
Ragusa, A., Svelato, A., Santacroce, C., Catalano, P., Notarstefano, V., Carnevali, O., Papa, F., Rongioletti, M. C. A., Baiocco, F., Draghi, S., D'Amore, E., Rinaldo, D., Matta, M., & Giorgini, E. (2021). Plasticenta: First evidence of microplastics in human placenta. *Environment International, 146*(January), 106274. https://doi.org/10.1016/j.envint.2020.106274
Ricker, T. (2017, February 15). Lightlines Are humanity's latest attempt to protect smartphone zombies. *The Verge*. https://www.theverge.com/2017/2/15/14621968/lightlines-protect-distracted-smartphone-users
Scully, K. (2017, February 16). Special traffic lights in Bodegraven to alert smartphone addicts. *I Am Expat*. https://www.iamexpat.nl/read-and-discuss/expat-page/news/bodegraven-special-traffic-lights-to-alert-smartphone-addicts
Simondon, G. (2017). *On the mode of existence of technical objects*. C. Malaspina and J. Rogove (Trans.). University of Minnesota Press (original work published 1958).
Star, S. L., & Ruhleder, K. (1996). Steps toward an ecology of infrastructure: Design and access for large information spaces. *Information Systems Research, 7*(1), 111–134. https://doi.org/10.1287/isre.7.1.111
Steinhardt, S. B. (2016). Breaking down while building up: Design and decline in emerging infrastructures. In J. Kaye, A. Druin, C. Lampe, D. Morris, & J. P. Hourcade (Eds.), *CHI '16: Proceedings of the 2016 CHI Conference on Human Factors in Computing Systems* (pp. 2198–2208). ACM. https://doi.org/10.1145/2858036.2858420
Stevens, E. S. (2001). *Green plastics: An introduction to the new science of biodegradable plastics*. Princeton University Press.
Sundberg, J. (2014). Decolonizing posthumanist geographies. *Cultural Geographies, 21*(1), 33–47. https://doi.org/10.1177/1474474013486067
Thompson, C. (2002). When elephants stand for competing models of nature. In J. Law, A. Mol, B. Herrnstein Smith, & E. R. Weintraub (Eds.,) *Complexities: Social studies of knowledge practices* (pp. 166–190). Duke University Press.
Thulin, S. G. (1965). Bag with handle of weldable plastic material. United States US3180557A, filed 10 July 1962, and issued 27 April 1965. https://patents.google.com/patent/US3180557/en
Todd, Z. (2015). Indigenizing the Anthropocene. In H. Davis & E. Turpin (Eds.), *Art in the Anthropocene: Encounters among aesthetics, politics, environments and epistemologies* (pp. 241–254). Open Humanities Press.
Tsing, A. L. (2015). *The mushroom at the end of the world: On the possibility of life in capitalist ruins*. Princeton University Press.
Tuhiwai Smith, L. (2021). *Decolonizing methodologies: Research and Indigenous peoples*. Zed Books.
Van Cauwenberghe, Vanreusel, L., A., Mees, J., & Janssen, C. R. (2013). Microplastic pollution in deep-sea sediments. *Environmental Pollution, 182*(November), 495–499. https://doi.org/10.1016/j.envpol.2013.08.013
Wakkary, R. (2021). *Things we could design: For more than human-centered worlds*. MIT Press.
Watts, V. (2013). Indigenous place-thought and agency amongst humans and non-humans (First Woman and Sky Woman go on a European world tour!). *Decolonization: Indigeneity, Education & Society, 2*(1), 20–34. https://jps.library.utoronto.ca/index.php/des/article/view/19145
Winner, L. (1980). Do artifacts have politics? *Daedalus, 109*(1), 121–136.
Wolfe, C. (2010). *What is posthumanism?* University of Minnesota Press.
van der Zee, R. (2015, May 5). How Amsterdam became the bicycle capital of the world. *The Guardian*. https://www.theguardian.com/cities/2015/may/05/amsterdam-bicycle-capital-world-transport-cycling-kindermoord

Epilogue

Six Lessons for a More-than-Human 'Smart' City from a Disabled Cyborg

Laura Forlano

'I am not a robot', I confirmed—dutifully checking the box on the left—while knowing full well that it was a lie. reCAPTCHA requires that I verify my humanity daily to perform simple tasks on the web. My robotic pancreas would probably disagree. For I am a Disabled Cyborg. As a Type 1 diabetic, my 'smart' insulin pump and sensor system are an essential part of my identity, as well as important for keeping me alive.

A few years ago, in 2019, I spent the month of July transcribing alert and alarm data from my 'smart' insulin pump and sensor system to better understand my own experience as well as to gain insight into what it means to 'live with' machines. Here is a small excerpt from the 'History' log of the device:

Day 32—August 1

4:46 am Alert on low [did not feel low, was sleeping]
5:11 am Alert on low
5:36 am Alert on low
5:51 am BG required
5:51 am BG required
5:51 am Low SG
6:01 am Alert on low
6:10 am BG required [sensor read 43 but was actually 179]
6:10 am Calibration not accepted
6:11 am Low battery Pump
6:12 am Insert battery
6:26 am Calibrate now
6:36 am BG required
6:37 am BG required
6:46 am Low reservoir
8:01 am Sensor updating
8:36 am Sensor updating
9:06 am Sensor updating
9:36 am BG required

In this small fragment of data, it is possible to read the future of the more-than-human 'smart' city. A more-than-human 'smart' city is a collection of people and both living and non-living things—from trees to terabytes, and from mushrooms

Laura Forlano, *Six Lessons for a More-than-Human 'Smart' City from a Disabled Cyborg.* In: *Designing More-than-Human Smart Cities.* Edited by: Sara Heitlinger, Marcus Foth, and Rachel Clarke, Oxford University Press. © Oxford University Press (2024). DOI: 10.1093/9780191980060.003.0018 to microbes—that are connected by sensors, networks, applications, and databases. Below, I'll elaborate on the key observations about the more-than-human 'smart' city that one can learn by analysing the short excerpt of data above.

First, I'll start with my own experience as a Disabled Cyborg.

As a Disabled Cyborg, I know that my life, my identity, and my Crip subjectivity are mutually shaped through my participation and engagement with my medical devices. My medical devices are me and not me at the same time. Living with machines is not the same as merely 'using' them. To live with someone or something requires co-habitation, mutual entanglement, interdependence, and reciprocity. For me, medical devices are 'intimate infrastructures' that can be compared to urban infrastructures (Forlano 2017).

More-than-human 'smart' cities require citizens with such sensitivities, a recognition that technologies are not only tools; they are both figuratively (and, quite literally, in the case of Disabled Cyborgs) part of us. Technologies are socially constructed in that they are shaped by humans, and they also shape our social, cultural, and political realities. And, for disabled people living with technology, it is not only our machines but also our politics that are cyborg.

Second, I'll describe the phenomenon of algorithmic error.

Let's look at the first line of data: '4:46 am Alert on low [did not feel low, was sleeping]'. In brackets, I annotate the machine data in my field notes with the text 'did not feel low, was sleeping'. This annotation reveals that according to the sensor system, when I was awakened at 4:46 am, my blood sugar was low. For many people, 4:46 am might be considered an ungodly hour but, in this case, the time of day or night is irrelevant to the machine.

In a medical emergency, certainly, one would want to be awakened. But my point here is that *it was not a medical emergency*, and I did not want to be awakened. Data is meant to represent the real world, but it is not actually the real world. I write 'did not feel low was sleeping' because, here, I do not trust the accuracy of the machine data. I checked the alert, dismissed the alarm, and went back to sleep.

As I annotated a few lines later: '6:10 am BG required [sensor read 43 but was actually 179]'. Thus, I do not use the machine data in isolation; I use it in combination with my own experience of 'being low' (or experiencing an episode of extreme low blood sugar). An interesting phenomenon is that machines use thresholds to understand the world. For example, while 79 might indicate low blood sugar, 81 does not if the threshold is set to be 'below 80'. For a human, 79 and 81 might be a very similar experience. They might signal danger if you are out jogging a mile from one's house, but not if you are sitting watching TV. But the machine generally does not have any way of understanding the context.

Error and failure are part of what it means to be human, as well as what it means to live with machines. Rather than eliminate error, we should learn to live with it as the default condition. For me, the notion of Cyborg Disability captures the reality that both humans and machines are disabled (Forlano 2023).

Third, I'll emphasise the vast amounts of (often invisible) human labour that is required for machines to function.

The word robot—derived from the Czech word robota, meaning 'forced labour'—was coined by Karel Capek in his science fiction play *R.U.R. (Rossum's Universal Robots)*. While many current discussions about robots, machines, and related technologies such as artificial intelligence (AI) cast them as working on behalf of (or even replacing) humans as mere tools, other narratives highlight the need for human labour. In fact, reCAPTCHA itself, mentioned above, is an excellent example. How many seconds, minutes, and hours are we collectively logging to keep websites secure from malicious software?

In the dataset above, each alert signals a different task that must be completed by the human for the continued function of the machine. For example, each of the alerts above must be manually dismissed. These constant alerts and alarms, contributing to a phenomenon known as 'alert fatigue'. At 5:51 am, the pump prompts: 'BG required' (short for blood glucose required). In this case, the human must prick her finger with a tiny needle called a lancet and feed the blood into a test trip, which is then read by a device called a glucose meter, which then sends the data wirelessly to the pump and sensor system. While it takes less than a minute, those minutes certainly add up, hour after hour, day after day.

Later that morning, the data shows the following alert: '6:46 am Low reservoir'. This means that the pump is running out of insulin. Approximately every three days, according to US Food and Drug Administration guidelines, the human needs to change and replace the tubing and the reservoir, another few minutes that is necessary to keep the system functioning. This labour of caring for machines is not insignificant. In my case, I often remark that I am not sure whether the machine is taking care of me, or whether I am taking care of the machine.

All computational systems require such ongoing work of maintenance, repair, and care. Much of the work that keep systems and infrastructures running is hidden, out of sight, behind the scenes or, even, overseas. There is no such thing as 'fully automated'.

Fourth, power and energy are essential to keep machines running.

In my field notes, the alert data reads: '6:11am Low battery Pump'. And then: '6:12am Insert battery'. Without a source of power, machines can no longer function. Despite significant advances in renewable energy from sources such as the sun, wind, and water, computers cannot power themselves or, for example, mine their own precious minerals.

For me, this might mean changing a battery every few months or, with my current devices, plugging myself into the wall for thirty minutes every few days. The thought of a power outage for more than a few hours can be existentially scary both because of the constant need for power as well as the need to refrigerate the insulin.

Since the climate crisis promises more frequent and more damaging events that will disrupt our power grids, transportation networks, and medical infrastructure, it is also more dangerous for Disabled Cyborgs like me, that cannot go days without the conveniences of electricity and refrigeration. In response to this and other threats, we can learn from disabled activists that have experience with organising mutual aid networks that foster interdependence, which will be increasingly necessary for survival in the more-than-human 'smart' city (Hamraie & Fritsch 2019).

Fifth, data privacy and data ownership are potential sites of economic value as well as conflict.

With this small excerpt of data and similar data from medical devices, people are generally required and/or incentivised to share it both with their medical providers as well as to device manufacturers. This data sharing happens through portals and applications that communicate with one another as well as with health systems. In a more-than-human 'smart' city, data commons, in which data is owned, managed, and/or controlled by collectives, could be integrated with other public commons.

Lastly, artistic projects expand our understanding of ourselves and the world.

' *... did not feel low, was sleeping*' from my fieldnote in the dataset above, became the title of interdisciplinary artist Itziar Barrio's exhibition at Smack Mellon Gallery in DUMBO, New York, in spring 2023, which included a series of robotic sculptures on which she and I collaborated (Figures 16.1 and 16.2). The sculptures use my data both as design material to program their movements—twisting and writhing, inflating and deflating—as well as a text that is printed on the circuit boards. Unlike the latest mobile phones, tablets, and computers, the sculptures suggest an alternative narrative of computing, communicated through earlier technologies of cement, spandex, and rubber.

A more-than-human 'smart' city must embrace artistic and cultural expression to support human flourishing. Art provokes reflection about technology through active experimentation, uncovering new potential, and asking essential questions about the human condition. These critical and generative questions are important in that they are not only in service to the economy, but they also open up spaces for debate and for doing things differently.

At first glance, these observations might seem obvious. But they are frequently overlooked in corporate boardrooms and behind the desk at city hall. This is perhaps because we prefer the myths of computing rather than the realities (Dourish & Bell 2011). These myths are frequently circulated on talk shows, senate hearings, and science fiction stories. A more-than-human 'smart' city must contend with these realities. In sum, a more-than-human 'smart' city might keep in mind the following statements, lessons that I am reminded of on a daily basis through my experience living with technology:

> First, ask Disabled Cyborgs!!!;
> Second, error and failure is the default condition;
> Third, labour is essential, but it is often invisible;
> Fourth, without energy, nothing can function;
> Fifth, data ownership and privacy have value, but for whom?; and,
> Lastly, art offers generative possibility for reflection about ourselves and the world.

With that, I'll go back to dutifully declaring: 'I am not a robot'.

Figure 16.1

Figure 16.2

Figures 16.1 and 16.2 Robotic sculptures in progress at Itziar Barrio's studio for the artwork *was on low*, 2023. Concrete, spandex, lighting filters, hardware, epoxy resin, Arduino, motor, custom circuit board, and Laura Forlano's insulin pump alert data. Artist: Itziar Barrio. Source: Author.

References

Dourish, P., & Bell, G. (2011). *Divining a digital future: Mess and mythology in ubiquitous computing.* MIT Press.

Forlano, L. (2017). Data rituals in intimate infrastructures: Crip time and the disabled cyborg body as an epistemic site of feminist science. *Catalyst, 3*(2), 1–28. https://doi.org/10.28968/cftt.v3i2.28843

Forlano, L. (2023). Living intimately with machines: Can AI be disabled? *Interactions, 30*(1), 24–29. https://doi.org/10.1145/3572808

Hamraie, A., & Fritsch, K. (2019). Crip technoscience manifesto. *Catalyst, 5*(1), 1–33. https://doi.org/10.28968/cftt.v5i1.29607

Index

For the benefit of digital users, indexed terms that span two pages (e.g., 52–53) may, on occasion, appear on only one of those pages.

Designing More-than-Human Smart Cities